E-Business Strategy, Sourcing and Governance

Petter Gottschalk
Norwegian School of Management, Norway

IDEA GROUP PUBLISHING

Hershey • London • Melbourne • Singapore

Acquisitions Editor:	Michelle Potter
Development Editor:	Kristin Roth
Senior Managing Editor:	Amanda Appicello
Managing Editor:	Jennifer Neidig
Copy Editor:	Tom Papeika
Typesetter:	Sharon Berger
Cover Design:	Lisa Tosheff
Printed at:	Yurchak Printing Inc.

Published in the United States of America by
  Idea Group Publishing (an imprint of Idea Group Inc.)
  701 E. Chocolate Avenue
  Hershey PA 17033
  Tel: 717-533-8845
  Fax: 717-533-8661
  E-mail: cust@idea-group.com
  Web site: http://www.idea-group.com

and in the United Kingdom by
  Idea Group Publishing (an imprint of Idea Group Inc.)
  3 Henrietta Street
  Covent Garden
  London WC2E 8LU
  Tel: 44 20 7240 0856
  Fax: 44 20 7379 0609
  Web site: http://www.eurospanonline.com

Library of Congress Cataloging-in-Publication Data

Gottschalk, Petter, 1950-
  E-business strategy, sourcing, and governance / Petter Gottschalk.
    p. cm.
  Summary: "This book is based on the premise that it is difficult, if not impossible, to manage a modern business or public organization without at least some knowledge of the planning, use, control and benefits of information technology"--Provided by publisher.
  Includes bibliographical references and index.
  ISBN 1-59904-004-2 (hardcover) -- ISBN 1-59904-005-0 (softcover) -- ISBN 1-59904-006-9 (ebook)
  1. Electronic commerce--Management. 2. Internet in public administration. 3. Information technology--Management. 4. Strategic planning. I. Title.
  HF5548.32.G678 2006
  658'.054678--dc22
                              2005023874

British Cataloguing in Publication Data
A Cataloguing in Publication record for this book is available from the British Library.

E-Business Strategy, Sourcing and Governance

Table of Contents

Section III: Governance

Foreword

In this timely book, Dr. Gottschalk cogently tackles important subjects such as electronic business, strategic planning, sourcing of IT services, outsourcing, and IT governance. This book adds substantial knowledge from the author's expertise. The chapters are well-structured, interesting, and group ideas in a logical and appealing way. The model that is introduced for strategic planning (the Y model) is useful and well done. Many illustrations make the reading even more interesting.

This book provides a good and thorough overview of important aspects in IS/IT management and governance. It is very suitable as an excellent e-business textbook, and it appears very helpful for managers.

From the humble beginnings of a decade ago, e-business, sourcing, and governance have today become critical issues in strategic IT management in both private and public organizations all over the world. But are the organizations ready for this challenge? Some organizations might succeed, while others might fail — if they do not choose an approach that is suited for the maturity and the situation of each organization.

The resource-based theory of the firm is a useful entrance to the topics of e-business strategy, sourcing, and governance. The resource-based theory argues that performance differences across firms can be attributed to the variance in the firms' resources. Resources that are unique, non-transferable, non-imitable, non-substitutable, combinable, exploitable, and valuable are classified as strategic resources.

Strategic resources are required to succeed in selecting and implementing appropriate e-business models. Strategic IT resources are obtained in sourcing situations. Strategic resources are applied in IT governance arrangements. The availability and smart application of strategic resources can distinguish success from failure in organizations.

Many fail to understand that what, where, when, and how to outsource, how to select e-business model, and how to implement governance, are among the most demanding, vital and essential executive skills needed for a company's success. Executives and IT professionals are still failing to grasp what makes for a good e-business strategy, sourcing, and governance.

This book answers the entire range of above questions in a lucid yet exhaustive way. It covers both opportunities and threats. Towards the end, it makes a very interesting contribution of showing how IT governance has to change because of IT outsourcing.

All in all this book is a most comprehensive guide on all aspects of e-business, strategy, sourcing, and governance, and is highly commendable for practitioners, researchers, policy makers, and consultants alike.

Dr. Binshan Lin
BellSouth Corporation Professorship in Business Administration
Louisiana State University in Shreveport

Preface

E-Business Strategy, Sourcing and Governance is based on the premise that it is difficult, if not impossible, to manage a modern business or public organization without at least some knowledge of the planning, use, control, and benefits of information technology. Managers need to have an understanding of strategy development, including the current technology situation, the current and desired business situation, the need for changes, the application portfolio, and organizational and human resource issues in the area of information technology.

E-Business Strategy, Sourcing and Governance was written after several years of management education, training, and research. I have been conducting management education at the graduate and undergraduate levels in Norway and abroad. For example, the Master of Management program in Information Technology Management & E-Commerce that the Norwegian School of Management BI runs at Fudan University in China covers most of the material included in this book. I have also been conducting management training in organizations such as the telecom company Telenor. I have been conducting management research in areas such as key issues in technology management, critical success factors, knowledge management, leadership roles of technology managers, project management, outsourcing, and strategy implementation.

While this book is an updated text on current business-IT challenges, it is also tailor-made for courses at the master's level in China, Singapore, Egypt, and other countries where the Norwegian School of Management BI runs educational programs. In these programs, there will be more emphasis on strategic planning, e-business, IT sourcing, IT governance, and other topics that are covered in this new book.

Some areas of the book are better at covering the necessary material — for example, the outsourcing and governance chapters. This is done to expand our thinking of e-business strategy. However, many areas of the first chapters discuss topics very briefly and typically include only one reference as a source for what is being said. This is done to limit the presentation of general e-business material that is found in so many other textbooks.

Some readers will be disappointed with the second chapter. They would like to find more enthusiasm for emerging technologies and business models. However, from a business strategy perspective, even the second and third waves of e-business will foster both failures and successes, depending on the extent of realistic expectations and ambitions.

Some readers will find that many theories are reviewed but none is clearly highlighted as superior or "the way to go," so I am not sure how practical these parts of the book can be for a manager. It is my hope and belief, however, that practicing managers will be able and willing to appreciate good management theories.

This book is intended to discuss current topics (strategy, sourcing, and governance) in the e-business domain. These are important topics today. However, "e-business domain" is a vague concept, and it is expanding as you read, which has led me to discuss strategy, sourcing, and governance in a more general business context.

I am not sure that this is a book on e-business, as you would expect. It is, in a way, primarily a book on business, which, of course, includes e-business. This is maybe the only way e-business can be successful, by integrating e-business strategy into the larger picture of business strategy.

This is a book about how to manage information technology (IT). It is concerned with the planning, use, control, and benefits of IT in business and public organizations. It is not about information technology per se.

The main perspective in this book is change management. If a company stands still, it will not survive. To survive a company must be proactive rather than reactive. It must be proactive to external threats and opportunities and to internal strengths and weaknesses. The world around us is changing.

In general, we first have to find out **what** we would like to achieve, then we should discuss **how** we could go about achieving it.

1. **What** would we like to achieve?

2. **How** can we do it?

The same is true for an information system. We first have to find out **what** kind of information is needed, and then we can discuss **how** to provide it and how technology can help. The important lesson here is that **What** comes before **How**: The focus of an information system is always first on information (what), and then on technology (how).

However, technology also gives us new opportunities. Therefore, we do have to know the technology. So we can expand the sequence by **what** before **how** before **what**:

1. **What** kind of information is needed?   What

2. **How** can IT provide it?   What > How

3. **What** else are we able to achieve using IT?   What > How > What

In this book we present a procedure for developing and implementing IS/IT strategy. Chapter III presents strategy analysis, while Chapter IV covers strategy choice and Chapter IV discusses strategy implementation. These chapters cover the procedure of strategic planning.

We also need content in strategic planning. Content is provided in Chapter I about theories of the firm, Chapter II about electronic business, Chapters VII to XII about IT sourcing and Chapters XIII to XVIII about IT governance.

Overview of Book Chapters

Chapter I. Theories of the Firm provides a framework for understanding and analyzing modern business performance. According to the resource-based theory of the firm, performance differences across firms can be attributed to the variance in the firms' resources and capabilities. Resources that are valuable, unique, and difficult to imitate can provide the basis for firms' competitive advantages. In turn, these competitive advantages produce positive returns.

Chapter II. E-Business is the core chapter on electronic business, how it is evolving, and what decisions are to be made by executives concerning business models and infrastructure services. A business model can be defined as

Figure 1. Overview of book chapters

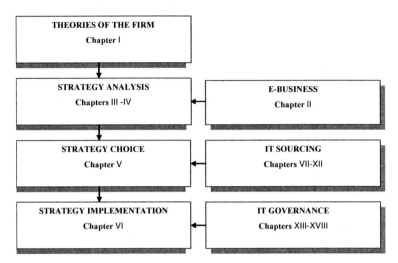

the method by which a firm builds and uses its resources to offer its customers better value than its competitors do and to take money doing so. It details how a firm makes money now and how it plans to do so in the long run. The model is what enables a firm to have a sustainable competitive advantage, to perform better than its rivals in the long-term do. An e-business model can be defined as a description of the roles and relationships among a firm's consumers, customers, allies, and suppliers that identifies the major flows of product, information, and money, and the major benefits to participants.

Chapter III. IS/IT Strategy Work introduces the Y model for strategic planning. In the Y model, stages 1 to 3 cover analysis, 4 and 5 cover choice, and 6 and 7 cover implementation. Stage 3 is a so-called gap analysis, and looks at the difference between the desired and actual situation. This stage also includes prioritizing. Stage 4 is a creative session as it calls for ideas and proposals for alternative actions. Stages 5 and 6 are typical planning stages. The final stage 7 is important because we can learn from performing an evaluation.

Chapter IV. Strategy Analysis introduces a number of methods to analyze the current and desired business situation. Methods included are concerned with benefits of IS/IT, stages of IS/IT growth, IS/IT in management activities, IS/IT in business processes, IS/IT support for value configuration, strategic integration, IS/IT support for knowledge management, IS/IT in e-business, and IS/IT enabled business transformation.

Chapter V. Strategy Choice introduces criteria and methods to be applied when making strategic IS/IT decisions, concerning both future applications and development approach. When needs for change have been identified and proposals for filling gaps have been developed, alternative actions for improving the current situation can be developed. New IS/IT can be developed, acquired, and implemented in alternative ways. Several decisions have to be made when a new IS/IT is chosen. Such decisions are called systems development strategy, and they are illustrated later when we discuss IT governance as allocation of decision rights.

Chapter VI. Strategy Implementation discusses enablers and barriers to successful implementation of e-business strategy. IS/IT strategy implementation can be defined as the process of completing the projects for application of information technology to assist an organization in realizing its goals. However, implementing an IS/IT strategy is not simply the act of implementing many projects and individual systems. Instead, implementing such a plan demands a gestalt view in the planning of individual systems. A gestalt view represents the implementation of the plan philosophy, attitudes, intentions, and ambitions associated with IS/IT use in the organization. It may include decisions about the IS organization and the implementation of IT architecture.

Chapter VII. Sourcing Management is the first chapter in the second part of the book concerned with sourcing of IS/IT services. An important point is made in this book about how strategy was absent from early e-business attempts. The first part of this book describes how strategy might be present. To establish and maintain a distinctive strategic positioning, an organization needs to follow six fundamental principles concerned with right goal, value proposition, value configuration, trade-off, fit, and continuity. One of the strategic choices often overlooked is concerned with IT sourcing. IT sourcing decisions are influenced by trade-off, fit and continuity principles.

Chapter VIII. Sourcing Theories presents a number of management theories that can be applied to our understanding of sourcing decisions. In Chapter I, general theories of the firm and value configurations of firms were introduced. Here we return to more theories. While theories and value configurations in Chapter I were introduced to develop e-business strategy, more theories are introduced here to understand the specifics of sourcing in general and outsourcing in particular. We want to understand why companies choose IT outsourcing in the middle of the Y model.

Chapter IX. IS/IT Outsourcing discusses opportunities and threats when outsourcing, as well as vendor value proposition, and outsourcing phases. Information technology outsourcing – the practice of transferring IT assets, leases, staff, and management responsibility for delivery of services from internal IT functions to third party vendors — has become an undeniable trend.

Chapter X. Sourcing Markets presents different areas for sourcing, such as infrastructure, applications, and processes. The paradigm shift in the possibilities of communication that the Internet and telecommunications revolution has brought about has opened up a plethora of opportunities in outsourcing business processes. Business process outsourcing involves transferring certain value contributing activities and processes to another firm to save costs, to focus on its areas of key competence, and to access resources. The possibilities of disaggregating value elements in terms of business processes for creating value in them at the vendor's premises and final aggregation and synthesis at the client organization are explored and exploited in business process outsourcing. Business process outsourcing includes enterprise services (human resources, finance and accounting, payment services, and administration), supply management (buying processes, storing processes, and moving processes), demand management processes (customer selection, customer acquisition, customer retention, and customer extension), and operations.

Chapter XI. Sourcing Practices is concerned with performance and outcome from sourcing arrangements. Termination of an IT outsourcing arrangement involves strategic decision-making. General studies of strategic decision making show how rapidly strategic decisions are made in small firms operating within high-velocity environments, and how decision speed is linked to performance. Fast decision makers use more, not less information than do slow decision makers. The former also develop more, not fewer, alternatives, and use a two-tiered advice process. Conflict resolution and integration between strategic managers are also critical to the pace of decision-making. Finally, fast decisions based on this pattern of behaviors lead to superior performance.

Chapter XII. Offshore IT Outsourcing discusses why offshoring has become so popular and the benefits and pitfalls. The shifting geography of business processes can de defined as the third wave of geography-related change in the design and operation of corporations. During the first wave, the improving transportation infrastructure of the 20th century enabled corporations to seek effective production capabilities in increasingly far-flung locations that provided access to new markets and tangible resources, land local factories, mines, and production workers. During the second wave, as capital markets became global and interconnected in the latter half of the 20th century, corporations began to capitalize on vibrant global financial markets for both debt and equity. Now we are in the midst of a third wave, in which digitized business processes like order processing, billing, customer service, accounts and payroll processing, and design and development can be carried out without regard to physical location.

Chapter XIII. IT Governance as Resource Mobilization is the first chapter in the third and final part of this book concerned with governance. In many organizations, information technology has become crucial in the support, the sustainability, and the growth of the business. This pervasive use of technology has created a critical dependency on IT that calls for a specific focus on IT governance. IT governance consists of the leadership and organizational structures and processes that ensure that the organization's IT sustains and extends the organization's strategy and objectives.

Chapter XIV. IT Governance as Allocation of Decision Rights discusses important aspects of who, what and when in decision-making. The first decision in the systems development strategy map is concerned with use of resources. Over the last two decades, the availability of standard application packages has risen. In most application areas, there are standard packages available today. Most organizations have changed from an in-house development strategy to a standard package strategy. Acquisition of standard application software is a very widespread strategy, especially among small and medium-sized companies that cannot afford large in-house staff for systems development.

Chapter XV. IT Governance as Strategic Alignment discusses alignment between business strategy and IS/IT strategy. While the business strategy is the broadest pattern of resource allocation decisions, more specific decisions are related to information systems and information technology. IS must be seen both in a business and an IT context. IS is in the middle because IS supports the business while using IT.

Chapter XVI. Implementing IT Governance presents implementation mechanisms for effective governance. Enterprises implement their governance arrangements through a set of governance mechanisms: structures, processes, and communications. Well-designed, well-understood, and transparent mechanisms promote desirable IT behaviors. Conversely, if mechanisms are poorly implemented, then governance arrangements will fail to yield the desired results.

Chapter XVII. IT Outsourcing Governance develops an extended governance model for successful outsourcing relationships. The overall objective of this chapter is to concentrate on the important issues of strategy, structure, and management of IT outsourcing arrangements. Using well-known theoretical perspectives described earlier in this book, a governance model for successful management of IT outsourcing relationships is presented. IT outsourcing governance can be defined as specifying the decision rights and accountability framework to encourage desirable behavior in the IT outsourcing arrangement, where resources are transferred from one party to the other in return for resources controlled by the other party. Governance is not about making specific decisions — management does that — but rather determines who systematically makes and contributes to those decisions. Governance reflects broader principles while focusing on the management of the outsourcing relationship to achieve performance goals for both client and vendor. Governance is the institutional framework in which contracts are monitored, adapted, and renewed. Effective outsourcing governance encourages and leverages the ingenuity of the vendor's and client's people in IT usage and ensures compliance with both enterprises' overall vision and values.

Chapter XVIII. Knowledge Management in Governance discusses the importance of knowledge transfer and alternative strategies and stages for knowledge management technology. The knowledge-based view of the firm has established itself as an important perspective in strategic management. This perspective builds on the resource-based theory of the firm. The knowledge-based view of the firm implies that information systems are designed to support knowledge management in organizations. Knowledge management can be defined as a method to simplify and improve the process of sharing, distributing, creating, capturing, and understanding knowledge in a company. Knowledge management is description, organization, sharing, and development of knowledge in a firm.

Chapter XIX. Case Studies are introduced at the end of the book for student term papers and class discussion. Rolls-Royce is a case from the manufacturing sector. UPS Logistics and Maersk Logistics are cases from the maritime industry. Telecom Italia Mobile, Netcom and Colt Telecom Group are cases from the telecom industry.

I hope you enjoy reading my book. Any comments you may have are appreciated. Please e-mail me at petter.gottschalk@bi.no.

Petter Gottschalk
Oslo, Norway, August 2005

SECTION I

STRATEGY

Chapter I

Theories of the Firm

In this book we need to develop a general understanding of business firms to enable strategic IS/IT planning. We will present the resource-based theory of the firm, the activity-based theory of the firm and the firm in terms of its value configuration.

An understanding of firm theories and value configurations is important to later discussions of the topics in the book. The resource-based theory is applied to understand resources needed for e-business, sourcing, and governance. An important resource is knowledge in terms of know-what, know-how and know-why.

Resource-Based Theory of the Firm

According to the resource-based theory of the firm, performance differences across firms can be attributed to the variance in the firms' resources and capabilities. Resources that are valuable, unique, and difficult to imitate can provide the basis for firms' competitive advantages. In turn, these competitive advantages produce positive returns. According to Hitt et al. (2001), most of the few empirical tests of the resource-based theory that have been conducted have supported positive, direct effects of resources. An important and often critical resource is IS/IT applications in the firm.

The essence of the resource-based theory of the firm lies in its emphasis on the internal resources available to the firm, rather than on the external opportunities and threats dictated by industry conditions. Firms are considered highly heterogeneous, and the bundles of resources available to each firm are different. This is both because firms have different initial resource endowments and because managerial decisions affect resource accumulation and the direction of firm growth as well as resource utilization (Loewendahl, 2000).

The resource-based theory of the firm holds that, in order to generate sustainable competitive advantage, a resource must provide economic value and must be presently scarce, difficult to imitate, non-substitutable, and not readily obtainable in factor markets. This theory rests on two key points. First, that resources are the determinants of firm performance and second, that resources must be rare, valuable, difficult to imitate and non-substitutable by other rare resources. When the latter occurs, a competitive advantage has been created (Priem & Butler, 2001).

Resources can simultaneously be characterized as valuable, rare, non-substitutable, and inimitable. To the extent that an organization's physical assets, infrastructure, and workforce satisfy these criteria, they qualify as resources. A firm's performance depends fundamentally on its ability to have a distinctive, sustainable competitive advantage, which derives from the possession of firm-specific resources (Priem & Butler, 2001).

The resource-based theory is a useful perspective in strategic management. Research on the competitive implications of such firm resources as knowledge, learning, culture, teamwork, and human capital, was given a significant boost by resource-based theory — a theory that indicated it was these kinds of resources that were most likely to be sources of sustainable competitive advantage for firms (Barney, 2001).

Firms' resource endowments, particularly intangible resources, are difficult to change, except over the long term. For example, although human resources may be mobile to some extent, capabilities may not be valuable for all firms or even for their competitors. Some capabilities are based on firm-specific knowledge, and others are valuable when integrated with additional individual capabilities and specific firm resources. Therefore, intangible resources are more likely than tangible resources to produce a competitive advantage. In particular, intangible firm-specific resources such as knowledge allow firms to add value to incoming factors of production (Hitt et al., 2001).

Resource-based theory attributes advantage in an industry to a firm's control over bundles of unique material, human, organizational, and locational resources, and skills that enable unique value-creating strategies. A firm's resources are said to be a source of competitive advantage to the degree that they are scarce, specialized, appropriable, valuable, rare, and difficult to imitate or substitute.

We will return to the topic of resources when we discuss IT governance as resource mobilization later in this book.

Activity-Based Theory of the Firm

The resource-based theory of the firm grew out of efforts to explain the growth of firms. Although its origins lay primarily in economics, researchers in strategy have developed the resource-based theory. The main attraction of the resource-based theory is that it focuses on explaining why firms are different and its effect on profitability. The main tenets of the resource-based theory are that firms differ in their resource endowments that these differences are persistent, and that firm-level performance differentials can be explained by analyzing a firm's resource position. Differences in resources are seen to lead to non-replicable efficiency rents.

Sheehan (2002) discussed comparing and contrasting the resource-based theory with the activity-based theory, and his discussion is presented in the following.

The activity-based theory conceives the firm as a bundle of activities, while the resource-based theory conceives the firm as a bundle of resources. The resource-based theory focuses on explaining why some firms create more value than others do by examining differences in resource stocks. However, the resource-based theory places little or no emphasis on resource flows. The role of the production function in transforming inputs into end products (other than having the latent ability to transform) is under-conceptualized in the resource-based theory. On the other hand, the activity-based theory focuses on flows of resources in activities. It emphasizes the impact of the firm's production function on creating value, while placing little attention on differences in stocks of resources. It is implicitly assumed that all necessary inputs (resources) can be acquired from the market.

Value Configuration of the Firm

To comprehend the value that information technology provides to organizations, we must first understand the way a particular organization conducts business and how information systems affect the performance of various component activities within the organization. Understanding how firms differ is a central challenge for both theory and practice of management. For a long time, Porter's (1985) value chain was the only value configuration known to managers. Stabell and Fjeldstad (1998) have identified two alternative value configurations. A value shop schedules activities and applies resources in a fashion that is dimensioned and appropriate to the needs of the client's problem, while a value chain performs a fixed set of activities that enables it to produce a standard product in large numbers. Examples of value shops are professional service firms, as found in medicine, law, architecture, and engineering. A value network links clients or customers who are or wish to be interdependent. Examples of value networks are telephone companies, retail banks and insurance companies.

A value configuration describes how value is created in a company for its customers. A value configuration shows how the most important business processes function to create value for customers. A value configuration represents the way a particular organization conducts business.

The Firm as a Value Chain

The best-known value configuration is the value chain. In the value chain, value is created through efficient production of goods and services based on a variety of resources. The company is perceived as a series or chain of activities. Primary activities in the value chain include inbound logistics, production, outbound logistics, marketing and sales, and service. Support activities include infrastructure, human resources, technology development, and procurement. Attention is on performing these activities in the chain in efficient and effective ways. In Figure 1.1, examples of IS/IT are assigned to primary and support activities. This figure can be used to describe the current IS/IT situation in the organization as it illustrates the extent of coverage of IS/IT for each activity.

The knowledge intensity of systems in the different activities can be illustrated by different shading, where dark shading indicates high knowledge intensity. In this example, it is assumed that the most knowledge intensive activities are computer aided design and customer relationship management.

The Firm as a Value Shop

Value cannot only be created in value chains. Value can also be created in two alternative value configurations: value shop and value network (Stabell & Fjeldstad, 1998). In the value shop, activities are scheduled and resources are applied in a fashion that is dimensioned and appropriate to the needs of the client's problem, while a value chain performs a fixed set of activities that enables it to produce a standard product in large numbers. The value shop is a company that creates value by solving unique problems for customers and clients. Knowledge is the most important resource, and reputation is critical to firm success.

While typical examples of value chains are manufacturing industries such as paper and car production, typical examples of value shops are law firms and medical hospitals. Often, such companies are called professional service firms or knowledge-intensive service firms. Like the medical hospital as a way to practice medicine, the law firm provides a standard format for delivering complex legal services. Many features of its style — specialization, teamwork, continuous monitoring on behalf of clients (patients), and representation in many forums — have been emulated in other vehicles for delivering professional services (Galanter & Palay, 1991).

Knowledge-intensive service firms are typical value shops. Sheehan (2002) defines knowledge-intensive service firms as entities that sell problem-solving services, where

Figure 1.1. Examples of IS/IT in the value chain

Infrastructure: Use of corporate intranet for internal communications				
Human resources: Use of corporate intranet for competence building				
Technology: Computer Aided Design (CAD)				
Procurement: Use of electronic marketplaces				
Inbound logistics: Electronic Data Interchange (EDI)	**Production**: Computer Integrated Manufacturing (CIM)	**Outbound logistics**: Web-based order-tracking system	**Marketing and sales**: Customer Relationship Management (CRM)	**Service**: System for local troubleshooting

the solution chosen by the expert is based on real-time feedback from the client. Clients retain knowledge intensive service firms to reduce their uncertainty. Clients hire knowledge-intensive service firms precisely because the client believes the firm knows something that the client does not and believes it is necessary to solve their problems.

While expertise plays a role in all firms, its role is distinctive in knowledge-intensive service firms. Expert, often professional, knowledge is at the core of the service provided by the type of firm.

Knowledge-intensive service firms not only sell a problem-solving service, but also and equally a problem-finding, problem-defining, solution-execution, and monitoring service. Problem finding is often a key for acquiring new clients. Once the client is acquired and their problem is defined, not all problems will be solved by the firm. Rather the firm may only clarify that there is no problem (i.e. the patient does not have a heart condition) or that the problem should be referred to another specialist (i.e. the patient needs a heart specialist). If a problem is treated within the firm, then the firm needs to follow up the implementation to assure that the problem in fact has been solved (i.e. is the patient's heart now working properly?). This follows from the fact that there is often uncertainty in both problem diagnosis and problem resolution.

Sheehan (2002) has created a typology of knowledge-intensive service firms consisting of the following three types. First, knowledge-intensive search firms search for opportunities. The amount of value they create depends on the size of the finding or discovery, where size is measured by quality rather than quantity. Examples of search firms include petroleum and mineral exploration, drug discovery in the pharmaceutical industry, and research in the biotechnology industry. Second, knowledge-intensive diagnosis firms create value by clarifying problems. Once the problem has been identified, the suggested remedy usually follows directly. Examples of diagnosis firms include doctors, surgeons, psychotherapists, veterinarians, lawyers, auditors and tax accountants, and software support. Finally, knowledge-intensive design firms create value by conceiving new ways of constructing material or immaterial artifacts. Examples of design firms include architecture, advertising, research and development, engineering design, and strategy consulting.

Figure 1.2. Examples of IS/IT in the value shop

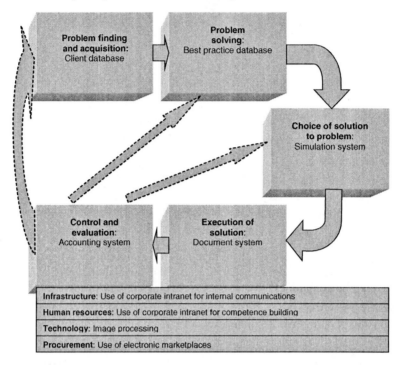

Knowledge-intensive service firms create value through problem acquisition and defi-nition, alternative generation and selection, implementation of an alternative, and follow up to see if the solution selected resolves the problem. To reflect this process, Stabell and Fjeldstad (1998) have outlined the value configuration of a value shop.

A value shop is characterized by five primary activities: problem finding and acquisition, problem solving, choice, execution, and control and evaluation, as illustrated in Figure 1.2. Problem finding and acquisition involves working with the customer to determine the exact nature of the problem or need. It involves deciding on the overall plan of approaching the problem. Problem solving is the actual generation of ideas and action (or treatment) plans.

Choice represents the decision of choosing between alternatives. While choice is the least important primary activity of the value shop in terms of time and effort, it is also the most important in terms of customer value. Execution represents communicating, orga-nizing, and implementing the decision, or performing the treatment. Control and evalu-ation activities involve monitoring and measurement of how well the solution solved the original problem or met the original need.

This may feed back into the first activity, problem finding and acquisition, for two reasons. First, if the proposed solution is inadequate or did not work, then it feeds back into learning why it was inadequate and begins the problem-solving phase anew. Second, if the problem solution was successful, the firm might enlarge the scope of the problem-

Figure 1.3. Examples of IS/IT in the value shop

Activities	Tasks	IS/IT
Problem finding and acquisition	Register client information	Financial system
	Register case information	Case database
Problem solving	Do case analysis	Case-based reasoning
	Do reference search	Library search engine
Choice	Evaluate alternatives	Case-based reasoning
	Make recommendation to client	Office systems
Execution	Participate at meetings	Office systems
	Revise recommendation	Office systems
Control and evaluation	Register recommendation	Case database
	Check client satisfaction	Financial system

solving process to solve a bigger problem related to or dependent upon the first problem being solved (Afuah & Tucci, 2003).

Figure 1.2 can be used to identify current IS/IT in the organization. We let a law firm serve as example in Figure 1.3. Within each of the five activities, there are many tasks in a law firm. For each task, there may be IS/IT support. For example, problem solving may consist of the two tasks of case analysis and reference search. Lawyers will be eager to discuss the case and to search more information on similar cases. A system for case-based reasoning may be installed, where the current case can be compared to similar cases handled by the law firm. Also, intelligent search engines with thesaurus may be available in the law firm to find relevant information on the Internet and in legal databases.

The Firm as a Value Network

The third and final value configuration is the value network. A value network is a company that creates value by connecting clients and customers that are, or want to be, dependent on each other. These companies distribute information, money, products, and services. While activities in both value chains and value shops are done sequentially, activities in value networks occur in parallel. The number and combination of customers and access points in the network are important value drivers in the value network. More customers and more connections create higher value to customers.

Stabell and Fjeldstad (1998) suggest that managing a value network can be compared to managing a club. The mediating firm admits members that complement each other, and in some cases exclude those that do not. The firm establishes, monitors, and terminates direct or indirect relationships among members. Supplier-customer relationships may exist between the members of the club, but to the mediating firm they are all customers.

Examples of value networks include telecommunication companies, financial institutions such as banks and insurance companies, and stockbrokers. Value networks perform three activities (see Figure 1.4):

Figure 1.4. Examples of IS/IT in the value network

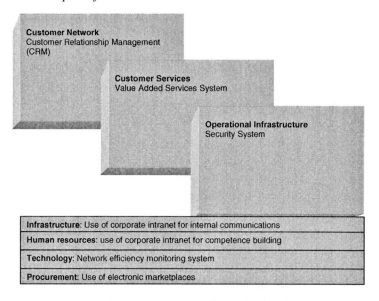

- Development of customer network through marketing and recruiting of new customers, to enable increased value for both existing customers and new customers

- Development of new services and improvement in existing services

- Development of infrastructure so that customer services can be provided more efficiently and effectively

The current IS/IT situation in a value network will mainly be described through the infrastructure that typically will consist of information technology. In addition, many of the new services may be information systems that will be used by customers in their communication and business transactions with other customers. The knowledge component will mainly be found in the services of a value network, as information systems are made available to customers to exchange relevant information.

Comparison of Value Configurations

Value chain, value shop and value network are alternative value configurations that affect the use of information technology in the company as illustrated in Figure 1.5. While the role of IT is to make production more efficient in a value chain, IT creates added value in the value shop, while IT in the form of infrastructure is the main value in the value network. Some companies have more than one value configuration, but most companies have one dominating configuration.

Figure 1.5. Characteristics of value configurations

Characteristics	Value Chain	Value Shop	Value Network
Value creation	Transformation of input to output	Solving clients and customers problems	Connecting clients and customers to each other
Work form	Sequential production	Integrated and cyclical problem solving	Monitored and simultaneous connections
Information systems	Making production more efficient	Adding value to the knowledge work	Main value by use of IT infrastructure
Example	Paper factory	Law firm	Telecom company

In the long term, business organizations can choose to change their value configurations. A bank, for example can be a value shop when it focuses on converting inputs to outputs. The value resides in the output and once you have the output, you can remove the production organization. This removal does not have an impact on the value of the output. The value shop is a solution provider. It is somebody that solves problems. The input is a problem. The output is a solution to the problem. A bank that does this would view itself as a financial service operator, a financial advisor that also has the ability to provide the money. But what it would do is identify client problems; it would address those problems; it would select a solution together with the client and help to implement it; it would have stringent quality controls. As part of its offering, it would probably supply the client with some cash as a loan or accept some of the clients cash for investment (Chatzkel, 2002).

Alternatively, the bank can be a value network, which is the logic of the marketplace. The bank would define its role as a conduit between people that do not have money and those people that do have money. What the bank does is arrange the flow of cash between them. The bank will attract people with money to make deposits and investments. The bank will also attract people without money to obtain loans. As a value network, the bank will connect people with opposite financial needs. The network consists of people with different financial needs. Over time, persons in the network may change status from money *needer* to money *provider* and vice versa (Chatzkel, 2002).

Both as a value shop and as a value network, the business organization can be identified as a bank. But it would have completely different consequences for what it will focus on doing well, what it will focus on doing itself, vs. what it would not want to do itself. This provides a kind of strategic systems logic. It asks, "Which strategic system in terms of value configuration are we going to operate in?" Choosing an appropriate value configuration is a long-term decision with long-term consequences.

Chapter II

E-Business

Concepts and Trends

Internet

The Internet is an extremely important new technology, and it is no surprise that it has received so much attention from entrepreneurs, executives, investors, and business observers. Caught up in the general fervor, many have assumed that the Internet changes everything, rendering all the old rules about companies and competition obsolete. According to Porter (2001), that may be a natural reaction, but it is a dangerous one. It has led many companies, dot-coms and incumbent alike, to make bad decisions — decisions that have eroded the attractiveness of their industries and undermined their own competitive advantage. The time has come to make a clearer view of the Internet.

Internet technology provides better opportunities for companies to establish distinctive strategic positioning than did previous generations of information technology. The Internet's greatest impact has been to enable the reconfiguration of existing industries that had been constrained by high costs for communicating, gathering information, or accomplishing transactions. For example, the Internet tends to dampen the bargaining power of channels to providing companies with new, more direct avenues to customers (Porter, 2001).

The Internet has many properties, but 10 of them stand out (Afuah & Tucci, 2003):

- *Mediating technology.* The Internet is a mediating technology that interconnects parties that are independent or want to be. The interconnection can be business-to-business (B2B), business-to-consumer (B2C), consumer-to-consumer (C2C), or consumer-to-business (C2B). It can also be within a firm or any other organization, in which case it is called an intranet.

- *Universality.* Universality of the Internet refers to the Internet's ability to both enlarge and shrink the world. It enlarges the world because anyone anywhere in the world can potentially make his or her products available to anyone anywhere else in the world. It shrinks the world in that distance is reduced on electronic highways.

- *Network externalities.* A technology or product exhibits network externalities when it becomes more valuable to users as more people take advantage of it. A classic example is the telephone, where the value for each subscriber increases with number of subscribers. The more people that are connected to a network within the Internet, the more valuable the network is.

- *Distribution channel.* The Internet acts as a distribution channel for products that are largely information bits, such as software, music, video, news, and tickets. There is a replacement effect if the Internet is used to serve the same customers serviced by the old distribution channel without bringing in new customers. There is an extension effect if the Internet is used by more people and for new services.

- *Time moderator.* The fifth property of the Internet is time moderation, or its ability to shrink and enlarge time. It shrinks time for customers who want information on products when regular stores are closed. It enlarges time when related work can be done at different points in time.

- *Information asymmetry shrinker.* An information asymmetry exists when one party to a transaction has information that another party does not — information that is important to the transaction. The Web reduces such information asymmetries, as the other party can find the same information on the Web.

- *Infinite virtual capacity.* Access to the Internet is perceived as unlimited; you do not have to wait on hold or in a long line. For example, virtual communities like chat houses have infinite capacity for members who can talk anytime of the day for as long as they want.

- *Low cost standard.* Firms could not exploit the properties of the Internet if they did not adopt it. For two reasons, adoption has been easy. First and most important, the Internet and the Web are standards open to everyone everywhere and are very easy to use. Second, the cost of the Internet is a lot lower than that of earlier means of electronic communications.

- *Creative destroyer.* These properties of the Internet have enabled it to usher in a wave of creative destruction in many industries. Newspapers, for example, offer their readers material on their web sites. The Internet is a low cost standard printing press of sorts and a distribution network with unlimited capacity that reaches more people than any newspaper could ever hope to reach. This tears down a large part of the barriers to entry that exist in the newspaper business.

- *Transaction cost reducer.* The Internet also reduces transaction costs for many industries — thanks in part to the universality, distribution channel, low cost standard, and information asymmetry reduction properties. Transaction costs are the costs of searching for sellers and buyers; collecting information on products; negotiating, writing, monitoring, and enforcing contracts; and the costs of transportation associated with buying and selling.

However, as supply chains are becoming more dispersed and global in their orientation, and thereby have given rise to the problem of coordinating flow of information and materials across organizations that are linked together, transaction costs will rise (Grover & Malhotra 2003).

The Internet provides a global infrastructure that enables compression of time and space, integrated supply chains, mass customization and navigational ability. The impact of the Internet can be described as breaking down traditional trade-offs between richness of interaction possible with a customer and the number of customers a business can access or products it can offer. Internet-based businesses can compete on huge selections of products, as they are not constrained by physical stores. Also, richer interaction (e.g. check order status, seek online advice) and customized relationships with large numbers of customers at incremental costs are increasingly feasible with the economics of information (Grover & Saeed 2004).

Digital Transformation

The digital transformation of traditional businesses is occurring (Andal-Ancion, Cartwright, et al. 2003). New information technologies, such as broadband networks, mobile communications and the Internet, have well-known, but often unrealized, potential to transform businesses and industries. The key to success is knowing how and when to apply technologies. Companies should look at 10 specific drivers to help determine their best strategy.

Fro a study of large corporations in North America and Europe, Andal-Ancion, Cartwright, et al. (2003) identified the different drivers that determine the competitive advantage of deploying new information technology. Each of the drivers is very specific to how new IT can be applied in a particular industry. They are not general factors, such as the overall cost of a technology. In addition, they are different from the critical success factors that affect the implementation of information technology and that are mostly specific to a company, as opposed to being characteristic of an industry. There are ten drivers to help determine strategy:

1. *Electronic deliverability.* Some products have a large component that can be delivered electronically. Airline companies, for instance, enable customers to book reservations online, after which the confirmations and tickets can be delivered efficiently through e-mail.

2. *Information intensity.* Nearly all products and services have some information content, but the amount varies dramatically. Cars come with volumes of operating instructions, for instance.

3. *Customizability.* New information technology allows many companies to tailor an overall offering to the specific needs and preferences of individual customers. In the past, newspapers were a one-size-fits all product. Today, online editions can be customized to include just the news and information that a particular is subscriber likely to want.

4. *Aggregation effects.* Products and services differ in the way they can be aggregated or combined. Thanks to new information technology, institutions can offer customers bundled services.

5. *Search costs.* Before the advent of Internet companies such as Amazon.com, finding an out-of-print book could require considerable time and effort. Now, the Web provides people with vast amounts of information, regardless of their location or time zone, lowering the search costs for finding exactly the product or service they want.

6. *Real-time interface.* A real-time interface is necessary for companies and customers dealing with important information that changes suddenly and unpredictably. A good example is online trading, in which rapid fluctuations in the stock market can be devastating for those who lack instantaneous access to that information.

7. *Contracting risk.* Buying new books online has little contracting risk for customers. Prices are relatively low, and specifying the exact titles is straightforward. Buying cars online is a completely different matter. Prices are substantially higher.

8. *Network effects.* In many industries, the utility of a good or service increases with the number of people who are using it (or one that is compatible). A key benefit of using Microsoft Office, for instance, is that the suite of programs is ubiquitous in the business world, enabling people to share Word, PowerPoint and Excel documents easily.

9. *Standardization benefits.* New information technology enabled companies to synchronize and standardize certain processes, resulting in greater efficiency in business-to-business transactions as well as increased convenience for customers.

10. *Missing competencies.* New information technology can facilitate company alliances in which partners use each other to fill in missing competencies.

These ten drivers can be classified into three types of drivers. The first four drivers are inherent characteristics of product or service, drivers 5-7 are concerned with interactions between company and its customers, while the last three are concerned with interactions between company and its partners and competitors.

The ten drivers determine what type of mediation approach is most likely to succeed in particular industries. For each of three defined strategies, a couple of drivers are dominant, several are ancillary, and others have little consequence. The three strategies classic disintermediation, remediation, and network-based mediation are explained in terms of drivers by Andal-Ancion, Cartwright, et al. (2003) as follows:

A.   *Classic disintermediation* is cutting away layers of intermediaries, such as distributors, that separate the company from its customers. Disintermediation is the elimination of traditional intermediaries, be they retail stores, direct mail operations, or 800-number-style telephone support operations. With market-facing systems, the selling of products directly to consumers and businesses has become a powerful force in many industries. This strategy is affected mainly by the drivers that pertain to the inherent characteristics of a product or service. Specifically, electronic deliverability is a major factor. That is, why use a distributor when a product or service can be delivered electronically to the customer? Information intensity is another dominant driver. Before new information technology, products or services with high information intensity often needed intermediaries, such as an insurance agent, to explain a complex policy. Now, a sophisticated Web site can perform much of that functionality. Less powerful drivers of disintermediation include customizability, search costs, real-time interface, and low contracting risk. An industry that benefits from technology that provides a real-time interface, for instance, will favor disintermediation in order to eliminate the time lag caused by intermediaries.

B.   *Remediation* is introducing and embracing intermediaries. Historically, whenever transportation and communications infrastructures have markedly improved, industry value chains have tended to lengthen, with products and services becoming increasingly specialized. This has led many to suggest that the Web will also create whole new classes of intermediaries: market-facing enterprises whose primary presence is on the Web and who will provide portals that allow online users to access producers of goods and services. Remediation is affected mainly by two drivers: aggregation effects and high contracting risk. When there are benefits to combining products or services, companies can use technology to work more closely with their intermediary's partners, building strong, ongoing relationships. Some insurance companies, for example, now provide potential customers with online estimates of different policies through the Web site of the Automobile Association of America (www.aaa.com). High contracting risks also encourage companies to use technology to establish closer — and more secure — relationships. Ford, for instance, relies on the Web-based applications of intermediary Vastera Inc., a Virginia-based firm, to handle import and export processes, customs clearance, trade regulation compliance and cost calculations for shipments to Mexico and Canada. Other drivers of remediation are customizability (if the intermediary can contribute to the customization process rather than get in its way), real-time interface (if the interface is between the intermediary and either the producer or customer — and not between the producer and customer, which would instead encourage disintermediation) and missing competencies. High search costs tend to favor disintermediation instead of remediation.

C.   *Network-based mediation* is building strategic alliances and partnerships with new and existing players in a tangle of complex relationships. This mediation is affected mainly by drivers that pertain to a company's interactions with its partners and competitors. Specifically, network effects and standardization benefits are clearly important reasons for industry players to work more closely together. Other drivers include high search costs (which favor the use of a network for locating products and information), the need for a real-time interface (which encourages partners to build a system that enables them to deal with each other in real time) and missing competencies (which encourages companies, even competitors, to partner with one another to fill those gaps).

Electronic Commerce

Electronic commerce (EC) is an important concept that describes the process of buying, selling, or exchanging products, services, and information, via computer networks, including the Internet (Turban, et al. 2002). From a communications perspective, EC is the delivery of goods, services, information, or payments over computer networks or by any other electronic means. From a business process perspective, EC is the application of technology toward the automation of business transactions and workflow. From a service perspective, EC is a tool that addresses the desire of firms, consumers, and management to cut service costs while improving the quality of goods and increasing the speed of service delivery. From an online perspective, EC provides the capability of buying and selling products and information on the Internet and other online services. From a collaboration perspective, EC is the framework for inter- and intra-organizational collaboration. From a community perspective, EC provides a gathering place for community members, to learn, transact, and collaborate.

Electronic commerce over large ubiquitous networks will be conducted soon in routine fashion. While some may question the timeframe involved, few will question its imminence. In this transient phase of rapid technological change, it is difficult to see the real implications of these changes for both business and society. Recent writings have elaborated on the power of information technologies to reduce the costs of coordination and transactions and consequently to influence governance structures between buyers and sellers. Much of the popular press is also aggressive in providing anecdotes of innovative companies that have leveraged web-based technologies by expanding, improving, or modifying product and service offerings. A subliminal theme in all this hyperbole is the notion that these technologies are good and will provide the consumer with many more options, services, and advantages. Grover and Ramanlal (1999) challenged this theme by presenting alternative scenarios in which these technologies did not necessarily work in the best interest of the customer. For example, product customization, enabled by IT networks, can allow sellers to exploit buyers rather than benefit buyers.

The emergence of e-commerce is creating fundamental change to the way that business is conducted. These changes are altering the way in which every enterprise acquires wealth and creates shareholder value. The myriad of powerful computing and communications technology enabling e-commerce allow organizations to streamline their business processes, enhance customer service, and offer digital products and services. This shift underlying marketing fundamentals is now the driving force that is luring many organizations to embrace e-commerce. However, as they are learning, organizations must proceed with caution, as the road to e-commerce is littered with failed initiatives (Chang, Jackson, et al. 2003).

While engaging in e-commerce undoubtedly has substantial benefits, this marketplace is also quite competitive. E-commerce reduces customer search and switching costs, has the ability to distribute information on new products, access new sales channels and reduce entry-level capital requirements, thereby lowering barriers to entry. Companies that exhibit a market orientation by being vigilant regarding the needs of customers and the actions of competitors tend to achieve better performance. Over-emphasizing one dimension at the cost of the other tend to lead to sub-optimization in an environment that rewards the ability to sense and respond to a variety of information cues (Chang, Jackson, et al., 2003).

Electronic Business

The term *commerce* is defined by some as describing transactions conducted between business partners. When this definition of commerce is used, some people find the term electronic commerce to be narrow. Thus, many use the term e-business. E-business refers to a broader definition of EC, not just the buying and selling of goods and services, but also servicing customers, collaborating with business partners, and conducting electronic transactions within an organization (Turban, et al., 2002).

E-commerce is part of e-business, as illustrated in Figure 2.1. The difference can be demonstrated using a business example. The business example is concerned with handling of customer complaints. As long as customers do not complain, then e-commerce may be sufficient for electronic transactions with customers. The front end of

Figure 2.1. E-commerce is part of e-business

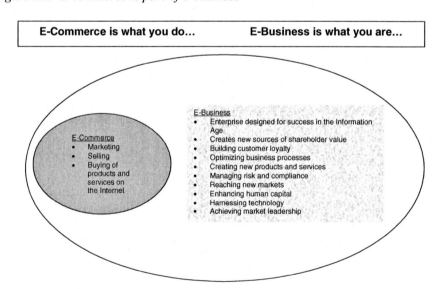

the business is electronic, and this front end is the only contact customers have with the business.

However, if a customer complains, then other parts of the business may have to get involved. For example, if the customer has received a computer which is found deficient, then the customer gets in touch with the vendor. The vendor has to decide whether the complaint is justified. If it is, then the vendor has to decide whether to (a) fix the product, (b) replace the product, or (c) refund the money paid for the product.

This kind of decision-making will typically involve other departments in addition to marketing and sales departments. These other departments may be the technical department, the production department, and the finance department. While the marketing and sales departments have electronic communication with the customer using information systems, other departments may not be connected to the same information systems.

In this situation, the internal handling of a customer complaint in the business is not transparent to and accessible for the customer. The customer may experience time passing by, without any information from the vendor. A complaining customer was angry already at the time of the complaint. The anger and frustration are rising, as the customer receives no response. The customer is unable to obtain information from the vendor by electronic means, since the vendor is doing e-commerce, not e-business.

If the vendor would be an e-business, then the business process of customer complaints handling would be an integrated information system to which the customer has access. Then it is possible for the customer to follow the complaint handling process, and it is possible for other departments than marketing and sales, to stay in direct contact with the complaining customer to resolve the issues. This business process is illustrated in Figure 2.2.

Weill and Vitale (2001) uses the following working definition of e-business: Marketing, buying, selling, delivering, servicing, and paying for products, services, and information

Figure 2.2. Customer complaint handling business process in company with e-commerce but no e-business

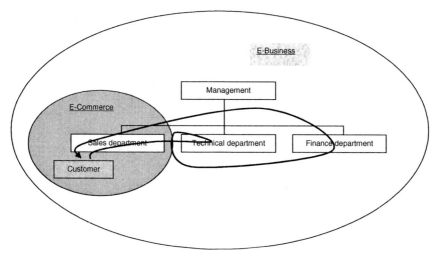

across (nonproprietary) networks linking an enterprise and its prospects, customers, agents, suppliers, competitors, allies, and complementors. The essence of this definition is the conduct of business and business processes over computer networks based on nonproprietary standards. The Internet is the exemplar of a nonproprietary network used today for e-business. Given its low cost and universal access, the Internet will be the major infrastructure for the near future. However, new access technologies already on the horizon (e.g., use of wireless application protocol from mobile telephones) will supplement the Internet.

E-business embodies the most pervasive, disruptive, and disconcerting form of change: it leaves no aspect of managing organizations untouched, it challenges long-accepted business models, and organization leaders have little to draw on from their experience to manage its effects. In particular, its capacity to transform business processes is no longer in dispute. The new technologies at the heart of e-business open up myriad possibilities not just to reconsider the re-engineering of existing processes but also to design, develop, and deploy fundamentally new ways of conceiving and executing business processes. Senior executives in every organization thus confront a central challenge: How should they endeavor to capture, analyze, and project the transformational impact of e-business on their organization's most critical or core processes? Later in this book, we put forward that knowledge management provides one useful vehicle for doing so (Fahey, Srivastava, et al., 2001).

In spite of its pervasiveness, visibility, and impact, e-business often remains a poorly understood phenomenon in many industries. E-business constitutes the ability of a firm to connect electronically, in multiple ways, many organizations, both internal and external, for many different purposes. It allows an organization to execute electronic transactions with any individual entity along the value creation — suppliers, logistics providers, wholesalers, distributors, service providers, and end customers. Increasingly, e-business allows an organization to establish real-time connections simultaneously among numerous entities for some specific purpose, such as optimizing the flow of physical items (raw materials, components, finished products) through the supply chain (Fahey, Srivastava,, et al., 2001).

E-business raises a number of critical business issues, each of which in turn generates distinct knowledge issues and challenges specific to the e-business transformation of processes. First, e-business is transforming the *solutions* available to customers in almost every industry, that is, the breadth of solutions and how the solutions are obtained and experienced. Consumers can now buy books, food, clothing, and many other goods over the Internet in ways that allow distinct forms of customization. Industrial purchasers can now use the Internet to scour the offerings of many providers and procure components and supplies in combinations, prices, and delivery schedules that dramatically lower the costs of search, speed delivery, and reduce prices. These new solutions open up possibilities for customer value creation and delivery that were simply unimaginable few years ago (Fahey, Srivastava, et al., 2001).

Second, the creators and purveyors of the new customer value propositions represent new types of *rivals*. Traditional booksellers are confronted by Amazon.com; Merill Lynch faces E*TRADE. These new entities recast the profile of rivals in many industries and, partly as a consequence, reshape the contours and boundaries of most traditional competitive spaces or industries (Fahey, Srivastava, et al., 2001).

Third, in part due to the competitive context changes just noted, the nature and content of *strategy*, and by implication, the dynamics of marketplace rivalry, are undergoing profound change. No longer can most firms rely on making modest, incremental changes to long-established strategy success formulas. Strategy in product domains as diverse as financial services, household furnishings, computers, automobiles, and industrial components, increasingly revolves around inventing new product solutions, and/or new ways of interacting with customers in designing, developing, and delivering these solutions. In fact, organizations are adjusting their strategies according to the new notion of the customer where customer intimacy, customer relationship management, one-to-one marketing, and the concept of the customer as opposed to the product as the new asset of the organization and real carrier of value, dominate. In short, e-business offers the platform for new forms of marketplace strategy models — a significant element of any firm's business model — that will change the competitive rules of the game (Fahey, Srivastava, et al., 2001).

Fourth, e-business requires firms to refocus and reconfigure almost every type of tangible and intangible asset. It places an especially heavy premium on developing and leveraging intangible assets, including many different types of new skills, new forms of integrated and intensive relationships with external entities, new sets of perceptions held by customers, channels, and suppliers, and significant new knowledge (Fahey, Srivastava, et al., 2001).

Fifth, e-business is dramatically reshaping every traditional business process: from developing new products and managing customer relationships to acquiring human resources and procuring raw materials and components. By enabling major new tasks to be added to individual processes, e-business broadens their scope, content, and value-generating capability. For example, customer relationship management essentially has been reinvented through e-business's ability to access large bodies of heretofore-unavailable data, massage and mine such data in radical new ways, and customize the outputs of such analysis to customer segments, and in many cases, to individual customers. And, by integrating traditionally largely separate processes, e-business in effect creates what might well be described as new business processes (Fahey, Srivastava, et al., 2001).

Competitive Strategy

A study conducted by Chang, Jackson, et al. (2003) proposed that e-commerce initiatives are important strategic initiatives and that firms with a stronger e-commerce market orientation would be more successful. Content analysis of CEO's letter to shareholders of 145 Fortune 500 firms was conducted to evaluate the importance of e-commerce and strategic orientation. The results provide support to the studies proposition and indicate that e-commerce must be pursued carefully as a strategic initiative rather than as an appendage to an existing organization.

Strategy is an ongoing process of evaluating purpose as well as questioning, verifying and redefining the manner of interaction with the competitive environment. Complexity of the strategy process can be simplified by searching for patterns of behavior in organizations. These patterns of emergent behavior can be used to describe the underlying processes of organizational adaptation. Basic strategic orientation of organizations can be described in terms of a typology of defenders, prospectors, analyzers, and reactors. Each orientation differs with respect to risk disposition, innovativeness, and operational efficiencies. Strategic orientation such as low cost or differentiation is means of altering the firm's position vis-à-vis competitors and suppliers. Strategy involves mustering resources and creating capabilities that are difficult to imitate by competitors, resulting in superior rents. Strategic orientation is both an issue of how firms position themselves with respect to competitors and an issue of how firm-specific resources are exploited (Grover & Saeed, 2004).

Much strategic management literature has been devoted to identifying attributes or dimensions of a company's strategic orientation. Internet-based businesses include portals, travel sites, e-tailers, and providers of financial and informational services. These businesses attempt to leverage the internet infrastructure and digital economics in order to gain strategic positioning within the marketplace. For internet-based businesses, four major dimensions of strategic orientation are particularly pertinent: risk disposition, innovativeness, operational efficiency, and marketing intensity (Grover & Saeed, 2004).

Internet Strategy

Many of the pioneers of Internet business, both dot-coms and established companies, have competed in ways that violate nearly every precept of good strategy. There was for a long time an absence of strategy. According to Porter (2001), the time has come to take a clearer view of the Internet. It is necessary to move away from rhetoric — such as Internet industries, e-business strategies, and a new economy — and see the Internet for what it is. It is an enabling technology, a powerful set of tools that can be used, wisely or unwisely, in almost any industry and as part of almost any strategy.

Strategy is neither the quest for the universally best way of competing nor an effort to be all things to every customer. It defines a way of competing that delivers unique value in a particular set of uses or for a particular set of customers. To establish and maintain a distinctive strategic positioning, a company needs to follow six fundamental principles (Porter, 2001):

- It must start with the *right goal*: superior long-term return on investment. Only by grounding strategy in sustained profitability will real economic value be generated. Economic value is created when customers are willing to pay a price for a product or service that exceeds the cost of producing it.

- A company's strategy must enable it to deliver a *value proposition*, or set of benefits, different from those that competitors offer.

- Strategy needs to be reflected in a *distinctive value configuration*. To establish a sustainable competitive advantage, a company must perform different activities than rivals or perform similar activities in different ways.

- Robust strategies involve *trade-offs*. A company must abandon or forgo some product features, services, or activities in order to be unique at others.

- Strategy defines how all the elements of what a company does *fit* together. A strategy involves making choices throughout the value configuration that are independent; all a company's activities must be mutually reinforcing.

- Strategy involves *continuity* of direction. A company must define a distinctive value proposition that it will stand for, even if that means forgoing certain opportunities.

- The absence of strategy in may pioneering Internet businesses have mislead them to focus on revenues rather than profits, indirect values rather than real value, every conceivable product rather than trade-offs, activities of rivals rather than tailor the value configuration, and rash of partnerships rather than build control. To capitalize on the Internet's strategic potential, executives and entrepreneurs alike will need to develop a strategy that exploits this potential. In some industries, the use of the Internet represents only a modest shift from well-established practices. Virtual activities do not eliminate the need for physical activities, but often amplify their importance. The complementarity between Internet activities and traditional activities arises for a number of reasons. First, introducing Internet applications in one activity often places greater demands on physical activities elsewhere in the value configuration. Second, using the Internet in one activity can have systemic consequences, requiring new or enhanced physical activities that are often unanticipated. Third, most Internet applications have some shortcomings in comparison with conventional methods, such as customers being unable to physically examine products (Porter, 2001).

Competing on Reach, Affiliation and Richness

A new generation of electronic commerce is emerging, one that will be shaped more by strategy than by experimentation. The battle for competitive advantage will be intensified. According to Evans and Wurster (1999), the battle will be waged along three dimensions: reach, affiliation, and richness.

To the extent that information was embedded in physical modes of delivery, a basic law governed its economics: there was a universal trade-off between richness and reach. Richness means the quality of information, as defined by the user. Reach means the number of people who participate in the sharing of that information. Until recently, it has been possible to share extremely rich information with a very small number of people and less rich information with a larger number, but it was impossible to share simultaneously as much richness and reach as one would like. This trade-off is at the heart of the old economics of information, as illustrated in Figure 2.3 (Evans & Wurster, 2000).

Figure 2.3. Traditional trade-off between richness and reach

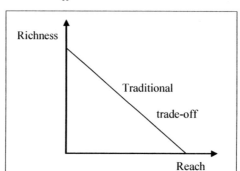

Communicating rich information has required proximity (people working in the same physical location) or dedicated channels (such as proprietary computer networks, retail stores, or a sales force). The costs or physical constraints of these channels have limited the number of people who can access the information. Conversely, communicating information to a large audience has required compromises in the quality of that information. Technologies have not allowed us to achieve simultaneously as much richness and reach we would like.

Two forces drive the fundamental change taking place now. First, the explosion of connectivity has caused information to reach almost anybody. Second, the adoption of common information standards that allows everybody to communicate with everybody else at essentially zero cost.

Future business competition will not only be along the dimensions of reach and range. It will also be concerned with affiliation. The same technological forces that blow up the trade-off between richness and reach also opens a change in interests the business represents. Evans and Wurster (2000) describe the three dimensions of competition as follows.

- *Competing on reach.* Before the emergence of e-commerce, retail stores competed on reach by offering convenient physical locations and broad selections of goods and services at these locations. But the number of physical locations and the product selections had to be limited. Each physical location had its costs, and broader selection of products in these locations was associated with higher costs. Electronic commerce offers a dramatic improvement in reach because the navigation function (catalog) is separated from the physical function (inventory). There is no limit to locations, and there is no limit to selections.

  Reach is about access and connection. It means how many customers a business can connect with and how many products it can offer to those customers. Reach is the most visible difference between electronic and physical businesses, and it has been the primary competitive differentiator for e-commerce thus far.

- *Competing on affiliation.* Before the emergence of e-commerce, suppliers were focused on their products and services. They were concerned with their own interests. Until now, affiliation has not been a serious competitive factor in physical commerce because, in general, no company ever devised a way to make money by taking the consumers' side. However, it is a natural progression, as navigators emerge. Navigators may be software programs, evaluators or search engines. They are not selling anything except, possibly, information.

Affiliation is about whose interests the business represents. Affiliation does not mean caring for the customer: any supplier, retailer, or navigator has to do that. It does not refer to any of the helpful, positive-sum activities by which sellers further their own interests by furthering those of their customers. That is simply good business. The test of affiliation is where the consumer's gain is the seller's loss. Informing the consumer of purchasing alternatives available from other suppliers; explaining why a premium feature is not worth the money; sharing unflattering information on product performance or customer satisfaction: these are the kinds of navigational services that consumers would expect from a navigator serving their interests.

- *Competing on richness.* When competing on reach and affiliation, traditional players have to struggle to keep abreast of electronic retailers and pure navigators. But they have natural advantages when it comes to richness. Traditional retailers can exploit their detailed information about customers. Suppliers can use extensive product information to their advantage.

Richness is the depth and detail of information that the business can give the customer, as well as the depth and detail of information it collects about the customer. Electronic businesses have not yet learned to compete seriously on the richness dimension. But richness holds enormous potential for building close relationships with customers in a future dominated by e-commerce. Rich product information encompasses all the obvious categories of technical facts, product background, and troubleshooting advice. Rich consumer information is variously described as database marketing, data mining, or mass customization.

Figure 2.4. Emerging trade-off between richness, reach, and affiliation

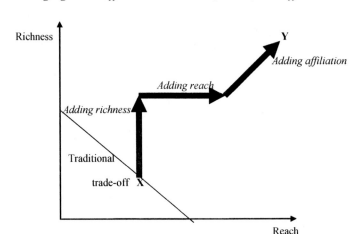

Competition in the second generation of electronic commerce is illustrated in Figure 2.4. The old point of competition X is transformed into the new point of competition Y through added richness, reach, and affiliation.

The Internet provides access to a *virtual territory* for each company. While a physical territory is an area of land (terra = earth) which has been expanded to include ocean parts and air parts, a virtual territory can be defined as a combination of reach, affiliation and richness which has achieved a combined effect of being in control of the virtual area. This virtual territory then belongs to the company. A virtual territory assumes the combined successful effects of reach, affiliation, and richness.

If a company is primarily successful along less than three dimensions, it has no virtual territory. For example, if a company is only successful along the richness dimension, the Internet provides information embassies for the company. An *information embassy* can be defined as a representation of the company on foreign territory.

Block, Run and Alliance Strategies

If a firm's business model enables it to gain a competitive advantage, the chances are that its competitors would like to catch up or maybe even leapfrog it. What can a firm do to maintain its competitive advantage? To sustain a competitive advantage, a firm can — depending on its capabilities, environment, and technology in question — pursue some subset of the three generic strategies block, run, and alliance (Afuah & Tucci, 2003):

- *Block strategy* is the firm erecting barriers around its product market space. A firm can block in two ways. First, if its capabilities are inimitable and distinctive enough to offer customers unique value, the firm can limit access to them and thereby keep out competitors. That would be the case, for example, when the firm has intellectual property that can be protected and sends signals to potential imitators that it means business in protecting the property. Second, if all firms are equally capable of performing these activities, incumbents may still prevent entry by signaling that post-entry prices will be low. There are several ways a firm can achieve this. For example, it can establish a reputation for retaliating against anyone who tries to imitate any component of its business model. It can also do so by making heavy, nonreversible investments in relevant assets. For example, if a firm spends billions of dollars installing fiber optics capability for the households in a town, the chances are that it will lower prices if another firm wants to offer high-speed access to the same customers. In general, such signals can prevent profit-motivated potential competitors from entering.

  Blocking works only as long as a company's capabilities are unique and inimitable or as long as barriers to entry last. But competitors can, for example, circumvent patents and copyrights or challenge them in court until they are overturned. Moreover, the usefulness of such capabilities lasts only until discontinuities such as deregulation/regulation, changing customer preferences and expectations, or radical technological change render them obsolete. The information asymmetry reduction property of the Internet also suggests that blocking is not going to be very effective.

- *Run strategy* admits that blockades to entry, no matter how formidable they may appear, are often penetrable, or eventually fall. Sitting behind these blockades only gives competitors time to catch up or leapfrog the innovator. An innovator often has to run. Running means changing some subset of components or linkages of business models or reinventing the whole business model to offer the customer better value. Running can give a firm many first-mover advantages, including the ability to control parts of its own environment. In an age of rapid technological change, the run strategy becomes extremely important because blocking is more difficult. Running sometimes means the cannibalization — eating into existing sales — of one's own products before competitors do.

- *Alliance strategy* enables a firm to do it with others through some kind of strategic teaming-up, joint venture, acquisition, or equity position. Teaming up allows a firm to share in resources that it does not possess and may not want to acquire or cannot acquire even if it wanted to. Shared resources also facilitate knowledge transfer. Alliance has its disadvantages too. It is not easy for a firm to protect its technology or other aspects of its business that it would like to keep proprietary. In teaming up, a firm also risks becoming too dependent on another firm's resources. Often, running also requires teaming up.

Attaining and maintaining a competitive advantage often requires some combination of the three strategies. An important question is, "When is each strategy or combination of strategies appropriate?" Two factors influence the choice of strategy. First, the choice depends on what it takes for a firm to build a profitable business model. It depends on what determines profitability in the face of the technology in question. After all, a business model is about how to make money over the long run. Second, timing is of the essence. The strategy pursued is a function of the stage of evolution of the technology — the Internet in our case. It is also a function of when existing and potential competitors have pursued related strategies or plan to (Afuah & Tucci, 2003).

Value Creation

New value can be created in e-business by the ways in which transactions are enabled. The term value refers to the total value created in e-business transactions regardless of whether it is the firm, the customer, or any other participant in the transaction who appropriates that value. Amit and Zott (2001) identified four major value drivers in e-business: efficiency, complementarities, lock-in, and novelty. Each of these four drivers and the linkages among them enhance the value-creation potential of e-business:

- *Efficiency*. Transaction cost theory suggests that transaction efficiency increases when the costs per transaction decrease. Therefore, the greater the transaction efficiency gains that are enabled by a particular e-business, the lower the costs and hence the more valuable it will be. Efficiency enhancements relative to offline businesses (i.e., those of companies operating in traditional markets), and relative to other online businesses (i.e., those of companies operating in virtual markets), can be realized in a number of ways. One is by reducing information asymmetries between buyers and sellers through the supply of up-to-date and comprehensive information. The speed and facility with which information can be transmitted via the Internet makes this approach convenient and easy. Improved information can also reduce customers' search and bargaining costs. By leveraging the cheap interconnectivity of virtual markets, e-businesses further enhance transaction efficiency by enabling faster and more informed decision-making. Also, they provide for greater selection at lower costs by reducing distribution costs, streamlining inventory management, simplifying transactions (thus reduce the likelihood of mistakes), allowing individual customers to benefit from scale economies through demand aggregation and bulk purchasing, streamlining the supply chain, and speeding up transaction processing and order fulfillment, thereby benefiting both vendors and customers.

- *Complementarities*. Whenever having a bundle of goods together provides more value than the total value of having each of the goods separately, complementarities are present. For a company, another company is a complementor if customers value the company's product more when they have the other company's product than when they have the company's product alone. The resource-based theory of the firm also highlights the role of complementarities among strategic assets as a source of value creation. E-businesses leverage this potential for value creation by offering bundles of complementary products and services to their customers. These complementary goods may be vertical complementarities (e.g., after-sales services) or horizontal complementarities (e.g., one-stop shopping, or cameras and films) that are provided by partner firms. They are often directly related to a core transaction enabled by the firm. Furthermore, offline assets can complement online offerings. Customers who buy products over the Internet value the possibility of getting after-sales services offered through bricks-and-mortar retail outlets, including the convenience of returning or exchanging merchandise. E-businesses may also create value by capitalizing on complementarities among activities such as supply-chain integration, and complementarities among technologies such as linking the imaging technology of one business with the Internet communication technology of another, thereby unleashing hidden value.

- *Lock-in*. The value-creating potential of an e-business is enhanced by the extent to which customers are motivated to engage in repeat transactions (which tends to increase transaction volume), and by the extent to which strategic partners have incentives to maintain and improve their associations (which may result in both increased willingness to pay of customers and lower opportunity costs for firms). These value-creating attributes of an e-business can be achieved through lock-in. Lock-in prevents the migration of customers and strategic partners to competitors, thus creating value in the aforementioned ways. Lock-in is manifested as switching costs, which has its roots in network theory. It should also be noted that, as the resource-based theory of the firm suggests, a firm's strategic assets, such as its brand name, and buyer-seller trust, both contribute to lock-in. Customer retention can be enhanced in several ways. First, loyalty programs rewarding repeat customers. Second, firms can develop dominant design proprietary standards. Third, firms can establish trustful relationships with customers, for example, by offering them transaction safety and reliability guaranteed by independent and highly credible third parties. Virtual markets also enable e-business firms to create virtual communities that bond participants to a particular e-business.

- *Novelty*. E-businesses innovate in the ways they do business, that is, in the structuring of transactions. The unique characteristics of virtual markets make the possibilities for innovation seem endless. For example, e-business firms can identify and incorporate valuable new complementary products and services into their bundle of offerings in novel ways. Another dimension of innovation in e-business refers to the appropriate selection of participating parties. For example, firms can direct and intensify traffic to their web site by initiating affiliate programs with third parties, who are compensated for enabling the execution of transactions from their own web sites. Novelty is also linked to complementaries. The main innovation of some e-businesses resides in their complementary elements, such as the resources and capabilities they combine. There is also an important relationship between novelty and efficiency. Certain efficiency features of e-businesses may be due to novel assets that can be created and exploited in the context of virtual markets.

Launching a Business on the Internet

Launching a business on the Internet requires careful planning, understanding the target customer base, and choosing the right products and services to offer. This first planning step involves strategic questions such as, "Who will buy the product? How familiar are you with the Internet? Are you planning to be a short-termer or a long-termer? Who are your competitors? How good will your product(s) look? How will you present your product offerings? How will you manage and process transactions? How will the product be shipped? How will you handle unexpected change? How will you get and use feedback?" (Awad, 2002).

The next step in launching a business on the Internet is resolving the software and hardware issues, especially with respect to linking to the Internet Service Provider (ISP) that will put the business on the Internet. For a fee, the ISP gives the new firm a software package, user name, password, and access phone number. Equipped with a modem, the firm can then log onto the Internet and browse the World Wide Web, send and receive e-mail, and download software packages or text files. Nearly every ISP today offers what is called virtual hosting or a virtual domain as well. This allows the firm to have its own domain name, such as http://www.thefirm.com (Awad, 2002).

The firm's site should capture customers' attention and retain them long enough to result in a sale. The site should also generate repeat customers. Assuming the buyer has gone through the ordering process, how can the experience end on a good note? The delivery of the product is critical. The system should include a tracking system to let the shopper know when and who received the product. A follow-up e-mail after the order has been filled is a tactful method of thanking the customer and confirming the order (Awad, 2002).

Customer service contributes a great deal to creating customer loyalty. In addition to being enjoyable, the shopping experience should be risk-free for the firm and the firm customer. That means implementing powerful security measures for the Web site and the servers to protect them and the transactions from hackers. Security is concerned with protection of data, software, and hardware against accidental or intentional damage from a defined threat (Awad, 2002).

When it comes to security, Web site planners look at three overlapping types of risk: document security, privacy, and overall system security. Document security entails the integrity of the Web site and its information. There must be security features in Web design that ensure no one can corrupt the integrity of the site itself, let alone the information in its content or its layout. Customer privacy has to do with embedding devices in the visitor's hard disk to track site usage. The visitor should be aware of such marketing tactics and should be able to choose whether the merchant is allowed to secure such a link. System security deals with the way the network, the Web server, and the e-business infrastructure prevent unauthorized access and tampering with e-commerce traffic (Awad, 2002).

In launching a business on the Internet, we can define several phases. The business planning and strategizing phase is followed by the hardware, software, security, and setup phase, the design phase, the marketing phase, the fulfillment phase, and finally the maintenance and enhancement phase. Maintenance means keeping a system or a business on course, based on the initial design or plan. Enhancement means implementing upgrades or changes that are designed to improve the system's productivity. The focus in this phase is on managing the e-business. When customer messages pile up unanswered, something is wrong. The source of the pileup could be a poor Web site, a congested communication line, or an understaffed e-merchant (Awad, 2002).

Regardless of the reasons or circumstances, the goal of maintenance is to ensure the usability of the Web site. The goal of enhancement is to upgrade the Web site and the business-to-consumer connection to meet the latest standards and customer expectations. The bottom line is customer attraction and retention (Awad, 2002).

E-Business Models

A business model can be defined as the method by which a firm builds and uses its resources to offer its customers better value than its competitors use and to take money doing so. It details how a firm makes money now and how it plans to do so in the ling run. The model is what enables a firm to have a sustainable competitive advantage, to perform better than its rivals in the long-term do. A business model can be conceptualized as a system that is made up of components, linkages between the components, and dynamics (Afuah & Tucci, 2003).

Weill and Vitale (2001) define an e-business model as a description of the roles and relationships among a firm's consumers, customers, allies, and suppliers that identifies the major flows of product, information, and money, and the major benefits to participants.

There are many different ways to describe and classify e-business models. Weill and Vitale (2001) propose that there are a finite number of atomic e-business models, each of which captures a different way to conduct e-business. Firms can combine atomic e-business models as building blocks to create tailored e-business models and initiatives, using their competencies as their guide. Weill and Vitale (2001) identified a small number of eight atomic e-business models, each of which describes the essence of conducting business electronically.

1. **Direct to customer.** The distinguishing characteristic of this model is that buyer and seller communicate directly, rather than through an intermediary. The seller may be a retailer, a wholesaler, or a manufacturer. The customer may be an individual or a business. Examples of the direct-to-customer model are Dell Computer Corporation (www.dell.com) and Gap, Inc. (www.gap.com).

    - *Infrastructure.* The direct-to-customer model requires extensive electronic connection with the customer, including online payment systems. Many direct-to-customer implementations include an extranet to allow customized Web pages for major B2B customers. Operating a direct-to-customer e-business requires significant investment in the equivalent of the store: the Web site. Direct-to-customer businesses spend millions of dollars developing easy-to-navigate and easy-to-use Web sites with the goal of improving the B2B or B2C shopping experience online. Lands End (www.landsend.com) has devised a feature by which women can build and store a three-dimensional model of themselves to "try on" clothes electronically.

      In their field research, Weill and Vitale (2001) found that firms with e-business initiatives containing the direct-to-customer e-business model needed and were investing more heavily in three areas of infrastructure services: application infrastructure, communications, and IT management.

      Direct-to-customer firms particularly needed payment transaction processing to process online customer payments, enterprise-wide resource planning (ERP) to process customer transactions, workflow infrastructure to optimize business process performance, communication network services linking all points in the enterprise to each other and the outside world (often using TCP/IP protocol), the installation and maintenance of workstations and local area networks supporting the large number of people required to operate a direct-to-customer model, and service-level agreements between the business and the IT group or outsourcer to ensure, monitor, and improve the systems necessary for the model.

    - *Sources of revenue.* The main source of revenue in the direct-to-customer model is usually direct sales to customers. Supplemental revenues come from advertising, the sale of customer information, and product placement fees.

    - *Critical success factors.* Critical success factors are the things a firm must do well to flourish. The following list shows the critical success factors for the direct-to-customer model: create and maintain customer awareness, in order to build a critical mass of users to cover the fixed cost of building an electronic presence; reduce customer acquisition costs; strive to own the customer relationship and understand individual customer needs; increase repeat purchases and average transaction size; provide fast and efficient transaction processing, fulfillment, and payment; ensure adequate security for the organization and its customers; and provide interfaces that combine ease of use with richness of experience, integrating multiple channels.

2.   **Full-service provider.** A firm using the full-service provider model provides total coverage of customer needs in a particular domain, consolidated via a single point of contact. The domain could be any major area of customer needs requiring multiple products and services, for example, financial services, health care, or industrial chemicals. The full-service provider adds value by providing a full range of products, sourced both internally and externally, and consolidated them using the channel chosen by the customer. Examples of the full-service provider are the Prudential Advisor (www.prusec.com) and GE Supply Company (www.gesupply.com).

- *Infrastructure.* Virtually all businesses aspire to getting hundred percent of their customers' business, or at least to getting as much of that business as they can profitably handle. Yet the number of full-service providers remains small. Part of the reason for this is required infrastructure. The missing piece of infrastructure in many businesses is often a database containing information about the customer and the products that the customer owns. Without owning these data, a provider does not own the customer relationship, and therefore some of the customer's transactions are likely to take place directly with other providers. All of the important interactions with customers occurring across any channel or business unit must be recorded in the firm-wide customer database.

  Weill and Vitale (2001) identified in their field research databases and data warehouses as some of the most important infrastructure services associated with the full-service provider model. Other important infrastructure services included the following: the ability to evaluate proposals for new information systems initiatives to coordinate IT investments across a multi-business-unit firm with the goal of a single point of contact for the customer; centralized management of IT infrastructure capacity to integrate across multiple business units within the firm and third-party providers, the full-service provider model is not readily workable if each business unit optimizes its own IT needs; installation and maintenance of workstations and local area networks to operate the online business linking all the business units and third-party providers; electronic support for groups to coordinate the cross-functional teams required to implement this model; and the identification and testing of new technologies to find cost-effective ways to deliver this complex business model to the customer across multiple channels.

- *Sources of revenue.* A full-service provider gains revenues from selling its own products and those of others, and possibly also from annual membership fees, management fees, transaction fees, commissions on third-party products, advertising or listing fees from third-party providers, and fees for selling aggregated data about customers.

- *Critical success factors.* One important critical success factor is the brand, credibility and trust necessary for a customer to look to the firm for its complete needs in an area. Another is owning the customer relationship in one domain and integrating and consolidating the offering of many third parties into a single channel or multiple channels. A third factor is owning more of the customer data in the relevant domain than any other player. A final factor is enforcement of policies to protect the interests of internal and external suppliers, as well as customers.

3.   **Whole of enterprise.** The single point of contact for the e-business customer is the essence of the whole-of-enterprise atomic business model. Although many of this model's breakthrough innovations have occurred in public-sector organizations, the model is applicable in both the for-profit and the public sectors. An example of this model is the Australian state of Victoria with its Business Channel (www.business.channel.vic.gov.au) and Health Channel (www.betterhealth.vic.gov.au).

- *Infrastructure.* For the whole-of-enterprise model, infrastructure needs to link the different systems in the various business units and provide a firm-wide perspective for management. The field research by Weill and Vitale (2001) revealed that the following infrastructure services are the most important for implementing this model: centralized management of infrastructure capacity to facilitate integration and capture economies of scale; identification and testing of new technologies to find new ways to integrate the often different systems in many business units into a single point of customer contact; management of key data independent of applications and the creation of a centralized repository for firm-wide information; electronic means of summarizing data from different applications and platforms to manage the complexity arising from a single point of contact for multiple business units; development of an ERP service to process the transactions instigated by customers interacting with several different business units, often requiring consolidating or linking several ERPs in the firm; payment transaction processing, either on a firm-wide basis or by linking several systems across the business units; large-scale data-processing facilities to process transactions from multiple business units, often centralized to achieve economies of scale; and integrated mobile computing applications, which provide another channel to the customer.

- *Sources of revenue.* In the for-profit sector, revenues are generated by provision of goods and services to the customer by the business units. There may also be the opportunity to charge an annual service or membership fee for this level of service. In the government sector, the motivation is usually twofold: improved service and reduced cost. Service to the community is improved through continuous, round-the-clock operation and faster service times. Government costs can potentially be reduced by sharing more infrastructure and eliminating the need to perform the same transaction in multiple agencies.

- *Critical success factors.* The following list details the critical success factors for the whole-of-enterprise model: changing customer behavior to make use of the new model, as opposed to the customer continuing to interact directly with individual units; reducing costs in the individual business units as the direct demands on them fall, and managing the transfer pricing issues that will inevitably arise; altering the perspective of the business units to take an enterprise-wide view, which includes broad product awareness, training, and cross-selling; in the integrated implementation, reengineering the business processes to link into life events at the front end and existing legacy processes and systems at the back end; and finding compelling and practical life events that customers can use as triggers to access the enterprise.

4. **Intermediaries** such as portals, agents, auctions, aggregators, and other intermediaries. E-business is often promoted as an ideal way for sellers and buyers to interact directly, shortening old-economy value chains by disintermediating some of their members. Yet some of the most popular sites on the Internet, both for consumers and for business users, are in fact intermediaries — sites that stand between the buyer and the seller. The services of intermediaries include search (to locate providers of products and services), specification (to identify important product attributes), price (to establish the price, including optional extras such as warranties), sale (to complete the sales transaction, including payment and settlement), fulfillment (to fulfill the purchase by delivering the product or service), surveillance (to conduct surveillance of the activities of buyers and sellers in order to report aggregate activity and prices and to inform and regulate the market), and enforcement (to enforce proper conduct by buyers and sellers). Examples of intermediaries are electronic malls, shopping agents, specialty auctions, electronic markets, electronic auctions, and portals.

    - *Infrastructure.* Intermediaries generate value by concentrating information and bringing together buyers and sellers, operating entirely in space and thus relying on IT as the primary infrastructure. Weill and Vitale (2001) found in their field interviews that the most important infrastructure services for firms pursuing the intermediary atomic business model are the following: knowledge management, including knowledge databases and contact databases that enable the codification and sharing of knowledge in this highly information-intensive business; enforcing Internet and e-mail policies to ensure proper and consistent use of electronic channels to buyers, sellers, and intermediaries; workstation networks to support the products and services of this all-electronic business model; centralized management of e-business applications, ensuring consistency and integration across product offerings; information systems planning to identify the most effective uses of IT in the business; and information systems project management to ensure that business value is achieved from IT investments.

    - *Sources of revenue.* An intermediary may earn revenues from buyers, sellers, or both. Sellers may pay a listing fee, a transaction fee, a sales commission, or some combination. Similarly, buyers may pay a subscription fee, a success fee, or a sales commission.

- *Critical success factors.* The chief requirement for survival as an intermediary is sufficient volume of usage to cover the fixed costs of establishing the business and the required infrastructure. Attracting and retaining a critical mass of customers is therefore the primary critical success factor. Another important critical success factor is building up infrastructure just quickly enough to meet demand as it increases.

5. **Shared infrastructure.** The firm provides infrastructure shared by its owners. Other suppliers, who are users of the shared infrastructure, but not owners, can also be included. Customers who access the shared infrastructure directly are given a choice of suppliers and value propositions. The owner and the non-owner suppliers are generally represented objectively. In some situations, goods or services flow directly from the shared infrastructure to the customer. In other situations, a message is sent by the shared infrastructure to the supplier, who then completes the transaction by providing the goods or services to the customer.

- An example illustrating the features of the shared-infrastructure business model is the system from 2000 by America's largest automakers, some of their dealers, and IBM, Motorola, and Intel. The initiative was named Covisint (collaboration vision integrity). General Motors, Ford, and DaimlerChrysler see stronger potential benefits from cooperating on supply-chain logistics than from competing.

- *Infrastructure.* The shared-infrastructure business model requires competitors to cooperate by sharing IT infrastructure and information. This level of cooperation requires agreement on high-level IT architectures as well as operational standards for applications, data communications, and technology. Effective implementation of the shared-infrastructure model also requires enforcement of these standards, and most shared-infrastructure models have a joint committee to set and enforce standards. Another role of these committees is to implement the policies of the shared infrastructure about what information, if any, is hared and what information is confidential to partner firms. Weill and Vitale (2001) found in their field research that the most important infrastructure services required by firms implementing the shared-infrastructure atomic business model all concerned architectures and standards: specification and enforcement of high-level architectures for data, technology, applications, communications, and work that are agreed to by alliance partners; and specification and enforcement of detailed standards for the high-level architectures.

- *Sources of revenue.* Revenues can be generated both from membership fees and from transaction fees. The alliance may be run on a nonprofit basis or on a profit-making basis. Not-for-profit shared infrastructures are typically open to all eligible organizations and distribute any excess revenues back to their members. The for-profit models are typically owned by a subset of the firms in a given segment, which split up any profits among themselves.

- *Critical success factors.* Critical success factors for the shared-infrastructure model include the following: no dominant partner that gains more than any other partner; an unbiased channel and objective presentation of product and service information; critical mass of both alliance partners and customers; management of conflict among the ongoing e-business initiatives of the alliance partners; compilation and delivery of accurate and timely statements of the services and benefits provided to each member of the alliance; and interoperability of systems.

6.   **Virtual community.** Virtual communities deserve our attention, and not only because they are the clearest, and perhaps the last, surviving embodiment of the original intent of the Internet. By using IT to leverage the fundamental human desire for communication with peers, virtual communities can create significant value for their owners as well as for their members. Once established, a virtual community is less susceptible to competition by imitation than any of the other atomic business models. In this business model, the firm of interest — the sponsor of the virtual community — sits in the center, positioned between members of the community and suppliers. Fundamental to the success of this model is that members are able, and in fact are encouraged, to communicate with one another directly. Communication between members may be vial e-mail, bulletin boards, online chat, Web-based conferencing, or other computer-based media, and it is the distinguishing feature of this model. Examples of this model are Parent Soup (www.parentsoup.com), a virtual community for parents, and Motley Fool (www.motleyfool.com), a virtual community of investors.

   •   *Infrastructure.* Virtual communities depend on IT to exist. In particular, the creation and continual enhancement of an Internet site is essential if a virtual community is to survive. Many virtual-community sites include not only static content and links, but also tools of interest to potential members. Weill and Vitale (2001) found in their field research that the infrastructure services most important for the virtual-community business model are the following: training in the use of IT for members of the community; application service provision (ASP) to provide specialized systems virtual communities need such as bulletin boards, e-mail, and ISP access; IT research and development, including infrastructure services for identifying and testing new technologies and for evaluating proposals for new information systems initiatives; information systems planning to identify and prioritize potential investments in IT in this completely online business; and installation and maintenance of workstations and local area networks to support the electronic world of the virtual community.

   •   *Sources of revenue.* A sponsoring firm can gain revenue from membership fees, direct sales of goods and services, advertising, click-throughs and sales commissions. A firm sponsoring a virtual community as an adjunct to its other activities may receive no direct revenue at all from the virtual community. Rather, the firm receives less tangible benefits, such as customer loyalty and increased knowledge about its customer base.

   •   *Critical success factors.* The critical success factors for a virtual community include finding and retaining a critical mass of members; building and maintaining loyalty with an appropriate mix of content and features; maintaining privacy and security for member information; balancing commercial potential and members' interests; leveraging member profile information with advertisers and merchants; and engendering a feeling of trust in the community by its members.

7.   **Value net integrator.** Traditionally, most firms operate simultaneously in two worlds: the physical and the virtual. In the physical world, goods and services are created in a series of value-adding activities connecting the supply side (suppliers, procurement, and logistics) with the demand side (customers, marketing, and shipping). In the virtual world, information about the members of the physical value chain are gathered, synthesized, and distributed along the virtual value chain. E-business provides the opportunity to separate the physical and virtual value chains. Value net integrators take advantage of that split and attempt to control the virtual value chain in their industries by gathering, synthesizing, and distributing information. Value net integrators add value by improving the effectiveness of the value chain by coordinating information. A pure value net integrator operates exclusively in the virtual value chain, owning a few physical assets. To achieve the gathering, synthesizing, and distributing of information, the value net integrator receives and sends information to all other players in the model. The value net integrator coordinates product flows form suppliers to allies and customers. The product flows from the suppliers to customers may be direct or via allies. In some cases, the value net integrator may sell information or other products to the customer. The value net integrator always strives to own the customer relationship with the other participants in the model, thus knowing more about their operations than any other player. Examples of value net integrators are Seven-Eleven Japan and Cisco Systems (www.cisco.com).

-    *Infrastructure.* The value net integrator succeeds in its role by gathering, synthesizing, and distributing information. Thus, for a value net integrator, data and electronic connectivity with allies and other players are very important assets. Field research carried out by Weill and Vitale (2001) suggests that the most important infrastructure services required for a value net integrator include middleware, linking systems on different platforms across the many players in the value net; a centralized data warehouse that collects and summarizes key information for analysis from decentralized databases held by several players across the value net; specification and enforcement of high-level architectures and detailed standards for data, technology, applications, and communications to link together different technology platforms owned by different firms; call centers to provide advice and guidance for partners and allies in getting the most value from the information provided by the value net generator; and high-capacity communications network service to support the high volumes of information flowing across the value net.

-    *Sources of revenue.* In this model, revenues are generally earned by fees or margins on the physical goods that pass through the industry value net. By using information about consumers, the value net integrator is able to increase prices by meeting consumer demand. By using information about suppliers, the value net integrator reduces costs by cutting inventories and lead times.

- *Critical success factors*. The critical success factors for the value net integrator atomic business model are as follows: reducing ownership of physical assets while retaining ownership of data; owning or having access to the complete industry virtual value chain; establishing a trusted brand recognized at all places in the value chain; operating in markets where information can add significant value, such as those that are complex, fragmented, regulated, multilayered, inefficient, and large with many sources of information; presenting the information to customers, allies, partners, and suppliers in clear and innovative ways that provide value; and helping other value chain participants capitalize on the information provided by the value net integrator.

8.   **Content Provider.** Like many terms associated with e-business, content provider has different meanings to different people. We define content provider as a firm that creates and provides content (information, products, or services) in digital form to customers via third parties. The physical-world analogy of a content provider is a journalist, recording artist, or stock analyst. Digital products such as software, electronic travel guides, and digital music and video are examples of content. A virtual-world example of a content provider is weather forecasters such as Storm Weather Center (www.storm.no).

- *Infrastructure*. Content providers must excel at tailoring and manipulating their core content to meet the specific needs of customers. Content providers must categorize and store their content in well-indexed modules so it can be combined and customized to meet customer needs via a wide variety of channels. Customers and transactions tend to be relatively few, at least compared with the number of end consumers and their transactions. Often complex and unique IT infrastructures are needed to support the particular needs of the specialized professionals employed by the content provider. Field research by Weill and Vitale (2001) identified the most important infrastructure services: multimedia storage farms or storage area network infrastructures to deal with large amounts of information; a strong focus on architecture, including setting and enforcing standards particularly for work; detailed data architectures to structure, specify, link manipulate, and manage the core intellectual property; workstation network infrastructures to enable the fundamentally online business of a content provider; and a common systems development environment to provide compatible and integrated systems, ensuring the systems can provide content across multiple channels to their customers.

- *Sources of revenue*. The primary source of revenue for a content provider is fees from its third parties or allies. These fees may be based on a fixed price per month or year, or on the number of times the third party's own customers access the content. In some situations, the fees paid are lower for content branded by the provider, and higher for unbranded content, which then appears to the customer to have been generated by the third party itself.

Figure 2.5. E-business models integration with customers vs. partners

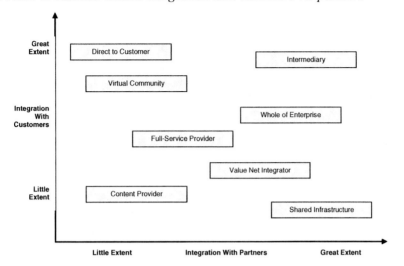

- *Critical success factors.* To succeed, a content provider must provide reliable, timely content in the right format and at the right price. The critical success factors for this model include the following: branding (the value of content is due in part to reputation), recognized as best in class (the business of content provision will be global and competitive), and network (establishing and maintaining a network of third parties through which content is distributed.

One way of comparing these e-business models is to analyze to what extent each model creates integration with customers and to what extent each model creates integration with partners. As illustrated in Figure 2.5, the business model of Direct to Customer creates mainly integration with customers, while Shared Infrastructure creates mainly integration with partners.

Determining Appropriate Models

Despite works by Weill and Vitale (2002) and others, how an e-business model must be defined and specified is largely an open issue. Business decision makers tend to use the notion in a highly informal way, and usually there is a big gap between the business view and that of IT developers.

The electronic business landscape is confusing for many new entrants, and many of them face the paradox that hesitation would run the risk of being left behind, but rushing in and making an incorrect choice regarding electronic business initiatives could have dire consequences for organizations. According to Hayes and Finnegan (2005), Internet-only or "dot.com" models have proven particularly vulnerable. For example, the dot.com implosion of Spring 2000 led to a large number of high-profile collapses including boo, ClickMango and eToys. "Clicks and Mortar" strategies have also met with mixed success e.g., Wall Street Journal Interactive and Fyffes' World-of-Fruit.

The Internet age has produced many Internet business models. For example, Afuah and Tucci (2003) distinguish between the following nine: brokerage model, advertising model, infomediary model, merchant model, manufacturing model, affiliate model, community model, subscription model, and utility model. An Internet business model — sometimes labeled b-web — is a business on the Internet that represents a distinct system of suppliers, distributors, commerce service providers, infrastructure providers, and customers that use the Internet for their primary business communication and transactions.

Another classification of Internet business models is presented by Laudon and Laudon (2005):

- *Virtual storefront:* Sells physical products directly to consumers or to individual businesses (Amazon.com, EPM.com)

- *Information broker:* Provides product, pricing, and availability information to individuals and businesses. Generates revenue from advertising or from directing buyers to sellers (Edmunds.com, Kbb.com, Insweb.com, IndustralMall.com)

- *Transaction broker:* Saves users money and time by processing online sales transactions, generating a fee each time a transaction occurs. Also provides information on rates and terms (E*TRADE.com, Expedia.com)

- *Online marketplace:* Provides a digital environment where buyers and sellers can meet, search for products, display products, and establish prices for those products (eBay.com, Priceline.com, ChemConnect.com, Pantellos.com)

- *Content provider:* Creates revenue by providing digital content, such as digital news, music, photos, or video, over the web (WSJ.com, CNN.com, TheStreet.com, Gettyimages.com, MP3.com)

- *Online service provider:* Provides online service for individuals and businesses. Generates revenue from subscription or transaction fees, from advertising, or from collecting marketing information from users (@Backup.com, Xdrive.com, Employease.com, Salesforce.com)

- *Virtual community:* Provides online meeting place where people with similar interests can communicate and find useful information (Motocross.com, iVillage.com, Sailnet.com)

- *Portal:* Provides initial point of entry to the web along with specialized content and other services (Yahoo.com, MSN.com, StarMedia.com)

Hayes and Finnegan (2005) present several classifications of e-business models. One classification includes e-shop, e-mall, e-procurement, third-party marketplace, e-auction, virtual community, collaboration platform, value chain service provider, value chain integration, information brokerage, and trust services. Another classification includes aggregation, agora/open market, alliance, and value chain. Next classification includes catalogue hubs, other hubs, yield managers, exchanges, forward aggregator, and reverse aggregator. A final classification consists of a long list including click and mortar merchant model, virtual merchant, catalogue merchant, virtual mall, metamediary, distributor, manufacturer model, buy/sell fulfillment, market exchange, bounty broker, auction broker, reverse auction, vertical web community, specialized portal, knowledge networks, open source model, content services, trust services, and transaction broker.

Electronic business poses significant challenges for organizations as it affects both how organizations relate to external parties (customers, suppliers, partners, competitors, and markets) and how they operate internally in managing activities, processes, and systems. Porter (2001) argues that the companies that succeed with e-business will be those that use the Internet in conjunction with their traditional business models and activities.

Hayes and Finnegan (2005) argue that business models are possibly the most discussed, yet least understood area of electronic business. They refer the point that consultants, executives, researchers and journalists have abusively used the phrase business model but have rarely given a precise definition of what they exactly meant by using it, and that this has lead to the loss of credibility of the concept.

A business model can be understood as a blend of three streams: value, revenue, and logistics. The value stream is concerned with the value proposition for buyers, sellers, and market makers. The revenue stream identifies how the organizations will earn revenue, and the logistics stream involves detailing how supply chain issues will affect the organizations involved (Hayes & Finnegan, 2005).

A business model can also be understood as an architecture for product, service and information flows, incorporating a description of the sources of revenue, the actors involved, their roles, and the benefits to them. An electronic business model is comprised of components, linkages, and dynamics. Components are factors such as customer scope, product (goods and services) scope, customer value, pricing, revenue sources, connected activities, implementation, capabilities of the firm, and sustainability. Linkages exist when one activity affects another in terms of cost-effectiveness, and trade-offs and optimization are sought to find the right blend to achieve competitive advantage. The dynamics represent how a firm reacts to or initiates change to attain a new competitive advantage, or to sustain an existing one, to have sustainable competitive advantage and to perform better than its rivals in the long term (Hayes & Finnegan, 2005).

While the atomic business models by Weill and Vitale (2002) were distinguished along dimensions such as infrastructure, sources of revenue and critical success factors, we can think of other criteria to classify e-business model. For example, three major areas that affect the sustainability and growth of an e-business are revenue streams, value streams and logistical streams. These three elements are interrelated with changes in any one affecting the other. Furthermore, e-business models can be classified in terms of integration with customers vs. integration with partners, as illustrated in Figure 2.5.

At the moment, there is no single, comprehensive, and cogent taxonomy of the web business models. Businesses face questions as to what is their appropriate business model. This is made more difficult when we consider that companies in the same industry often pursue different Internet business models. For example, companies in the automobile industry have industry consortia models such as shared infrastructure, while others have virtual community models.

As a result, determining and employing an appropriate Internet business model has become a major business issue. The problem is that there is no well-developed or complete framework to aid the decision of choosing a model.

In addition to outlining the components of a business model, some authors offer a set of business model representation tools. Weill and Vitale (2001) have developed a formalism to assist analyzing e-business initiatives, which they call e-business model schematic. The schematic is a pictorial representation, aiming to highlight a business model's important elements. This includes characteristics of the firm of interest, its suppliers and allies, the major flows of product, information, and money, and finally the revenues and other benefits each participant receives.

In determining an appropriate e-business model, several criteria can be used, such as:

- *Involved parties*, such as business-to-business, business-to-consumer, and/or consumer-to-consumer.

- *Revenue sources*, such as transaction fee, product price, and/or exposure fee.

- *Value configuration,* such as value chain, value shop and/or value network.

- *Integration* with customers and/or partners.

- *Relationships,* such as one-to-many, many-to-many, and/or many-to-one.

- *Knowledge,* such as know-how, know-what and know-why.

Unfortunately, e-business models still fall under open and weak theory domains. An open domain is one that cannot be realistically modeled. A weak theory domain is a domain in which relationships between important concepts are uncertain. General knowledge in such domains is theoretically uncertain, incomplete, and subject to changes. Methods that rely on deductive proofs are not readily applicable. Concepts and statements in Internet business models are more or less plausible, stronger or weaker supported, rather than true or false.

Fortunately, new research on e-business models is emerging. For example, Hayes and Finnegan (2005) present different approaches to understanding e-business models. One approach is e-business model *ontology*, which can be defined as a rigorous definition of the e-business issues and their interdependencies in a company's business model. The e-business model ontology focuses on four aspects of the organization, product innovation, infrastructure management, customer relationship, and financials.

Dimensions of product innovation are target customer segment, value proposition, and capabilities. Dimensions of customer relationship are information strategy, feel and serve, and trust and loyalty. Dimensions of infrastructure management are resources, activity configuration, and partner network, while dimensions of financials are revenue model, cost structure, and profit/loss.

Architectures for business models can be identified through the deconstruction and reconstruction of the value configuration. Value configuration elements are identified as well as the possible ways that information can be integrated in the value configuration and between the respective value configurations of the parties that are interacting.

As we have seen, decision makers are faced with an enormous range of electronic business models from which to choose. The process of fully researching each of these models can prove daunting. Such research is a feature of what has been termed the intelligence phase of decision-making. This phase is important as options excluded at this stage are not considered at a later stage. Hayes and Finnegan (2005) developed a framework for use at the intelligence phase to exclude models that are incompatible with prevailing organizational and supply chain characteristics.

The framework assesses the following characteristics: economic control, supply chain integration, functional integration, innovation, and input sourcing:

- *Economic control* refers to the degree to which a market is hierarchical or self-organizing. This characteristic can be measured in terms of the extent of regulatory bodies, government policy, customers, asset specificity, switching costs, proprietary products, capital requirements, and access to necessary inputs for new entrants in this industry.

- *Supply chain integration* is considered a measure of the degree to which the business functions and processes of an organization are integrated with those of their supply chain partners. This characteristic can be measured in terms of shipping scheduling, transportation management, tax reporting, negotiating customer credit terms, negotiating supplier credit terms, determining freight charges and terms, resource planning, and inventory control.

- *Functional integration* refers to the degree to which multiple functions are integrated in a business model. In order to measure the degree to which functions within an organization are integrated, a scale that considers a detailed list of processes can be applied. Examples of process integrations are purchase order processing with servicing functions, shipping scheduling with manufacturing, transportation management with financial functions, tax reporting with financial functions, negotiating customer credit terms with distribution, and negotiating supplier credit terms with distribution.

- *Innovation* is the degree of innovation of an e-business model, which can be defined as the extent to which processes can be performed via the Internet that were not previously possible. Innovation can be divided into internal and external components based on the firm's ability (internal) to innovate or assimilate innovations within the innovative environment of the industrial sector (external).

- *Sourcing* refers to the way in which inputs are sourced by the organization, either systematically from a long-term supplier or through spot markets. The issue of sourcing raw materials is more straightforward as manufacturing and operating inputs are sourced either systematically or on spot markets.

Hayes and Finnegan (2005) believe that their framework has the potential to help decision makers by providing a method of excluding from consideration those electronic business models that are unsuitable given prevailing organizational and environmental characteristics. Business models are excluded based on scale ratings for items measuring economic control, supply chain integration, functional integration, innovation, and sourcing. For each scale, the decision-maker needs to determine the number of attributes that are applicable to their organization.

Infrastructure Capabilities

As firms integrate e-business into their existing business, they migrate from traditional physical business models to combined physical and virtual models. This shift increases the role of the information technology infrastructure because information and online transaction processing become more important. However, the large number of infrastructure investment options can easily overwhelm senior management. To help, Weill and Vitale (2002) classified e-business initiatives by the building blocks they use (which are called atomic e-business models), and they examined the main IT infrastructure services that these models need. The business models require surprisingly different IT infrastructure services, so categorization should help executives prioritize their IT infrastructure investments based on their business goals. At the heart of this prioritization process is the firm's IT governance process, which should ensure that IT knows of upcoming IT infrastructure needs early in the strategizing process.

Weill and Vitale (2002) define a firm's information technology portfolio as its total investment in computing and communications technology. The IT portfolio thus includes hardware, software, telecommunications, electronically stored data, devices to collect and represent data, and the people who provide IT services.

IT Infrastructure

The foundation of an IT portfolio is the firm's information technology infrastructure. This internal IT infrastructure is composed of four elements: IT components (the technologist's view of the infrastructure building blocks), human IT infrastructure (the intelligence used to translate the IT components into services that users can draw upon), shared IT services (the user's view of the infrastructure), and shared and standard applications (fairly stable uses of the services) as illustrated in Figure 2.6.

IT components. At the base of the internal infrastructure are the technical components, such as computers, printers, database software packages, operating systems, and scanners. These components are commodities and are readily available in the marketplace. Traditionally, IT infrastructures have been described in terms of these components. Unfortunately, while technologists understand the capabilities of these components, business people do not — components are not business language to them. Thus, technologists and business people have had difficulty discussing infrastructure needs and business models because they have not had a common language (Weill & Vitale, 2002).

Figure 2.6. The hierarchy of IT infrastructure

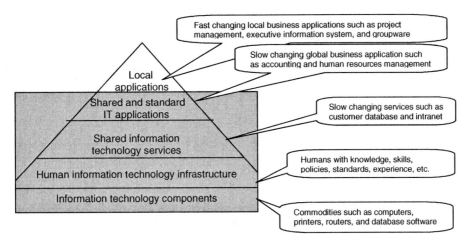

Human IT infrastructure. Describing IT components in business terms requires a translation. That translation is handled by people, and is performed in this layer, which builds on the IT components layer. The human IT infrastructure layer consists of knowledge, skills, standards, and experience. These tools are used to bind IT components into reliable services, which are services business people can understand (Weill & Vitale, 2002).

Shared IT services. This layer views the infrastructure as a set of services that users can understand, draw upon, and share, to conduct their business. For example, to link with customers and partners, they can draw on channel management services. To manage data, they can draw on data management services. To handle security, they can draw on security and risk services. In all, Weill and Vitale (2002) identified nine service areas needed by IT-enabled business models — with 70 services in all. Therefore describing IT infrastructure as a set of reliable services allows business people and technologists to discuss business models and their underlying infrastructure needs because the two parties speak the same language.

Shared and standard applications. The top piece of the IT infrastructure consists of stable applications, such as human resource management, budgeting, and accounting. In the last five to seven years, there has been a significant trend by multi-business firms to standardize their common business processes and the associated IT applications. The driver for some firms was improving and reengineering their business processes; for others, it was implementation of large enterprise resource planning (ERP) systems. As a result, shared and standard applications have been added to the typical firm's IT infrastructure (Weill & Vitale, 2002).

Based on these layers, a firm's IT infrastructure capability is its integrated set of reliable IT infrastructure services available to support both existing applications and new initiatives.

The time required to implement a new e-business initiative depends in part on the firm's infrastructure capability. For example, in building a new web-based housing loan system, a large bank needed to use the following information technology infrastructure services: mainframe and server processing, customer databases, both local area and national communications networks, and security procedures and systems. Having most of these infrastructure services already in place significantly reduced the time and cost to build the loan system (Weill & Vitale, 2002).

Infrastructure Services

Weill and Vitale (2002) identified nine service areas with 70 services needed by IT-enables e-business models. The service areas were (number of services in parenthesis): applications infrastructure (13), communications (7), data management (6), IT management (9), security (4), architecture and standards (20), IT research and development (2), and IT education (2):

Applications infrastructure

1.   Internet policies such as employee access
2.   Enforce internet policies
3.   E-mail policies such as inappropriate and personal mail, harassment policies, filtering policies
4.   Enforce e-mail policies
5.   Centralized management of e-business applications such as common standards
6.   Centralized management of infrastructure capacity such as server traffic
7.   Integrated mobile computing applications such as access for internal users
8.   ERP (enterprise resource planning) services
9.   Middleware linking systems on different platforms
10.   Wireless applications such as web applications for wireless devices
11.   Application services provision to business units
12.   Workflow applications such as groupware
13.   Payment transaction processing such as EFT (electronic funds transfer)

Communications

14.   Communications network services
15.   Broadband communication services
16.   Intranet capabilities to support publishing, directories, etc.
17.   Extranet capabilities to support information and applications
18.   Workstation networks
19.   EDI (electronic data interchange) linkages to customers and suppliers
20.   Electronic support to groups

Data management

21. Manage key data independent of applications

22. A centralized data warehouse that summarizes key information from decentralized databases

23. Data management advice and consultancy

24. Electronic provision of management information

25. Storage farms or storage area networks

26. Knowledge management in terms of contract database, information databases and communities of practice

IT management

27. Large scale data processing facilities

28. Server farms including mail server, web servers and printer servers

29. Installation and maintenance of workstations and LANs (local area networks)

30. Information systems planning for strategy

31. Information systems project management

32. Negotiate with suppliers and outsourcers

33. Service levee agreements

34. Common systems development environment

35. Pilot e-business initiatives such as pilot web shop fronts

Security

36. Security policies for use of information systems

37. Enforce security policies for information systems

38. Disaster planning for business applications

39. Firewall on secure gateway services

Architecture and standards

40. Specify architectures for data by setting high level guidelines for data use and integration

41. Specify architectures for technology by setting high level guidelines for technology use and integration

42. Specify architectures for communications by setting high level guidelines for communications use and integration

43. Specify architectures for applications by setting high level guidelines for applications use and integration

44. Specify architectures for work by setting high level guidelines for the way work will be conducted

45. Enforce architectures for data

46. Enforce architectures for technology

47. Enforce architectures for communications
48. Enforce architectures for applications
49. Enforce architectures for work
50. Specify architecture standards for data
51. Specify architecture standards for technology
52. Specify architecture standards for communications
53. Specify architecture standards for applications
54. Specify architecture standards for work
55. Enforce architecture standards for data
56. Enforce architecture standards for technology
57. Enforce architecture standards for communications
58. Enforce architecture standards for applications
59. Enforce architecture standards for work

Channel management

60. Electronic file transfer protocols
61. Kiosks
62. Web sites
63. Call centers
64. IVRs
65. Mobile phones
66. Mobile computing

IT research and development

67. Identify and test new technologies for business purposes
68. Evaluate proposals for new information systems initiatives

IT education

69. Training and use of IT
70. Management education for generating value from IT use

These 70 infrastructure services were identified by Weill and Vitale (2002) when they studied IT infrastructure services and e-business. They studied 50 e-business initiatives in 15 firms. Based on their study, they identified eight atomic business models, 9 infrastructure areas with 70 infrastructure services. The nine infrastructure areas were defined as follows.

Applications infrastructure. An application is a software program that resides on a computer for translating electronic input into meaningful form. Applications management includes purchasing software, developing proprietary applications, modifying applications, providing installation and technical support, and other tasks related to ensuring that applications are meeting the needs of the organization.

Communications. Technology that facilitates digital communication both within the organization and with the outside world is relevant here. It includes the management of hardware and software to facilitate communication via computer, telephone, facsimile, pagers, mobile phones, and other communication and messaging services. It includes the cabling and any other communication linkages required to create an effective communications network, in addition to the necessary hardware and applications to meet the needs of the organization.

Data management. This refers to the way the organization structures and handles its information resources. Data may be sourced from internal or external databases. Data management includes data collection, database design, sorting and reporting information, creating links to external databases, assuring data compatibility, and other activities surrounding the effective management of electronic information.

IT management. Information technology management includes many of the professional and strategic activities of the information technology group including negotiation, IS planning, project management, and other tasks. IS project management is defined as the coordination and control of all of the activities required to complete an information systems project.

Security. To protect data, equipment, and processing time, organizations restrict access to certain data and protect data and applications from manipulation and contamination. Recovery refers to the need for a plan to maintain computer operations and information should a disaster occur.

Architecture and standards. Information technology architecture is a set of policies and rules that govern the use of information technology and plot a migration path to the way business will be done in the future. In most firms, it provides technical guidelines rather than rules for decision-making. Architecture has to cope with both business uncertainty and technological change, making it one of the most difficult tasks for a firm. A good architecture evolves over time and is documented and accessible to all managers in the firm. Each architecture decision needs a sound business base to encourage voluntary agreement and compliance across the business. A standard is a detailed definition of the technical choices to implement architecture. Five elements of architectures and standards are important: data, technology, communications, applications, and work. It can be distinguished between specifying architecture or standards and enforcement.

Channel management. New and emerging technologies allow direct connections or distribution channels to customers.

IT research and development. The information systems market develops rapidly, particularly with the rise of new e-business technologies. It is thus necessary to test continually applications and hardware to assist with planning decisions. IT research and development includes identifying and testing new technologies for business purposes and evaluating proposals for new information systems initiatives.

IT education. Training and education in the use of IT can be defined as formal classes, individual training, and technology-based self-training programs for users ensuring hands-on computer proficiency levels meeting corporate requirements. IS management education can be defined as education aimed at senior levels in the firm designed to generate value from IT use.

Our presentation of Weill and Vitale's (2002) work on infrastructure services indicate the number and complexity of services that constitute the IT infrastructure in an organization to enable electronic business. Successfully implementing e-business initiatives depends on having the necessary IT infrastructure in place. E-business initiatives can be decomposed into their underlying atomic e-business models, which can have quite different IT infrastructure requirements.

For example, the most critical IT infrastructure service for the first business model of content provider might be storage farms or storage area networks, which is a data management service number 25 on the list. Here it can be argued that as a content provider, the quality, quantity and availability of content by electronic means is the most critical service. For the next e-business model of direct to customer, getting paid in an efficient way might be the most critical factor for success, leading to the need for IT infrastructure service number 13 which is payment transaction processing.

Strategic Agility

Companies need to build IT infrastructure for strategic agility. Strategic agility is defined by the set of business initiatives an enterprise can readily implement. Many elements contribute to agility, including customer base, brand, core competence, infrastructure, and employees' ability to change. Organizing and coordinating those elements into an integrated group of resources results in an enterprise capability, which, if superior to that of competitors, becomes a distinctive competence. Research conducted by Weill, et al. (2002) demonstrated a significant correlation between strategic agility and IT infrastructure capability. This suggests that if managers can describe their desired strategic agility, they then can identify the IT infrastructure service clusters that need to be above the industry average — and thus can create a distinctive competence.

Strategic agility is the ability of a firm to continually sense and explore customer and marketplace enrichment opportunities and respond with the appropriate configurations of capabilities and capacities to exploit these opportunities with speed, surprise, and competitive success. According to Sambamurthy and Zmud (2004), enriching customers, leveraging capabilities and capacities, nurturing inter-organizational cooperation, and mastering change and uncertainty are the four building blocks of strategic agility.

Enriching customers can include the following activities:

- *Solution-centricity:* Deliver total solutions for current and anticipated customer needs. Solutions are customizable bundles of products and services.

- *Customer-centricity:* Heighten customer convenience, including space, time, speed, and personalized convenience.

- *Accelerate solution and product innovation to refresh continually customer offerings:* Portfolio of incremental, architectural, and radical innovation projects.

- *Co-opt customers in the innovation process:* Customers are sources of ideas for product and solution offerings. Customers are co-creators of innovative ideas.

Leveraging capabilities and capacities is the next building block. First, an ecosystem of capabilities has to be built. The ecosystem might consist of customer relationship management, selling chain management, supply-demand synchronization, manufacturing management, financial engineering, brand management, human capital management, and information technology management. Next, world-class excellence has to be nurtured. This implies focus on a balanced set of metrics, such as adaptiveness, responsiveness, speed, cost, effectiveness, and quality. This also implies applying continuous improvement methods for capability enhancement and investing in and developing enabling information infrastructures and services platforms.

Nurturing inter-organizational cooperation is concerned with value net concept, value net posture, and value net integration. In the context of strategic agility, value nets are configurations of sourcing and partnership structures for building the extended enterprise. This definition is different from our main definition of value network as a value configuration in this book. In the context of strategic agility, value nets are architected to leverage other firms' capabilities and assets that complement core capabilities and assets within a firm. Value net posture is concerned with the governance of the value net, which can be either prescriptive or collaborative. Value net integration requires focus on the value net and expertise replication or expertise integration. In addition, the following actions are important in nurturing inter-organizational cooperation:

- Identify and certify potential partners with regard to desired competencies (assets, capabilities) and their financial solvency

- Develop and continually assess working relationships with partners

- Develop abilities to work with partners through a variety of contractual mechanisms

- Develop competencies to quickly establish (and remove) the technology, process and managerial interfaces needed when initiating business arrangements with new partners

Mastering change and uncertainty is the fourth and final building block of strategic agility. It requires strategic foresight, strategic insight, and organizational learning. The following actions are important in mastering change and uncertainty:

- Sense, anticipate and exploit trends, opportunities, and threats

- Quickly and seamlessly marshal the combinations of capabilities necessary in shaping innovative moves

- Quickly reconfigure capabilities necessary in shaping innovative moves

- Execute and learn from strategic experiments and from strategic actions

The evidence from leading enterprises indicates that implementing different types of electronic business initiatives based on atomic e-business models requires different high-capability IT infrastructures. Strategic agility requires time, money, leadership and focus — an understanding of which distinct patterns of high-capability infrastructures are needed where. Investing in IT infrastructure is like buying an option. If used successfully, infrastructure enables faster time to market; if not, it will prove an unnecessary cost. To ensure that investments in IT infrastructure support the organization's strategic goals and business initiatives, Weill, et al. (2002) consider it critical for the enterprise's most senior executives to understand which specific IT infrastructure capabilities are needed for which kinds of initiatives. That way, they can have some assurance that the investments they make today will serve the strategies of tomorrow.

One approach to improving strategic agility is utility computing. Utility computing proposes to allow clients to buy computing capacity as they do electricity — just by plugging in. For clients the cost is variable and based on the actual capacity they demand, rather than a fixed cost for a capacity they only use during peak periods. They can get the capacity they need whenever they need it, without expending resources and effort to regularly monitor and upgrade capacity (Ross & Westerman, 2004)

The vision of utility computing goes beyond traditional outsourcing of IT services. It includes all potential combinations of sourcing options, as we shall see in part II of this book. Vendors are promising to offer applications and business processes, including computing, applications, and expert staff, in an on demand format, just as many firms now buy call center and payroll processes (Ross & Westerman, 2004).

Utility computing relies on several important technical capabilities to deliver these promised services. First, grid computing enables a network of processors to provide shared processing capacity by seamlessly accessing unused capacity elsewhere. Second, autonomic computing technology enables a network to be self-healing, and thus provides higher reliability across a system than is currently available. Third, web services provide technical standards that facilitate integration across systems. In combining these three capabilities in a one-to-many business model, vendors expect to offer on demand computing capacity and a wide range of plug-and-play technology and process components (Ross & Westerman, 2004).

Another approach to improving strategic agility is organizational architecture work. Organizations often relegate the job of aligning business needs and technology support to IT or operations, but with the strategic uncertainties of e-business, Sauer and Willcocks (2002) find that a separate coordinating role of organizational architect may be the only solution.

The shifting competitive landscape is creating a larger gap between strategists and technologists. Executives are busy creating and refining visions and have little time to focus on technology. Technologists are busy keeping the platform current and have little time to understand the business in depth. Without a mechanism to force communication, each group retreats into its specialty.

Among companies that were successfully aligning business and technology in e-business, Sauer and Willcocks (2002) identified a series of bridging activities that amounted to the creation of what they call organizational architect. An organizational architect is someone who is neither all strategist nor all technologist, who guides the translation of a strategic vision to a flexible, integrated platform. Organizational architects sustain a dialogue between visionaries and technologists as they define and design the right combination of structures, processes, capabilities and technologies. This combination has a greater chance of improving strategic agility by being responsive to shifting organizational goals.

Sauer and Willcocks (2002) surveyed chief executive officers and chief information officers at 97 companies in the United States, Europe and Australia that had moved or were moving to e-business. Most were responding to an increasingly volatile business environment by shrinking their development and planning cycles. Half of the companies did not extend their plans beyond one year, and half of those with infrastructure plans updated them quarterly.

Lacking some mechanism to bridge the interests of strategists and technologists, information technology cannot prepare for change, and senior business executives end up guiding and funding short-term technology initiatives. Organizational architects work with both strategists and technologists to identify and grow the organizational and technical capabilities needed to see a vision through to its supporting platform. The architect sees the vision through three main translation phases (Sauer & Willcocks, 2002):

- **Phase 1:** *From vision to organization.* The organizational architect sets design parameters for the organizational structures, processes and capabilities that make the vision possible.

- **Phase 2:** *From organization to technology requirements.* The architect now works to map the organizational needs to platform characteristics.

- **Phase 3:** *From technology requirements to actual platform.* The architect is now ready to get a fix on reality by talking with technology experts about what they can actually do.

An organizational architect is a significant investment for a business, so it will be important to underwrite the position even though it is essentially a staff function with no immediately visible commercial benefits. Sauer and Willcocks (2002) argue that persistence will be required particularly in difficult economic times.

Sambamurthy and Zmud (2004) define the evolution toward strategic agility in terms of four generations. The first generation was total quality management, while the second was lean management and mass customization. Then followed organizational adaptiveness before strategic agility emerged. Each generation of corporate transformation has emphasized specific types of capabilities and performance enhancement. Path dependent progression through each of these waves is essential as the learning that occurs within each wave produces necessary changes in orientation and capacity.

Total quality management had efficiency as its competitive base, while lean management and mass customization had customer centricity and product variety as its base. Organizational adaptiveness was characterized by flexibility and partnerships, while strategic agility has entrepreneurial sense-making and improvisation as its competitive base. Furthermore, strategic agility has the design objective of innovation and disruption and the decision architecture of external-internal collaboration.

The evolution toward agility in terms of information architecture started with data and metrics rationalization (total quality management), moved on to process rationalization and data integration (lean management and mass customization), then to meta process rationalization and meta data integration (organizational adaptiveness), and finally to information visibility and information probing (strategic agility).

According to Sambamurthy and Zmud (2004), information technologies can enable agility in several ways. First, the strategic role of IT can shift to fluid decision, authority, and collaboration structures. Second, the IT architecture can shift to modular form. Next, key technologies will be web services, objects, intelligent agents, and distributed collaboration technologies. Fourth, key IT partnerships will include partners' market experts. Finally, IT investment focus will no longer be cost reduction, productivity improvement, time-to-market, or product life cycle refreshment. Rather, IT investment will focus on real options, market prototyping, time-to-solution, and relationship capital.

Of critical importance is IT investment in IT infrastructure. Strategic agility requires a distinct pattern of high-capability infrastructures. Getting the right balance is difficult. Under-investing reduces strategic agility and slows time to market. Also, infrastructure investments must be made before investments in business applications because doing both at the same time results in infrastructure fragmentation. But if the infrastructure is not used or is the wrong kind, a company is over-investing and wasting resources (Weill, et al., 2002).

Sambamurthy and Zmud (2004) provide the following managerial guidelines for strategic agility:

- Adaptiveness enables competitive success in the digital economy
- Strategic agility enables competitive leadership
- Adaptiveness requires the co-integration of customer- and solution-centricity, capabilities built around information, process, and information technology infrastructures, and value net architectures
- Additionally, strategic agility requires the mastery of change and uncertainty through entrepreneurial orientation and sensing capabilities
- Strategic agility is nurtured at multiple levels: competitive agility, innovation agility, and functional agility
- The evolution toward strategic agility occurs through the learning gained by prior investments in total quality management, lean management and value net integration
- Information technology management facilitates strategic agility as a digital options generator by representing a platform for process innovation, for value net integration, and for innovation and strategic experimentation
- Attention must be focused on significant transformations of the IT function, such as IT architecture, IT investment, IT partnerships, and organizing logic

Strategic agility is an emerging concept that needs research concerning both organizational and technology issues. Organizational issues include competency development and organizational architecture as demonstrated by the need for organizational architects. Technology issues include distributed intelligence, interfacing intelligent agents and humans, knowledge discovery technologies and processes, rapid start-up and integration initiatives, meta data and process architectures, and end-to-end value chain information visibility (Sambamurthy & Zmud, 2004).

One approach to organizational actions for strategic agility is organization capital readiness. Kaplan and Norton (2004) define organization capital as the ability of the organization to mobilize and sustain the process of change required to execute strategy. Organization capital provides the capability for integration so that individual intangible human and information capital assets, as well as tangible physical and financial assets, are not only aligned to the strategy, but are all integrated and working together to achieve the organization's strategic objectives. An enterprise with high organization capital has a shared understanding of vision, mission, values and strategy, is strongly led, has created a performance culture around the strategy, and shares knowledge across the organization.

If managers can describe their desired strategic agility, they then can identify the IT infrastructure services that need to be above the industry average — and thus can create a distinctive competence. Although none of the enterprises Weill, et al. (2002) evaluated had all 70 infrastructure services presented earlier, those with the highest degree of strategic agility had more services in each of the 10 clusters, broader implementations of each service and more demanding service level agreements.

Important drivers of strategic agility are strategy, sourcing and governance. Strategy describes paths to the desired future, sourcing describes access to resources for the desired future, while governance describes management mechanisms to lead into the desired future.

Chapter III

IS/IT Strategy Work

Strategy can be defined simply as principles, a broad based formula, applied in order to achieve a purpose. These principles are general guidelines guiding the daily work to reach business goals. Strategy is the pattern of resource allocation decisions made throughout the organization. These encapsulate both desired goals and beliefs about what are acceptable and, most critically, unacceptable means for achieving them.

While the business strategy is the broadest pattern of resource allocation decisions, decisions that are more specific are related to information systems and information technology. IS must be seen both in a business and an IT context. IS is in the middle because IS supports the business while using IT. This will be discussed later in this book in terms of IT governance as strategic alignment.

Why is strategic IS/IT planning undertaken within business organizations? Hann and Weber (1996) see IS/IT planning as a set of activities directed toward achieving the following objectives:

1. Recognizing organizational opportunities and problems where IS/IT might be applied successfully

2. Identifying the resources needed to allow IS/IT to be applied successfully to these opportunities and problems

3. Developing strategies and procedures to allow IS/IT to be applied successfully to these opportunities and problems

4. Establishing a basis for monitoring and bonding IT managers so their actions are more likely to be congruent with the goals of their superiors

5. Resolving how the gains and losses from unforeseen circumstances will be distributed among senior management and the IT manager

6. Determining the level of decision rights to be delegated to the IT manager.

Empirical studies of information systems / information technology planning practices in organizations indicate that wide variations exist. Hann and Weber (1996) found that organizations differ in terms of how much IS/IT planning they do, the planning methodologies they use, the personnel involved in planning, the strength of the linkage between IS/IT plans and corporate plans, the focus of IS/IT plans (e.g., strategic systems vs. resource needs), and the way in which IS/IT plans are implemented.

It has been argued that the Internet renders strategic planning obsolete. In reality, it is more important than ever for companies to do strategic planning (Porter, 2001, p. 63):

Many have argued that the Internet renders strategy obsolete. In reality, the opposite is true. Because the Internet tends to weaken industry profitability without providing proprietary operational advantages, it is more important than ever for companies to distinguish themselves through strategy. The winners will be those that view the Internet as a complement to, not a cannibal of, traditional ways of competing.

After having presented strategic planning in general, the Y model for strategy work is discussed and applied later in this chapter. The model provides a coherent systematic procedure for development of an IS/IT strategy.

Strategic Planning

Often, strategy development is equated with strategic planning procedures. They represent the design approach to managing strategy. Such procedures may take the form of highly systematized, step-by-step, chronological procedures involving many different parts of the organization. For example, the annual strategic planning cycle in a company may follow a procedure like this:

1. *May*. Broad strategic direction.
2. *June*. Review of current strategy.
3. *August*. Goals for business units.
4. *September*. Strategies for business units.
5. *October*. Board meeting to agree strategic plan.
6. *November*. Board meeting to agree operational plan and budget.

Some of the key concepts in strategic planning are future thinking, controlling the future, decision-making, integrated decision-making and a formalized procedure to produce an articulated result in the form of an integrated process of decisions. Strategic planning is the process of deciding on the projects that the organization will undertake and the approximate amount of resources that will be allocated to each program over the next several years.

Planning represents the extent to which decision-makers look into the future and use formal planning methodologies. Planning is something we do in advance of taking action; it is anticipatory decision-making. We make decisions before action is required. The focus of planning revolves around objectives, which are the heart of a strategic plan. According to Mintzberg (1994), planning has the following characteristics:

- *Planning is future thinking.* It is taking the future into account. Planning denotes thinking about the future. Planning is action laid out in advance.

- *Planning is controlling the future.* It is not just thinking about it but achieving it—enacting it. Planning is the design of a desired future and of effective ways of bringing it about. It is to create controlled change in the environment.

- *Planning is decision making.* Planning is the conscious determination of courses of action designed to accomplish purposes. Planning are those activities which are concerned specifically with determining in advance what actions and/or human and physical resources are required to reach a goal. It includes identifying alternatives, analyzing each one, and selecting the best ones.

- *Planning is integrated decision making.* It means fitting together of ongoing activities into a meaningful whole. Planning implies getting somewhat more organized, it means making a feasible commitment around which already available courses of action get organized. This definition may seem close to the preceding one. But because it is concerned not so much with the making of decisions, as with the conscious attempt to integrate different ones, it is fundamentally different and begins to identify a position for planning.

- *Planning is a formalized procedure to produce an articulated result, in the form of an integrated system of decisions.* What captures the notion of planning above all—most clearly distinguishes its literature and differentiates its practice from other processes—is its emphasis on formalization, the systemization of the phenomenon to which planning is meant to apply. Planning is a set of concepts, procedures, and tests. Formalization here means three things: (a) to decompose, (b) to articulate, and (c) to rationalize the process by which decisions are made and integrated in organizations.

Given that this is planning, the question becomes — why do it? Mintzberg (1994) provides the following answers:

- Organizations must plan to coordinate their activities.

- Organizations must plan to ensure that the future is taken into account.

- Organizations must plan to be rational in terms of formalized planning.

- Organizations must plan to control.

Strategy is both a plan for the future and a pattern from the past, it is the match an organization makes between its internal resources and skills (sometimes collectively called competencies) and the opportunities and risks created by its external environments. Strategy is the long-term direction of an organization. Strategy is a course of action for achieving an organization's purpose. Strategy is the direction and scope of an organization over the long term, which achieves advantage for the organization through its configuration of resources within a changing environment and to fulfill stakeholder expectations (Johnson & Scholes, 2002).

Strategy as a plan is a direction, a guide, or course of action into the future, a path to get from here to there. Strategy as a pattern is a consistency in behavior over time. Strategy as a position is the determination of particular products in particular markets. Strategy as perspective is an organization's way of doing things (Mintzberg, 1994).

Strategic planning does not attempt to make future decisions, as decisions can be made only in the present. Planning requires that choices be made among possible events in the future, but decisions made in their light can be made only in the present. Once made, these decisions may have long-term, irrevocable consequences. Strategic planning has many benefits for an organization (Johnson & Scholes, 2002, p. 61):

- It can provide a structured means of *analysis and thinking* about complex strategic problems, at its best requiring managers to *question and challenge* the received wisdom they take for granted.

- It can encourage a *longer-term view* of strategy than might otherwise occur. Planning horizons vary, of course. In a fast-moving consumer goods company, 3-5 year plans may be appropriate. In companies that have to take very long-term views on capital investment, such as those in the oil industry, planning horizons can be as long as 14 years (in Exxon) or 20 years (in Shell).

- It can be used as a means of *control* by regularly reviewing performance and progress against agreed objectives or previously agreed strategic direction.

- It can be a useful means of *coordination*, for example by bringing together the various business unit strategies within an overall corporate strategy, or ensuring that resources within a business are coordinated to put strategy into effect.

- Strategic planning may also help to *communicate* intended strategy.

- It can be used as a way of involving people in strategy development, therefore perhaps helping to create *ownership* of the strategy.

- Planning systems may provide a sense of security and logic for the organization and, in particular, management who believe they *should* be proactively determining the future strategy and exercising control over the destiny of the organization.

In the strategic planning perspective on strategy formation, strategies are intentionally designed, much as an engineer designs a bridge. Building a bridge requires a long formulation phase, including extensive analysis of the situation, the drawing up of a number of rough designs, evaluation of these alternatives, choice of a preferred design, and further detailing in the form of a blueprint. Only after the design phase has been completed do the construction companies take over and build according to plan. Characteristic of such a planning approach to producing bridges and strategies is that the entire process can be disassembled into a number of distinct steps that need to be carried out in a sequential and orderly way. Only by going through these steps in a conscious and structured manner will the best results be obtained (Wit & Meyer, 2004).

The whole purpose of strategizing is to give organizations direction, instead of letting them drift. Organizations cannot act rationally without intentions—if you do not know where you are going, any behavior is fine. By first setting a goal and then choosing a strategy to get there, organizations can get organized. A structure can be chosen, tasks can be assigned, responsibilities can be divided, budgets can be allotted, and targets can be set. Not unimportantly, a control system can be created to measure results in comparison to the plan, so that corrective action can be taken (Wit & Meyer, 2004).

Another advantage of the planning approach to strategy formation is that it allows for the formalization and differentiation of strategy tasks. Because of its highly structured and sequential nature, strategic planning lends itself well to formalization. The steps of the strategic planning approach can be captured in planning procedures to enhance and organize the strategy formation process. In such planning procedures, not all elements of strategy formation need to be carried out by the same person, but can be divided among a number of people. The most important division of labor is often between those formulating the plans and those implementing them (Wit & Meyer, 2004).

In many large companies the managers proposing the plans are also the ones implementing them, but deciding on the plans is passed up to a higher level. Often other tasks are spun off as well, or shared with others, such as diagnosis (strategy department or external consultants), implementation (staff departments), and evaluation (corporate planner and controller). Such task differentiation and specialization can lead to better use of management talent, much as the division of labor has improved the field of production. At the same, having a formalized procedure allows for sufficient coordination and mutual adjustment, to ensure that all specialized elements are integrated back into a consistent organization-wide strategy (Wit & Meyer, 2004).

An important advantage of strategic planning is that it encourages long-term thinking and commitment. Strategic planning directs attention to the future. Managers making strategic plans have to take a more long-term view and are stimulated to prepare for, or even create, the future. Instead of just focusing on small steps, planning challenges managers to define a desirable future and to work towards it. Instead of wavering and opportunism, strategic planning commits the organization to a course of action and allows investments to be made at the present that may only pay off in the long run (Wit & Meyer, 2004).

Corporate strategy is concerned with the strategic decisions at the corporate level of organizations; decisions which may affect many business units. Managers at this level are acting on behalf of shareholders, or other stakeholders, to provide services and, quite possibly, strategic guidance to business units which, themselves, seek to generate value by interacting with customers. In these circumstances, a key question is to what extent and how might the corporate level add value to what the businesses do; or at the least how it might avoid destroying value (Johnson & Scholes, 2002).

A multi-business company structure may consist of a number of business units grouped within divisions and a corporate center or head office providing, perhaps, legal services, financial services and the staff of the chief executive. There are different views as to what is meant by corporate strategy and what represents corporate at distinct from business-level strategy. Johnson and Scholes (2002) argue that anything above the business unit level represents corporate activity.

Figure 3.1. Corporate strategy above other levels

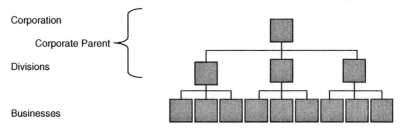

The levels of management above that of business units are often referred to as the corporate parent. So, for example, the divisions within a corporation that look after several businesses act in a corporate parenting role. The corporate parenting role can be as (Johnson & Scholes, 2002):

- *The portfolio manager.* A corporate parent acting as an agent on behalf of financial markets and shareholders with a view to enhancing the value attained from the various businesses in a more efficient or effective way than finical markets could. Their role is to identify and acquire under-valued assets or businesses and improve them.

- *The restructurer.* A corporate parent identifying restructuring opportunities in businesses and having the skills to intervene to transform performance in those businesses. They may well hold a diverse range of businesses within their portfolio. However, they do have a limited role at business-unit level, which is to identify ways in which businesses can be turned around or fitness improved and to manage the restructuring period.

- *The synergy manager.* Synergy is often seen as the main reason for the existence of the corporate parent. Potentially, synergy can occur in situations where two or more activities or processes complement each other, to the extent that their combined effect is greater than the sum of the parts. In terms of corporate strategy, the logic is that value can be enhanced across business units. This can be done in a number of ways: activities might be shared, and there may exist common skills or competences across businesses.

- *The parental developer.* A corporate parent seeks to employ its own competences as a parent to add value to its businesses. Here, the issue is not so much about how it can help create or develop benefits across business units or transference between business units, as in the case of managing synergy. Rather, parental developers have to enhance the potential of business units.

In our strategic planning perspective, corporate strategy will depend on the main role of the corporate parent. The portfolio manager is not directly intervening in the strategies of business units. Rather, they are setting financial targets, making central evaluations about the well-being and future prospects of such businesses and investing or divesting accordingly. The restructurer is directly intervening in business units, as it is likely that the business restructuring opportunities that will be sought will be those that match the skills of the corporate center. The synergy manager will initiated activities and develop resources that are shared across business units. Managers in the businesses have to be prepared to co-operate in such transference and sharing (Johnson & Scholes, 2002).

Finally, the parental developer has to enhance the potential of business units in various ways. Suppose, for example, it has a great deal of experience in globalizing domestically based businesses; or a valuable brand that may enhance the performance of image of a business; or perhaps specialist skills in financial management, brand marketing or research and development. If such parenting competences exist, corporate managers then need to identify a parenting opportunity — a business or businesses that are not fulfilling their potential but where improvement could be made by the application of the competences of the parent (Johnson & Scholes, 2002).

Strategic management includes understanding the strategic position of an organization, strategic choices for the future and turning strategy into action. Understanding the strategic position is concerned with impact on strategy of the external environment, internal resources and competences, and the expectations and influence of stakeholders. Strategic choices involve understanding the underlying bases for future strategy at both the corporate and business unit levels and the options for developing strategy in terms of both the directions in which strategy might move and the methods of development. Translating strategy into action is concerned with ensuring that strategies are working in practice. A strategy is not just a good idea, a statement, or a plan. It is only meaningful when it is actually being carried out (Johnson & Scholes, 2002).

Generally, there are some characteristics of strategic decisions that are usually associated with the word strategy (Johnson & Scholes, 2002):

- Strategy is likely to be concerned with long-term direction of an organization.
- Strategic decisions are normally about trying to achieve some advantage for the organization over competition.
- Strategic decisions are likely to be concerned with the scope of an organization's activities.
- Strategy can be seen as the matching of the resources and activities of an organization to the environment in which it operates.
- Strategy can also be seen as building on or expanding an organization's resources and competences to create opportunities or to capitalize on them.
- Strategies may require major resource changes for an organization.
- Strategic decisions are likely to affect operational decisions.
- The strategy of an organization is affected not only by environmental forces and resource availability, but also by the values and expectations of those who have power in and around the organization.

The notion of *strategic fit* is developing strategy by identifying opportunities in the business environment and adapting resources and competences to take advantage of these. The correct *positioning* of the organization is important, for example in terms of the extent to which it meets clearly identified market needs. *Strategic position* is concerned with impact on strategy of the external environment, internal resources and competences, and the expectations and influence of stakeholders (Johnson & Scholes, 2002).

Strategy development is here equated with strategic planning procedures. They represent the design approach to managing strategy, which views strategy development as the deliberate positioning of the organization through a rational, analytic, structured a directive process. *Strategy as design* is an important strategy lens. Alternative and supplementing lenses are strategy as experience and strategy as ideas. *Strategy as experience* suggests that strategies develop in an adaptive fashion and change gradually. Strategy is here understood in terms of continuity; once an organization has adopted a particular strategy, it tends to develop from and within that strategy, rather than fundamentally changing direction. *Strategy as ideas* sees strategy as the emergence of order and innovation from the variety and diversity that exists in and around an organization. New ideas and therefore innovation may come from anywhere in an organization or from stimuli in the world around it (Johnson & Scholes, 2002).

In addition to strategic planning, strategy development and strategy formation is also concerned with concepts such as strategic leadership, organizational politics, strategic incrementalism, the learning organization, imposed strategy, and multiple processes of strategy development. A *strategic leader* is an individual upon whom strategy development and change are seen to be dependent. Managers often suggest that the strategy being followed by the organization is really the outcome of *organizational politics* in terms of the bargaining and power politics that go on between important executives. Managers may have a view of where they want the organization to be in years to come and try to move towards this position incrementally, where *strategic incrementalism* can be though of as the deliberate development of strategy by learning through doing over time. The concept of the *learning organization* and strategy as a learning process implies continual regeneration of strategy from the variety of knowledge, experience, and skills of individuals with a culture that encourages mutual questioning and challenge around a shared purpose or vision. Forces or agencies external to the organization may cause *imposed strategy* that the organization has to follow. Different lenses and different strategy development processes may cause *multiple processes of strategy development*, since there is no right way in which strategies are developed (Johnson & Scholes, 2002).

At the beginning of this subchapter on strategic planning, strategy was defined as a course of action for achieving an organization's purpose. Where managers have a clear understanding of their organization's purpose, this can provide strong guidance during processes of strategic thinking, strategy formation, and strategic change. The *organizational purpose* can function as a fundamental principle, against which strategic options can be evaluated. Organizational purpose can be defined as the reason for which an organization exists. The broader set of fundamental principles giving direction to strategic decision-making, of which organizational purpose is the central element, is referred to as the *corporate mission*. The corporate mission may have elements such as organizational beliefs, organizational values, and business definition (Witt & Meyer, 2004).

Some authors distinguish between deliberate strategy and emergent strategy as two alternative processes of strategy formulation. According to Christensen and Raynor (2003), *deliberate strategy* — such as strategic planning — is the appropriate tool for organizing action if three conditions are met. First, the strategy must encompass and address correctly all of the important details required to succeed, and those responsible for implementation must understand each important detail in management's deliberate strategy. Second, if the organization is to take collective action, the strategy needs to make as much sense to all employees as they view the world from their own context as it does to top management, so that they will all act appropriately and consistent. Finally, the collective intentions must be realized with little unanticipated influence from outside political, technological and market forces.

Emergent strategy bubbles up from within the organization, is the cumulative effect of day-to-day prioritization and investment decisions made by middle managers, engineers, salespeople, and financial staff. These tend to be tactical, day-to-day operating decisions that are made by people who are not in a visionary, futuristic, or strategic state of mind (Christensen & Raynor, 2003).

Some authors distinguish between intended strategy and realized strategy. *Intended strategy* is an expression of desired strategic direction deliberately formulated and planned by managers. *Realized strategy* is the strategy actually being followed by an organization in practice. *Strategic drift* occurs when an organization's strategy gradually moves away from relevance to the forces at work in its environment. (Johnson & Scholes, 2002).

As we will see throughout this book, strategic planning procedures apply methods for analysis, choice, and implementation. A general method is available in terms of strategy maps as defined by Kaplan and Norton (2004), which represent interesting perspectives on strategy development and strategy formation. Strategy maps are used to describe how the organization creates value, and they were developed for the balanced scorecard. The strategy map is based on several principles:

- *Strategy balances contradictory forces.* Investing in intangible assets for long-term revenue growth usually conflicts with cutting costs for short-term financial performance.

- *Strategy is based on a differentiated customer value proposition.* Satisfying customers is the source of sustainable value creation.

- *Value is created through internal business processes.* The financial and customer perspectives in strategy maps and balanced scorecards describe the outcomes, that is, what the organization hopes to achieve.

- *Strategy consists of simultaneous, complementary themes.* Operations management, customer management, innovation, regulations, and societal expectations deliver benefits at different points in time.

- *Strategic alignment determines the value of intangible assets.* Human capital, information capital and organization capital are intangible assets.

Understanding the strategic position of an organization and considering the strategic choices open to it, are of little value unless the strategies managers wish to follow, can be turned into organizational action. Strategies cannot take effect until they take shape in action. Such action takes form in the day-to-day processes and relationships that exist in organizations; and these need to be managed, desirably in line with the intended strategy (Johnson & Scholes, 2002).

Translating strategies into action is no simple task. First, it is important to organize for success by introducing appropriate structure, processes, relationships, and boundaries. Second, it is important to enable success by managing people, managing information, managing finance, managing technology, and integrating resources. Finally, strategic change has to be managed by diagnosing the change situation, applying relevant styles and roles, and implement levers for managing strategic change, such as organizational routines and symbolic processes (Johnson & Scholes, 2002).

The design school of strategic planning is built on the belief that strategy formation is a process of conception — the use of a few basic ideas to design strategy. Of these, the most essential is that of congruence, or fit, between external and organizational factors. A number of premises underlie the design school (Mintzberg, 1994):

1. Strategy formation should be a controlled, conscious process of thought.

2. Responsibility for the process must rest with the chief executive officer; that person is *the* strategist.

3. The model of strategy formation must be kept simple and informal.

4. Strategies should be unique: the best ones result from a process of creative design.

5. Strategies must come out of the design process fully developed.

6. The strategies should be made explicit and, if possible, articulated, which means they have to be kept simple.

7. Finally, once these unique, full-blown, explicit, and simple strategies are fully formulated, they must then be implemented.

Strategic Planning and Firm Performance

Numerous researchers and executives advocate strategic planning. They argue that an explicit planning process rather than haphazard guesswork results in the collection and interpretation of data critical to creating and maintaining organization-environment alignment. They argue that planning generally produces better alignment and financial results than does trial-and-error learning (Miller & Cardinal, 1994).

Despite the intuitive appeal of these arguments, several researchers have countered that explicit strategic planning is dysfunctional, or at best irrelevant. One of the most widely circulated criticisms is that planning yields too much rigidity. Proponents of the rigidity hypothesis maintain than a plan channels attention and behavior to an unacceptable degree, driving out important innovations that are not part of the plan. Given that the future parameters of even relatively stable industries are difficult to predict, these theoreticians consider any reduction in creative thinking and action dysfunctional (Miller & Cardinal, 1994).

Miller and Cardinal (1994) developed a model that might explain the inconsistent planning-performance findings reported in previous research. Results from the model suggest that strategic planning positively influences firm performance. Researchers who have concluded that planning does not generally benefit performance appear to have been incorrect.

Measurement of Competitive Strategy

The measurement of competitive strategy is an important issue in strategic management. Porter (1985) first defined three generic competitive strategies—cost leadership, differentiation, and focus. Attempts to measure these strategies seek to capture differences in the extent to which firms emphasize various competitive dimensions. Competitive strategy is traditionally measured at the business level. Yet businesses often consist of product portfolios in which a different competitive strategy is used for each product. Thus, business-level measures may not be good indicators of product-level competitive strategy. Further, business-level analyses have found combined cost-leadership and differentiation strategies. But if competitive strategies are formulated at the product level, it is unclear whether combined strategies exist at that level.

Nayyar (1993) examined these issues. He found that business-level measures are not good indicators of product-level competitive strategies. I also found no evidence supporting the existence of combined competitive strategies at the product level. He found that cost-leadership and differentiation are mutually exclusive at the product level. They do not appear to be two dimensions of any strategy. Previously used business-level measures tend to identify combined competitive strategies, a result that may reflect the existence of product portfolios rather than combined competitive strategies.

These findings suggest a need for a reexamination of the concept of competitive strategies. It appears that firms use competitive strategies for products and then construct product portfolios to obtain overall cost, differentiation, and preemption advantages. Within any industry, different firms may construct different product portfolios.

In his measurement of competitive strategy, Nayyar (1993) used the following competitive dimensions associated with a cost-leadership strategy: operating efficiency, cost control, pricing below competitors, managing raw materials cost and availability, trade sales promotion, manufacturing process improvements and innovation, and product cost reduction. The following competitive dimensions were associated with a differentiation strategy: new product development, extensive customer service, building and maintaining brand equity, marketing innovation, influence over distribution channels, targeting high-priced segment(s), advertising, building and maintaining the firm's reputation, providing product(s) with many features, and premium product quality. The following competitive dimensions were associated with a focus strategy: serving special market segment, manufacturing, and selling customized products.

Instead of measuring competitive strategy in terms of alternative strategies, Julien and Ramangalahy (2003) measured competitive strategy in terms of intensity. The more competitive a strategy is, the more intense is the competitive strategy. The intensity was measured in terms of marketing differentiation, segmentation differentiation, innovation differentiation, and products service. Marketing differentiation is based on competitive pricing, brand development, control over distribution, advertising and innovation in terms of marketing techniques. Segmentation differentiation relies on the ability to offer specialized products to specific customer groups. Innovation differentiation is based on the ability to offer new and technologically superior products. Product service is based on the quality of the products and services provided by customers.

Competitive strategy must drive other strategies in the firm, such as knowledge strategy. Executives must be able to articulate why customers buy a company's products or services rather than those of its competitors. What value do customers expect from the company? How does knowledge that resides in the company add value for customers? Assuming the competitive strategy is clear, managers will want to consider three further questions that can help them choose a primary knowledge management strategy (Hansen et al., 1999):

- *Do you offer standardized or customized products?* Companies that follow a standardized product strategy sell products that do not vary much, if at all. A knowledge management strategy based on reuse fits companies that are creating standardized products.

- *Do you have a mature or innovative product?* A business strategy based on mature products typically benefits most from a reuse of existing knowledge.

- *Do your people rely on explicit or tacit knowledge to solve problems?* Explicit knowledge is knowledge that can be codified, such as simple software code and market data.

Strategic planning in a turbulent environment is challenging. The challenge of making strategy when the future is unknowable encouraged reconsideration of both the process of strategy formulation and the nature of organizational strategy. Attempts to reconcile systematic strategic planning with turbulent, unpredictable business environments included the following (Grant, 2003):

- *Scenario planning.* Multiple scenario planning seeks not to predict the future but to envisage alternative views of the future in the form of distinct configurations of key environmental variables. Abandoning single-point forecasts in favor of alternative futures implies forsaking single-point plans in favor of strategy alternatives, emphasizing strategic flexibility that creates option values.

- *Strategic intent and the role of vision.* If uncertainty precludes planning in any detailed sense, then strategy is primarily concerned with establishing broad parameters for the development of the enterprise with regard to domain selection and domain navigation. Uncertainty requires that strategy is concerned less with specific actions and the more with establishing clarity of direction within which short-term flexibility can be reconciled with overall coordination of strategic decisions.

- *Strategic innovation.* If established companies are to prosper and survive, new external environments require new strategies. Strategic planning may be a source of institutional inertia rather than innovation. Yet, systematic approaches to strategy can be encouraging to managers to explore alternatives beyond the scope of their prior experiences. Strategic inertia may be more to do with the planners than of planning per se.

- *Complexity and self-organization.* Often faced with a constantly changing fitness landscape, maximizing survival implies constant exploration, parallel exploration efforts by different organizational members, and the combination of incremental steps. A key feature of strategic processes is the presence of semi structures that create plans, standards, and responsibilities for certain activities, while allowing freedom elsewhere. One application of the semi structure concept to strategy formulation concerns the use of simple rules that permit adaptation while establishing bounds that can prevent companies from falling off the edge of chaos.

Hopkins and Hopkins (1997) investigated relationships among managerial, environmental, and organizational factors, strategic planning intensity, and financial performance in U.S. banks. The results suggested that the intensity with which banks engage in the strategic planning process has a direct, positive effect on banks' financial performance, and mediates the effects of managerial and organizational factors on banks' performance. Results also indicated a reciprocal relationship between strategic planning intensity and performance. That is, strategic planning intensity causes better performance and, in turn, better performance causes greater strategic planning intensity.

Strategic planning takes many different forms in different organizations. However, Boyd and Reuning-Elliotts (1998) study of strategic planning provide strong support for the measurement properties of the strategic planning construct. In particular, the study results indicate that strategic planning is a construct that can be reliably measured through seven indicators: mission statement, trend analysis, competitor analysis, long-term goals, annual goals, short-term action plans, and ongoing evaluation. This evidence is important because previous researchers rarely tested for dimensionality of the planning construct, nor did most studies report tests of the reliability of their measures.

A small, entrepreneurial startup may operate without any explicit strategy. The firm's strategy is likely to exist only in the head of the founder, and apart from being articulated through verbal communication with employees, suppliers, and other interested parties, may have been made explicit only when a business plan was required by outside investors. Most corporations with an established management structure tend to have some form of strategic planning process, through in small, single-business companies the strategy process may be highly informal, with no regular cycle, and may result in little documentation. Most larger companies, especially those with multiple businesses, have more systematic strategic planning processes, the outcome of which is a documented plan that integrates the business plans of the individual divisions (Grant, 2002).

Whether formal or informal, systematic or ad hoc, documented or not, the strategy formulation process is an important vehicle for achieving coordination within a company. The strategy process occupies multiple roles within the firm. It is in part a coordination device encouraging consistency between the decisions being made at different levels and in different parts of the organization. And it is in part a mechanism for driving performance by establishing consensus around ambitious long-term targets and by inspiring organizational members through creating vision and a sense of mission. In these roles, the strategy process can be important in achieving both coordination and cooperation (Grant, 2002).

The system through which strategy is formulated varies considerably from company to company. Even after the entrepreneurial startup has grown into a large company, strategy making may remain the preserve of the chief executive. Medium-sized, single-business companies typically have simple strategic planning processes where functional managers provide key inputs such as financial projections and market analysis, but the key elements of strategy — goals, new business developments, capital investment, and key competitive initiatives — are decided by the chief executive (Grant, 2002).

The more systematized strategic planning processes typical of large companies with separate divisions or business units traditionally follow an annual cycle. Strategic plans tend to be for three to five years and combine top-down initiatives (indications of performance expectations and identification of key strategic initiatives) and bottom-up business plans (proposed strategies and financial forecasts for individual divisions and business units). After discussion between the corporate level and the individual businesses, the business plans are amended and agreed and integrated into an overall corporate plan that is presented to and agreed by the board of directors (Grant, 2002).

The resulting strategic plan typically comprises the following elements (Grant, 2002):

• A statement of the goals the company seeks to achieve over the planning period with regard to both financial targets and strategic goals.

• A set of assumptions or forecasts about key developments in the external environment to which the company must respond.

• A qualitative statement of how the shape of the business will be changing in relation to geographical and segment emphasis, and the basis on which the company will be establishing and extending its competitive advantage.

• Specific action steps with regard to decisions and projects, supported by a set of mileposts stating what is to be achieved by specific dates.

• A set of financial projections, including a capital expenditure budget and outline operating budgets.

Although directed toward making decisions that are documented in written strategic plans, the important elements of strategic planning form the strategy process: the dialog through which knowledge is shared and ideas communicated the establishment of consensus, and the commitment to action and results (Grant, 2002).

The Y Model for Strategy Work

In all kinds of strategy work, there are three steps. The first step is concerned with analysis. The second step is concerned with choice (selection and decision), while the final step is concerned with implementation.

We now introduce a model for strategy work. This is illustrated in Figure 3.2. The model consists of seven stages covering analysis, choice, and implementation. The stages are described in the following list.

Figure 3.2. The Y model for IS/IT strategy work

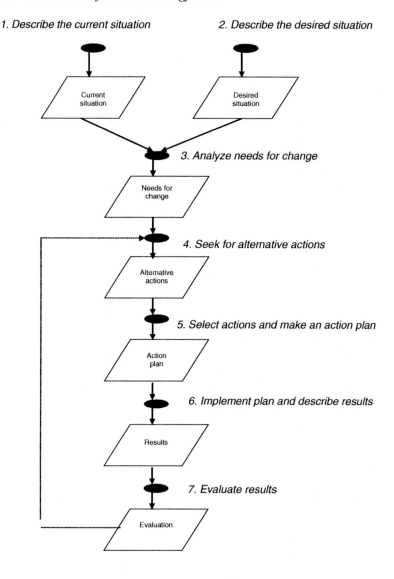

1. *Describe current situation.* The current IS/IT situation in the business can be described using several methods. The benefits method identifies benefits from use of IS/IT in the business. Distinctions are made between rationalization benefits, control benefits, organizational benefits, and market benefits. Other methods include the three-era model, management activities, and stages of growth.

2. *Describe desired situation.* The desired business situation can be described using several methods described in the first chapter. Value configurations, competitive strategy, management strategy, business process redesign, knowledge management, the Internet and electronic business, and information technology benefits.

3. *Analyze and prioritize needs for change.* After descriptions of the current situation and the desired situation, needs for change can be identified. The gap between desired and current situation is called needs for change. Analysis is to provide details on needs, what change is needed, and how changes can take place. *What*-analysis will create an understanding of vision and goals, knowledge strategy, market strategy, and corporate problems and opportunities. *How*-analysis will create an understanding of technology trends and applications. These analyses should result in proposals for new IS/IT in the organization.

4. *Seek for alternative actions.* When needs for change have been identified and proposals for filling gaps have been developed, alternative actions for improving the current situation can be developed. New IS/IT can be developed, acquired, and implemented in alternative ways. For example, an information system can be developed in-house by company staff, it can be purchased as a standard application from a vendor, or it can be leased from an application systems provider (ASP).

5. *Select actions and make an action plan.* When needs for change and alternative actions have been identified, several choices have to be made and documented in an action plan. Important issues here include development process, user involvement, time frame and financial budget for IS/IT projects.

6. *Implement plan and describe results.* This is the stage of action. Technical equipment such as servers, PCs, printers and cables are installed. Operating systems are installed. Application packages, software programs, programming tools, end user tools, and database systems are installed. Development projects are organized. Management and user training takes place. Document results over time.

7. *Evaluate results.* Implementation results are compared with needs for change. It is determined to what extent gaps between desired and current situation have been closed. This is the beginning of the IS/IT strategy revision process, where a new process through the Y model takes place. Typically, a new IS/IT strategy process should take place every other year in business organizations.

While stages 1 to 3 cover *analysis*, 4 and 5 cover *choice*, and 6 and 7 cover *implementation*. In some strategy models, stage 2 is listed as the first stage. It is here recommended to do stage 1 before stage 2. It is easier to describe the ideal situation when you know the current situation. If you start out with stage 2, it often feels difficult and abstract to describe what you would like to achieve. Having done stage 1 first makes the work more relevant. Stage 3 is a so-called gap analysis, looking at the difference between the desired and actual situation. This stage also includes prioritizing. Stage 4 is a creative session as it calls for ideas and proposals for alternative actions. Stages 5 and 6 are typical planning stages. The final stage 7 is important because we can learn from performing an evaluation.

A graphical representation of the Y model is shown in Figure 3.2, using the description technique provided earlier in this book. It is called the Y model as it looks like the letter Y. There is one feedback-arrow to compare the evaluation with the desired situation. In this chapter, we will follow the Y model in our discussions.

Resource-Based Strategy

Strategic management models traditionally have defined the firm's strategy in terms of its product/market positioning— the products it makes and the markets its serves. The resource-based approach suggests, however, that firms should position themselves strategically based on their unique, valuable, and inimitable resources and capabilities rather than the products and services derived from those capabilities. Resources and capabilities can be thought of as a platform from which the firm derives various products for various markets. Leveraging resources and capabilities across many markets and products, rather than targeting specific products for specific markets, becomes the strategic driver. While products and markets may come and go, resources and capabilities are more enduring. Therefore, a resource-based strategy provides a more long-term view than the traditional approach, and one more robust in uncertain and dynamic competitive environments. Competitive advantage based on resources and capabilities therefore is potentially more suitable than that based solely on product and market positioning (Zack, 1999).

According to Hitt et al., (2001), scholars argue that resources form the basis of firm strategies and are critical in the implementation of those strategies as well. Therefore, firm resources and strategy seem to interact to produce positive returns. Firms employ both tangible resources (such as buildings and financial resources) and intangible resources (like human capital and brand equity) in the development and implementation of strategy. Outside of natural resource monopolies, intangible resources are more likely to produce a competitive advantage because they are often rare and socially complex, thereby making them difficult to imitate.

According to Barney (2001), resource-based theory includes a very simple view about how resources are connected to the strategies a firm pursues. It is almost as though once a firm becomes aware of the valuable, rare, costly to imitate, and nonsubstitutionable resources it controls, the actions the firm should take to exploit these resources will be self-evident. That may be true some of the time. For example, if a firm possesses valuable, rare, costly to imitate, and nonsubstitutionable economies of scale, learning curve economies, access to low-cost factors of production, and technological resources, it seems clear that the firm should pursue a cost leadership strategy.

However, it will often be the case that the link between resources and the strategy of a firm is not being so obvious. Resource-based strategy has to determine when, where and how resources may be useful. Such strategy is not obvious, since a firm's resources may be consistent with several different strategies, all with the ability to create the same level of competitive advantage. In this situation, how should a firm decide which of these several different strategies it should pursue? According to Barney (2001) this and other questions presented by Priem and Butler (2001) concerning the resource-based theory of the firm indicate that the theory is still a theory in many respects, and that more conceptual and empirical research has to be conducted to make the theory more useful to business executives who develop resource-based strategies for their firms.

Resource-based strategy is concerned with the mobilization of resources. Since perceived resources merely represent potential sources of value-creation, they need to be mobilized to create value. Conversely, for a specific resource to have value it has to increase or otherwise facilitate value-creation. The activity whereby tangible and intangible resources are recognized, combined and turned into activities with the aim of creating value is the process here called resource mobilization. The term *resource mobilization* is appropriate, as it incorporates the activity-creation based on both individual and organizational resources, as well as tangibles and intangibles. According to Haanaes (1997), alternative terms such as resource allocation, resource leveraging or resource deployment are appropriate when describing the value-creation based on tangible resources, but less so for intangibles. For example, a competence cannot be allocated, as the person controlling it has full discretion over it. Moreover, the competence can be used in different ways. An engineer can choose to work for a different organization and to work with varying enthusiasm. Also, the same engineer can choose not to utilize his or her competence at all. The term resource mobilization is, thus, meant to cover the value-creation based on all types of resources, and it recognizes that all activity creation has a human aspect.

In strategic management and organization theory, the importance for the firm of reducing uncertainty and its dependence on key resources that it cannot fully control has received much attention. If a large part of the resource accumulation takes place in terms of increased competences that key professionals could easily use for the benefit of other employers, the firm needs to set priorities in terms of linking these individually controlled resources to the firm. Loewendahl (2000) suggests three alternative strategies. The simplest strategy, which may be acceptable to some firms, involves minimizing the dependence on individual professionals and their personal competence. In this sense, the firm chooses to avoid the dependence on individual tangibles. A second strategy is that of linking the professionals more tightly to the firm and reducing the probability of losing them. The third alternative strategy involves increasing the organizationally controlled competence resources without reducing the individually controlled resources. Such a strategy leads to a reduction in the relative impact of individual professionals on total performance, without reducing the absolute value of their contributions. Firms that have been able to develop a high degree of organizationally controlled resources, including relational resources that are linked to the firm rather than to individual employees, are likely to be less concerned about the exit and entry of individual professionals and more concerned about the development and maintenance of their organizational resource base.

According to Maister (1993), there is a natural, but regrettable, tendency for professional firms, in their strategy development process, to focus on new things: What new markets does the firm want to enter? What new clients does the firm want to target? What new services does the firm want to offer? This focus on new services and new markets is too often a cop-out. A new specialty (or a new office location) may or may not make sense for the firm, but it rarely does much (if anything) to affect the profitability or competitiveness of the vast bulk of the firm's existing practices.

On the other hand, an improvement in competitiveness in the firm's core businesses will have a much higher return on investment since the firm can capitalize on it by applying it to a larger volume of business. Enhancing the competitiveness of the existing practice will require changes in the behavior of employees. It implies new methods of operating, new skill development, and new accountabilities. Possible strategies for being more valuable to clients can be found in answers to the following questions (Maister, 1993):

- Can we develop an innovative approach to *hiring* so that we can be more valuable to clients by achieving a higher caliber of staff than the competition?

- Can we *train* our people better than the competition in a variety of technical and counseling skills so that they will be more valuable on the marketplace than their counterparts at other firms?

- Can we develop innovative *methodologies* for handling our matters (or engagements, transactions or projects) so that our delivery of services becomes more thorough and efficient?

- Can we develop systematic ways of helping, encouraging, and ensuring that our people are skilled at client *counseling* in addition to being top suppliers?

- Can we become better than our competition at accumulating, disseminating, and building our firm-wide expertise and experience, so that each professional becomes more valuable in the marketplace by being *empowered* with a greater breadth and depth of experience?

- Can we organize and *specialize* our people in innovative ways, so that they become particularly skilled and valuable to the market because of their focus on a particular market segment's needs?

- Can we become more valuable to our clients by being more systematic and diligent about *listening* to the market: collecting, analyzing, and absorbing the details of their business than does our competition?

- Can we become more valuable to our clients by investing in research and *development* on issues of particular interest to them?

In resource-based strategy, there has to be consistency between resources and business. The logic behind this requirement is that the resources should create a competitive advantage in the business in which the firm competes. To meet this requirement, corporate resources can be evaluated against key success factors in each business. When doing so, it is important to keep in mind that in order to justify retaining a business, or entering a business, the resources should convey a substantial advantage. Merely having pedestrian resources that could be applied in an industry is seldom sufficient to justify entry or maintain presence in an attractive industry (Collis & Montgomery, 1997).

Moreover, managers must remember that, regardless of the advantage of a particular corporate resource appears to yield, the firm must also compete on all the other resources that are required to produce and deliver the product or service in each business. One great resource does not ensure a successful competitive position, particularly if a firm is disadvantaged on other resource dimensions (Collis & Montgomery, 1997).

Activity-Based Strategy

The goal of strategy formulation in the resource-based theory is to identify and increase those resources that allow a firm to gain and sustain superior rents. Firms owning strategic resources are predicted to earn superior rents, while firms possessing no or few strategic resources are thought to earn industry average rents or below average rents. The goal of strategy formulation in the activity-based theory is to identify and explore drivers that allow a firm to gain and sustain superior rents. Drivers are a central concept in the activity-based theory. To be considered drivers, firm level factors must meet three criteria: they are structural factors at the level of activities, they are more or less controllable by management, and they affect the cost and/or differentiation position of the firm. The definition of drivers is primarily based on what drivers do. Drivers are abstract, relative, and relational properties of activities. For example, scale of an activity is a driver, as the size of the activity relative to competitors may represent a competitive advantage.

The analytical focus of the resource-based theory is potentially narrower than that of the activity-based theory. While the activity-based theory takes the firm's entire activity set as its unit of analysis, the resource-based theory focuses on individual resources or bundles of resources. Having a narrower focus means that the resource-based theory may not take into account the negative impact of resources, how a resource's value may change as the environment changes, or the role of non-core resources in achieving competitive advantage.

The activity-based and resource-based theories are similar as they both attempt to explain how firms attain superior positions through factors that increase firm differentiation or lower firm cost. While drivers and resources share a common goal of achieving and sustaining superior positions, the manner by which they are seen to reach a profitable position is different. With the resource-based theory, it is the possession or control of strategic resources that allow a firm to gain a profitable position. On the other hand, drivers within the activity-based theory are not unique to the firm. They are generic, structural factors, which are available to all firms in the industry, in the sense that they are conceptualized as properties of the firm's activities. A firm gains a profitable position by configuring its activities using drivers. It is this position that a firm may own, but only if it is difficult for rivals to copy the firm's configuration.

The sustainability of superior positions created by configuring drivers or owning resources is based on barriers to imitation. The sustainability of competitive advantage as per the activity-based theory is through barriers to imitation at the activity level. If the firm has a competitive advantage, as long as competitors are unable to copy the way activities are performed and configured through the drivers, the firm should be able to achieve above average earnings over an extended period. The sustainability of superior profitability in the resource-based theory is through barriers to imitation of resources and immobility of resources. If resources are easily copied or substituted then the sustainability of the position is suspect.

Sheehan (2002) concludes his discussion by finding similarities between the resource-based theory and the activity-based theory. Resources in the resource-based theory are similar to drivers in the activity-based theory as both are based on earning efficiency rents. Furthermore, capabilities in the resource-based theory are similar to activities in the activity-based theory as both imply action.

Chapter IV

Strategy Analysis

Stages 1 to 3 cover strategy analysis in the Y model. While stage 1 is concerned with describing the current IS/IT situation, stage 2 is concerned with describing the current and desired business situation, and stage 3 is concerned with analyzing needs for change based on the gap identified when comparing current and desired situation as illustrated in Figure 4.1.

Describing Current IS/IT Situation

The Y model starts with a description of the current situation. We focus on the IS/IT situation, as this will be the subject of change later in the model. First of all, we have to understand in what ways the company is using IS/IT. Many approaches can help us gain an understanding of the present IS/IT situation. We will look at some of them:

I.   *Benefits of IS/IT*. IS/IT is applied in business organizations to achieve benefits. We can study current IS/IT in the organization to understand what benefits have been achieved so far. Here we can determine what main benefit categories are currently the case. We will make distinctions between rationalization benefits, control benefits, organizational benefits, and market benefits.

II. *Stages of IS/IT growth*. IS/IT in business organizations change over time. New hardware and software, new areas of applications, and new IS/IT support functions emerge. Most business organizations develop through stages over time. Here we can determine at what stage the business organization is for the time being. We will make distinctions between a total of nine stages. These nine stages are classified into three eras: data processing, information systems, and information networks.

III.   *IS/IT in management activities.* Management activities can be studied in a hierarchical perspective of operational, tactical, and strategic management. Current IS/IT in the organizations can be assigned to these levels to determine the extent of support at each level.

IV.   *IS/IT in business processes.* In a company, many business processes take place at the same time. Some of the processes may rely heavily on IS/IT, while others are mainly manual at the current point in time.

V.   *IS/IT support for value configuration.* We make distinctions between value chain, value shop and value network. In each of these value configurations, IS/IT can support activities. The current IS/IT situation is described by identifying activities in the value configuration depending on the extent of technology support.

VI.   *Strategic integration.* Business strategy and IT strategy have for a long time suffered from lack of coordination and integration in many organizations. Here we measure the current IS/IT situation by use of ten integration mechanisms to determine integration stage in an organization.

VII.   *IS/IT support for knowledge management.* We have introduced four ambition levels for knowledge management, so here we can determine at what level a business organization is.

VIII.   *IS/IT in e-business.* For most firms, becoming an e-business is an evolutionary journey. We introduce six stages to describe the evolving e-business: external communications, internal communications, e-commerce, e-business, e-enterprise, and transformation.

IX.   *IS/IT enabled business transformation.* IT-enabled transformation can include business direction change, but more often, we find examples at lower levels, such as business design change and business process change.

Description of the current situation assumes that we have been able to define borders for our study. Borders exist for both breath and depth. Breath is a question of whether the whole company or only one division should be studied. Depth is a question of whether all aspects such as technology, marketing, management, and finance should be included in the study. We recommend both extensive breath and thorough depth to ensure that a wide range of alternative solutions and alternative actions can be identified in later stages of the Y model. In the case of breath, this may imply that both suppliers and customers are included because there may be electronic market places used by our suppliers and customers. In the case of depth, this may imply that analysis of top management is included because management competence in the area of IS/IT can influence both management attitudes and ambitions concerning future applications of IS/IT.

Description of the current IS/IT situation should focus on issues of importance in technology and knowledge management. Less emphasis should be put on technology

Figure 4.1. The three stages of strategy analysis

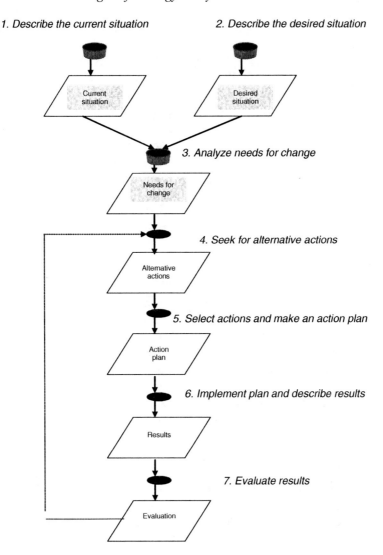

1. Describe the current situation

2. Describe the desired situation

Current situation

Desired situation

3. Analyze needs for change

Needs for change

4. Seek for alternative actions

Alternative actions

5. Select actions and make an action plan

Action plan

6. Implement plan and describe results

Results

7. Evaluate results

Evaluation

itself, such as drawings of company networks and servers. Technology management is focused on the management of information technology, while knowledge management is focused on knowledge strategy and knowledge management systems.

Method I: Benefits of IS/IT

The main reason for using IS/IT in organizations is the achievement of benefits. There are several kinds of benefits: rationalization benefits, control benefits, organizational benefits and market benefits. These benefits are at different levels and have different implications. Rationalization benefits are found at the operational level and imply cost reductions. Control benefits are at the operational management level and imply both cost reductions and increased revenues. Organizational benefits are found at middle management and top management levels and imply both cost reductions and increased revenues. Market benefits are found externally and imply increased revenues. Each benefit category can be described as follows:

- *Rationalization benefits* occur when IS/IT is taking the place of people through automation. Person-years may be saved when replacing people with IS/IT. Personnel costs drop while IS/IT costs rise. Benefits are the net difference. A necessary requirement for achieving this kind of benefit is that there are other tasks for the people released of their duties, or that people can be dismissed from their jobs if it is socially acceptable in the corporate culture. Rationalization benefits were the typical justification of early investments, even if they created unemployment. For example, when lawyers revise a document, they no longer get a printout on paper to correct and be typed by secretaries. Instead, lawyers correct their own documents on the screen.

- *Control benefits* occur when employees are able to make better and different decisions and actions than they would have done without the information. For example, when secretaries make appointments for lawyers, information on client profitability and importance can make them schedule more meetings in the law office, thereby reducing travel time for lawyers.

- *Organizational benefits* occur when IS/IT opens up for organizational structures (more decentralization, flatter), which create higher motivation, better work from the employees and better economic results. Some tasks in the organization were previously worked on sequentially, while IS/IT today enable parallel work. For example, an updated document can be accessed by lawyers at different locations at the same time.

- *Market benefits* occur when the IS/IT provides the business with competitive advantages leading to more sales and higher profits. Information systems can make the company look distinctly different from its competitors. The Internet has created new opportunities for e-commerce and e-business. For example, online legal services can generate an additional revenue source for law firms.

This analysis of current IS/IT benefits will provide information on the current IS/IT situation. If most benefits are found within rationalization and control, then there has been a cost control approach to IS/IT applications in the organization. If most benefits are found within organizational and market effects, then there has been a revenue increase approach to IS/IT applications in the organization.

IS/IT in knowledge management can create some or all four kinds of benefits. Although the typical expectation will be concerned with organizational benefits and market benefits, efficient and effective use of IS/IT in knowledge management will also create rationalization benefits and control benefits.

Figure 4.2. Example of IS/IT benefits distribution

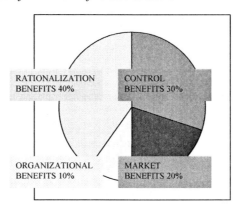

A new IS/IT may cause some or all four kinds of benefits. The challenge when deciding to make an IS/IT is to identify and quantify the benefits in monetary terms. Companies with little experience using IS/IT will look for mainly rationalization benefits, while more experienced companies will look for control and organizational benefits. The most experienced companies will look for market benefits.

What kind of benefits the company has utilized in the present IS/IT will tell us the current situation of the company when it comes to the use of IS/IT. For example, we may find a distribution of benefits as illustrated in Figure 4.2. A possible interpretation of this distribution is that the company has been good at exploring rationalization and control benefits, but not so good at achieving market benefits and organizational benefits.

Method II: Stages of IS/IT Growth

Over time, business organizations have developed and advanced in their use of IT. In the beginning, there were data processing (DP) and data processing systems. Then there were management information systems (MIS) and strategic information systems (SIS). Organizations in the DP era will improve operational efficiency by automating informa-tion-based processes. Organizations in the MIS ear will improve management effective-ness by satisfying their information requirements. Organizations in the SIS era will improve competitiveness by changing the nature or conduct of business.

This is sometimes called the EEC model, where organizations move from concerns about efficiency (E) to effectiveness (E) and finally to competitiveness (C). In the DP era, efficiency (E) is about doing things right. In the MIS era, effectiveness (E) is about doing the right things. In the SIS era, competitiveness (C) is about gaining competitive advantage in the market place. Based on the EEC model, we now have a method of distinguishing between three eras of IS/IT growth to describe the current IS/IT situation in a company:

*   *Era 1*. Data processing to achieve efficiency. Here focus is on *data*, where humans have to interpret data to make information out of it.

- *Era 2*. Management information systems to achieve effectiveness. Here focus is on *information*, where access to information is achieved.

- *Era 3*. Strategic information systems to achieve competitiveness. Here focus is on *knowledge*, where information is organized to support knowledge work.

The EEC model is only one of many stages of IS/IT growth models. Nolan (1979) introduced a model with six stages, which later has been expanded to nine stages. It has been suggested as a theory of IS/IT development over time in organizations. *Nolan's model* focuses on the level of IS/IT expenditures as illustrated in Figure 4.3.

Nolan's model suggests that organizations slowly start out in the initiation stage. Then a period of rapid spreading of IT use takes place in the contagion stage. After a while, the need for control emerges. Control is followed by integration of different technological solutions. The data management enables a development without rising IS/IT expenditures. Then constant growth will take place as the stage of maturity is reached.

To understand the current IS/IT situation in a specific business organization, IS/IT expenditures can be mapped over time. Hopefully, there are historical accounting figures available at least for the last decade to draw the curve and to judge what stage in the curve the business is at right now. We can get more help to identify the appropriate stage by looking at specific characteristics of each stage as described in the following.

The stage of IS/IT maturity of an organization is not only indicated by the level of IS/IT expenditures. We can also look at the application portfolio, the IS/IT organization, the IS/IT planning and control, and the user awareness to estimate stage of growth of an organization. For example, an organization in the initiation stage will have an application portfolio of functional cost-reduction applications, while an organization in the maturity stage will have an application portfolio of applications integrated to handle information flows as illustrated in Figure 4.4.

Figure 4.3. Nolan's six stage model of IS/IT evolution in organizations

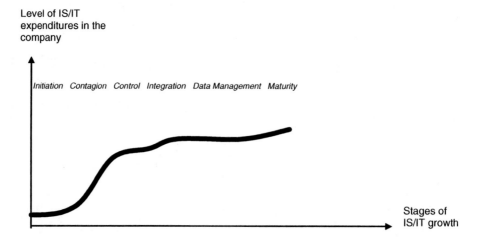

Figure 4.4. Characteristics of stages in Nolan's model

Growth Characteristics	Stage 1 Initiation	Stage 2 Contagion	Stage 3 Control	Stage 4 Integration	Stage 5 Data	Stage 6 Maturity
Application portfolio	Functional cost-reduction applications	Rapid increase in all application areas	Upgrade documentation, simplifying existing applications	Restructuring existing applications in a systems architecture	Restructuring existing applications in a data architecture	Application integration supporting information flows
IS/IT organization	Specialization for technological learning	User-oriented computer programmers	Middle management	Establish IS/IT support function and user accounts	Establish data administration function	Establish IS/IT resource management function
IS/IT planning	No planning, operational managers taking initiatives on an individual basis	No planning, operational managers and IT experts taking initiatives on an individual basis	Formal planning and control procedures for IS/IT	Focused planning concerned with integration of information systems	Focused planning concerned with integration of databases	Strategic IS/IT planning
User influence	No influence, trained to use technology	No influence, trained to use technology	Some influence concerned with efficient use of technology	Some influence concerned with control of IS/IT costs	Some influence concerned with data flows in systems	Significant influence concerned with effective use of technology

Figure 4.4 can be compared with Leavitt's Diamond introduced earlier. Leavitt's Diamond argues that everything is connected, requiring changes in tasks (applications), people, structure (organization), and technology to move from one stage to the next. We see from the figure that application portfolio (tasks), IS/IT organization and user influence (people), as well as IS/IT planning (organization) all change from one stage to the next. Each stage represents the technology level itself.

Figure 4.5. Extended Nolan's six stage model to nine stages of IS/IT evolution in organizations

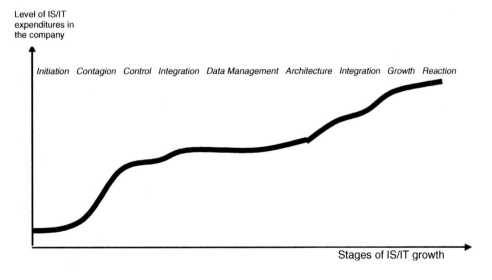

Level of IS/IT expenditures in the company

Initiation Contagion Control Integration Data Management Architecture Integration Growth Reaction

Stages of IS/IT growth

Figure 4.6.   Characteristics of revised and extended Nolan model

Growth Characteristics	Stage 4 Integration	Stage 5 Data	Stage 6 Architecture	Stage 7 Integration	Stage 8 Growth	Stage 9 Reaction
Application portfolio	Restructuring existing applications in a systems architecture	Restructuring existing applications in a data architecture	Application integration supporting information flows	Intra- and interorganizational communication	Systems connecting business with vendors and customers	Extended infrastructure to support tailor-made applications
IS/IT organization	Establish IS/IT support function and user accounts	Establish data administration function	Establish IS/IT resource management function	Central IS/IT coordination and local helpdesks	IS/IT operations outsourcing and ASP	Network of system owners
IS/IT planning	Focused planning concerned with integration of information systems	Focused planning concerned with integration of databases	Strategic IS/IT planning	Focused strategic IS/IT planning such as standardization and open systems	Focused strategic IS/IT planning such as e-business strategy	Focused strategic IS/IT planning such as infrastructure strategy
User influence	Some influence concerned with control of IS/IT costs	Some influence concerned with data flows in systems	Significant influence concerned with effective use of technology	Significant influence as project managers	Significant influence as system owners	Significant influence as strategic partners
Knowledge management	End-user tools for knowledge workers	End-user tools for knowledge workers	End-user tools for knowledge workers	Information about knowledge sources	Information from knowledge sources	Information processing as knowledge work

Figure 4.7.   Example of current IS/IT stage of growth in an organization

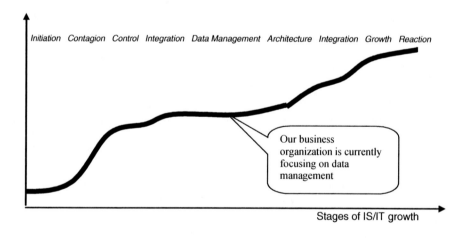

Nolan's stages of growth were introduced three decades ago. Several revisions have been done to the model. In the 1990s, three more stages were added to the model to cover recent developments in IS/IT in companies. These stages are labeled functional integration, tailored growth, and rapid reaction as illustrated in Figures 4.5 and 4.6.

Figure 4.8. Comparative maturity of IS/IT in various geographic regions

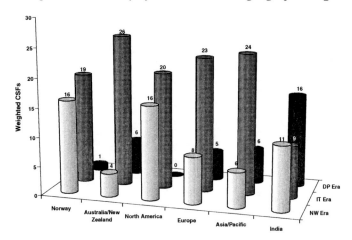

To describe the current IS/IT situation in a business organization using the method of stages of growth, we can circle our finding as illustrated in Figure 4.7. Assuming that our business organization is at stage 5, concentrating on data management, we can indicate that the next natural step in the future will be to work on architecture.

The nine stages can be divided into three eras, each era consisting of three stages. The first era is called data processing (DP) era; the second is information technology (IT) era, while the third is network (NW) era.

In a study conducted by Gottschalk and Khandelwal (2002), the extent to which business organizations were in these areas, was measured. The approach was through identification of critical success factors (CSF). As illustrated in Figure 4.8, Norwegian business organizations have left the DP era. Half of them are now in the IT era, while the other half is in the NW area.

Method III: IS/IT in Management Activities

Management activities can be studied in a hierarchical perspective as illustrated in Figure 4.9. This is an old, famous representation of the company. The company is a pyramid with different layers of functions. When assessing the current situation, the challenge is to find where IS/IT supports functions in the pyramid. Different kinds of IS/IT support different aspects of the business. The different IS/IT are related to the pyramid. An IS/IT may cover several functions in the pyramid.

In the following three Figures 4.10-12, we see how the five levels in the pyramid may have support from IS/IT. In the first figure, strategic control is concerned with products, markets, and objectives. The main purpose of IS in this function is control by providing information for decision making. In the next figure, we see characteristics of IS depending on level in the pyramid. While an IS for strategic control has very few users, an IS for

Figure 4.9. Management activities in a hierarchical perspective

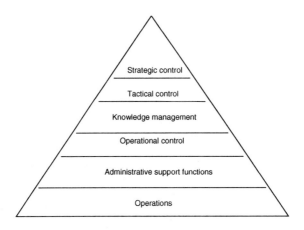

operations has very many users. In the last figure, only three of the levels in the pyramid are illustrated. We see that while strategic control is based on external information, operational control is based on internal information. Both strategic and operational control use information independent of the context in which it was previously used.

We will use the Norwegian School of Management BI (NSM) to illustrate this approach. NSM is in the business of economic and administrative education, undergraduate and graduate and extended management education, as well as classroom teaching and distant learning. Products include bachelor, master and doctoral degrees as well as different

Figure 4.10. Purpose of IS/IT applications

Tasks	Kind of Problems	Purpose of IS
Strategic control	What kind of business? Which products? Which markets? How reach objectives?	Control benefits Market benefits
Tactical control	Given business, what kinds of resources are needed and how are they best developed?	Control benefits Organizational benefits
Knowledge management	Given business, what kind of knowledge is needed in knowledge work?	Organizational benefits Market benefits
Operational control	Given business, what kind of resources, how are they utilized?	Control benefits Rationalization benefits
Administrative support functions	How to do these functions in the best way?	Rationalization benefits Control benefits
Operations	How to make the products in the best way?	Rationalization benefits Control benefits

Figure 4.11. Information processing of IS/IT applications

Type of IS	Users	User requirements	Information processing
IS for strategic control	Very few	Unstable, non-repetitive and unpredictable	Aggregation and combination of large volumes of data from many sources
IS for tactical control	Not so many, but in different departments	Unstable, repetitive and predictable	Calculations to determine performance
IS for knowledge management	All knowledge workers and managers who provide input and receive output from knowledge work	Unstable, non-repetitive and predictable	Communication and combination of information
IS for operational control	Many in different departments	Stable, repetitive and unpredictable	Optimization of performance
IS for administrative support functions	Few when administrative support functions centralized, more if decentralized	Stable, non-repetitive and predictable	Combination of information
IS for operations	Many in different departments, also customers and suppliers	Stable, repetitive and predictable	Transactions to be handled efficiently

kinds of diplomas. The market is mainly Norway with some activities abroad. An example of a management problem at the strategic level might be, "Should NSM start IT education and offer a Master of Science in Technology and Knowledge Management?" We might wonder what kind of IS/IT would help at this strategic control level. Management would need an IS/IT, which provides information about educational needs of society and what competitors are doing and intend to do. At the tactical control level, resource issues arise: Teachers, administrative staff, school buildings, computers and classroom equipment. The management problem at the tactical level might be: How do we combine our resources? Here management needs an IS/IT that provides information that can enable trade-offs between different kinds of resources.

At the knowledge management level, information needs arise: the knowledge workers (e.g., professors) need to make existing knowledge explicit and to acquire and develop new knowledge through research. The knowledge management problem might be, "How do we organize knowledge creation, sharing, and distribution in new educational

Figure 4.12. IS for strategic control, knowledge management and operational control

Information Characteristics	Strategic control	Knowledge management	Operational control
Sources of information?	External	Internal and external	Internal
Which time period?	Future (forecasts, plans)	Past (history)	Past (history)
Degree of detail?	Low degree	Low and high	High degree
How frequent?	Infrequent	Frequent	Frequent
Is it correct?	No, based on judgment	Yes, based on experience	Yes, based on actual data
Information context?	Context independent	Context dependent	Context independent

Figure 4.13. Example of current IS/IT situation based on a hierarchical perspective

programs? At the operational control level, the problem is to allocate teachers to courses, classrooms, and hours. Do we have IS/IT for this purpose? Finally, for operational functions: Do we use computers in our teaching?"

Here we have illustrated how we can describe the IS/IT situation in the company by identifying IS/IT in management activities. We can describe the situation by documenting at what hierarchical levels there is IS/IT support currently and the extent of this support as illustrated in the example in Figure 4.13. According to this example, current IS/IT provide strong support for administrative support functions as well as operational control. Operations do also rely heavily on IS/IT. The top three layers have only marginal support from IS/IT.

Method IV: IS/IT in Business Processes

Information systems in an organization have three purposes:

- *Management purpose*: To make information available that can be used in planning and decision-making.

- *Communication purpose*: To create contact and dialog between various parts of the organization and between the organization and its environment.

- *Learning purpose*: To develop knowledge about the company, its operations, and its environment.

Management, communication, and learning purposes are tightly linked to tasks in the company. Persons in the company perform tasks in business processes. A business process can be defined as a structured and organized collection of activities and duties that exist to produce a result in the form of goods or services for an internal receiver in the company or an external customer in the market place. A business process has a beginning and an end, uses one or more resources, and creates a result of value for the receiver in the organization or the customer in the market place. Activities in the business process are primarily important to the extent that they contribute to complete the process, i.e. that the business process delivers expected results in the form of goods or services. Typical examples of business processes include mortgage application handling in a bank, order execution in a net shop, product development in manufacturing industry, and client problem solving in a law firm.

In a company, many business processes take place at the same time. These processes are often dependent on each other, as they produce goods and services through process interactions. The company also interacts with its environment. The environment includes everything and everyone influencing the company, such as competitors, suppliers, customers, authorities and interest groups.

Business processes are concerned with how work is organized, coordinated, staffed, and focused to produce goods and services of value to receivers and customers. Business processes are workflows in the form of materials and information. Hence, business processes are collections of activities. Furthermore, business processes are the very special way the company has chosen to coordinate work and knowledge, and the way management chooses to coordinate all production of goods and services. For example, all companies have a workflow to handle customer complaints. This workflow will be organized differently in different companies.

Today, executives are interested in identifying and improving business processes. This interest has emerged as executives realize that company success is dependent on the ability to deliver products at low prices, with high quality and professional service to customers. This interest has also emerged as more and more business processes have important interactions with the environment, such as supply and delivery business conducted over the Internet.

Figure 4.14. The business process of customer complaint handling

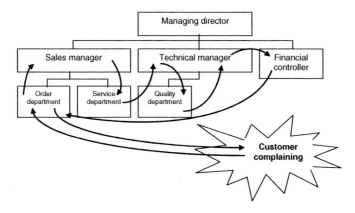

Business processes do normally cross departmental borders. A business process can involve sales department, technical department and service department. Business processes may involve several levels in the hierarchy. Figure 4.14 illustrates an example of a customer complaint handling process. The customer is dissatisfied with a PC ordered over the Internet and returns the PC. The order department gets a notice and informs the sales manager. The service department receives the PC and sends it to the technical manager. Then the PC moves on to the product control department, which concludes that the PC is defect and that the customer should be offered the opportunity to get it repaired for free. However, the customer had asked for the money back, so the matter is forwarded to the financial controller who decides that the customer may choose between repair and money return. The financial controller informs the service department of this decision, and the service department sends an e-mail to the customer.

IS/IT supports business processes. Information-intensive business processes will typically find intensive support by information systems. Business processes that were manual and inefficient may have been restructured and activities in the processes may have been automated using information technology.

The current IS/IT situation in the company can be described by linking applications of information technology to businesses processes. Sometimes a company has defined a few core business processes, and the description can then focus on the extent to which IS/IT support these core business processes.

In knowledge management, our focus is on knowledge in business processes. We want to identify and describe how knowledge workers participate and contribute in business processes, and how IS/IT support their work. Figure 4.15 may illustrate this point. This is an example where we have identified two core business processes of client problem analysis and solution and human resources management in a consulting firm. While the first process involves heavy knowledge work as indicated with the dark color, human resources management is just as much an administrative task. On the other hand, the current situation in the organization is such that human resources management receives more support from IS/IT than does the business process of client problem analysis and solutions.

Figure 4.15. Business processes with different knowledge intensity and IS/IT support

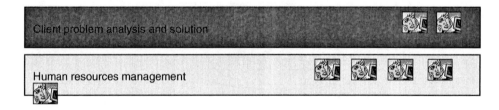

Method V: IS/IT Support for Value Configuration

The most important business processes are often found in the company's value configuration. A value configuration describes how value is created in a company for its customers. A value configuration shows how the most important business processes function to create value for customers. A value configuration represents the way a particular organization conducts business. The best-known value configuration is the value chain.

In the *value chain*, value is created through efficient production of goods and services based on a variety of resources. The company is perceived as a series or chain of activities. Primary activities in the value chain include inbound logistics, production, outbound logistics, marketing and sales, and service. Support activities include infrastructure, human resources, technology development, and procurement.

Value cannot only be created in value chains. Value can also be created in two alternative value configurations: value chop and value network (Stabell & Fjeldstad, 1998). In the *value shop*, activities are scheduled and resources are applied in a fashion that is dimensioned and appropriate to the needs of the client's problem, while a value chain performs a fixed set of activities that enables it to produce a standard product in large numbers. The value shop is a company that creates value by solving unique problems for customers and clients. Knowledge is the most important resource, and reputation is critical to firm success.

The third and final value configuration is the *value network*. A value network is a company that creates value by connecting clients and customers that are, or want to be, dependent on each other. These companies distribute information, money, products, and services.

These value configurations were thoroughly presented in Chapter I.

Method VI: Strategic Integration

The current IS/IT situation in a company can be measured through the extent of integration between business strategy and IS/IT strategy. King and Teo (1997) have defined four stages of integration. The first is separate planning with administrative integration. The second is one-way linked planning with sequential integration, while the third is two-way linked planning with reciprocal integration. The fourth stage is integrated planning with full integration.

The four stages of integration can be described in terms of benchmark variables as shown in Figure 4.16. Benchmark variables indicate the theoretical characteristics at each stage of integration. For example, firms at Stage 1 can theoretically be expected to conform to values of benchmark variables listed under Stage 1. However, this does not mean that it is not possible for firms at Stage 1 to have values of benchmark variables applicable to other stages.

Figure 4.16.   Stages of integration between business strategy and IS/IT strategy

Benchmark Variables	Stage 1 Administrative Integration	Stage 2 Sequential Integration	Stage 3 Reciprocal Integration	Stage 4 Full Integration
Purpose of integration	Administrative and nonstrategic	Support business strategy	Support and influence business strategy	Joint development of business and IS strategies
Role of the IS function	Technically oriented and nonstrategic	Resource to support business strategy	Resource to support and influence business strategy	Critical to long-term survival of organization
Primary role of the IS executive	Functional administrator responsible for back room support	IS expert who formulates IS/IT strategy to implement business strategy	IS expert who provides valuable inputs during strategy formulation and implementation	Formal and integral member of top management who is involved in many business matters
Performance criteria for the IS function	Operational efficiency and cost minimization	Contribution to business strategy implementation	Quality of IS inputs into business strategy formulation and implementation	Long-term impact on organization
Triggers for developing IS applications	Need to automate administrative work processes	Business goals considered first	Business goals and IS capabilities considered jointly	IS applications are critical to success of business strategy
Top management participation in IS/IT planning	Seldom	Infrequent	Frequent	Almost always
User participation in IS/IT planning	Seldom	Infrequent	Frequent	Almost always
IS executive participation in business planning	Seldom	Infrequent	Frequent	Almost always
Assessment of new technologies	Seldom	Infrequent	Frequent	Almost always
Status of IS executive (Number of levels below the CEO)	Four or more	Three	Two	One

Each of the 10 benchmark variables can be explained more in detail as follows:

1. *Purpose of integration.* At Stage 1, integration focuses primarily on the support of administrative work processes. This gradually changes as the IS function begins to support business strategy (Stage 2) or influence business strategy (Stage 3). At Stage 4, there is joint strategy development for both business and IS strategies.

2. *Role of the IS function.* The general transition from being technically oriented to business oriented is a trend for most IS functions. At Stage 1, the IS function is viewed as being primarily technically oriented. Gradually, this role changes when the IS function is used as a resource to support the implementation (Stage 2) and formulation (Stage 3) of business strategies. At Stage 4, the IS function is viewed as critical to the long-term success of the organization.

3. *Primary role of the IS executive.* There seems to be a general decrease in the size of the central IS function. This may have resulted in a shift in the responsibilities of the IS function from systems design to systems integration, and from the role of a developer to that of an advisor. Due to increasing decentralization, the IS function may assume a staff role similar to a federal government in coordinating dispersed IS resources. The skill requirements of the senior executive have also changed over the years with increasing emphasis on both knowledge about

changing technology and knowledge about the business. In addition, significant political and communication skills are required. The role of the IS executive gradually changes from being a functional administrator responsible for providing back room support (Stage 1), to being an IS expert who formulates IS strategy to implement business objectives (Stage 2). As the firm begins to apply IT for strategic purposes, the role of the IS executive becomes more important. He or she begins to play a major role in facilitating and influencing the development and implementation of IS applications to achieve business objectives (Stage 3). Finally, in Stage 4, the IS executive becomes a formal and integral member of the top management team, and provides significant inputs in both IS and non-IS related matters.

4.   *Performance criteria for the IS function.* As the IS function matures, the performance criteria for the IS function change from a structured focus on operational efficiency to a more unstructured concern for the impact of IS on strategic direction. It follows that the early performance criteria (Stage 1) for the IS function are primarily concerned with operational efficiency and cost minimization. When the IS function begins to play a more strategic role, the emphasis gradually shifts to effective strategy implementation (Stage 2), and then to the quality of IS inputs into business strategy formulation and implementation (Stage 3). Ultimately, the performance criteria for the IS function should be its long-term impact on the organization (Stage 4).

5.   *Triggers for developing IS applications.* Initially, the triggers for the development of new IS applications are opportunities for achieving greater efficiencies through process automation. As IS applications begin to be increasingly used to support business strategies, business goals become trigger mechanisms in deciding appropriate IS applications to be developed (Stage 2). At Stage 3, the joint consideration of business goals and IS capabilities becomes important as the firm attempts to develop systems for sustainable competitive advantage. Finally, in Stage 4, IS applications are developed because they are critical to the success of the firm's strategy and the creation of business value.

6.   *Top management participation in IS/IT planning.* Traditionally, as in Stage 1, top management had not paid great attention to the IS function because it was an overhead function that generated only cost. At Stage 2, greater top management participation in IS/IT planning begins when IS strategies come to be used to support business strategies. The realization that strategic IS/IT planning can also influence business strategy motivates top management to participate more actively in this kind of strategy work (Stage 3). Finally, in Stage 4, when the IS function becomes critical for the survival of the organization, top management and the senior IS executive jointly formulate business and IS plans.

7.   *User participation in IS/IT planning.* Before the availability of end-user computing, user management was generally not significantly involved (Stage 1). However, as end-user systems and tools begin to dominate individual work, and the IS function begins to influence functional units in terms of its effects on business strategies, participation of users becomes more important in order to fully exploit the potential of information technology. User participation gradually increases through the stages, until at Stage 4, users participate extensively in IS/IT planning.

8. *IS executive participation in business planning.* The other side of business management participation in IS/IT planning is having IS executives participate in business planning. The traditional role of the IS function in providing administrative support does not require the senior IS executive to participate in business planning (Stage 1). The senior IS executive reacts to business plans and does not have any influence on their formulation. At Stage 2, the senior IS executive participation is initiated. As the IS function becomes more important in achievement of business objectives, it becomes necessary to include more frequent participation of the senior IS executive in business planning because the traditional participants are relatively unfamiliar with the potential of information technology (Stage 3). With greater participation, the senior IS executive becomes more informed about business objectives and is better able to provide higher quality inputs into the planning process. At Stage 4, the senior IS executive becomes an integral member of the top management team and participates extensively in both business planning and IS/IT planning.

9. *Assessment of new technologies.* During IS/IT planning, new technologies, which can affect the firm, are usually assessed. The level of sophistication involved in assessing new technologies is the basis for this ninth benchmark variable. In the early stages of IS/IT planning (Stages 1 and 2), assessment of the impact of new technologies, if any, is usually done rather informally and infrequently. At Stage 3, the need for formal and frequent procedures for assessing new technologies becomes apparent as the IS function begins to play a more important role in business planning. At Stage 4, assessment of the impact of new technologies becomes an integral part of business planning and IS/IT planning.

10. *Status of IS executive.* The responsibilities of the IS function have changed over the years due to technological and conceptual changes that made information technology more important to organizations. IS line responsibilities are being rapidly distributed in many organizations as the IS function begins to take on more staff responsibilities. With these changing responsibilities of the IS function, the status of the senior IS executive is likely to become higher. The position of the senior IS executive—in terms of the number of levels below the CEO—can serve as an indication of the importance of the IS function to the firm's strategy.

Method VII: IS/IT Support for Knowledge Management

Information technology can be applied at four different levels to support knowledge management in an organization. At the first level, end user tools are made available to knowledge workers. At the second level, information on who knows what, is made available electronically. At the third level, some information representing knowledge is stored and made available electronically. At the fourth level, information systems capable of simulating human thinking are applied in the organization. These four levels are illustrated in Figure 4.17, where they are combined with knowledge management tasks. The entries in the figure only serve as examples of current systems.

Figure 4.17. Examples of IS/IT at different knowledge management levels

LEVELS / TASKS	I END USER TOOLS	II WHO KNOWS WHAT	III WHAT THEY KNOW	IV WHAT THEY THINK
Distribute knowledge	Word Processing Desktop Publishing Web Publishing Electronic Calendars Presentations	Word Processing Desktop Publishing Web Publishing Electronic Calendars Presentations	Word Processing Desktop Publishing Web Publishing Electronic Calendars Presentations	Word Processing Desktop Publishing Web Publishing Electronic Calendars Presentations
Share knowledge		Groupware Intranets Networks E-mail	Groupware Intranets Networks E-mail	Groupware Intranets Networks E-mail
Capture knowledge			Databases Data Warehouses	Databases Data Warehouses
Apply knowledge				Expert systems Case based reasoning

The four different levels of support for knowledge management in an organization are described in Chapter IV. The levels are discussed in the context of the stages of growth model for knowledge management technology.

Method VIII: IS/IT in E-Business

For most firms, becoming an e-business is an evolutionary development (Porter, 2001). Earl (2000) has described the typical six-stage journey that corporations are likely to experience. The six stages are not necessarily definitive periods of evolution, as companies may have activities at several neighboring stages at the same time. The six stages are illustrated in Figure 4.18.

Each of the six stages of evolving the e-business as illustrated in Figure 4.18 can be described as follows (Earl, 2000):

1. *External communication.* It was more than a decade ago that most corporations wanted a home page on the Internet for the first time. The realization that the Internet was a potential communications channel to external stakeholders such as investors, analysts, customers, potential recruits, and suppliers, was matched by the recognition that the Web provided an interesting and not too difficult means of designing and publishing corporate public relations material.

   The vision behind creating such Web sites rarely extends beyond external corporate communications. Perhaps the only interactive aspect is a provision for e-mailed questions to corporate departments from external stakeholders.

2. *Internal communication.* Intranets, using the Internet and Web techniques, are introduced at this stage to raise the information and communication capacity of the

Figure 4.18. Stages of e-business maturity

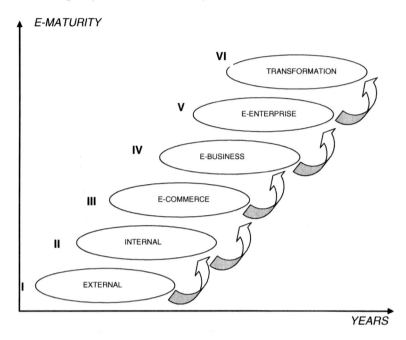

organization. An integrated, familiar front end to frequently-used internal applications does appeal to end-users. Knowledge management applications have evolved from this stage. And sometimes having internal access to the same information that is provided externally is well received.

Information technology is applied to design consistent and user-friendly front ends to e-mail, groupware, administrative support systems, and other systems used by most people in the organization.

3.   *E-commerce.* Buying and selling on the Internet take place at this stage. Electronic channels and services are promoted to complement traditional forms of distribution. In the case of start-ups, customers are identified and attracted by using the Web and other advertising channels.

At this stage, organizations struggle with questions such as: What and how do we tell customers and suppliers that they can trade with us online? What pricing policies do we adopt and how do they relate to pricing in our traditional channels? Which products and services are suited to electronic market trading? What IS/IT applications and functions are needed to support e-commerce?

4.   *E-business.* Many companies discover a critical lesson at the e-commerce stage. Building an online channel on top of inadequate or inefficient business processes achieves only one thing: it broadcasts and magnifies the fact that the company's back office systems or operational processes are really bad. So this fourth stage is about re-engineering and redesigning business processes to match customers' expectations.

Customers already recognize the signs of business processes that are not synchronized with the demands and expectations of e-commerce: goods that do not arrive on time; e-mailed requests that do not receive response; clumsy handling of returns; inability to track order status; network access that breaks down; and telephone requests where persons answering the phone have no idea what you are talking about.

Most firms learn the hard way and treat stage 3 as inevitable, evolutionary, experiential learning. Then they accept the costs of stage 4, where reengineering of business processes and redesign of architecture and infrastructure of their technology base have to be implemented. The lesson at stage 4 is that high-performance processes are needed to stay in e-business.

5.   *E-enterprise.* Web-enabled online business puts new pressures on management processes. Decision-making occurs increasingly on the network, rather than in meeting rooms. Transactions can be monitored and analyzed in real time. Information can be collected online. New ways of representing and analyzing these data are being developed. We are witnessing new ways of communicating across the enterprise using wireless and mobile technologies.

Wireless and mobile technologies are about to change Internet business. This is being driven by customer demand for wireless devices and the desire to be connected to information and services available through the Internet from anywhere and at any time. Similarly, company employees see no reason anymore for showing up in the office at eight o'clock and leave again at five. Resulting, telecommunications, the Internet, and mobile computing are merging their technologies to form the basis for mobile work and management.

In stage 5, decision-making is becoming entrepreneurial and about communicating decisions across the enterprise. This stage is the dawn of cybernetic models of management where traditional top managers find the time to leave the company. The critical success factor is to recruit, develop, and empower people who have the skills to use information and act on it.

6.   *Transformation.* The company has successfully made the journey of e-business. The challenges of the previous stages have been met, and the new business and management solutions required for the e-enterprise are embedded. In many ways, this is the goal. However, we know that nothing stabilize, market forces and emerging technologies drive continuous change.

E-commerce and e-business are discussed in Chapter IV.

Method IX: IS/IT-Enabled Business Transformation

The role of IS/IT in shaping business operations is a distinctive one. IS/IT has become a fundamental enabler in creating and maintaining flexible business activities. Using a framework that breaks IS/IT-enabled business transformation into five levels, Venkatraman (1994) provides a description of each level's characteristics and offers guidelines for deriving maximal benefits. He suggests that each organization first determines the level at which the benefits are in line with the costs or efforts of the needed changes and then proceed to higher levels as the demands of competition and the need to deliver greater value to the customer increases as illustrated in Figure 4.19.

Level One: Information technology efficiency. The first level is the basic one for leveraging IS/IT functionality within a business through localized exploitation. The expression 'localized exploitation' is chosen to indicate that, in many cases, decisions to deploy isolated systems (e.g., a customer order-entry system, inventory control system, internal electronic mail system) are decentralized to the appropriate functional, operational managers. Typically, managers initiate and deploy these systems to respond to operational problems or challenges. This level one is best viewed as the deployment of standard IS/IT applications with minimal changes to the business processes.

This underutilizes IS/IT's potential capabilities and fails to provide organizations with as many possible advantages if the company attempted to change the business processes to leverage the technical functionality. The main weakness is that competitors can easily imitate standard technical applications with minimal changes to the underlying business processes to neutralize sources of strategic advantage.

Level Two: Information systems integration. The second level is a logical extension of the first, reflecting a more systematic attempt to leverage IS/IT capabilities throughout the entire business process. This level involves two types of internal systems integration: technical inter-connectivity (dealing with the inter-connectivity and interoperability of the different systems and applications throughout a common IT platform) and business process interdependence (dealing with the interdependence of organizational roles and responsibilities across distinct functional lines). Neither type alone is sufficient. Often, firms allocate more attention to technical inter-connectivity than to business process interdependence. Efforts at technical inter-connectivity have been enhanced by significant developments in connectivity capabilities during the past decade, such as increased availability of integrated technological solutions and favorable cost-performance trends.

Efforts at business process interdependence should first emphasize the view that the firm should develop its own vision for internal integration after assessing the benefits of integrating current businesses processes. If a company deems the current processes to be effective, then it is important to articulate the specific objectives of internal integration: for instance, some firms may seek to create cross-functional, horizontal business processes that are parallel to the traditional organization. Alternatively, the logic for internal integration may reflect a transition toward fundamentally redesigning the business processes over a period of time.

Efforts at business processes interdependence should then emphasize the need to ensure that marketplace considerations guide internal integration efforts. Simply fine-tuning existing outmoded processes through current technological capabilities does not create the required organizational capabilities.

Level Three: Business process change. The third level reflects a strong view that the benefits from IS/IT functionality are not fully realized if superimposed on the current business processes—however integrated they might be. This is because the current business processes subscribe to a set of organizational principles that responded to the

Figure 4.19. Level of IT-enabled transformation as identity of current IS/IT situation

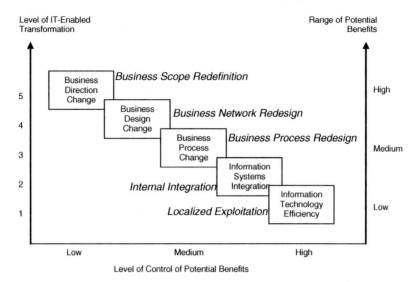

industrial revolution. Organizational concepts such as centralization vs. decentralization, span of control, line vs. staff, functional specialization, authority-responsibility balance, and administrative mechanisms for coordination and control are all derived from the general principles. Although these concepts are still valid, IS/IT functionality can significantly alter some of these old principles. Some modes of organizing may be rendered relatively inefficient. In the opinion of professionals and academics, the new logic of organization should be predicated on current and emerging IS/IT capabilities. IS/IT functionality should not be simply overlaid on existing business processes but should be used as a lever for designing the new organization and associated business processes.

Three critical questions for exploiting IS/IT-related benefits at the level of business process redesign are: (i) what is the rationale for the current organizational design? (What are its strengths and limitations?), (ii) what significant changes in business processes are occurring in the marketplace? (What are the likely impacts?). (iii) What are the costs of continuing with the status quo? (When should we redesign the business process? what should be our pace of redesign?).

A company should initiate business process redesign after ascertaining the significant changes in its key competitors' business processes — especially those of new entrants — so that it can formulate appropriate responses beforehand.

Benefits from business process redesign are limited in scope if the processes are not extended outside the focal organizational boundary to identify options for redesigning relationships with the other organizations that participate in ultimately delivering value to the customer.

Level Four: Business design change. The three levels discussed thus far have focused on IS/IT-enabled business transformation within a single organization. These levels — either implicitly or explicitly — assumed that the boundary of the focal organization is fixed or given. Even when there are interconnections with external businesses — such as suppliers, buyers, and other intermediaries — the distribution of business activities across the different firms is not altered. In contrast, this level represents the redesign of the nature of exchange among multiple participants in a business network through effective deployment of IS/IT capabilities.

If this is the current IS/IT level in the company, then we should see evidence of a strategic logic influencing related participants in the business network to provide products and services in the marketplace, exploiting IS/IT functionality for learning from the extended network as well as for coordination and control. We should further see evidence of elimination of activities where our organization may not have the required level of competence, streamlining business scope to remain flexible as well as responsive to fast-changing and diverse customer needs, and ability to exploit sources of competence in the larger business network (beyond what is available in our organization).

Level Five: Business direction change. Strategy analysis typically starts with the mission and vision. When the mission describes the business we are in, then the vision describes what we want to achieve in that business. At the fifth level, IS/IT will play a role in influencing mission and vision.

If this is the current IS/IT level in the company, then we should see evidence of a business scope redefinition that is enabled and facilitated by IS/IT functionality. We should see evidence of opportunities and actions to take advantage of IS/IT capabilities to create a more flexible and effective business entity. We should see substitution of inter-firm business relationships as an effective alternative to vertical integration.

Describing Current and Desired Business Situation

We have used a series of methods to describe the current situation of IS/IT. Now we have to consider whether the current IS/IT applications are what the company needs or if there might be changes needed. We use the Y model as our guiding approach. We compare the present business situation (with its support from IS/IT) with the desired business situation. If the current IS/IT applications are not able to serve the needs of the future desired business, then there are needs for change in IS/IT applications and the way we do business. At this point, we are moving into stage 2 of the Y model.

There are many techniques for business analysis. Some are general, while others are more specific. General analysis techniques include SWOT analysis and the X model. Specific analysis techniques include business direction (mission, vision, objectives), market strategy, value system, competitive forces, and product life cycle. We will the following methods:

I.   *SWOT analysis.* SWOT analysis is an analytical tool for assessing the present and future situation focusing on strengths (S), weaknesses (W), opportunities (O), and threats (T). The whole company may be the object of analysis, but also a department in a company or a project in a company may be the study object. How can knowledge management exploit our strengths, compensate our weaknesses, use opportunities, and avoid threats? How can knowledge management technology help make it happen?

II.   *X model.* The X model is a tool for description and analysis of both the current and a desired situation. It is a method for assessing the situation within a company, a project, or a department. The situation consists of a time period in which work is done. In the beginning of the time period, there are both factual and personal inputs, and at the end of the period, there are both factual and personal outputs. How can knowledge management improve factual and personal outputs? How can knowledge management technology help make it happen?

III.   *Business direction.* Important business concepts are mission, vision, and objectives. How can knowledge management make the firm achieve its vision? How can knowledge management make the firm reach its objectives? How can knowledge management technology help make it happen?

IV.   *Market strategy.* The market strategy shows our position and ambition in the market place. Either we can have the same product as our competitors, or we can have a different product. If we have the same product as everyone else, it has to be sold at the same price as all the others (as in a vegetable market or through the Internet). It is not possible for an Internet bookstore to sell at a higher price than others, when there is perfect information and information searching is associated with no costs. This is called the law of indifference. In order to survive, the company must have a cost advantage that will give higher profits and result in higher earnings for the owners. How can knowledge management cause a cost advantage? How can knowledge management technology help make it happen? If we are selling a product that our customers perceive to be different from our competitors' product, then we have differentiation. A service may in its basic form be the same for all companies, like an airline travel, in the sense that all airlines are supposed to bring you safely to your destination. The product is differentiated by supplementary services. How can knowledge management make our customers perceive our products and services to be different from our competitor's? How can knowledge management technology help make it happen?

V.   *Competitive forces.* The basis of this method is that a company exists within an industry and to succeed, it must effectively deal with the competitive forces that exist within the particular industry. For example, the forces in an emerging industry such as mobile communication are considerably different from those of established industries such as financial services. The company interacts with its customers, suppliers, and competitors. In addition, there are potential new entrants into the particular competitive marketplace and potential substitute products and services. To survive and succeed in this environment, it is important to understand these interactions and the implications in terms of what opportunities or competitive advantage can occur. How can knowledge management reduce the threat of new entrants, reduce the bargaining power of suppliers, reduce the bargaining power of buyers, reduce the threat of substitute products and services, and reduce the rivalry among existing competitors? How can knowledge management technology help make it happen?

VI.   *Product portfolio analysis.* There are a number of approaches that aim to relate the competitive position of an organization to the maturity of its product. The models assume there is a basic S-shaped curve description to the growth phenomenon of products. Four stages in the life cycle of any product can be identified as introduction, growth, maturity, and decline. When we look at the life cycle of all products in the firm, we can apply product portfolio analysis. This method shows the relationship between a product's current or future revenue potential and the appropriate management stance. The two by two matrix names the products in order to chart symptoms into a diagnosis so that effective management behavior can be adopted. The matrix classifies products according to the present market share and the future growth of that market. A successful product that lasts from emergent to mature market goes around the matrix. This strategy is simply to milk the cows, divest the dogs, invest in the stars and examine the wild cats. How can knowledge management get more milk for a longer period of time from the cows? How can knowledge management explore and exploit the stars? How can knowledge management eliminate the dogs? How can knowledge management develop the wild cats into stars? How can knowledge management technology help make it happen?

VII. *Environmental analysis.* Environmental analysis is concerned with the external corporate environment. An analysis of the environment is important because it increases the quality of the strategic decision-making by considering a range of the relevant features. The organization identifies a threats and opportunities facing it, and those factors that might assist in achieving objectives and those that might act as a barrier. The strategy of the organization should be directed at exploiting the environmental opportunities and blocking environmental threats in a way that

Figure 4.20. Example of SWOT analysis

Strengths	Opportunities
Distribution	Market growth
Knowledge	Supplementary services
Reputation	Globalization
Weaknesses	Threats
Management	New competitors
Costs	New technology
Infrastructure	Low-cost producers

is consistent with internal capabilities. This is a matter of environmental fit that allows the organization to maximize its competitive position. An external analysis can investigate politics, the economy, the society, and the technology. This is sometimes called PEST analysis. If we include the study of legal and environmental matters, we call it PESTLE. The analytical work that has to be done in the company when doing environmental analysis is concerned with questions such as: What are the implications of the trends (changes in the environment)? What can the company do in order to meet the opportunities and threats that follow? How can knowledge management meet the opportunities and threats that follow? How can knowledge management technology help make it happen? For example, how can knowledge management technology help in global competition (politics)? How can knowledge management technology help in alliances and partnerships (economy)? How can knowledge management help serve an increasing number of older people (society)?

VIII. *Knowledge analysis.* Distinctions can be made between core knowledge, advanced knowledge and innovative knowledge. While core knowledge is required to stay in business, advanced knowledge makes the firm competitively visible, and innovative knowledge allows the firm to lead its entire industry. The knowledge map can be applied to identify firm position. The map in terms of the strategic knowledge framework presented earlier in this book, illustrates firm knowledge levels compared with competitors' knowledge levels.

Method I: SWOT Analysis

SWOT analysis is an analytical tool for assessing the present and future situation focusing on strengths (S), weaknesses (W), opportunities (O), and threats (T). The whole company may be the object of analysis, but also a department in a company or a project in a company may be the study object. As illustrated in Figure 4.20, strengths and weaknesses are concerned with the internal situation, while opportunities and threats are concerned with the external situation.

The main advantage of this technique is its readiness for application. The main disadvantage is that it will represent subjective views. Furthermore, management has to be aware of employee expectations if employees are invited to contribute in a SWOT analysis, as they will expect something to happen after the analysis is completed.

The SWOT model reveals the needs for changes in business. The company has to change in order to take advantage of tomorrow's opportunities and to avoid future threats. The company does also need to change to utilize strengths and to avoid weaknesses. For example, the company in Figure 4.26 could:

• Seek more benefits from distribution, knowledge and reputation

• Improve management, reduce costs and improve infrastructure

• Find ways of participating in the market growth

• Develop supplementary services

- Expand market activities worldwide

- Develop entry barriers for competitors

- Learn and introduce new technology

- Cut costs where there are low-cost producers.

Method II: X Model

The X model is a tool for description and analysis of both the current and a desired situation. It is a method for assessing the situation within a company, a project, or a department. The situation consists of a time period in which work is done. In the beginning of the time period, there are both factual and personal inputs, and at the end of the period, there are both factual and personal outputs, as illustrated in Figure 4.21.

This technique is called the X model because of the visual image we see illustrated in Figure 4.22. It uses the same description technique as the Y model, where a rectangle represents an information set and a dot represents an information process.

The personal inputs consist of people with knowledge, experience, attitudes, needs, and ambitions. The factual inputs consist of tasks, objectives, plans, procedures and resources. The working manners and procedures consist of working styles, cooperation, and communication. Personal outputs consist of people with new knowledge, new experience, new attitudes, new needs, and new ambitions. Similarly, factual outputs consist of executed tasks, objectives achieved or not, plans implemented or not, new procedures installed and used resources.

The main advantage of the X model is its very compressed description; a description of a comprehensive situation is condensed onto a page. Thereby, it gives a very good overview of what has happened or will happen. Another advantage is that the model focuses both on factual and personal inputs, thereby providing a good starting point for business analysis. An example of a knowledge management project will illustrate the X model in Figure 4.23.

Figure 4.21. The X model in a time perspective

Figure 4.22. Inputs and outputs of the X model

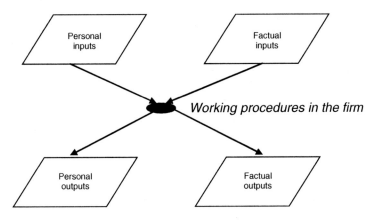

We see in this example that the expected outcome is reduced motivation. Reasons for this may be too much work close to milestones as well as medium quality communication. Probably, we may be able to achieve improved motivation if these two factors are changed as illustrated in Figure 4.24. The working manner is determined by the factual and personal inputs. The reason for two much work close to milestones might be that there is too short time allocated to the work. We would also like to change the inputs, but that might not always be possible as they are given or determined by others.

When we have described the current situation and working manners, we can explain why personal and factual outputs become what they do. The next step is to describe the desired situation. It is easy to say what we would like the desired situation to be. Then we can go backwards in the X model to revise personal and factual inputs as well as working procedures.

Figure 4.23. The X model applied to a project in the company

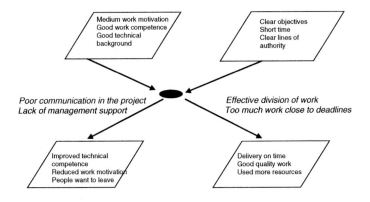

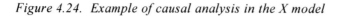

Figure 4.24. Example of causal analysis in the X model

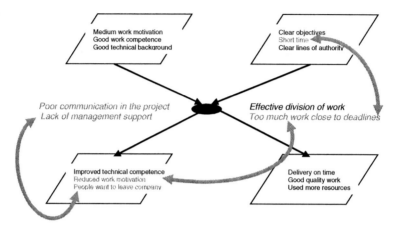

Method III: Business Direction

Important business concepts are mission, vision, and objectives. A *mission* is an unambiguous statement of what the company does and its long-term, overall purpose. It indicates what kind of business the company is in, and which markets it serves. For example, a telecom corporation such as Telenor in Norway is in the business of providing connections, while a power corporation such as Statnett is in the business of providing energy. The mission of a law firm is to provide legal advice. The mission describes a justification for firm existence; it states the purpose of the organization. The mission answers the question: What business are we in?

A *vision* is a statement of what the business will be in the future (three to five years), and how the company will operate. It indicates how good the company wants to be. Given the mission that describes the justification for existence, the vision is to describe what ambitions the firm has for the future. For example, the vision of Telenor may be to develop from a local operator in Norway to a global player in the telecommunications market. For Statnett the vision might be to expand into other energy sources than hydroelectric power. For a law firm, the vision might be to become the leader in business law. The vision represents the view that senior management has for the future of the organization; it is what they want it to become or achieve. The vision answers the question: What do we want to achieve in this business?

Objectives are long-term targets that management is setting to take the company toward its vision. Objectives are quantified targets, such as financial returns, customer service, manufacturing performance, staff moral, and social and environmental contributions. For example, the objective of Telenor may be to double its income from foreign business. For Statnett it may be to have a fraction of its business in non-hydropower. For a law firm, an objective might be to recruit all the best business lawyers. Objectives define the desired future positions of the organization; they are specific and tangible measures of future targets. Objectives answer the questions: What should be our future positions in this business?

The Norwegian School of Management BI (NSM) will serve as an example. The mission of NSM is teaching business administration and management, and doing research. Its vision is to be one of the leading research-based business schools in Europe and an attractive workplace for leading faculty members within important management areas such as marketing, finance, and technology. Objectives include the number of doctoral students and the amount of research funding in the future.

Method IV: Market Strategy

The market strategy shows our position and ambition in the market place. Figure 4.25 provides an illustration of generic market strategies. Either we can have the same product as our competitors, or we can have a different product. If we have the same product as everyone else, it has to be sold at the same price as all the others (as in a vegetable market or through the Internet). It is not possible for an Internet bookstore to sell at a higher price than others are, when there is perfect information and information searching is associated with no costs. This is called the law of indifference. In order to survive, the company must have a cost advantage that will give higher profits and result in higher earnings for the owners.

If we are selling a product that our customers perceive to be different from our competitors' product, then we have differentiation. A service may in its basic form be the same for all companies, like an airline travel, in the sense that all airlines are supposed to bring you safely to your destination. The product is differentiated by supplementary services. For example, some airlines give you the option of booking certain seats in advance; some airlines have frequent flyer programs, while others have better meals.

The two generic market strategies are concerned with cost leadership or differentiation. In Figure 4.26, required skills and resources as well as organizational requirements are listed for the two strategies.

Cost leadership means the organization aims to be the lowest-cost producer in the marketplace. The organization enjoys above-average performance by minimizing costs. The product or service offered must be comparable in quality to those offered by others

Figure 4.25. Generic market strategies

	Same product	Different product
Broad market scope (all markets)	Overall cost leadership	Differentiation
Narrow market scope (selected markets)	Cost based focus	Differentiation based focus

Figure 4.26.   Characteristics of generic market strategies

Generic strategy	Required skills and resources	Organizational requirements
Cost leadership	• Frequent investments and easy access to capital • Process skills • Intensive supervision of labor	• Tight cost control; frequent, detailed control reports • Structured organization and responsibilities • Incentives based on meeting quantitative targets
Differentiation	• Strong on marketing and creativity • Product skills • Strong capability in basic research • Corporate reputation for quality or technological leadership • Strong cooperation with distribution channels	• Strong coordination in research and development (R&D), product development, and marketing • Market based incentives • Ability to attract highly skilled labor and creative people • Looser, more trusting organizational relationships

in the industry in order that customers perceive its relative value. Typically, there is only one cost leader. If more than one organization seek advantage with this strategy, a price war ensues, which eventually may drive the organization with the higher cost structure out of the marketplace.

Differentiation means the organization qualifies its products or service in a way that allows it to appear unique in the marketplace. The organization has identified which qualitative dimensions are most important to its customers, and it has found ways to add value along one or more of those dimensions. In order for this strategy to work, the price charged customers by the differentiator must seem fair relative to the price charged by competitors. Typically, multiple firms in any given market will employ this strategy (Pearlson, 2001).

Method V: Competitive Forces

The basis of this method is that a company exists within an industry and to succeed, it must effectively deal with the competitive forces that exist within the particular industry. For example, the forces in an emerging industry such as mobile communication are considerably different from those of established industries such as financial services.

The company interacts with its customers, suppliers, and competitors. In addition, there are potential new entrants into the particular competitive marketplace and potential substitute products and services. To survive and succeed in this environment, it is important to understand these interactions and the implications in terms of what opportunities or competitive advantage can occur. Figure 4.27 illustrates the competitive forces model (Porter, 1985).

At any one time, one or more of the forces may be exerting particular pressure on the competing company. The competitive forces method models the competitive world in which any organization exists and the forces that play upon it. The current competitive position of any organization will be the net force of these five aggregated. In order to understand the strength of any one of these forces, an understanding must be built up of the contributory factors to its power. Theoretically, there are a large number of these but for any given organization many of them will not be relevant (Robson, 1997):

- *Rivalry among existing competitors.* This rivalry can range from intense in a cutthroat industry to mild in an affluent one. When rivalry is high profits tend to be low. Industries that are static or in decline will have more intense rivalry than those which are rapidly growing. When there are high fixed costs or high storage costs, then the volume of sales must be maintained and so rivalry heightens. Rivalry is more intense when there is over-capacity caused by demand fluctuations or production constraints. Where there is no brand loyalty, i.e. no differentiation, then demand depends on price, and when switching costs are small, this is very elastic, so rivalry will be heated. If there are many organizations of a similar size in the same pool then rivalry will be intense. If leaving the industry will cost a lot either physically or emotionally then the rivalry will tend to be intense.

- *Threat of new entrants.* The height of the barriers against this threat and the determination to get over them defines the industry's profitability. Government policy can represent such a barrier when a license to operate is required or strict safety rules have to be applied. The threat of reactions to a new entrant acts as a barrier, since dealing with aggressive counter-moves needs strong capabilities and significant advantages. For example, Color Air was a new entrant that was met by aggressive counter-moves by existing airlines in Norway. After having lost five hundred million Norwegian Kroner, Color Air gave up. If existing firms have lower costs than new entrants can have, then this absolute cost advantage is a very high barrier. A new entrant must establish access to distribution channels so the

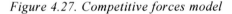

Figure 4.27. Competitive forces model

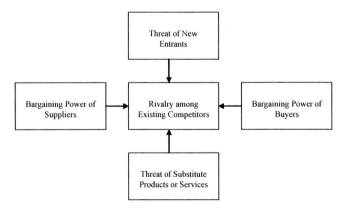

difficulties of access act as a barrier to entry. If buyers would have to face extra costs to change suppliers, or have a reluctance to do so, this acts as an entry barrier. If economies of scale are an important pricing factor then new entrants either need large markets straightaway or must face higher costs. The degree of product differentiation and brand loyalty is directly related to the height o the entry barrier. Some industries involve major start-up costs and obviously, in them the barriers to entry are very high.

- *Threat of substitute products or services*. When this threat is high then the profit margin is low as customers more readily change when prices are high. If a similar product or service is available at the same, or lower, price then the threat is high. If potential substitutes are more expensive, or inferior, then the threats are low. Switching costs for customers determine the threat of substitutes as well as determining the height of the entry barrier. If no extra costs are incurred then change is likely. Apathetic or satisfied buyers are not likely to change, militant or dissatisfied ones are. Generally the more significant the purchase is to the customer the higher is their propensity to switch.

- *Bargaining power of buyers*. This primarily depends on their price sensitivity and their bargaining leverage. The bargaining power of buyers depends on the purchaser's relative cost importance. A number of things can reduce price sensitivity: brand loyalty and differentiation, impacts of the product on their product, and customer's own profitability. The bargaining power of buyers depends on buyer concentration and volume, buyer switching costs, buyer information, threat of backward vertical integration by buyers, and existence of substitutes.

- *Bargaining power of suppliers*. This is the differentiation of the inputs, and matters when the organization's process needs a rare commodity. When switching costs of changing to an alternative supplier are high then suppliers are relatively powerful since the organization would face significant costs if it were to leave them. When substitute suppliers are available, the power of the supplier is reduced. The higher supplier concentration the higher supplier power is. If the supplier has to achieve high volume sales then they hold less bargaining power. Supplier power is low when the costs of goods provided are high relative to the purchasing industry's total costs. Supplier power is higher when their product is significant to the buyer organization's chances of product differentiation. When suppliers will find it easy to forward integrate into the purchaser's industry then they have high bargaining power.

To produce a model of the competitive forces playing upon an organization requires detailed research into its industry, but it then allows the net power of the five forces as well as extreme single powers to be judged in order to concentrate attention on those most significant.

Method VI: Product Portfolio Analysis

There are a number of approaches that aim to relate the competitive position of an organization to the maturity of its product. The models assume there is a basic S-shaped curve description to the growth phenomenon of products. Four stages in the *life cycle* of any product can be identified as illustrated in Figure 4.28:

- *Introduction.* The product is new and there is an initial stage of experimentation and gradual acceptance. IS/IT can support product specification, customer requirements, process design, market research and forecasting, logistics planning, and cost estimation.

- *Growth.* There is a rapid increase in sales. IS/IT can support product enhancement, customer service, capacity development and utilization, new distribution channels, monitoring price margins, service from suppliers, promotion to expand customer base, and identifying competitors' position.

- *Maturity.* Sales remain high but there is no further increase. IS/IT can support product variations, customer segmentation, product cost reduction, costing and sourcing of components, inventory control, pricing flexibility, analysis of contribution, and targeting specific competitors.

- *Decline.* Competition, product displacement or other factors cause a decline in sales. IS/IT can support reduced inventory levels, sales forecasting, subcontracting, release of capacity for other uses, rationalization of distribution channels, and reduction in administrative costs.

When we look at the life cycle of all products in the firm, we can apply product portfolio analysis. This method shows the relationship between a product's current or future revenue potential and the appropriate management stance as illustrated in Figure 4.29. The two by two matrix names the products in order to chart symptoms into a diagnosis so that effective management behavior can be adopted. The matrix classifies products according to the present market share and the future growth of that market. A successful product that lasts from emergent to mature market goes clockwise around the matrix.

Figure 4.28. Product life cycle

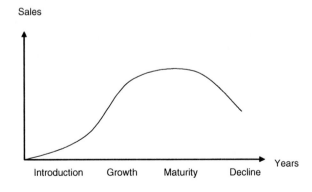

Figure 4.29. Product portfolio analysis

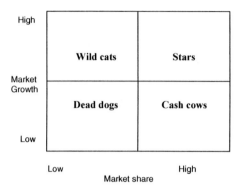

The matrix segments summarize the expected profit and cash flow and recommends an outline strategy to follow. This strategy is simply to milk the cows, divest the dogs, invest in the stars, and examine the wild cats (Robson, 1997):

- *Cash cows*. Products in this segment are those that are the current high-income earners for the organization. They are expected to provide the major part of current profits and form the major source of funding for future developments. Cash cows are relatively short-term so they are not expected to provide significant future revenues. Management will try to increase profitability by milking more intensively and by extending the lifetime. IS/IT will tend to focus on control of the business environment rather than innovation—to defend the current position.

- *Stars*. Products in this segment are the ones that provide significant revenue now and are expected to continue to do so in the future. In this segment, the organization will wish to seek opportunities to increase profits and extend the life of the product. IS/IT will tend to focus on the customer — identifying customers and their requirements to achieve a better understanding of demand than actual and potential competitors do.

- *Dead dogs*. Products in this segment provide little or no contribution to profits today, and it is not expected that this situation will change. Such products should be removed. IS/IT will tend to focus on reducing costs and securing customers.

- *Wild cats*. Products in this segment are those that the organization is currently prepared to continue, although they make little or no contribution to revenue now, they are expected to in the future. These are usually young products and are probably still being developed. Investments should be made cautiously in this segment since the risks associated with it are higher than with others. The organization will seek ways to ensure that products quickly mature into highly profitable stars. IS/IT will tend to focus on innovative product and process improvements.

Method VII: Environmental Analysis

Environmental analysis is concerned with the external corporate environment. An analysis of the environment is important because it increases the quality of the strategic decision-making by considering a range of the relevant features. The organization identifies a threats and opportunities facing it, and those factors that might assist in achieving objectives and those that might act as a barrier. The strategy of the organization should be directed at exploiting the environmental opportunities and blocking environmental threats in a way that is consistent with internal capabilities. This is a matter of environmental fit that allows the organization to maximize its competitive position.

An external analysis can investigate politics, the economy, the society, and the technology. This is sometimes called PEST analysis. If we include the study of legal and environmental matters, we call it PESTLE. In Figure 4.30 some examples of external factors are listed and their implications for the company. The analytical work that has to be done in the company when doing environmental analysis is concerned with questions such as: What are the implications of the trends (changes in the environment)? What can the company do in order to meet the opportunities and threats that follow?

The success of an environmental is largely dependent on the characteristics of the environment: the complexity of it, that is how many variables are in the environment, the rate of change and the amount (and cost) of available information about it. Environmental analysis considers the external situation within which the organization exists. It is important to audit the environmental influences, assess the nature of the environment to judge whether it is simple or complex, identify the key environmental forces, and identify the key opportunities and threats to be handled by the company (Robson, 1997).

Figure 4.30. External factors for environmental analysis

External Factor	Examples of Trends	Implications for Company
Politics	Less trade barriers	Global competition
Economy	Deregulation	Global competition
	Larger, freer markets	Alliances and partnerships
Society	Increasing number of older people	New services and products
	Growing unemployment	Market decrease
	More knowledge	Changing customer needs
Technology	IT can support knowledge work	Technology to achieve benefits
	New communications networks	Technology to become global
Legal issues	Privacy legislation	Data security
	Electronic signature	Paperless trading
Ecology	Green movements	Reusable resources
	Terrorism	Contingent plans

Method VIII: Knowledge Analysis

Distinctions can be made between core knowledge, advanced knowledge and innovative knowledge. While core knowledge is required to stay in business, advanced knowledge makes the firm competitively visible, and innovative knowledge allows the firm to lead its entire industry. The knowledge map in Figure 4.31 can be applied to identify firm position. The map illustrates firm knowledge levels compared with competitors' knowledge levels.

While the knowledge map represents an external analysis of the firm's current knowledge situation, the knowledge gap in Figure 4.32 represents an internal analysis of the firm's current knowledge situation. The knowledge gap is dependent on business strategy. What the company does is different from what the company will do, creating a strategy gap. What the company knows is different from what the company has to know, creating a knowledge gap. Two important links emerge: the strategy-knowledge-link and the knowledge-strategy-link (Tiwana, 2000).

Figure 4.31. Knowledge map for external analysis

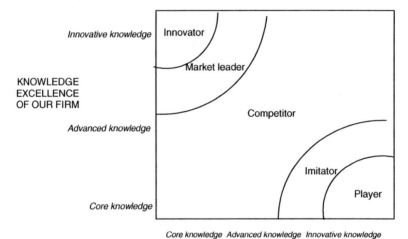

KNOWLEDGE EXCELLENCE OF COMPETING FIRMS

Figure 4.32. Identifying knowledge gap in internal analysis

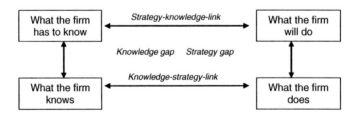

Analyzing Needs for Change

After descriptions of the current situation and the desired situation, needs for change can be identified. The gap between desired and current situation is called needs for change. In Figure 4.33, all business analysis methods presented earlier are listed, and examples of desired and current situation are presented to illustrate this third stage of the Y model. Needed changes are exemplified, and potential IS/IT are suggested. We see many changes needed, and IS/IT solutions include executive information system (EIS), project management system (PMS), research library system (RLS), customer relationship management (CRM), enterprise resources planning (ERP), electronic market places (EMS), and knowledge management system (KMS). Many of these systems will rely on Internet technology. For example, EIS, PMS and KMS will use both intranet and extranet as well as the Internet.

The same kind of analysis should be done for the current and desired IS/IT situation as illustrated in Figure 4.34. Again, we see IS/IT solutions include customer relationship management (CRM), knowledge management system (KMS), and executive information system (EIS). The column "change needed" in both Figures 4.39 and 4.40 represent answers to the what-question, while the column "IS/IT potential" suggests answers to the how-question.

One of the elements of the IS/IT strategy is identification of future applications. In order to discuss this subject, we have to familiarize ourselves with what kinds of application software a company might have, and how applications are developed or acquired.

Figure 4.33. Identification of potential IS/IT based on needs for business change

Business Analysis	Desired Situation	Current Situation	Change Needed	IS/IT Potential
SWOT analysis	Strong management	Weak management	Strengthen management	Executive Information System (EIS)
X model	Even distribution of work	Too much work close to milestones	Improve work scheduling	Project Management System (PMS)
Business direction	Research-based business school	Education-based business school	Strengthen research	Research Library System (RLS)
Market strategy	Strong differentiation	Weak differentiation	Add services to base product	Customer Relationship Management (CRM)
Competitive forces	High entry barriers for new entrants	Low entry barriers for new entrants	Achieve economies of scale	Enterprise Resources Planning (ERP)
Product portfolio analysis	Many stars	Many cash cows	Extend life of products	Knowledge Management System (KMS)
Environmental analysis	Reach young people	Customers are old people	Apply new technology-based market channels	Electronic Market Places (EMP)
Knowledge analysis	Market leader	Imitator	Share and develop advanced and innovative knowledge	Knowledge Management System (KMS)

Figure 4.40. Identification of potential IS/IT based on needs for technology change

IS/IT Analysis	Desired Situation	Current Situation	Change Needed	IS/IT Potential
Benefits of IS/IT	Market benefits	Rationalization benefits	Achieve competitive advantage	Customer Relationship Management (CRM)
Stages of IS/IT growth	Growth stage	Architecture stage	Improve internal and external communication	Knowledge Management System (KMS)
IS/IT in management activities	Knowledge management	Administrative and support functions	Improve support for knowledge workers	Knowledge Management System (KMS)
IS/IT in business processes	Excellent human resources management	Poor human resources management	Improve human resources management	Knowledge Management System (KMS)
IS/IT support for value configuration	Excellent problem solving in value shop	Poor problem solving in value shop	Improve problem solving	Knowledge Management System (KMS)
Strategic integration	Reciprocal integration	Administrative integration	Top management participation	Executive Information System (EIS)
IS/IT support for knowledge management	What they know stage	End user tools stage	Coding information from knowledge sources	Knowledge Management System (KMS)
IS/IT in e-business	E-business stage	Internal communication stage	Business process reengineering and design	New IS/IT infrastructure

A company seldom starts from scratch. There are already computers, terminals, printers, operating systems, application software, databases, and communication networks in the firm. This implies that potential IS/IT as listed in Figures 4.39 and Figure 4.40 have to be considered in view of existing infrastructure, architecture and applications.

Furthermore, at this stage of the Y model, needs for change have to be prioritized. This implies that not all needs can get attention and not all potential IS/IT can be implemented.

Analyzing needs for change, identifying potential IS/IT, comparing with current IS/IT in the company, and then prioritizing needs for change, should result in proposals for new IS/IT in the organization. For example, our company may prioritize extending product lives, sharing and developing advanced and innovative knowledge, improving internal and external communication, improving support for knowledge workers, improving human resources management, improving problem solving, and coding information from knowledge sources. If such needs for change have priority, then a knowledge management system (KMS) should be implemented in the organization.

Resource-Based IS/IT Strategy

One of the key resources in business firms is knowledge. We have seen that method VII for describing the current situation is concerned with IS/IT support for knowledge management in terms of person-to-tools, person-to-person, person-to-information and person-to-system. Similarly, method VIII for describing the desired situation is concerned with knowledge analysis in terms of core, advanced and innovative knowledge. When developing a resource-based IS/IT strategy, this will typically be the focus of strategy work.

Activity-Based IS/IT Strategy

When developing an activity-based IS/IT strategy, the current situation will typically be described in terms of IS/IT support for value configuration, IS/IT in e-business and other methods. The desired situation may be described using methods such as market strategy, competitive forces, and product portfolio analysis.

Most methods can be applied for both resource-based and activity-based IS/IT strategy work. Some methods enable integration of both resource-based and activity-based strategy work. A good example is SWOT analysis. Strengths (S) and Weaknesses (W) can be understood in terms of the resource situation, while Opportunities (O) and Threats (T) can be understood in terms of the activity situation of the firm.

Therefore, resource-based and activity-based strategy work are not necessarily alternatives. Rather, they complement each other as perspectives when developing an IS/IT strategy.

Chapter V

Strategy Choice

Stages 4 to 5 cover strategy choice in the Y model. While stage 4 is concerned with seeking alternative actions, stage 5 is concerned with selecting actions and making an action plan as illustrated in Figure 5.1.

Identifying Alternative Actions

When needs for change have been identified and proposals for filling gaps have been developed, alternative actions for improving the current situation can be developed. New IS/IT can be developed, acquired, and implemented in alternative ways. Several decisions have to be made when a new IS/IT is chosen. Such decisions are called systems development strategy, and they are illustrated later when we discuss IT governance as allocation of decision rights.

New IS/IT can be developed using analytical or experimental methodology. Analytical methodology implies defining the needs of users through intellectual reasoning techniques. Such techniques define stages of systems study, systems design, programming, installation, testing, implementation, and maintenance. Experimental methodology is showing the users alternative computer screens with information and asking for their

Figure 5.1. The two stages of choice

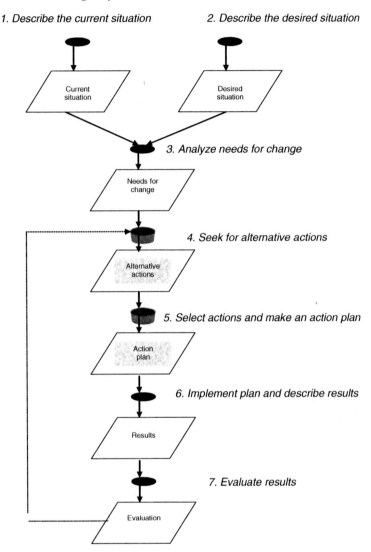

1. Describe the current situation   2. Describe the desired situation

opinions. This is sometimes called prototyping. Through iterations, we might improve and create even better systems. The decision here will depend on systems complexity and the available time for development.

A common analytical methodology is the systems life cycle. The *systems life cycle* partitions the systems development process into formal stages that must be completed sequentially with a formal definition of labor between end users and information systems specialists. The life cycle for an information system has six stages: (1) project definition, (2) system study, (3) design, (4) programming, (5) installation, and (6) maintenance. Figure 5.2 illustrates these stages. Each stage consists of basic activities that must be performed before the next stage can begin.

Figure 5.2. The life cycle methodology for information systems development

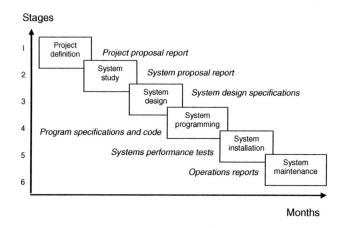

The systems life cycle is useful for building large complex systems in-house that require a rigorous and formal requirements analysis, predefined specifications, and tight controls over the systems-building process. However, the systems life cycle methodology is costly, time consuming, and inflexible. Often, volumes of new documents must be produced and steps repeated if requirements and specifications need to be revised. Because of the time and cost to repeat the sequence of life cycle activities, the methodology encourages freezing of specifications early in the development process, discouraging change.

A common experimental methodology is prototyping. *Prototyping* consists of building an experimental system rapidly and inexpensively for end users to evaluate. By interacting with the prototype, users can get a better idea of their information requirements. The prototype accepted by the users will be the basis for creating the final system. The prototype is a working version of an information system or part of the system, but it is

Figure 5.3. The prototyping methodology for systems development

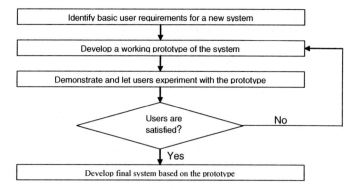

meant only to be a preliminary model. The process of building a preliminary system, trying it out, improving it, and trying it again is called an iterative process of systems development because the steps required to build a system can be repeated over and over again. In Figure 5.3, a four-step model of the prototyping process is illustrated.

Prototyping is most useful when there is some uncertainty about requirements or design solutions. Prototyping encourages end-user participation in building a system; therefore, it is more likely to produce a system that fulfills user requirements. However, rapid prototyping runs the risk of ignoring essential steps in systems development. Such ignorance may later cause rise in maintenance costs.

A systems project can either be completely expert-driven or completely user-led, or something in between. It is an important part of Scandinavian culture to have user participation. Totally user-led may be difficult, as technical problems will require the assistance of IS/IT experts. The decision here will depend on technical skills needed as well as availability of competent and motivated users. We can distinguish between the following four user participation roles:

- *Resources manager*. This is a user who has management responsibility and makes decisions concerning resources for new IS/IT, including people involved in systems development and money for procurement of equipment.

- *Solutions entrepreneur*. This is a user who has ideas about new information systems, both related to applications areas and systems design.

- *Requirements developer*. This is a user who has strong opinions about functions in a new information system.

- *System champion*. This is a user who is enthusiastic and dedicated to the successful implementation of the new system.

The result of a systems project can be a product and/or a process. Product means only the new IS/IT. Process means paying attention to the learning and increased insight gained from participating in the IS/IT development activity. The decision here will depend on systems complexity as well as company culture for learning. We can distinguish between the following four kinds of results:

- *Systems success*: the benefits from the new information system in terms of rationalization benefits, control benefits, organizational benefits, and market benefits.

- *User success*: the extent of user satisfaction with the new system.

- *Development success*: the extent to which the new IS/IT was developed on time and within budget.

- *Learning success*: the extent to which participating persons have improved their skills in IS/IT development.

Coordination of systems development can be defined along a scale. This scale runs from one-sided systems development to a balanced development of personnel, system, and organization. A completely one-sided systems development may create an efficient technological solution, but it may not work in the organization as personnel and organizational issues were not considered. The decision here will depend on company culture for linking human resources management to information technology management. We can distinguish between four alternative coordination approaches:

- *One-sided*: Attention is concentrated on the technical solution of the new IS/IT. We put all our efforts into optimizing both hardware and software by selecting machines, servers and network, as well as database system and application software, so that the technology itself works as efficient as possible.

- *Two-sided*: Attention is expanded to users, where solutions may be tailor-made to individual users.

- *Three-sided*: Attention is further expanded to the organization, where solutions are designed in such a way that business processes are improved.

- *Four-sided*: Attention is further expanded to the environment, where solutions are designed in such a way that stakeholders may find it attractive to do business with us.

Selecting Appropriate Actions

At this stage, we have to make final decisions concerning content of actions and development actions. While content of actions is our final priority of needed changes, development actions is our final systems development strategy.

In stage 3 of the Y model, we analyzed needs for change, identified potential IS/IT, compared them with current IS/IT in the company, prioritized needs for change, and proposed new IS/IT in the organization. We are going to look a little closer at the task of choosing which IS/IT to develop/acquire when discussing IT governance as allocation of decision rights later in this book.

Making the Plan

The Y model focuses on the different steps in strategy work, including making an IS/IT strategy. We have discussed in depth the analysis part of an IS/IT strategy. The analysis covered description of the current situation, description of desired situation, analysis of needs for change, and priority of needs for change. When the analysis part was complete, decisions had to be made. The choices should be made by business management, preferably by the chief executive of the organization. When all necessary decisions have been made, then the important task of implementation can start, as described in the next chapter.

The Y model outlines the working steps. Analysis and choice should result in an approved IS/IT strategy, that is, a strategy which is decided to be implemented. An approved strategy is the product of strategy work. We may distinguish between product (plan) and process (learning). The process should ideally involve all affected and give them access to all the analyses of the work and give them a possibility for voicing their opinions and listen to the viewpoints of others. In that way the process will give learning to all involved and might be a way of securing support for the strategy.

The work of developing an IS/IT strategy for the first time might be organized as a project. A project is a unique task, which can be contrasted by continuous line activities. Later on, the updating and maintenance of the strategy might be part of the responsibilities of the line organization. Even then, they have to involve all the necessary parties in the work.

We might focus even more on what is involved in a process. There are three well-known stages in an organizational development process, and making an IS/IT strategy might well be looked at as organizational development. The first stage is unfreeze. Here it is important to create a climate for change, getting acceptance and readiness for change. In the analysis part, it is certainly of importance to focus on the need for changes and create a common understanding of the need for changes. Such needs should be recognized by all involved. The second stage is change. In the implementation part, we have to be aware that it is a change process. Growth and changes might hurt. They can result in opposition and counter attacks. It is necessary to alter attitudes, beliefs, and values of individuals directly, or indirectly, by changing the structure, goals, or technology of the organization. The final stage is refreeze. Here the new state is institutionalized. The new situation is stabilized. Here we sum up what we have achieved, and are happy about it, before we start over again.

There should be some clear goals set for what we would like to achieve during the process. We want the commitment of management, and we should also use the process to educate management about benefits and risks of IS/IT. We want management to understand how IS/IT is applied, and we want to increase managers' own use of IS/IT. At the same time we want the commitment of users, and we want to educate them as well concerning the importance of IS/IT for the business. Changes in users' attitudes toward IS/IT will create commitment to strategy and implementation plans as well as better understanding of business and its dependence on IS/IT. Hopefully the process will lead to better relationships between the IS/IT department and user departments. The close cooperation in the strategy process should lead to such a result.

At the outset there might be resistance among management against getting involved in the process, and they may oppose any new strategies for IS/IT. The problem might be that top management belongs to an older generation and are subject to a general resistance to change. There may also be some specific explanations for resistance. One such explanation might be the uncertainty about benefits of IS/IT. Generally, resistance of management can be identified as:

•   Ignorance of IS/IT and its potential uses and benefits

•   Poor communication between the IS/IT department and the rest of the business

•   General resistance to change

- Lack of focus on opportunities for competitive advantage

- Lack of instruments for decisively measuring the benefits of IS/IT

There are several approaches to overcoming management resistance. Education or information — creating knowledge — is of importance, if it is possible to get management involved. If they do not want to listen to IS/IT people from the company, then it might be a good idea to have management meet with managers from other companies that have experienced the benefits of IS/IT themselves. All the time it is of importance to link IS/IT to business needs. It is also of importance to involve management in the decision-making. A good idea might be a kind of steering committee, which should consist of all the functional managers. Functional budgets for IS/IT would make the functional managers strongly involved. Quick positive results might also convince management about the benefits of IS/IT. It is not certain that such applications are available, but in prioritizing one should look for applications that are low risk, relatively quick to acquire/develop and give good, fast results. In summary, here are some tactics for involving and influencing management:

- Educate management about use and benefits of IS/IT

- Have management meet other managers who are enthusiastic about IS/IT

- Link IS/IT to business management needs

- Form a steering committee

- Develop functional IS/IT budgets

- Rapid development of low-risk, managerially useful systems

The development of an IS/IT strategy might be organized as a project, as we discussed earlier. As illustrated in Figure 5.4, we can have a traditional organizational structure with a steering committee, project manager and project team (consisting of both business people and IS/IT people). One special aspect is that one should look for a management

Figure 5.4. Strategy project organization structure

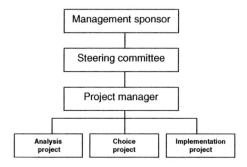

sponsor, that is, a member of the top management group of the company that would like to sponsor the work. A sponsor serves as a change agent and is a strong supporter of change using IS/IT.

The management sponsor is crucial for project success. The perfect sponsor does the following tasks:

- Chairing the steering committee meetings
- Assuring top management participation and commitment, through active backing and allocation of the right resources
- Representing the interests and priorities of the business
- Heading the marketing effort — the effort of selling the project to the whole organization should not be underestimated
- Acting as the focal point for decisions about scope, priority, and conduct of project work.

The steering committee is of key importance for project success. We are here focusing on what should be done by the steering committee in order to get a positive decision by top management concerning IS/IT strategy:

- Providing strategic direction and guidance on business requirements, and priorities to the project team
- Reviewing and approving plans and raising risk management issues
- Conducting checkpoint reviews and authorizing continuation of work
- Reviewing and contributing to final result, before submission to top management.

We advocate strong interaction between the steering committee and the project team. The steering committee gives its general directions at the outset and gives feedback several times on the material presented to them by the project manager.

The IS/IT strategy document may be long or short depending on traditions and expectations in the company. In large organizations, the strategy document will typically have the following elements:

1. Introduction
   - Purpose (its use, distribution of plan)
   - Background (why and the way it was developed, participants, methods)
   - Qualifications (what is not covered)
2. Current business situation
   - Analysis of business direction, market strategy, and competitive forces
   - SWOT analysis, X model, product portfolio analysis, and environmental analysis

- Knowledge analysis

3. Future business situation
   - Changes in business direction
   - Changes in business activities
   - Changes in knowledge management

4. Current IS/IT situation
   - Benefits, stages, management activities, strategic integration
   - Business processes, value configuration, e-business
   - IS/IT support for knowledge management

5. IS/IT vision and overall strategy
   - Important IS/IT trends
   - IS/IT vision (for the next 3-5 years)
   - Main priorities

6. IS/IT applications
   - Needs for changes in application portfolio
   - Required development portfolio
   - Existing portfolio upgrade
   - Future potential portfolio
   - Analysis of applications and portfolios, cost-benefit analysis
   - Proposed priorities

7. IS/IT organization
   - Need for changes
   - Strategy, general guidelines

8. IS/IT human resources
   - Need for changes
   - Strategy, general guidelines

9. IT infrastructure
   - Need for changes
   - Strategy, general guidelines

One important ambition of the IS/IT strategy is to align business and IS/IT. There are both enablers and inhibitors of business — IS/IT alignment. Such enablers and inhibitors should be identified, analyzed, and solved while making the plan. Solutions should be described in the IS/IT strategy document. The two most significant enablers are often senior executive support for IS/IT and IT involved in strategy development:

1.   Senior executive support for IS/IT can be documented by asking them to define and describe strategies that include the role of IS/IT. These descriptions from executives should be included in section 5 of the plan.

2.   IT's participation in creating business strategy can be documented by asking the CIO to define and describe the future business situation. These descriptions from the CIO should be included in section 3 of the plan.

Senior executive support for IS/IT strategy is the effort of executives to contribute to strategy analysis, choice and implementation. Management support includes management expectations, participation, monitoring, knowledge, time, and enthusiasm. Senior executive support is widely recognized as an important factor in the implementation of information systems and information technology strategy. Management may be hesitant to IS/IT strategy work, hence representing a problem. Some top executives may seem committed to the status quo.

Both middle management attitudes and senior management attitudes towards strategy are important influences on the extent of plan success. It may be difficult to secure top management commitment for a strategic plan; commitment being defined as acceptance of plan values and willingness to exert effort on its behalf.

The planning methodology itself may require too much top management involvement. The output of planning is not necessarily in accordance with management expectations. Top management monitoring of strategy work may represent an effective planning mechanism. Management control systems may in this context provide a comprehensive mechanism for effective planning. Management monitoring and control of strategic planning may be organized through a steering committee.

Generally, senior executive support is pivotal to the adoption of innovations. CEOs in particular have a major impact on changes in their organizations. A plan must be a call for action, one that recognizes management's responsibility to fix what is broken and to harvest opportunities proactively and in real time. It is imperative that IT personnel educate their top managers and make them aware of the importance of their support in major IT initiatives. Top management support is a key recurrent factor critical for effective IS/IT strategy.

Chapter VI

Strategy Implementation

Stages 6 and 7 cover strategy implementation in the Y model. While stage 6 is concerned with implementing the plan and describing results, stage 7 is concerned with evaluating results as illustrated in Figure 6.1.

The creation of IS/IT strategy has become a major challenge to business executives and IS/IT executives in recent years. Investments in information technology have been large, and many failed investments reflect this challenge. The impact of IT on organizational performance has grown in strategic importance, and thus the significance of failed IT investments is even greater. Information processing and information technology are becoming critical to many business and government operations, and the technology itself is changing at a rapid rate. New information technology will continue to transform organizations, and changes in how industry participants use IT can alter established relationships in an industry. Strategic IS/IT planning can play a critical role in helping organizations to increase efficiency, effectiveness and competitiveness. Although organizations use different methods in their analysis of current and desired situation, the resulting plans are to be implemented.

Figure 6.1. The two stages of implementation

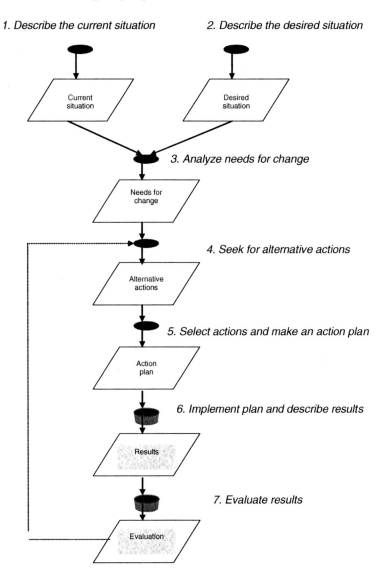

The importance of the implementation of strategic IS/IT plans is illustrated by the significant attention paid to it in recent years. Studies show that implementation is important for four reasons. First, the failure to carry out the strategic IS/IT plan can cause lost opportunities, duplicated efforts, incompatible systems, and wasted resources. Second, the extent to which strategic IS/IT planning meets its objectives is determined by implementation. Third, the lack of implementation leaves firms dissatisfied with and reluctant to continue their strategic planning. Fourth, the lack of implementation creates problems establishing and maintaining priorities in future strategic IS/IT planning.

Implementing Plan

IS/IT strategy implementation can be defined as the process of completing the projects for application of information technology to assist an organization in realizing its goals. However, implementing an IS/IT strategy is not simply the act of implementing many projects and individual systems. Instead, implementing such a plan demands a gestalt view in the planning of individual systems. A gestalt view represents the implementation of the plan philosophy, attitudes, intentions, and ambitions associated with IS/IT use in the organization. It may include decisions about the IS organization and the implementation of IT architecture.

The term implementation is given a variety of meanings in the literature. Implementation can be described as a procedure directed by a manager to install planned change in an organization. Change is an empirical observation of difference in form, quality, or state over time in an organizational entity. Implementation can be the process of gaining targeted organizational members' appropriate and committed use of an innovation. Information technology implementation from strategic IS/IT planning is a typical innovation.

When is an IS/IT application implemented? Is it implemented when it is approved by top management as part of the IS/IT strategy? When it is installed on a company computer? When it is put into its first use? When it is widely accepted by people in the company? When it is modified as a result of use, based on both detected errors and needs for improvement? When the benefits of the IS/IT strategy are finally appearing? There is no unified answer to this question, but most scholars agree that installation of a system is too early, while benefits are too late to wait for. This is illustrated in Figure 6.2. Most scholars agree that an IS/IT application is implemented when it is used and accepted by users. So in the example in Figure 11.2, we would say that implementation occurred in 2003.

Using the gestalt view, we can say that an IS/IT strategy implementation is defined by a degree of implementation. If the complete IS/IT strategy is implemented, we can talk about 100 percent implementation. If nothing is implemented, we can talk about zero implementation. A strategic IS/IT plan is implemented over time, as illustrated in Figure 6.3. The process of implementation can follow different paths. In Figure 6.3, there are two examples of early and late implementation respectively, both ending at an implementation degree of 60 percent.

Figure 6.2. Implementation of an IS/IT application

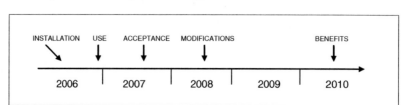

Figure 6.3. Implementation of IS/IT strategy over time

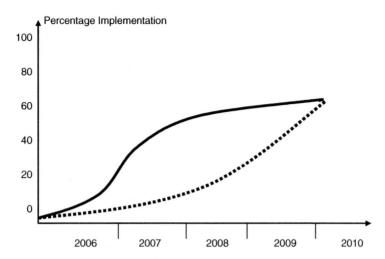

There is no optimal extent of implementation. It depends on the situation in the company over time. If the IS/IT strategy has an excellent match with desired business situation and actual business development, then more of the strategy is likely to be implemented. If the IS/IT strategy consists of a few large, focused projects that, when first started, have to be finished, then more of the strategy is likely to be implemented. If the organization has a culture of walk and talk consistency, then more of the strategy is likely to be implemented. Walk and talk consistency implies that management actual does what it says it is going to do. If the IS/IT strategy has a short time horizon, then more of the strategy is likely to be implemented. If management is able to predict the future, then more of the strategy is likely to be implemented.

While there is no optimal extent of implementation generally, we would be surprised to find everything or nothing implemented. If everything is implemented, then it creates an impression of ignoring changes over time that should influence implementation. If nothing is implemented, then it creates an impression that the organization is completely unable to create change, and there is complete inconsistency between talk and walk. An empirical study of Norwegian business organizations tells us that on average 60 percent of an IS/IT strategy was implemented. Whether this is good or bad is hard to tell. We may suggest a rule of thumb that two-thirds should be implemented.

We have to remind ourselves that initially, at the start of implementation, the complete IS/IT strategy is to be implemented. All actions were written into the plan to be executed. Nothing was written into the plan without the intention of being executed. What we are saying about implementation extent is that environmental changes as well as internal changes over time may create a situation where some of the plan contents are not smart to do anymore. Such evaluation of the plan after some time, often after one or two years, may cause revision of the plan.

Barriers to Implementation

At this stage 6 in the Y model of implementing the plan, all attention should be focused on implementation of the whole plan. This is the stage of action. Technical equipment such as servers, PCs, printers and cables are installed. Operating systems are upgraded. Application packages, software programs, programming tools, end user tools, and database systems are installed. Development projects are initiated. Management and user training takes place.

At this stage, we should focus on the tackling of implementation challenges. The literature on implementation challenges is steadily growing. A series of factors influencing implementation have been identified. In the following, we will discuss some important factors for implementation of IS/IT strategy:

- Resources needed for the implementation

- User involvement during the implementation

- Solutions to potential resistance during the implementation

- Responsibility for the implementation

- Management support for the implementation

- Information technology needed for implementation

Resources Needed for the Implementation

One reason for the lack of implementation is that resources are not made available. The answer to the simple question "Can it be done?" is dependent on competence and resources. It is important to identify the resources and actions needed to implement new applications and development tools. Resource mobilization for implementation is an effective implementation mechanism to secure quality of implementation. An important resource issue in the field of strategic IS/IT is the difficulty of recruiting IS specialists and defining their role in projects. In an IS/IT strategy written in English in a Norwegian organization, this problem was confirmed: "Technological expertise is a precondition for development and migration of new and complicated technology in the institution, but the dependence on such expertise also represents a problem to management." Some information systems professionals are systems rationalists preoccupied with new capabilities of technology, tending to ignore goal incongruence and assuming consensus on goals. Generally speaking, information systems innovations are dependent on an IS professional environment. Just as important, there is a need for those users who will champion the new systems and have the drive and vision to push the projects forward. In addition, many businesses are dependent on external expertise such as consultants for implementation. In summary, the following resources are important:

- Financial resources needed for the implementation

- Technical abilities needed for the implementation

- Human resources needed for the implementation
- Project team time needed for the implementation
- External consultants needed for the implementation
- A project champion needed for the implementation

User Involvement During the Implementation

Both resources for and extensive performance of user training are necessary to secure implementation of IS/IT strategy. Education, training and other implementation activities are generally viewed as outside the IS role, in part because formal authority for training usually is assigned elsewhere. Training may consist of both formal and informal training. Formal training can be long-term as well as short-term instruction received through seminars, classes, conventions, and private lessons, while informal training can be on-the-job training received from co-workers and supervisors as the need arises. Many training efforts are based on needs analysis, needs assessment, or performance analysis. User involvement in implementation is an effective implementation mechanism to secure quality of implementation. It is usually better to use a high-involvement process that utilizes the knowledge and creativity of the people who actually do the work. Implementation represents a situation of transition in which users experience a threat to their sense of control over their work, if not direct loss of control. Interventions, which restore the users' sense of control, will reduce the threatening quality of the implementation experience, and, as a result, heighten the users' satisfaction with the new systems. In this view, the active ingredient for user involvement is the perceived control. User needs are the source of benefits, which motivate the use of an information technology application, and user satisfaction increases the implementability. In summary, the following user involvement issues are important:

- Training of information systems users
- Users' understanding of systems' functional features
- Users' participation in systems projects
- Users' involvement in the operation of information systems
- Participation in the ongoing development of information systems
- Users' support for the implementation

Solutions to Potential Resistance During the Implementation

Solutions to potential resistance during the implementation are methods and processes of solving problems created by latent opposition to the implementation. Resistance involves stubbornness in fulfilling the expectations of others. Resistance to implementation may have many facets, such as quite ignorance, active argumentation, low priority put on implementation compared with other assignments etc. Potential bases of resistance to the adoption of the plan should be identified, and the plan should define solutions needed for avoiding and/or dampening potential resistance to the necessary changes. Resistance may be caused by uncertainty, lack of competence, or commitment to the status quo. Some may find their influence threatened, others that implementation may be harmful to the organization, and still some that the plan should be improved before implementation. In summary, the following resistance issues are important:

- Solutions to potential resistance caused by job security

- Solutions to potential resistance caused by change of position

- Solutions to potential resistance caused by new skills requirements

- Solutions to potential resistance caused by skepticism about results

- Solutions to potential resistance caused by functional units' interests

- Solutions to potential resistance of our customers

Responsibility for the Implementation

During implementation, the frames of implementers (those responsible for the introduction of the technology to prospective users) will influence the extent of implementation. Most IS units do not have responsibility for key organizational results. Line managers are increasingly assuming responsibility for planning, building, and running information systems that affect their operation. It is important to identify the IT department's actions necessary to expedite adoption of the plan. A monitoring system to review implementation and provide feedback is an effective implementation mechanism. For each benefit desired from the implementation, specific responsibility for realizing benefits should be allocated within the business. Only when specific people are responsible for implementation actions, is implementation likely to occur. Responsibility has to be defined in such detail that responsible people take expected initiatives when problems occur during implementation. It may also be valuable to consider whether the chief executive responsible for strategy is willing to accept the personal risk involved. If not, the strategy may be good but is unlikely to be implemented. Implementation participants must accept responsibility for their own behavior, including the success of the actions they take to create change. Responsibility as such may take on two forms, negative duty and positive duty. Negative responsibility implies that action be taken due to threats and is often motivated by loyalty, while positive responsibility implies that action be taken due to commitment. In summary, the following responsibility issues are important:

- Responsibility for implementation on time

- Responsibility for implementation within budget

- Responsibility for implementation with intended benefits

- Responsibility for stepwise implementation of large projects

- Responsibility for implementation of high priority projects
- Responsibility for short-term benefits from initial projects
- Personnel rewards from successful implementation

Management support for the implementation

Management support is widely recognized as an important factor in the implementation of information systems. Management may be hesitant to the implementation of IS/IT strategy, hence representing an implementation problem. Some top executives are in reality committed to the status quo. Both middle management attitudes and senior management attitudes toward implementation are important influences on the extent of plan implementation. It may be difficult to secure top management commitment for implementation; commitment being defined as acceptance of plan values and willingness to exert effort on its behalf. The planning methodology itself may require too much top management involvement. The output of planning is not necessarily in accordance with management expectations. Top management monitoring of implementation may represent an effective implementation mechanism. Management control systems provide a comprehensive mechanism for implementing plans. Management monitoring and control of the implementation may be organized through a steering committee. Management support is pivotal to the adoption of innovations. CEOs in particular have a major impact on changes in their organizations. A plan must be a call for action, one that recognizes management's responsibility to fix what is broken proactively and in real time. It is imperative that IT personnel educate their top managers and make them aware of the importance of their support in major IT initiatives. Top management support is a key recurrent factor critical for effective implementation. In summary, the following management issues are important:

- Management expectations of the implementation
- Management participation in the implementation
- Management monitoring of the implementation
- Management knowledge about the implementation
- Management time needed for the implementation
- Management enthusiasm for the implementation

Information Technology Needed for Implementation

Information technology to be implemented is the hardware and software to be developed, acquired, installed, used, and modified. Information technology is developing rapidly, but in many organizations, IT is still lagging behind users' needs. For example, artificial intelligence is still in its infancy as a technology. This implies that a firm that wants to implement knowledge management level IV may have problems finding suitable technology. It is, therefore, important that the IS/IT strategy has identified available technology.

It is seldom smart to trust vendors' promises concerning future features of new technology when developing the IS/IT strategy. Instead, technological constraints should be identified and accepted. It is often emphasized that information architecture is not enough unless data access issues can be resolved. In summary, the following technology is important:

- Hardware to be implemented
- Communications technology to be implemented
- Databases to be implemented
- Applications software to be implemented
- Operating systems to be implemented
- A data infrastructure for the organization

Implementation Predictors

Resources needed for the implementation, user involvement during the implementation, solutions to potential resistance during the implementation, responsibility for the implementation, management support for the implementation, and information technology needed for the implementation are all considered important factors for IS/IT strategy implementation. These factors were empirically evaluated first in Norway and then in Australia (Gottschalk & Khandelwal, 2002).

In addition to the six factors listed above, four more factors were added in the empirical studies: analysis of the organization, anticipated changes in the external environment, projects' relevance to the business plan, and clear presentation of implementation issues.

In Norway, two factors were significant: responsibility for the implementation and user involvement during the implementation. In Australia, one factor was significant: projects' relevance to the business plan.

The average extent of strategic IS/IT plan implementation in Australia was 3.4, while the average plan implementation in Norway was 3.3, on a scale from one (little extent) to five (great extent). These results indicate that in both Australia and Norway, roughly 60% of a strategic IS/IT plan is implemented on average.

In Australia, responding organizations had an extensive description of projects' relevance to the business plan (3.7), while they had a limited description of solutions to potential resistance (1.9). In Norway, responding organizations had an extensive description of technology to be implemented (3.6), while they had a limited description of solutions to potential resistance (2.0).

The significant predictor in Australia was projects' relevance to the business plan, which had the highest overall description rating (3.7), indicating that relevance is both important and taken care of in many Australian firms. The two significant predictors in

Norway were responsibility of implementation and user involvement during implementation, which had high overall description ratings of 2.7 and 3.0.

The interesting difference between Australia and Norway lies in the finding that strategic descriptions are more important for implementation in Australia, while resource descriptions are more important for implementation in Norway. Given that both have about the same extent of plan implementation, 3.4 and 3.3, there is little reason to argue that firms in one nation are more successful than firms in the other.

One emerging proposition is that smaller organizations will tend to be more dependent on resources to get a plan implemented, while larger organizations will tend to be more dependent on strategic relevance to get a plan implemented. This proposition is relevant as responding Australian firms were much larger than the Norwegian respondents were. However, no significant relationship was found between organization size and the extent of relevance description (Gottschalk & Khandelwal, 2002).

Another emerging proposition is related to cultural differences. According to the Scandinavian research on information systems development, Scandinavia has high living standards and educational levels, an advanced technology infrastructure, an open community and key innovative leaders. This tradition seems different from research in other countries such as the UK with control structures, which may imply different strategic IS/IT plan implementation problems (Gottschalk & Khandelwal, 2002).

Evaluating Results

At this final stage of the Y model, implementation results are compared with needs for change. It is determined to what extent gaps between desired and current situation have been closed. This is the beginning of the IS/IT strategy revision process, where a new process through the Y model takes place. Typically, a new IS/IT strategy process should take place every other year in business organizations.

Let us look at an evaluation example. We assume that the company now has implemented an e-business system or a knowledge management system (KMS). The system may have been implemented to achieve results such as:

- Both organizational and market benefits

- Move from architecture stage to integration stage

- Improved communication and combination of information

- Improved business processes

- Improved efficiency and effectiveness in value shop activities

- Reach knowledge management level III

- Enable e-business at level IV

- Develop supplementary services to take advantage of opportunities

- Improve working procedures in accordance with firm vision

- Create different product according to market strategy

- Create entry barriers according to competitive forces model

- Extend the life of products classified as stars

- Attract knowledgeable people in the labor market

- Move from imitator to competitor according to the knowledge map

As this list illustrates, there may have been a variety of reasons for implementing a knowledge management system in the organization. When we do the evaluation of results, we will evaluate to what extent such results have been achieved. But the evaluation should not be limited to such planned, positive effects of a new system. The evaluation should investigate all kinds of effects as illustrated in Figure 6.4.

All planned, positive effects listed above belong in the upper-left quadrant for planned benefits. Here we evaluate to what extent we have achieved results in accordance with the IS/IT strategy. However, we will also have achieved other benefits from systems implementation that we did not think of when the IS/IT strategy was developed. These benefits may be just as valuable as the results as we aimed for. Hence, results are both planned and unplanned results.

At the other side of Figure 6.4, there are negative effects of implementing the IS/IT strategy. Some problems were known, and these problems have been dealt with. However, we will also experience new problems from systems implementation that we did not think of when the IS/IT strategy was developed. These new problems cause an increase in negative effects from implementing the IS/IT strategy.

Evaluating results at this final stage 7 of the Y model implies that all effects have to be considered, both positive and negative effects, as well as planned and unplanned effects. This total picture of effects is now compared with the original needs for change from stage 3 of the Y model. Discrepancies will be identified and have several consequences:

- Learning will occur from evaluating results

- Revision of implementation approach may be needed, including systems development strategy

- Revision of the IS/IT strategy may be needed

- A new IS/IT strategy may be needed

So far, we have discussed evaluating results in terms of strategy content. We also need to evaluate results in terms of plan implementation. An important result of IS/IT strategy is the extent of plan implementation. Implementation can be operationalized in several ways:

- *Implementation rate to date*. Implementation rate to date is the extent to which projects scheduled to be implemented to date have actually been implemented to

Figure 6.4. Evaluating effects from IS/IT

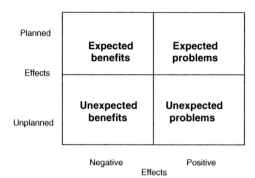

date. The number of projects in the IS/IT strategy actually implemented to date is divided by the number of projects in the IT strategy scheduled to be implemented to date. If the number of projects actually implemented is greater than the number of projects scheduled to be implemented, then the implementation rate is set to one (or hundred percent) in line with the spirit of implementation research measuring exclusively the extent to which a plan — here scheduled projects — is implemented.

- *Implementation rate to end.* Implementation rate to end is the extent to which projects will be implemented by the end of the implementation horizon assuming that the implementation extent to date will continue for the remaining implementation horizon. The number of projects in the IS/IT strategy actually implemented to date is divided by the fraction of implementation horizon expired. If the implementation rate to end is greater than one (or hundred percent) in line with the spirit of implementation research measuring exclusively the extent to which a plan — here planned projects is expected to be implemented.

- *Implementation extent.* Implementation extent is the degree to which the plan has been carried out. Implementing an IS/IT strategy provides a gestalt view of the organization whereas implementing several separate projects can be viewed more in a more piece-meal manner. Gestalt thinking leads to a larger complete picture, which is often too easily ignored by looking at individual projects. The gestalt view represents the implementation of the plan philosophy, attitudes, intentions, and ambitions of the overall plan. Important dimensions of implementation extent are (i) implementation completed on time, (ii) implementation completed within budget, (iii) implementation completed as expected, (iv) implementation achieved desired results, (v) no deviations from the strategy occurred during implementation, and (vi) satisfaction with strategy implementation.

- *Contribution to improved organizational performance.* Contribution to improved organizational performance is the extent to which the IS/IT strategy implementation has an impact on organizational performance. Evaluating organizational performance is perhaps the oldest and most commonly used form of evaluation for planning systems. The link between strategic planning and organizational performance is often elusive. While the three preceding constructs attempt to measure actual implementation, this construct attempts to measure overall effect of implementation. Objectives of IS/IT strategy implementation include improved IS performance, alignment of IS with business needs, achievement of competitive advantage from IS, achievement of top management commitment, prediction of future trends, increased user satisfaction, and improved IS function. Contribution to improved organizational performance can be measured by (i) return on investment, (ii) increased market share of goods and services, (iii) improved internal efficiency of operations, (iv) increased annual sales revenue, (v) increased customer satisfaction, and (vi) alignment of IS with business needs.

The creation of IS/IT strategy has become a major challenge to executives. Investments in IT are large, and many failed investments reflect this challenge. The impact of IT on organizational performance has growth in strategic importance, and thus the significance of failed IT investments is even greater. Information systems and information technology are critical to many business and government operations. New information technology for e-business will continue to transform organizations, and changes in how industry participants use IT is altering established relationships in an industry. Strategic information systems and information technology planning can play a critical part in helping organizations to increase efficiency, effectiveness, and competitiveness.

SECTION II

SOURCING

Chapter VII

Sourcing Management

An important point is made about how strategy was absent from early e-business attempts. The first part of this book described how strategy might be present. To establish and maintain a distinctive strategic positioning, an organization needs to follow six fundamental principles concerned with right goal, value proposition, value configuration, trade-off, fit, and continuity (Porter, 2001). One of the strategic choices often overlooked is concerned with IT sourcing. IT sourcing decisions are influenced by trade-off, fit, and continuity principles.

IT sourcing is related to the previously discussed topics in various important ways. First, the resource-based theory influences the choice of sourcing options, as sourcing is dependent on the availability of IT resources from internal and external sources. Second, e-business has specific requirements for IT infrastructure services depending on e-business models, and these requirements will typically be met through sourcing of IT services. Furthermore, decisions concerning IT sourcing belong in the strategic IS/IT planning process at the middle stages of the Y model. Finally, while e-business represents an answer to the question "what" the organization wants to do, sourcing represents an answer to the question "how" the organization can do it.

More and more companies move into IT sourcing combinations that require proactive management, leading to an increased need for IT governance. This is the topic of the third and final part of this book.

IT Sourcing Options

IT sourcing is concerned with defining, planning, and managing how an enterprise deploys internal and external resources and services to ensure the continuous fulfillment of its business objectives. A variety of sources has emerged. This variety is illustrated in Figure 7.1. Here we find internal sourcing and external sourcing. Both can be managed either through organizational hierarchy or through market mechanism.

In general, organizations have three basic alternatives for acquiring technological know-how. They can (1) develop the technology independently, (2) acquire another company that already has the technology, or (3) enter into a technology-sourcing arrangement. If a firm lacks the capabilities needed to develop a technology independently and other organizations already have the technology, management can consider external sourcing. There is a continuum of external sourcing methods based on the level of mutual commitment between the firm that has the technology (the source firm) and the firm that desires the know-how (the sourcing firm). These methods range from arms-length licensing contracts, through more tightly coupled co-development partnerships and joint ventures, to the outright acquisition of the source firm (Steensma & Corley, 2001).

Steensma and Corley (2001) focused on the two polar extremes in their study of technology sourcing: market contracting through licensing vs. the use of firm hierarchy through acquisition. The polar cases are basic particles from which more elaborate arrangements are constructed. Hierarchy implies that the sourcing firm can hierarchically control the technology, personnel, and other assets of the IT function and apply it to its current needs at its discretion.

Internal market as illustrated with numbers 3 and 4 in Figure 7.1 has a different sourcing logic. The concept of internal market is not new. The concept was first perceived to have radical implications eliminating superior-subordinate relationships, organizing all activ-

Figure 7.1. Sourcing options

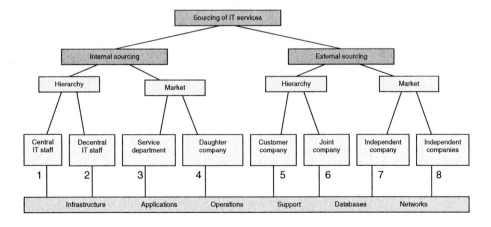

ity in terms of self-responsible profit centers, determining compensation objectively, eliminating internal monopolies, allowing freedom of access to information, and establishing a corporate constitution (King & Malhotra, 2000).

These appear to be less radical in today's environment of matrix organizations, self-managed teams, and re-engineered business processes. However, the notion of internal markets is not as simples as first suggested. The internal market is a mechanism for unleashing market forces inside the firm. Firms selecting this alternative might be able to retain control of the function while achieving the objectives of cost savings and service-responsiveness that are often ascribed to an external vendor (King & Malhotra, 2000).

Today, the internal market within an organization is characterized by a setup in which internal units are enabled to act autonomously by exerting self-control in conducting transactions with other internal units and with external entities within a framework of an overarching corporate vision, values, and precepts. This notion of internal markets may be best understood in terms of its potential broad applicability in an organizational context (King & Malhotra, 2000).

Implementation of the internal market concept requires the creation of a market economy inside a firm. In this, organizational units buy and sell goods and services among themselves and to others outside the firm at prices established in the open market. In contrast, the transfer prices that are used for internal transactions often represent a simulation of a marketing-clearing mechanism (King & Malhotra, 2000).

In IT sourcing, the term strategic sourcing is often used. Strategic sourcing has the following characteristics (Else, 2002):

- Systematic, ongoing effort to align individual sources and the portfolio of sources with broad high-level corporate strategy.

- Choosing and managing a set of specific sources in ways that advances one or more of strategic goals.

Figure 7.2. IT function specialization, as 'IS Lite' (Nielsen, 2004)

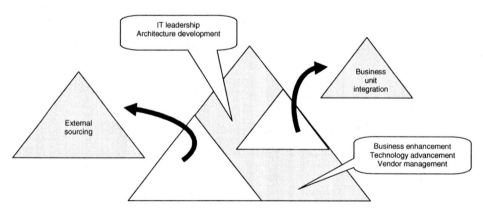

- Continuous business process — not a tactical procurement exercise — intended to map business requirements to service delivery options.

- Methodology to deploy technology strategy and the means, by which a business strategy is optimized.

- Highly multisourced environments will be the norm.

- Enterprises must develop new roles, processes, and governance structures to manage effectively the sourcing spectrum.

The increasing complexity of sourcing options and combinations has lead Computerworld (2005, p. 3) to stress qualifications needed by IT leaders:

Today's IT leaders operate in a vast sphere. They are multidimensional business executives, by turns global architects, employee boosters, and deal negotiators.

The purpose of IT sourcing can best be illustrated by sourcing principles developed for government agencies in the U.S. (Else, 2002, p. 35):

1. Support agency missions, goals, and objectives.

2. Be consistent with human capital practices designed to attract, motivate, retain, and reward a high-performing federal workforce.

3. Recognize that inherently governmental and certain other functions should be performed by federal workers.

4. Create incentives and processes to foster high-performing, efficient, and effective organizations throughout the federal government.

5. Be based on a clear, transparent, and consistently applied process.

6. Avoid arbitrary full-time equivalent (FTE) or other arbitrary numerical goals.

7. Establish a process that, for activities that may be performed by either the public or the private sector, would permit public and private sources to participate in competitions for work currently performed in-house, work currently contracted to the private sector, and new work, consistent with these guiding principles.

8. Ensure that, when competitions are held, they are conducted as fairly, effectively, and efficiently as possible.

9. Ensure that competitions involve a process that considers both quality and cost factors.

10. Provide for accountability in connections with all sourcing decisions.

Nielsen (2004) tried to study IT sourcing by looking at the IS organization. As illustrated in Figure 7.2, the IS organization can be divided into different parts that may be delegated and integrated into other organizational arrangements.

Dimensions of IT Outsourcing Strategy

IT outsourcing strategy can be defined as the logic underlying a firm's outsourcing decisions. This logic is visible in a firm's portfolio of IT outsourcing decisions. The logic either may have served to guide decisions regarding outsourcing of specific functions or may be revealed in the cumulative pattern visible in individual outsourcing decisions. Thus, strategy need not be a single decision that is consciously made, but rather the manifestation of multiple decisions (Lee et al., 2004).

Having defined strategy as such logic, we need to identify the decisions that are salient in constituting or reflecting an IT outsourcing strategy. Firms make decisions on the extent to which transactions will be vertically integrated (degree of integration), the extent to which they will relinquish control of transaction fulfillment (allocation of control), and the duration for which they will commit to a transaction decision (performance period). Lee et al. (2004) defined these decisions as dimensions of IT outsourcing strategy:

- *Degree of integration* has been the focus of much research on IT outsourcing. This focus stems from a recognition that the integration of the IS function is not an all-or-none activity. Outsourcing initiatives may be categorized as comprehensive, selective, and minimal outsourcing. Lacity and Willcocks (1998) found that firms predominantly engage in selective outsourcing, and that such selectivity yielded economies of scale, and resulted in the expected cost savings more often than comprehensive or minimal levels of outsourcing. Therefore, Lee et al. (2004) suggested a hypothesis that selective outsourcing will be more successful than comprehensive or minimal outsourcing. However, in their empirical research, this hypothesis was not supported.

- *Allocation of control* in outsourcing relationships refers to the manner in which compensation or reward structures are set up and the manner in which authority

Figure 7.3. Research model to study dimensions of IT outsourcing strategies and dimensions of outsourcing success (Lee et al., 2004)

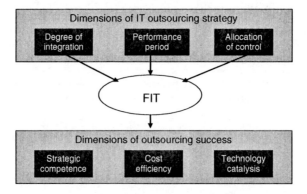

is exercised in the relationship. One control structure is the buy-in contract (Lacity & Willcocks, 1998). This entails the hiring of hourly workers, thereby subjecting them to the day-to-day authority of the client. Here, the client firm retains rights of control because it owns the assets, including labor power, necessary for the completion of work. A second control structure is a fee-for-service contract, which stipulates detailed bases for compensation. Here, rights of control are implicitly allocated to the provider firm that owns resources necessary for work completion. Finally, partnerships rely on complementary resources and voluntary resource allocations to benefit the partnership. Authority tends to be internalized within the relationship. Rights of control are therefore shared by client and provider firms. Under ideal conditions, the integrative nature of a partnership orientation minimizes problems stemming from equivocal contracts or uncertainty. However, as the interests of the client and provider diverge, partnerships may prove to be problematic. Therefore, Lee et al. (2004) suggested a hypothesis that buy-in or fee-for-service controls will be more successful than partnerships. However, in their empirical research, this hypothesis was not supported.

- *Performance periods* have been studied in the past. Research indicates that short-term contracts yield cost savings more often than long-term contracts (Lacity & Willcocks, 1998). Short-term contracts motivate providers toward higher performance and allow clients to recover quickly from contractual mistakes. Furthermore, it is difficult for the client to anticipate completely long-term requirements, and client and provider interests are likely to diverge over time. Therefore, Lee et al. (2004) suggested a hypothesis that short-term outsourcing relationships will be more successful than medium- or long-term relationships. However, in their empirical research, the reversed hypothesis was supported, suggesting that medium- and long-term outsourcing relationships will be more successful than short-term relationships. It may not be surprising that their findings contradicted conventional wisdom with respect to performance period of outsourcing relationships. Longer-term contracts are often preferable because they enable initial set-up costs to be distributed over a longer period of time. A long-term contract improves financial predictability and reduces the risk and uncertainties associated with important business functions. Time is a critical aspect in the development of relationships. While time introduces an element of risk in relationships, time also facilitates cooperation among self-interested parties and the development of trust. It enables voluntary sharing of resources, with anticipation of deferred compensation.

In their empirical study, Lee et al. (2004) defined outsourcing success in terms of three dimensions: strategic competence, cost efficiency, and technology catalysis. Strategic competence refers to a firm's efforts at redirecting the business and IT into core competencies, cost efficiency refers to improving the business' financial position, and technology catalysis refers to strengthening resources and flexibility in technology service to underpin business' strategic direction. Their research model is illustrated in Figure 7.3.

Chapter VIII

Sourcing Theories

In Chapter I, general theories of the firm and value configurations of firms were introduced. Here we return to more theories. While theories and value configurations in Chapter I were introduced to develop e-business strategy, more theories are introduced here to understand the specifics of sourcing in general and outsourcing in particular. We want to understand why companies choose IT outsourcing in the middle of the Y model.

We know that many companies choose IT outsourcing based on an analysis of core competencies. As we shall see, there are, however, many other theories that can be applied and that may provide both convergent and divergent answers to an outsourcing question. An example of divergent answer would be the theory of core competencies suggesting that non-core IT can be outsourced, while the resource-based theory suggests that non-core IT should be kept in-house if we have strategic IT-resources (valuable, non-imitable, non-substitutable, non-transferable, combinable, exploitable and available).

Theories of the Firm

Theory of Core Competencies

Based on the notion of core competency, issues of sourcing should hinge on the degree of criticality of a specific component or business activity to an organization. An extreme case would be for a company to strip itself down to the essentials necessary to deliver to customers the greatest possible value from its core skills — and outsource as much of the rest as possible. By limiting or shedding activities that provide no strategic advantage, a company can increase the value it delivers to both customers and shareholders and, in the process, lower its costs and investments (Ang, 1993).

Core competencies theory suggests activities should be performed either in house or by suppliers. Activities, which are not core competencies, should be considered for outsourcing with best-in-world suppliers. Some non-core activities may have to be retained in house if they are part of a defensive posture to protect competitive advantage. Although some authors indicate characteristics of core competencies, most of the literature on this subject seems tautological — core equals key, critical, or fundamental. Employees in non-core functions (even if not facing outsourcing) may feel excluded by the organization because they are a non-dominant discipline. For example, information technology employees working on Web based legal services in a law firm may feel excluded by lawyers in the firm. In the public sector, there may be particular uncertainty about what is core; and it has been suggested that government may aim to discover its core competencies via a residualisation process — outsourcing until and unless the shoe pinches, or a political backlash is triggered (Hancox & Hackney, 2000).

An organization may view IT itself as a core competence. It seems that most successful companies have a good understanding of IT's potential. However, some organizations outsource IT even though they see it as core and delivering competitive advantage. This may be because IT can be considered core at the corporate level, but some of its aspects, at lower levels, might be commodities. Thus the complexity of IT, and its (at least in part) core nature, may make the contracting out of IT a particularly challenging exercise. The ability to define IT requirements and to monitor their delivery by third parties may be some of the core IT competencies that any organization must have if it is to outsource IT successfully. It can even be argued that the very acts of specifying and managing supply contracts can themselves give competitive advantage (Hancox & Hackney, 2000).

Resource-Based Theory

The central tenet in resource-based theory is that unique organizational resources of both tangible and intangible nature are the real source of competitive advantage. With resource-based theory, organizations are viewed as a collection of resources that are heterogeneously distributed within and across industries. Accordingly, what makes the performance of an organization distinctive is the unique bland of the resources it possesses. A firm's resources include not only its physical assets such as plant and location but also its competencies. The ability to leverage distinctive internal and external competencies relative to environmental situations ultimately affects the performance of the business (Peppard et al., 2000).

The resource-based theory of the firm holds that, in order to generate sustainable competitive advantage, a resource must provide economic value and must be presently scarce, difficult to imitate, non-substitutable, and not readily obtainable in factor markets. This theory rests on two key points. First, that resources are the determinants of firm performance and second, that resources must be rare, valuable, difficult to imitate and non-substitutable by other rare resources. When the latter occurs, a competitive advantage has been created (Priem & Butler, 2001).

Resources can simultaneously be characterized as valuable, rare, non-substitutable, and inimitable. To the extent that an organization's physical assets, infrastructure, and workforce satisfy these criteria, they qualify as resources. A firm's performance depends fundamentally on its ability to have a distinctive, sustainable competitive advantage, which derives from the possession of firm-specific resources (Priem & Butler, 2001).

Investments in IT represent a major approach to asset capitalization in organizations. IT may symbolize firm growth, advancement, and progress. Because investments in IT can promote social prominence and public prestige, managers are induced to utilize slack resources to internalize IS services. Inducements toward investments in in-house IS services are further reinforced by well-publicized case studies that demonstrate the competitive advantage and new business opportunities afforded by IT (Ang, 1993).

The above reasoning suggests that managers may exhibit a penchant for building up internal IT resources such as IS employees, equipment, and computer capacity when organizations possess slack resources. In contrast, when slack resources are low, managers tend to conserve resources in response to the anxiety provoked by loss of financial resources. Anxiety is provoked because the loss of financial resources is often attributed to managerial incompetence and organizational ineffectiveness. As a result, leaders are more likely to be blamed and replaced when financial performance is poor. In response to the anxiety provoked by loss of financial resources, decision makers have been observed to reduce costs through downsizing the company by selling off physical assets and laying off workers (Ang, 1993).

Theory of Firm Boundaries

There has been renewed debate on the determinants of firm boundaries and their implications for performance. According to Schilling and Steensma (2002), the widely accepted framework of transaction cost economics has come under scrutiny as a comprehensive theory for firm scale and scope. At the heart of this debate is whether the underlying mechanism determining firm boundaries is a fear of opportunism (as posited by transaction cost economics), a quest for sustainable advantage (as posed by resource-based view theorists and others), a desire for risk-reducing flexibility (as has recently gained increased attention in work on options), or a combination of factors. Although perspectives on firm boundaries such as transaction costs or the resource-based view are based on fundamentally different motivations for pursuing hierarchical control over market contracts, they rely on common resource or context attributes as antecedents.

Afuah (2003) found that the literature on vertical firm boundaries could be divided into two perspectives. In the first, researchers argue that firms decide to organize activities internally or through markets for efficiency reasons. In the second, researchers argue that firms decide to organize activities internally or through markets for strategic positioning reasons. Since the Internet's largest potential is in reducing costs, Afuah (2003) focused only on the first perspective to keep the arguments traceable. Thus, the decision to outsource or to develop an input internally depends on weighing external component production and transaction costs, on the one hand, and internal component production and transaction costs, on the other hand. If the former are greater than the latter, a firm is better off integrating vertically backward to produce the input internally.

Most studies of firm boundaries emphasize relationships between the division of labor and firms' boundaries. One of the oldest ideas in economics is that returns to specialization increase with market size. In our case of IT outsourcing, firms' boundaries are determined by the extent to which there are large markets for specialization. If there are large markets for IT services available from vendors, then a client company will tend to outsource more of its internal IT function.

Economic Theories

Transaction Cost Theory

In transaction cost analysis, outsourcing decisions are typically framed as determination of firm boundaries. In this perspective, vertical integration can be described as involving a variety of decisions concerning whether corporations, through their business units, should provide certain goods or services in-house or purchase them from outside instead. The study of firm boundaries or vertical integration therefore involves the study of outsourcing, describing which activities are conducted within a firm's hierarchy, and which activities are conducted outside the hierarchy using market mechanisms or other forms of inter-organizational relationships (Ang, 1993).

Several studies have used the transaction cost perspective in their study of IT outsourcing (e.g., Ang & Straub, 1998; Grover, Teng et al., 1998; Langfield-Smith & Smith, 2003).

These studies generally support the thesis of transaction cost economics— that whenever an activity is conducted under conditions of high uncertainty, or whenever an activity requires specific assets, transaction costs, the costs of writing, monitoring and enforcing contracts, are likely to be high. When transaction costs are high, outsourcing is deemed to be relatively inefficient compared with internal, hierarchical administration. Therefore, central to the arguments of transaction cost analysis is the idea of achieving the economic goal of an efficient boundary in organization design (Ang, 1993).

Because production costs are objectively calculated by the accounting system, while transaction costs are assessed subjectively through indirect indicators, functional managers are likely to differ in the importance that they assign to reducing transaction costs. Consequently, the effect transaction costs have on a make-or-buy choice can partly reflect the influence exerted by the purchasing manager. Production cost differences seem more influential in sourcing decisions than transaction cost differences, and experience of the decision-maker is related to assessments of technological uncertainty. Profit center managers engage in influence activities that increase the costs of price renegotiations above the level that is observed in comparable external market transactions. Managers sometimes seem more reluctant to outsource when investments in specific assets are necessary; and contrary to theory, managers sometimes consider previous internal investments in specific assets a reason to insource. In certain circumstances decision-makers systematically misestimate (or fail to consider), transaction costs (Anderson, Glenn et al., 2000).

Neo-Classical Economic Theory

Neo-classical economic theory posits that firms outsource IT to attain cost advantages from assumed economies of scale and scope possessed by vendors (Ang & Straub, 1998). This theory is attained more empirical support in studies of outsourcing decisions than transaction cost economics. Neo-classical economic theory regards every business organization as a production function (Williamson, 1981), and where their motivation is driven by profit maximization. This means that companies offer products and services the market where they have a cost or production advantage. They rely on the marketplace where they have disadvantages.

According to neo-classical economic theory, companies will justify their sourcing strategy based on evaluating possibilities for production cost savings. Thus, the question of whether or not to outsource, is a question whether the marketplace can produce products and services at a lower price than internal production. In the context of IT outsourcing, a company will keep its IT-function internally if this has production cost advantages, and it will outsource when the marketplace can offer production cost savings.

However, defining outsourcing simply in terms of procurement activities does not capture the true strategic nature of the issues (Gilley & Rasheed, 2000). IT outsourcing is not only a purchasing decision — all firms purchase elements of their operations. This is done to achieve economic, technological, and strategic advantages. However, the economies of scale and scope argument would predict that outsourcing has little to offer to larger firms, because they can generate economies of scale and scope internally by reproducing methods used by vendors. As documented by Levina and Ross (2003), there are other reasons for large firms to move into outsourcing.

In neoclassical economic theory, outsourcing may arise in two ways. First, outsourcing may arise through the substitution of external purchases for internal activities. In this way, it can be viewed as a discontinuation of internal production (whether it be production of goods or services) and an initiation of procurement from outside suppliers.

To the extent this type of outsourcing reduces a firm's involvement in successive stages of production, substitution-based outsourcing may be viewed as vertical disintegration. This seems to be the most commonly understood type of outsourcing (Gilley & Rasheed, 2000).

Relational Theories

Contractual Theory

Luo (2002) examined how contract, cooperation, and performance are associated with one another. He argues that contract and cooperation are not substitutes but complements in relation to performance. Contracting and cooperation are two central issues in an IT outsourcing arrangement. A contract alone is insufficient to guide outsourcing evolution and performance. Since outsourcing involves repeated interorganizational exchanges that become socially embedded over time, cooperation is an important safeguard mechanism mitigating external and internal hazards and overcoming adaptive limits of contracts. The simultaneous use of both contractual and cooperative mechanisms is particularly critical to outsourcing arrangements in an uncertain environment.

An outsourcing contract provides a legally bound, institutional framework in which each party's rights, duties, and responsibilities are codified and the goals, policies, and strategies underlying the arrangement are specified. Every outsourcing contract has the purpose of facilitating exchange and preventing opportunism. Appropriate contractual arrangements can attenuate the leeway for opportunism, prohibit moral hazards in a cooperative relationship, and protect each party's proprietary knowledge. A complete contract reduces the uncertainty faced by organizational decision-makers and the risks stemming from opportunism on the part of one or more contracting parties. It provides a safeguard against ex post performance problems by restraining each party's ability to pursue private goals at the expense of common benefits. An incomplete contract may bring about ambiguity, which creates a breeding ground for shirking responsibility and shifting blame, raises the likelihood of conflict, and hinders the ability to coordinate activities, utilize resources, and implement strategies (Luo, 2002).

Contractual completeness is not just term specificity (i.e., the extent to which all relevant terms and clauses are specified), nor should every outsourcing contract maintain the same level of completeness. Previous studies that view contractual completeness and term specificity as equivalent have created a controversy about the role of the contract. For instance, it has been suggested that incomplete contracts are optimal in situations where some elements of enforcement are unverifiable. Similarly, it has been argued that economic agents rarely write contracts that are complete because boundedly rational parties may not be able to distinguish certain contingencies. By contrast, others demonstrate that contractual completeness reduces role conflict and role ambiguity for outsourcing managers, which then enhances outsourcing performance. Furthermore, it has been suggested that term specificity protects a partner's strategic resources and reduces operational and financial uncertainties through controlling opportunism and spurring information flow within an outsourcing arrangement.

Agency Theory

Agency theory has broadened the risk-sharing literature to include the agency problem that occurs when cooperating parties have different goals and division of labor (Eisenhardt, 1985). The cooperating parties are engaged in an agency relationship defined as a contract under which one or more persons (the principal(s)) engage another person (agent) to perform some service on their behalf, which involves delegating some decision-making authority to the agent (Jensen & Meckling, 1979). Agency theory describes the relationship between the two parties using the metaphor of a contract. In an IT outsourcing relationship this is a client-vendor relationship and an outsourcing contract.

The agency theory is applicable when describing client-vendor relationships in IT outsourcing arrangements. Typically, the client organization (principal) transfers property rights to the vendor organization (agent). In the context of IT assets transferred might be infrastructure, systems and documentation, and employees. For a certain amount of money, the vendor organization provides services to the client organization. This implies a change in legal relationships, and IT services are carried out using a more formal transaction process. The status of personal relationships also changes, from that of a manager and a subordinate, to that of a client-manager and a vendor. According to agency theory, control mechanisms also change, from that of behavioral control, to that of outcome-based control.

The technological and business complexity of IT means that there may be major problems for the principal in choosing a suitable agent and in monitoring the agent's work. Only the agent knows how hard he is working, and that can be especially important in multilateral contracting where one agent acts for several principals. This is often the case in IT outsourcing because of the market dominance of one large firm. Given the difficulties of behavior-based contracts suggested by agency theory, it is reasonable to assume that the overwhelming majority of clients would insist on outcome-based contracts when acquiring IT products and services. Such a strategy can only succeed if the client can confidently specify current and future requirements. But accurate predictions by the client may not always be in the vendor's interests; since vendor account managers often are rewarded according to contract profitability, which is principally achieved through charging the client extra for anything that is not in the contract (Hancox & Hackney, 2000).

Partnership and Alliance Theory

Partnership, often referred to as an alliance, has frequently been noted as a major feature of IT outsourcing. Partnership can reduce the risk of inadequate contractual provision, which may be comforting for clients about to outsource a complex and high-cost activity such as IT. However, in the relationship between vendor and client, the latter may be over dependent on the former, and goals are not necessarily shared. A client may be more comfortable if it knows the vendor already. In partner selection, cultural compatibility is vital and shared values and objectives inform all stages of the partnership development process. This may make a successful relationship especially difficult if the putative partners are from fundamentally different domains and bring fundamentally different perspectives, as might well be argued is the case in a private sector — public sector arrangement. The difficulty may be compounded where, as in the UK government's compulsory competitive tendering policy, the outsourcing can be involuntary (Hancox & Hackney, 2000).

Hancox and Hackney (2000) found that few organizations claim to be in a strategic partnership with their IT suppliers. The contract is more likely to favor the vendor because he has greater experience in negotiation. Clients with loose contracts were more likely to regard outsourcing as a failure; yet, most respondents in a study used the vendor's standard contract as a basis for outsourcing agreement and most did not use external technical or legal advice. It was found that 80% of clients wished that they had more tightly defined contracts. Partly the client's view of IT influences its relationship with the vendor, such that firms regarding IT as a core competence capability are more likely to look upon outsourcing as an alliance. Clients who view IT as a core are also more likely to be satisfied with the outsourcing arrangements because they negotiate from a more knowledgeable position (Hancox & Hackney, 2000).

Hancox and Hackney (2000) interviewed IT managers to find support for the partnership theory in IT outsourcing. Despite assurances found in vendors' marketing literature, most clients were skeptical about partnership. If partnership did exist, it was usually as a collection of some of the intangibles mentioned earlier, rather than as a formalized arrangement. Partnership was more likely to be claimed in the area of systems development, where vendors needed to have a greater understanding of the organization, than in outsourcing of operations and IT infrastructure support. There seemed to be no correlation between those organizations regarding IT as strategic and those regarding relationships with vendors as partnerships.

Relational Exchange Theory

Relational exchange theory is based on relational norms. According to this theory, the key to determining how efficiently contract governance is carried out lies in the relational norms between the transactors. For example, the degree to which transactors engage in joint-planning or their extent of inter-firm information sharing, are process elements that determine the costs associated with periodically renegotiating contracts. Those trans-actors who have established behavioral norms that can simplify and smooth the renegotiation process can reasonably expect to incur lower ex post bargaining costs than those who have not (Artz & Brush, 2000).

Artz and Brush (2000) examined supplier relationships that were governed by relational contracts, and they found support for the relational exchange theory. By altering the behavioral orientation of the alliance, relational norms lowered exchange costs.

In their measurement of relational norm, Artz and Brush (2000) included collaboration, continuity expectations, and communication strategies. Collaboration refers to the willingness of the client and vendor to work together to create a positive exchange relationship and improve alliance performance. Collaborative actions can act to enhance the client-vendor relationship as a whole and curtail opportunistic behaviors. For example, joint planning and forecasting can allow both the customer and the supplier to participate in determining each's roles and responsibilities and foster mutually beneficial expectations.

When one firm attempts to coerce another in order to gain a more favorable negotiation outcome, that firm is likely to be viewed by its alliance partner as exploitative rather than accommodative, and retaliatory behavior often results. In contrast, noncoercive strategies attempt to persuade rather than demand. Noncoercive communications center on beliefs about business issues and involve little direct pressure. Examples include simple requests or recommendations, in which one party stresses the benefits the other party will receive by complying.

Stakeholder Theory

As far as we know, there is no comprehensive use of stakeholder theory in IT outsourcing research. Although Lacity and Willcocks (2000) have used the term identifying four distinct customer stakeholders and three distinct supplier stakeholders, their research has not got any further on this path. In an IT outsourcing relationship, a stakeholder theory approach will describe the relationship as a nexus of cooperative and competitive interests possessing intrinsic value.

The term stakeholder is a powerful one. This is due, to a significant degree, to its conceptual breath. The term means many different things to many different people and hence evokes praise and scorn from a wide variety of scholars and practitioners of myriad academic disciplines and backgrounds. Such breadth of interpretation, though one of stakeholder theory's greatest strengths, is also one of its most prominent theoretical liabilities as a topic of reasoned discourse. Much of the power of stakeholder theory is a direct result of the fact that, when used unreflectively, its managerial prescriptions and implications are nearly limitless. When discussed in instrumental variation (i.e., that managers should attend to stakeholders as a means to achieving other organizational goals such as profit or shareholder wealth maximization) stakeholder theory stands virtually unopposed (Phillips et al., 2003).

Stakeholder theory is a theory of organizational management and ethics. Indeed all theories of strategic management have some moral content, though it is often implicit. Moral content in this case means that the subject matter of the theories are inherently moral topics (i.e., they are not amoral). Stakeholder theory is distinct because it addresses morals and values explicitly as a central feature of managing organizations. The ends of cooperative activity and the means of achieving these ends are critically examined in stakeholder theory in a way that they are not in many theories of strategic management (Phillips et al., 2003).

Social Exchange Theory

Typically, an IT outsourcing relationship will be a restricted social exchange.

Social exchange theory can be traced to one of the oldest theories of social behavior — any interaction between individuals is an exchange of resources. The resources exchange may be not only tangible, such as goods or money, but also intangible, such as social amenities or friendship. The basic assumption of social exchange theory is that parties enter into and maintain relationships with the expectation that doing so will be rewarding (Lambe et al., 2001).

Social exchange theory postulates that exchange interactions involve economic and/or social outcomes. Over time, each party in the exchange relationship compares the social and economic outcomes from these interactions to those that are available from exchange alternatives, which determines their dependence on the exchange relationship. Positive economic and social outcomes over time increase the partners' trust of each other and commitment to maintaining the exchange relationship. Positive exchange interactions over time also produce relational exchange norms that govern the exchange partners' interactions (Lambe et al., 2001).

Implicit in these postulates, the four foundational premises of social exchange theory are: (1) exchange interactions result in economic and/or social outcomes, (2) these outcomes are compared over time to other exchange alternatives to determine dependence on the exchange relationship, (3) positive outcomes over time increase firms' trust of their trading partner(s) and their commitment to the exchange relationship, and (4) positive exchange interactions over time produce relational exchange norms that govern the exchange relationship (Lambe et al., 2001).

Commitment is a widely used construct in social exchange research. It has been defined as an exchange partner believing that an ongoing relationship with another is so important as to warrant maximum efforts at maintaining it; that is, the committed party believes the relationship is worth working on to ensure that it endures indefinitely (Lambe et al., 2001).

Comparison of Theories

We have introduced eleven theories concerned with outsourcing. In Figure 8.1, these theories are compared in terms of what they recommend for outsourcing. We find that some theories indicate possibilities for outsourcing (theory of core competencies, resource-based theory, transaction cost theory, neoclassical economic theory, and theory of firm boundaries), while others indicate limitations (contractual theory, partnership and alliance theory, relational exchange theory, social exchange theory, agency theory, and stakeholder theory).

Figure 8.2 lists a comparison of the theories when it comes to the next stage. The next stage is when outsourcing has occurred and both client and vendor want the outsourcing

Figure 8.1. Possibilities and limitations in IT outsourcing based on theories

Theory	What should be outsourced?
Theory of core competencies	All IT functions which are peripheral to the company's production of goods and services for the market.
Resource-based theory	All IT functions where the company does not have sufficient strategic resources to perform in a competitive way. Strategic resources are unique, valuable, difficult to imitate, exploitable and difficult to substitute.
Transaction cost theory	All IT functions where benefits for the company are greater than the transaction costs. Benefits include increased revenues and reduced costs.
Contractual theory	Only IT functions where the company can expect and secure that vendor and customer will have the same contractual behavior. Common contract behavioral patterns include role integrity, reciprocity, implementation of planning, effectuation of consent, flexibility, contractual solidarity, reliance, restraint of power, proprietary of means and harmonization with the social environment.
Neoclassical economic theory	All IT functions that an external vendor can operate at lower costs than the company.
Partnership and alliance theory	Only IT functions where the company can expect and secure a partnership and alliance with the vendor that imply interdependence between the partners based on trust, comfort, understanding, flexibility, co-operation, shared values, goals and problem solving, interpersonal relations and regular communication.
Relational exchange theory	Only IT functions where the company easily can develop and secure common norms with the vendor. Norms determine behavior in three main dimensions: flexibility, information exchange, and solidarity.
Social exchange theory	Only IT functions where each of the parties can follow their own self-interest when transacting with the other self-interested actor to accomplish individual goals that they cannot achieve alone and without causing hazards to the other party.
Agency theory	Only IT functions where the agent (vendor) and the principal (client) have common goals and the same degree of risk willingness and aversion.
Theory of firm boundaries	All IT functions that satisfy several of the other theories, mainly resource-based theory and transaction cost theory.
Stakeholder theory	Only IT functions where a balance can be achieved between stakeholders. Stakeholders relevant in IT outsourcing include business management, IT management, user management and key IT personnel at the client, and business management, customer account management and key service providers at the vendor.

arrangement to be successful. What do the theories tell us? As is visible in Figure 8.2, the theories tell us a lot about what to do to be successful. Each theory provides recommendations for actions that will contribute to managing successful IT outsourcing relationships. From different theoretical perspectives, recommendations are made. Taken together, the list in Figure 8.2 represents critical success factors for an outsourcing arrangement.

An alternative taxonomy for outsourcing schools is presented in Figure 8.3. Kern (1999) applies here interorganizational theory and relational contract theory as a synthesis for studying IT outsourcing relationships.

Figure 8.2. Recommendations for managing successful IT outsourcing relationships based on theories

Theory	How to succeed in an outsourcing arrangement
Theory of core competencies	Capability to define IT needs and ability to manage IT services from the vendor represent the core competence within IT needed in the client organization to succeed in an IT outsourcing arrangement.
Resource-based theory	Capability to integrate and exploit strategic IT resources from the vendor together with own resources to produce competitive goods and services. An example of such a resource is the vendor's competence in an IT application area where the client has limited experience.
Transaction cost theory	Minimize transaction costs by reducing the need for lasting specific IT assets; increase transaction frequency; reduce complexity and uncertainty in IT tasks; improve performance measurements; and reduce dependence on other transactions.
Contractual theory	A complete IT contract based on information symmetry in a predictable environment with occurrence adaptation that prevents opportunistic behavior in an efficient collaborative environment with balance of power between client and vendor, where the contract is a management instrument that grants decision rights and action duties.
Neoclassical economic theory	Capability to integrate and exploit IT services from the vendor together with own services to produce competitive goods and services. An example of such a service is the vendor's operation of the client's communication network.
Partnership and alliance theory	Develop experience with alliances, develop alliance managers, and develop the ability to identify potential partners.
Relational exchange theory	Develop and secure common norms that are relevant to both parties. Norms determine behavior and are mainly concerned with flexibility, information exchange, and solidarity. Norms shall secure integration in the relation, which takes place through involvement. Involvement occurs by coordination of activities, adaptation of resources and interaction between individuals. The degree of involvement in these three dimensions is called activity link, resource link and actor link.
Social exchange theory	Enable social and economic outcomes in the exchange between client and vendor such that these outcomes outperform those obtainable in alternative exchanges. Positive economic and social outcomes over time increase the partners' trust of each other and commitment to maintaining the exchange relationship. Commitment is important, as it is an exchange partner's belief that an ongoing relationship with another is so important as to warrant maximum efforts at maintaining it.
Agency theory	It must be easy and inexpensive for the principal (client) to find out what the agent (vendor) is actually doing. In addition, both outcome-based and behavior-based incentives can be used to reduce and prevent opportunistic behavior.
Theory of firm boundaries	The supply of IT services from the organization's environment should change firm boundaries between the firm that desires the competence (sourcing firm) and the firm having the technology (source firm) in a clear and unambiguous manner. This can be achieved in a strict and rigid division of labor between client and vendor.
Stakeholder theory	Create efficient and effective communication with and between stakeholders to secure continued support from all stakeholders, to balance their interests and to make the IT outsourcing arrangement so that all stakeholders achieve their goals.

Figure 8.3. Theories studying IT outsourcing (partly adapted from Kern, 1999)

	Social and cognitive psychology	Strategic choice	Inter-organizational relationship view	Economic view	Relational contract view
Paradigm	Social and cognitive psychology	Resource-based theory Resource-dependence theory	Social exchange theory Power-political theory	Classical and neo-classical economics Transaction cost theory Agency theory	Classical and neo-classical contract theory Social exchange theory
Unit of analysis	Individual	Resources	Inter-organizational relationship	Relational transaction and agency costs	Contractual relations
Basic assumption	Physical, human, and organizational assets are unique	Outsourcing is a strategic decision which can be used to fill gaps	Inter-firm relations arise for a number of reasons and entail a particular set of behavioral and structural dimensions	Transaction and agency costs is critical for choice of governance structure	Business contracts are relational and entails a number of norms
Strengths			Examines the reasons, exchanges, behavioral and structural dimensions of inter-firm relationships	Analysis the efficiency and costs of governance structures	Holistic approach that considers the behaviors and dimensions of different contractual relations
Weaknesses			Determinants covered are fragmented, broad ranging and heterogeneous	Narrow focus on economic aspects	Discussed only polar archetypes of discrete and intertwined relations
Contribution to this study and potential predictors of PME	Individual cognitive characteristics-- need for cognition, belief perseverance	Human capital resources-- competence, capabilities	Exchange behaviors-- power, dependence, conflict, cooperation, trust	Human factors-- opportunism, bounded rationality	Personal relations-- social interaction and communication

Chapter IX

IS/IT Outsourcing

Information technology outsourcing—the practice of transferring IT assets, leases, staff, and management responsibility for delivery of services from internal IT functions to third party vendors—has become an undeniable trend ever since Kodak's 1989 landmark decision. In recent years, private and public sector organizations worldwide have outsourced significant portions of their IT functions, among them British Aerospace, British Petroleum, Canadian Post Office, Chase Manhattan Bank, Continental Airlines, Continental Bank, First City, General Dynamics, Inland Revenue, JP Morgan, Kodak, Lufthansa, McDonnell Douglas, South Australian Government, Swiss Bank, Xerox, and Commonwealth Bank of Australia (Hirsheim & Lacity, 2000).

How should firms organize their enterprise-wide activities related to the acquisition, deployment, and management of information technology? During the 1980s, IT professionals devoted considerable attention to this issue, primarily debating the virtues of centralized, decentralized, and federal modes of governance. Throughout the 1980s and 1990s, IT researchers anticipated and followed these debates, eventually reaching considerable consensus regarding the influence of different contingency factors on an enterprise's choice of a particular governance mode (Sambamurthy & Zmud, 2000).

Today, however, there are increasing signs that this accumulated wisdom might be inadequate in shaping appropriate insights for contemporary practice. The traditional governance logic has been turned upside down by utilizing other mechanisms, such as sourcing arrangements, strategic alliances, roles, teams, processes, and informal relationships, as the primary vehicles through which business executives orchestrate their IT organizational architectures (Sambamurthy & Zmud, 2000).

Today's IT organization must grapple with the unrelenting challenges associated with: acquiring current technical knowledge; attracting, retaining, motivating, and leveraging an IT workforce; distilling the confusion amid a proliferation in IT products, services, and vendors; and, contracting and managing a variety of relationships involved with selective outsourcing and multi-sourcing. Increasingly, the providers of IT products and services are being viewed as both arms-length suppliers of cost-effective technology and as vibrant business partners with an unlimited potential to enhance a firm's IT and business capabilities. IT procurement has moved from being operational to tactical to strategic, amidst networks of alliances with IT vendors, consultants, and third party service providers being built and managed in order to leverage their associated assets, competencies, and knowledge (Sambamurthy & Zmud, 2000).

As the outsourcing market evolves, a number of important aspects of IT outsourcing decisions have been explored. These studies can be categories as descriptive case studies and surveys of the current outsourcing practices, surveys of practitioners' perceptions of risks and benefits of outsourcing, and identification of best practices that distinguish success from failure (Hirshheim & Lacity, 2000).

In general, the current research indicates selective sourcing is still the norm but that outsourcing options are becoming more complex. There are many perceived benefits and risks of outsourcing, but these studies are based on respondents' perceptions rather than actual outcomes. The determinants of outsourcing research generally show that companies most likely to outsource on a large scale are in poor financial situations, have poor IT functions, or have IT functions with little status within their organizations. There is still considerable debate on best practices that distinguish successes from failures (Hirshheim & Lacity, 2000).

Outsourcing has become popular because some organizations perceive it as providing more value than an in-house computer center or information systems staff. The provider of outsourcing services benefits from economies of scale and complementary core competencies that would be difficult for a firm that does not specialize in information technology services to replicate. The vendor's specialized knowledge and skills can be shared with many different customers, and the experience of working with so many information systems projects further enhances the vendor's expertise. Outsourcing allows a company with fluctuating needs for computer processing to pay for only what it uses rather than to build its own computer center, which would be underutilized when there is no peak load. Some firms outsource because their internal information systems staff cannot keep pace with technological change or innovative business practices or because they want to free up scarce and costly talent for activities with higher paybacks (Laudon & Laudon, 2005).

Not all organizations benefit from outsourcing, and the disadvantages of outsourcing can create serious problems for organizations if they are not well understood and managed. Many firms underestimate costs for identifying and evaluating vendors of information technology services, for transitioning to a new vendor, and for monitoring vendors to make sure they are fulfilling their contractual obligations. These hidden costs can easily undercut anticipated benefits from outsourcing. When a firm allocates the responsibility for developing and operating its information systems to another organization, it can lose control over its information systems function. If the organization lacks the expertise to negotiate a sound contract, the firm's dependency on the vendor could result in high costs or loss of control over technological direction. Firms should be especially cautious when using an outsourcer to develop or to operate applications that give it some type of competitive advantage. A firm is most likely to benefit from outsourcing if it understands exactly how the outsourcing vendor will provide value and can manage the vendor relationship (Laudon & Laudon, 2005).

In this chapter, we mainly discuss threats associated with IT outsourcing. Threats are important to keep in mind when we move into later chapters of this book, as threats have to be solved and/or minimized through the outsourcing process. First, we start this chapter with typical outsourcing opportunities.

Outsourcing Opportunities and Threats

An empirical study of information technology sourcing in U.S. and UK organizations identified indicators of success. The objective of the study was to develop indicators of success based on participants' perceptions of whether the outcome of their IT sourcing decisions met their expectations. Participants cited a variety of expectations (anticipated and hoped-for outcomes) and reasons (justifications and explanations) for their sourcing decisions. Fifteen categories of expectations/reasons for sourcing were identified (Lacity & Willcocks, 1998):

1.   Reduce IT costs

2.   Improve technology or technical service

3.   Jump on the bandwagon; outsourcing perceived as a viable, irreversible trend within their industry

4.   Focus business on core competencies; IT perceived as non-core

5.   Restructure IT budgets from capital budgets to fixed operating budgets

6.   Play good corporate citizen; IT managers perceive an outsourcing evaluation demonstrates their willingness to subordinate the good of IT department for the good of the overall business

7.   Focus internal IT staff on critical IT activities, such as development, while outsourcing more stable and predictable IT activities, such as data center operations

8.   Prove efficiency; invite bids to receive a free benchmark

9.   Eliminate an IT burden; assume a vendor will solve problematic IT function(s)

10.   Downsizing — the entire company is pressured to reduce headcount

11.   Preemptive move by IT managers to expose exaggerated claims made to senior executives by consultants or vendors

12.   Improve cost controls

13.   Forced market testing by the government

14.   Justify new IT resources by bundling capital budget requests with a kind of proof that vendors cannot do it cheaper

15.   Facilitate mergers and acquisitions — vendors are perceived as experts in merging data centers quickly.

Each participant's expectations/reasons were mapped into the 15 chosen categories. In many instances, participants stated more than one expectation/reason. The ranking from one to 15 was based on total responses from participants.

Global outsourcing's defenders list a number of arguments in favor of outsourcing. Arguments in favor of outsourcing can be broken down to five areas: concentration on core business development by firms, cost control, access to state of the art technology, market discipline through greater transparency, and added flexibility to respond to demand changes (Clott, 2004).

While literature on outsourcing has often sought to draw lessons from highly visible companies that have been successful in outsourcing, Barthélemy (2003) in his article on "The seven deadly sins of outsourcing" sheds light on failed efforts. Failed outsourcing endeavors are rarely reported because firms are reluctant to publicize them. Firms do not like to report their failures because such information can damage their reputation.

Barthélemy's (2003) study was based on in-depth analysis of 91 outsourcing efforts carried out by European and North American firms. Through his survey, he found that the same mistakes underlie most failed outsourcing efforts. These mistakes have been termed the seven deadly sins of outsourcing:

1.   *Outsourcing activities that should not be outsourced.* Determining which activities can be best performed by outside vendors requires a good understanding of where the firm's competitive advantage comes from. Resources and capabilities that are valuable, rare, difficult to imitate, and difficult to substitute can be employed to create superior performance. Activities that are based on such resources and capabilities (i.e., core activities) should not be outsourced because firms risk loosing competitive advantage and becoming hollow corporations.

2.   *Selecting the wrong vendor.* Selecting a good vendor is crucial for successful outsourcing. The literature has identified numerous criteria for successful provider choice. A useful distinction can be made between hard and soft qualifications. Hard qualifications are tangible and can be easily verified by due diligence. They refer to the ability of vendors to provide low-cost and state-of-the-art solutions. Important criteria also include business experience and financial strength. Soft qualifications are attitudinal. They may be non-verifiable and may change depending on circumstances. Important soft criteria include a good cultural fit, a commitment to continuous improvement, flexibility, and a commitment to develop long-term relationships.

3.   *Writing a poor contract.* Since the 1980s, vendor partnerships have emerged as a model of purchasing excellence. Partnerships replace market competition by close and trust-based relationships with a few selected vendors. The notion that outsourcing vendors are partners and that contracts play a minor role was

popularized by early outsourcing deals. However, there are pitfalls in partnership management. A good contract is essential to outsourcing success because the contract helps establish a balance of power between the client and the vendor. Spending too little time negotiating the contract and pretending that the partnership relationship with the vendor will take care of everything is a mistake. Drafting a good contract is always important because it allows partners to set expectations and to commit themselves to short-term goals.

4. *Overlooking personnel issues.* The efficient management of personnel issues is crucial because employees generally view outsourcing as an underestimation of their skills. This may result in a massive exodus even before an actual outsourcing decision has been made. Firms that contemplate outsourcing must face two interrelated personnel issues. First, key employees must be retained and motivated. Second, the commitment of employees transferred to the vendor must also be secured.

5. *Loosing control over the outsourced activity.* When the performance quality of an activity is low, managers are often tempted to outsource it. If poor performance is attributable to factors such as insufficient scale economies or a lack of expertise, outsourcing makes sense. If poor performance is attributable to poor management, outsourcing is not necessarily the right solution. For an outsourcing client, it is particularly important to avoid losing control over an outsourced activity. It is critical to keep the outsourced activity in alignment with the overall corporate strategy. While vendor management skills are very important, they must also be complemented with technical skills. If no one in the company is able to assess technological developments, outsourcing is bound to fail.

6. *Overlooking hidden costs of outsourcing.* Outsourcing clients are generally confident that they can assess whether or not outsourcing results in cost savings. However, they often overlook costs that can seriously threaten the viability of outsourcing efforts. Transaction cost economics suggests two main types of outsourcing hidden costs. First, outsourcing vendor search and contracting costs are costs of gathering information to identify and assess suitable vendors and costs of negotiating and writing the outsourcing contract. Second, outsourcing vendor management costs include monitoring the agreement to ensure that vendors fulfill their contractual obligations, bargaining with vendors and sanctioning them when they do not perform according to the contract and negotiating changes to the contract when unforeseen circumstances arise.

7. *Failing to plan an exit strategy.* Many managers are reluctant to anticipate the end of an outsourcing contract. Therefore, they often fail to plan an exit strategy (i.e., vendor switch or reintegration of an outsourced activity). Outsourcing relationships can be viewed on a continuum. At one end are long-term relationships where investments specific to the relationship have been made by one or both partners. There is a considerable advantage in re-contracting with the same vendor because switching vendors or reintegrating the outsourced activity is very difficult. At the other end are market relationships where the client has a choice of many vendors and the ability to switch vendors with little cost and inconvenience. In this case, there is no real advantage in re-contracting with the same vendor.

Vendor Value Proposition

The value generation potential of an outsourcing relationship consists of three factors: client characteristics, the vendor-client relationship, and vendor characteristics. A key client characteristic is an understanding of how to manage resources that a firm does not own. A key in the vendor-client relationship is formal (contractual) aspects of the relationship.

The third factor shaping the outsourcing value proposition is the vendor's own capabilities. From an outsourcing vendor's perspective, there are many potential opportunities and benefits for the client. These opportunities and benefits can be derived from the IT outsourcing vendor's value proposition. Important vendor characteristics include capabilities such as technical competence, understanding of the customer's business, and relationship management. Our presentation and discussion in the following text of this third factor in terms of vendor value proposition is based on a research article by Levina and Ross (2003).

To date, most research on information technology outsourcing concludes that firms decide to outsource IT services because they believe that outside vendors possess production cost advantages. Yet it is not clear whether vendors can provide production cost advantages, particularly to large firms who may be able to replicate vendors' production cost advantages in-house. Mixed outsourcing success in the past decade calls for a closer examination of the IT outsourcing vendor's value proposition.

According to Levina and Ross (2003), the concepts of *complementaries* and *competencies* explain that outsourcing vendors can increase productivity and reduce costs on client projects by applying a set of complementary application management competencies. This is the vendor value proposition.

The concept of complementarity posits that firms can improve productivity by engaging in complementary activities where benefits from doing more of one activity increase if the firm is also doing more of the other activity. This concept of complementarity has been used in studies of manufacturing to show that modern manufacturing approaches work as a system, rather than as a set of independent factors. Those firms that invest simultaneously in several complementary activities perform better than those firms that increase the level of some of these activities, but not others. In fact, literature on complementarity argues that firms that increase one factor without also increasing complementary factors may be worse off than firms that keep the factors at the same lower level.

An outsourcing vendor may develop different competencies. In the case study by Levina and Ross (2003), the vendor developed a set of three competencies to respond to client needs and market demands: personnel development, methodology development and dissemination, and customer relationship management:

- *IT personnel development* addressed existing IT labor market constraints by the vendor in ways that the client had not. The vendor replaced experienced, high-cost client staff with mostly lower-cost, junior programmers and then developed their skills through training, mentoring, and team-based project work. Junior staff valued the professional growth while their mentors often relished opportunities to watch somebody take off. As a professional services firm, the vendor viewed maintenance work as a first step in a career development path, which involved rotating professionals within engagements, assigning personnel development managers, and creating both technical and management hierarchies.

- *Methodology development and dissemination* was necessary for consistent delivery of best of breed solutions to client problems. Whereas the client's staff focused on addressing users' immediate needs, the vendor introduced methodologies that focused on overall operational improvements on projects. The vendor had a long history of methodology development. The methodologies not only specified processes, they also standardized project documentation through forms and templates such as change request forms, lost time logs, and weekly status report forms, to closely monitor project status.

- *Customer relationship management* was formalized through level of service agreements. Each agreement set a fixed price for agreed-upon services. The major philosophy of outsourcing was that the vendor is taking a risk. The vendor is responsible for whatever is defined in that client interface document as being the vendor's responsibility. While agreements might not lead to greater user satisfaction with the level of IT services, it did reduce uncertainty, thereby creating clearer expectations and an acceptance of limits. As users accepted these limits, they recognized and appreciated services that exceeded contract requirements.

These three competencies turned out to be complementary by being mutually reinforcing. Management practices targeted at one competency tended to enhance the other competencies as well. This reinforcing pattern was apparent in all three pairings of the competencies:

- *Personnel development and methodology development and distribution are complementary competencies.* The methodology competency reinforced personnel development by helping junior staff learn quickly what they were expected to do. While methodologies were sometimes viewed as constraining individual initiative, one junior consultant argued that the methodology empowered her and others to challenge management directives that might be inconsistent with documented practices. In addition, standardization of practices around methodology facilitated staff rotations and scheduling. In the same way, personnel development practices, such as skill development, rotations, and promotion policies, provided training, encouragement, and incentives that led to consistent use and improvement of methodologies across the organization.

- *Methodology development and distribution and customer relationship are complementary competencies.* When methodology delivered operational improvements, the vendor could sometimes increase service levels with no added cost to the client. In some cases, the vendor had been able to pull people off a project and had elected to share the savings with the client. These very visible improvements in IT service levels reinforced the customer relationship. Methodological approaches also improved customer relationship management practices by defining and standardizing best practices for creating and managing level of service agreements. The customer relationship management competence similarly reinforced the methodology competence. The vendor regularly communicated with the client to discuss issues and expectations, and one outcome was to help the client managers understand the methodologies so that they could facilitate, rather than hinder, the vendor's ability to meet expectations. Thus, client managers shared their knowledge of systems with the vendor and provided early warnings, where possible, when business or corporate IT changes might have an impact on the vendor's responsibilities.

- *Personnel development and customer relationship are complimentary competencies.* Personnel development practices reinforced customer relationships by ensuring that staff understood and accepted accountability for meeting contractual obligations. Personnel development practices also developed communication skills to help staff establish customer expectations and build trust. At the same time, strong customer relationships led to better buy-in, on the customer's part, to personnel development policies that required release time or movement of personnel, such as training programs, mentoring, and job rotations.

The concepts of complementaries and core competencies explain that the vendor can increase productivity and reduce costs on client projects by applying this set of complementary application management competencies. Levina and Ross (2003) examined how the vendor delivers value to clients as a result of its ability to develop complementary competencies. First, they went beyond neoclassical economics theory to explain why potential clients are unlikely to develop these complementary competencies internally. They then explored the mechanisms that ensure that the benefits of the vendor's competencies are, in part, passed on to clients.

- *Why clients do not replicate and apply vendors' competencies.* Typically, clients have a different set of market structures and resource constraints than the IT services industry. Accordingly, clients have a different organization and different business processes. Clients have hired personnel to address the market conditions and customer demands of their industry. Clients can attempt to build IT application competencies rather than outsource to vendors, but, unlike vendors, they may find that optimizing the development and application of IT competencies will conflict with optimizing core business activities. Vendors, on the other hand, can shield themselves from these conflicts through the structure provided by contracts, which specify deliverables rather than levels of investment in competencies.

   For example, to address labor market constraints, clients could increase the compensation of technical specialists, but non-IT workers might perceive the inflated IT salaries as unfair. Similarly, clients are typically not as well positioned as vendors to institute an IT personnel career development office or a practice of IT personnel rotation and promotion.

- *Why vendors share productivity gains with clients.* From the client perspective, the vendor's value proposition would not exist if the benefits of complementary competencies accrued solely to the vendor. Contract-based, interpersonal, and reputation-based mechanisms encourage vendors to share advantages with clients. Clients may deploy some contract-based mechanisms including pilot projects, multi-phased contracting with penalties, interpersonal relationship building, carrot and stick incentives and short-term contracts, and competent contract monitoring. All of these mechanisms increase client control and motivate vendors to demonstrate value to the client. Since the value of outsourcing to the client is very hard to measure, most researchers have focused on client satisfaction.

Reputation-based mechanisms provide vendors with a strong incentive to share productivity gains with clients. IT service vendors focus on reputation building in their relationships with clients. In addition to their current contracting structure, vendors care about their long-term market position. Thus, the vendor is inclined to share benefits with the client so that the information about the vendor's contribution enables it to win future contracts. Developing a solid industry reputation helps a vendor win new, and extend existing, engagements, which lead to the acquisition of, and control over, more projects.

Knowledge-intensive service firms like outsourcing vendors are typical value shops, and such firms depend on reputation for success, as reputation is a key driver of firm value creation. Reputation is a relational concept, in the sense that firms are judged by their stakeholders relative to their competitors. Reputation is what is generally said or believed about an entity by someone, it is the net perception of a firm held by stakeholders judged relative to other firms. According to Sheehan (2002), there are four conditions, which must be present for reputation to work. Firstly, rents earned from maintaining a good reputation must be greater than not. Secondly, there must be a minimum of contact among stakeholders to allow for the changes in reputation to be communicated. Thirdly, there needs to be a possibility of repeat business. Lastly, there must be some uncertainty regarding the firm's type and/or behavior.

Reputation is related to the asymmetry of information, which is a typical feature of knowledge-intensive service firms. Asymmetry is present when clients believe the firm knows something that the clients do not and believe it is necessary to know to solve their problems.

Reputation can be classified as a strategic resource in knowledge-intensive firms. To be a strategic resource, it has to be valuable, rare, and costly to imitate, and possible to organize. Reputation is valuable as it increases the value received by the client. Reputation is rare as by definition only a few firms can be considered best in the industry. Reputation is costly to imitate, as it is difficult to build a reputation in the short run. Reputation is possible to organize in the general sense of controllability, which implies that a firm can be organized to take advantage of reputation as a resource.

The vendor's strategy and practices are depicted in Figure 2.2. This model of the IT vendor's value proposition suggests that client needs, as shaped by market constraints, specify the requirements for client satisfaction. Client satisfaction results from services provided by vendors through the application of a complementary set of core competencies targeted at delivering higher service at a lower marginal cost.

Figure 9.1. Vendor's value proposition (adapted from Levina & Ross, 2003)

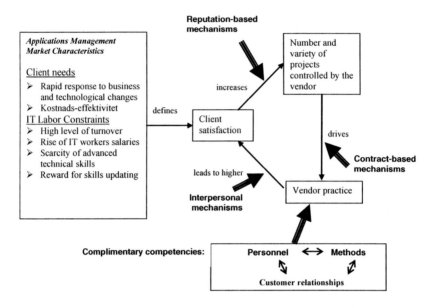

Client satisfaction is achieved in Figure 9.1 when the application of core competencies to projects is enabled by healthy client-vendor relationship, which is in part influenced by the vendor's expertise in managing client relationships. Competencies, in turn, grow through the vendor's firm-wide experience gained from controlling a large number and variety of projects, which, in turn, grow due to the reputation the vendor, develops through its ability to satisfy customers. The model represents a set of positive feedback loops, which will result in negative outcomes if, for example, the competencies do not match client needs.

Outsourcing Phases

Lacity and Willcocks (2000) identified six outsourcing phases. In these phases, a variety of stakeholders are involved, such as customer senior business managers, customer senior IT managers, customer IT staff, IT users, supplier senior managers, supplier account managers, supplier IT staff, and subcontractors. Stakeholder relationships vary during activities within phases, depending on goal alignment. For each of the phases, Lacity and Willcocks (2000) defined the major stakeholder goals, interactions, and outcomes witnessed in practice.

Phase 1: Vision

The customer goal in this first phase is to create a strategic vision of IT sourcing. The two main activities in this phase are identifying core IT capabilities and identifying IT activities for potential outsourcing. Typically, the customer senior business managers and customer senior IT managers are the primary stakeholders involved during this initial phase. Senior business managers have agendas prompted by financial pressures. Such pressures often lead to a core competency strategy by which the organization focuses on the core and downsized or outsourced rest. Because many senior business managers view much of IT as a non-core competency, they regularly question whether some or all of the IT function can be potentially outsourced.

Phase 2: Evaluation

The customer goal in this phase is to identify the best source for IT activities. The major activities during this phase include measuring baseline services and costs, creating a request for proposal, developing evaluation criteria, and inviting internal and external bids.

Phase 3: Negotiation

The customer goal in this phase is to negotiate a contract to ensure sourcing expectations are realized. The following activities may be included in this phase: conduct due diligence to verify claims in the request for proposals, negotiate service-level agreements for all IT services, create customer-supplier responsibility matrixes for all defined responsibilities, price all defined units of work, negotiate terms for transfer of employees, and agree on mechanisms for contractual change, including benchmarking, open-book accounting, non-exclusively clauses, and pricing schedules.

Phase 4: Transition

Customer goal in this phase is to establish precedents for operational performance. On large contracts, transition activities may last from 18 months to more than 2 years.

Phase 5: Improvement

Customer goal in this phase is to achieve value-added above or beyond operational performance. Customers seek to adapt and to improve the contract beyond the baseline. Cost reduction, service improvement, and more strategic views of IT service delivery are sought. The major activities in this phase include benchmarking performance, realigning the contract, and involving the supplier in value-added areas. Because of the history of working with the supplier, parties during the middle phase are typically comfortable changing hats from adversaries to cooperators to collaborators, depending on the task. By the middle phase, the complexity of relationships has become second nature, although the relational climate depends on how the overall outsourcing arrangement is turning out.

Phase 6: Performance

Customer goal in the mature phase is to determine and plan for the fate of current sourcing options. During the mature phase, the customer's goal is first to ensure continued operational performance if the relationship is not to be renewed. When relationships are extended, the mature phase provides an opportunity to learn from past experiences as well as to explore creative options when constructing a new deal. Assessment of these options depends as much on business strategic concerns and the nature of the current and future competitive climate as on the strength of relationships and past value of the outsourcing arrangement.

Chapter X

Sourcing Markets

IT Infrastructure Sourcing

According to Gartner (2004b), IT infrastructure consolidation and standardization characterized the largest multibillion IT outsourcing contracts during 2003 and 2004 and are expected to continue for the next several years. These contracts are not just exercises in cost reduction necessitated by economic doldrums, but they are also intended to advance clients toward becoming enterprises that are more efficient.

The foundation of an IT portfolio is the firm's information technology infrastructure. This internal IT infrastructure is composed of four elements as was illustrated in Figure 2.3. The presentation of Weill and Vitale's (2002) work on infrastructure services indicated the number and complexity of services that constitute the IT infrastructure in an organization to enable electronic business. Successfully implementing e-business initiatives depends on having the necessary IT infrastructure in place. E-business initiatives can be decomposed into their underlying atomic e-business models, which can have quite different IT infrastructure requirements.

It is important for outsourcing vendors providing IT infrastructure services to understand which atomic e-business models are represented in the firm's anticipated e-business initiative. Senior customer management has to design a process to involve vendor management in e-business strategizing, both to get IT input into business strategy and to provide the vendor with an early warning of what infrastructure services will be critical.

A conservative estimate for the extent of commoditization of adoption of real-time delivery offerings is about 5 percent of the total IT infrastructure outsourcing market. This is conservatively forecast to grow to about 20 percent within the next five years. Liberal estimates would be 10 to 30 percent.

Business process outsourcing is the factor likely to have the greatest influence over commoditization and maturity of IT infrastructure outsourcing. Business process outsourcing may largely eliminate the IT element in decision making for business unit managers and corporate-level executives looking for cost reduction. Enterprises are more likely to have separate IT and business process contracts than a business process contract that subsumes IT, but this is expected to shift over time with business process outsourcing maturity (Gartner, 2004b).

The creation and maintenance of a robust, enterprise-wide IT infrastructure might distinguish firms' ability to utilize IT. IT infrastructure is a critical resource of the firm. A more sophisticated infrastructure might represent a competitive advantage. IT infrastructure sophistication refers to the extent to which a firm has diffused key information technologies into its base foundation for supporting business applications. Theoretically, the resource-based view regards IT infrastructure as a strategic option. An option is a resource, whose possession enables firms to exploit emerging opportunities better than its competitors. Firms holding stronger options are positioned to obtain greater organizational advantage and create superior products and services from those assets (Armstrong & Sambamurthy, 1999).

Sophisticated infrastructure enhances the business degree of freedom by enhancing intra-organizational connectivity (across departmental units throughout the enterprise) and extra-organizational connectivity (with key external business partners). Further, a sophisticated infrastructure provides the flexibility to alter business strategies in response to competitive pressures (Armstrong & Sambamurthy, 1999).

IT Infrastructure as a Resource

One reason for outsourcing is access to resources. According to the resource-based theory of the firm, outsourcing is a strategic decision, which can be used to fill gaps in the firm's resources and capabilities (Grover, Teng et al., 1998). While the resource-based approach traditionally focuses on an internal analysis, a resource dependency theory focuses on the external environment of a firm and argues that all organizations find themselves dependent on some elements in their external environments.

The central tenet in resource-based theory is that unique organizational resources of both tangible and intangible nature are the real source of competitive advantage. With resource-based theory, organizations are viewed as a collection of resources that are heterogeneously distributed within and across industries. Accordingly, what makes the performance of an organization distinctive is the unique bland of the resources it possesses. A firm's resources include not only its physical assets such as plant and location but also its competencies. The ability to leverage distinctive internal and external competencies relative to environmental situations ultimately affects the performance of the business (Peppard et al., 2000).

Exploring competencies in the context of the management of information technology is a relatively recent development in the evolution of the information systems discipline. The importance of developing competencies that allow organizations to take success-fully advantage of information in their specific context has been noted. The concept of competence in the information systems literature is predominantly focused upon indi-vidual competence in the form of IT skill sets rather than treated as an organizational construct. The focus has been on the technology supply side and individuals' skills, emphasizing the requirement for IT professionals to have not just technical skills but also business and interpersonal skills (Peppard et al., 2000).

More recently, change agentry as a skill for IT professionals has been proposed. The implication of this literature stream is that the solution to the problem of lacking benefits from IT can be solved by equipping IT specialists with additional skills. The inference is that the inability to deliver value from information arises from shortcomings in the IT function and among IT professionals (Peppart et al., 2000).

Outsourcing gives a client organization access to resources in the vendor organization as the vendor handles IT functions for the client. Vendor resources can produce innovation, which is essential for long-term survival of the client. Quinn (2000) argues that the time is right for outsourcing innovation. Four powerful forces are currently driving the innovation revolution. First, demand is growing fast in the global economy, creating a host of new specialist markets sufficiently large to attract innovation. Second, the supply of scientists, technologists, and knowledge workers has skyrocketed, as have knowledge bases and the access to them. Third, interaction capabilities have grown. Fourth, new incentives have emerged.

Transformational outsourcing is an emerging practice to bring new capabilities to the organization (Linder, 2004). Resources are required to bring new capabilities, and resources bringing new capabilities can be found in an outsourcing vendor.

In this context, we apply the knowledge-based view of the firm that has established itself as an important perspective in strategic management. This perspective builds on the resource-based theory of the firm. According to the resource-based theory of the firm, performance differences across firms can be attributed to the variance in the firms' resources and capabilities. Resources that are valuable, unique, and difficult to imitate can provide the basis for firms' competitive advantages. In turn, these competitive advantages produce positive returns. According to Hitt et al. (2001), most of the few empirical tests of the resource-based theory that have been conducted have supported positive, direct effects of resources.

Slack Resources

Any analysis of outsourcing will typically incorporate the effects of managerial discre-tionary power on substantive administrative choices. Inclusion of managerial-behav-ioral factors to understanding outsourcing is consistent with the view of managerial choices to be the primary link between an organization and its environment (Ang, 1993).

The importance of managerial discretion in the operations of the firm has been widely acknowledged in organization theory. In general, the separation of ownership from control of the firm gives rise to problems of controlling managerial behavior. It can be emphasized that when ownership is thinly spread over a large number of shareholders in a firm, control lies in the hands of the managers who themselves own only a tiny fraction of the firm's equity. These circumstances permit managers greater discretion and decision latitude over substantive domains such as resource allocation, administrative choices, and product market selection (Ang, 1993).

Organizations with abundant slack tend to induce greater managerial discretion. Slack is defined as the difference between total resources and total necessary payments. It refers to the excess that remains once a firm has paid its various internal and external constituencies to maintain their cooperation. Slack can further be defined as a cushion of excess resources available in an organization that will either solve many organization problems or facilitate the pursuit of goals outside the realm of those dictated by optimization principles. An organization's slack reflects its ability to adapt to unknown or uncertain future changes in its environment. Accordingly, uncommitted or transferable slack resources would expand the array of options available to management (Ang, 1993).

Instead of distributing slack resources back to shareholders, managers tend to retain and invest slack resources in new employees, new equipment, and other assets to promote asset capitalization. One primary reason for retaining earnings within the organization is that increased asset capitalization, the primary indicator of firm size, enhances the social prominence, public prestige, and political power of senior executives (Ang, 1993).

Investments in IT represent a major approach to asset capitalization in organizations. IT may symbolize firm growth, advancement, and progress. Because investments in IT can promote social prominence and public prestige, managers are induced to utilize slack resources to internalize IS services. Inducements toward investments in in-house IS services are further reinforced by well-publicized case studies that demonstrate the competitive advantage and new business opportunities afforded by IT (Ang, 1993).

The above reasoning suggests that managers may exhibit a penchant for building up internal IT resources such as IS employees, equipment, and computer capacity when organizations possess slack resources. In contrast, when slack resources are low, managers tend to conserve resources in response to the anxiety provoked by loss of financial resources. Anxiety is provoked because the loss of financial resources is often attributed to managerial incompetence and organizational ineffectiveness. As a result, leaders are more likely to be blamed and replaced when financial performance is poor. In response to the anxiety provoked by loss of financial resources, decision makers have been observed to reduce costs through downsizing the company by selling off physical assets and laying off workers (Ang, 1993).

Companies may even sell IT assets at inflated rates to external service providers to generate short-term financial slack. The companies then reimburse the service provider by paying higher annual fees for a long-term outsourcing contract lasting eight to ten years. In other words, long-term facilities management contracts can be drawn where the service providers agree to purchase corporate assets, such as computer equipment, at prices substantially higher than the market value and to provide capital to the company by purchasing stock from the company. Arrangements such as these permit companies to maintain capital, defer losses on the disposition of assets, and at the same time, show an increase in financial value on the balance sheet. But, because these arrangements also involve companies paying higher fees over the life of the contract, company financial statements are thus artificially inflated and do not reflect the true financial picture of the institution (Ang, 1993).

Accordingly, when slack resources are low, we would expect firms to downsize internal IS services by selling off IT assets, and reducing IS personnel and occupancy expenses; in effect, outsourcing IS services. Thus, we would expect that firms are less likely to outsource when slack resources are high and more likely to outsource when slack resources are low (Ang, 1993).

Besides managerial discretion over slack resources, top management's perception of the criticality of IT may differ. According to the dependence-avoidance perspective of the firm, organizations will avoid comprising their autonomy, particularly when the resource is vital for the organization's survival. The strength of an organization's aversion to loss of autonomy is thus a function of the criticality of the resource. The organization will proactively struggle to avoid external dependency, that is, outsourcing, regardless of efficiency considerations as long as it depends on IT for survival. The value of IT for competitive advantage intensifies the pressure on firms to internalize sophisticated IS services to avoid leakage of competitive information (Ang, 1993).

Although it is generally accepted that IT is critical for information-intensive firms, not all members of top management teams attach the same degree of criticality to IT. Perceptions of the CIO's and CEOs of IT importance tend to be misaligned. While CIO's recognize IT as vital to an organization's strategy, CEOs with little background in IT tend to regard IS services as back-room operations, an expense to be controlled, rather than a strategic investment to be capitalized. Generally, CEOs' perceptions of IT criticality are as important as, if not more important than, those of the CIOs' with respect to IS sourcing decisions because IS investments represent a significant financial outlay for corporations. Sometimes management policies and direction of IT use are dictated by the CEOs' psychological involvement and participation in IS. Thus, we would expect that the greater the perceived criticality of IT to the firm, the less likely the firm will outsource its IS services (Ang, 1993).

Company Boundaries

Researchers have for many years sought to understand better why companies adopt different modes of governance. The resource-based view of the firm focuses on the opportunity for gain from transactions. A technology's potential for rendering a sustained competitive advantage will influence governance modes for external technology sourcing. The fundamental tenets of a resource-based perspective suggest a positive relationship between the perceived opportunity for sustainable advantage and the probability that a company will source technology with an acquisition from external sources (Steensma & Corly, 2001).

Sourcing technology from outside the organization changes company boundary between the firm that desires the know-how (the sourcing firm) and the firm that has the technology (the source firm). Managers must assess the governance alternatives for procuring desired technological know-how. According to classical decision theory, strategic decisions such as these entail a trade-off between risk and expected return, where risk is conceptualized as the variance of the probability distribution of the gains and losses of a particular alternative (Steensma & Coorly, 2001).

Steensma and Corley (2001) investigated organizational context as a moderator of theories on firm boundaries for technology sourcing. They found that the resource-based rationale, grounded on the opportunity to develop sustainable advantages, plays a larger role in explaining firm boundaries when a firm has lower levels of recoverable slack and a risk-seeking orientation than when a firm has higher slack and risk averseness. Organizational slack is defined as an organization's excess resources, while firm risk orientation is defined as expected outcome uncertainty (Steensma & Corley, 2001).

Contingency Model

Grover, Teng et al. (1998) developed a contingency model for IT outsourcing. Structural contingency theory has dominated the study of organizational design and performance during the past twenty years. It is the perspective underlying the prescribed dual approach to strategic analysis: environmental threats and opportunities analysis, and organizational strengths and weaknesses. Contingency perspectives indicate that the appropriateness of different strategies depend on the competitive setting of business. Further, the perspectives rest on the belief that no universal set of strategic choices exists that is optimal for all businesses, irrespective of their resource positions and environmental context. Thus, effective strategies are those that achieve a fit or congruence between environmental conditions and organizational factors.

The basic premise of contingency theory is that outsourcing strategy is only one of several types of economic restructuring by which an organization adapts to the environment. Therefore, there are situations under which outsourcing may or may not be appropriate. Figure 10.1 puts together the variety of contingency variables, including resource dimensions discussed earlier (Grover, Teng et al., 1998):

- *Resource base* emphasizes the necessity of critical IT resources and capabilities.

- *Resource dependence*, though emphasizing that much organizational action is determined by environmental conditions, recognizes the possibility of intentional adaptation to environmental conditions through management actions.

- *Agency costs* are based on agency cost theory that examines the reasons for principal-agent relationships and the problems inherent in them. An agency relationship can be defined as a contract under which one or more persons — principal(s) — engage another person — the agent — to perform some service on their behalf, which involves delegating some decision-making authority to the agent. Agency costs in terms of monitoring, bonding, and residual loss increase in outsourcing relationships with high uncertainty, high-risk aversion, low programmability, low outcome measurability, and greater length of relationship.

- Transaction costs are based on transaction cost theory that maintains that the organization of economic activity depends on balancing production economics, such as scale, against the cost of transacting. Transaction costs in terms of negotiating, monitoring, and enforcing contracts increase in outsourcing relationships by lower asset specificity, higher uncertainty, and lower frequency of contracting.

Activity-Based Theory of the Firm

The goal of strategy formulation in the resource-based theory is to identify and increase those resources that allow a firm to gain and sustain superior rents. Firms owning strategic resources are predicted to earn superior rents, while firms possessing no or few strategic resources are thought to earn industry average rents or below average rents. The goal of strategy formulation in the activity-based theory is to identify and explore drivers that allow a firm to gain and sustain superior rents. Drivers are a central concept in the activity-based theory. To be considered drivers, firm level factors must meet three criteria: they are structural factors at the level of activities, they are more or less controllable by management, and they affect the cost and/or differentiation position of the firm. The definition of drivers is primarily based on what drivers do. Drivers are abstract, relative, and relational properties of activities. For example, scale of an activity is a driver, as the size of the activity relative to competitors may represent a competitive advantage.

The analytical focus of the resource-based theory is potentially narrower than that of the activity-based theory. While the activity-based theory takes the firm's entire activity set as its unit of analysis, the resource-based theory focuses on individual resources or bundles of resources. Having a narrower focus means that the resource-based theory may not take into account the negative impact of resources, how a resource's value may change as the environment changes, or the role of non-core resources in achieving competitive advantage.

Figure 10.1. Contingency factors for outsourcing decisions

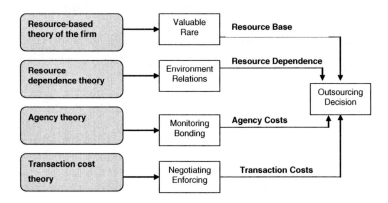

The activity-based and resource-based theories are similar as they both attempt to explain how firms attain superior positions through factors that increase firm differentiation or lower firm cost. While drivers and resources share a common goal of achieving and sustaining superior positions, the manner by which they are seen to reach a profitable position is different. With the resource-based theory, it is the possession or control of strategic resources that allow a firm to gain a profitable position. On the other hand, drivers within the activity-based theory are not unique to the firm. They are generic, structural factors, which are available to all firms in the industry, in the sense that they are conceptualized as properties of the firm's activities. A firm gains a profitable position by configuring its activities using drivers. It is this position that a firm may own, but only if it is difficult for rivals to copy the firm's configuration.

The sustainability of superior positions created by configuring drivers or owning resources is based on barriers to imitation. The sustainability of competitive advantage as per the activity-based theory is through barriers to imitation at the activity level. If the firm has a competitive advantage, as long as competitors are unable to copy the way activities are performed and configured through the drivers, the firm should be able to achieve above average earnings over an extended period. The sustainability of superior profitability in the resource-based theory is through barriers to imitation of resources and immobility of resources. If resources are easily copied or substituted then the sustainability of the position is suspect.

Sheehan (2002) concludes his discussion by finding similarities between the resource-based theory and the activity-based theory. Resources in the resource-based theory are similar to drivers in the activity-based theory as both are based on earning efficiency rents. Furthermore, capabilities in the resource-based theory are similar to activities in the activity-based theory as both imply action.

Business Application Sourcing

Dramatically reduced network cost due to the Internet and virtual private networks, the ever-increasing supply of bandwidth, and advances in the security of Internet based transactions have led to the emergence of application service providers (ASPs), a new category of IT service firms. ASP can be defined as an organization that manages and delivers application capabilities to multiple entities from a data center across a wide area network. User organizations can get access to software applications from one or more ASPs over the Internet for a subscription fee (Susarla et al., 2003).

In a typical business, we find several information systems applications. For example, Weill and Vitale (1999) identified an applications portfolio of 18 systems in a manufacturing business: budgeting, capital projects, customer complaints, debtors, general ledger, freight cost management, fixed assets, human resource management, inventory, market data, multi-plant accounting, office support, payroll management, pricing & sales, purchasing, sales forecasting, product safety system, and trading accounts management. These systems support tasks in peoples' jobs. For example, all systems help planning, investigating, coordinating, evaluating, supervising, staffing, negotiating, and representing to a varying extent.

User organizations can get access to software applications from one or more ASPs over the Internet for a subscription fee. A key selling point for ASP services involves a shorter time required to implement new software applications. For businesses plagued by high turnover of information technology staff, inadequate organizational resources to maintain and upgrade existing IT applications, and large capital requirements for major IT implementation projects, the ASP business model could be an attractive alternative with its off-the-shelf IT applications subscription approach. Sophisticated ASPs have gone as far as offering enterprise resource planning, electronic commerce, and supply chain applications, which may involve integration with existing information systems in a user organization (Susarla et al., 2003).

While the ASP model has the potential to change fundamentally the manner in which IT services are provided to user firms, to date ASPs have had a limited success in signing up customers. Moreover, several customers of ASPs are unsatisfied with their service, which questions the viability of the ASP business model and selection of ASP as an enter strategy for IT outsourcing. Evidence points also to the fact that ASPs themselves have to rework their service strategies in response to market demand. It has been long recognized that market success depends on designing services to match customer needs and that customer satisfaction has a positive impact on market share and profitability. Satisfied customers are more likely to engage in positive word of mouth, thus lowering the cost of attracting new customers. Satisfaction based on successful exploration and exploitation of the vendor value proposition plays an important role in building other important assets for the firm. A focus on satisfaction is important for ASPs if they have to retain existing customers as well as attract new customers (Susarla et al., 2003).

This calls for an assessment of the determinants of client satisfaction with ASP and evaluation of the effectiveness of the ASP mode of service delivery over the Internet. Susarla et al. (2003) analyzed the determinants of satisfaction in ASP service provision. Their analyzes shows that the satisfaction with an ASP is negatively affected by the disconfirmation effect, but positively influenced by the perceived provider performance and prior systems integration, which is a measure of integration of organizational systems prior to using ASP services. Disconfirmation is the negative discrepancy between expectation and performance.

Further, perceived provider performance is positively influenced by the functional capability of the ASP and the quality assurance by the ASP, but negatively influenced by the prior systems integration. These findings suggest that, to be successful, ASPs must strive to reduce the disconfirmation effect faced by adopting organizations and to enhance the perceived quality of their solution, possibly through partnerships with leading IT vendors. Further, ASPs must improve the integration of their offerings with existing applications in user organizations, which may require alliances with IT firms that specialize in integration services. From a client perspective, an enter strategy of ASP selection may thus focus on integration with existing IT, performance delivery, and standards of software capability.

From a vendor perspective, the findings of Susarla et al. (2003) indicate a need for ASPs to facilitate integration with existing IT in client organizations, ensure superior performance delivery, emphasize rigorous enforcement of service agreements, and ensure that their application meets standards of software capability. Their finding that ASPs are not evaluated on some of the prior experiences of the organizations is favorable to vendors, since it suggests that firms that are Internet savvy or that have a strong IT department are not going to have unreasonably high expectations from the ASPs.

A related area of exploration is an analysis of how organizational users form expectations about an ASP's services. The literature on outsourcing posits that the trade press, discussion with peers, consultants' forecasts, and the business strategy pursued by the company can contribute to the formation of expectations in the outsourcing context. As the IT outsourcing literature has documented, management defines the scope of the outsourcing and the sourcing criteria, while the IT department can provide insights on the technological reasons for outsourcing and judge the success of the outsourcing project in terms of performance outcomes that are met. Expectations that need to be realized in the outsourcing context may reflect the consensus among the different stakeholders in the organization (Susarla et al., 2003).

Business Process Sourcing

The paradigm shift in the possibilities of communication that the Internet and the telecommunications revolution has brought about and opened up a plethora of opportunities in outsourcing business processes. Business process outsourcing involves transferring certain value contributing activities and processes to another firm to save costs, to focus on its areas of key competence, and to access resources. The possibilities of disaggregating value elements in terms of business processes for creating value in them at the vendor's premises and final aggregation and synthesis at the client organization are explored and exploited in business process outsourcing (Ramachandran & Voleti, 2004).

Business process outsourcing includes enterprise services (human resources, finance and accounting, payment services, and administration), supply management (buying processes, storing processes, and moving processes), demand management processes (customer selection, customer acquisition, customer retention, and customer extension), and operations. A typical business process outsourcing contract includes discrete project-based IT services, ongoing IT management services, and general process management (Gartner, 2004a).

Business process outsourcing often fills human resources (HR) practitioners with fear, but handled properly it can help the HR function become more efficient and strategic, according to HR (2004). Of all the business-related acronyms that are filtering through to the corporate consciousness, BPO — business process outsourcing — is certainly one that appears to be raising interest.

Business process outsourcing, although often seen as the next evolutionary step in IT outsourcing, is also very different from it. BPO is about delegating the ownership, administration, and operation of a process to a specialist third party in order to solve a business problem. And because BPO is about delivering outcomes — higher performing business processes — it aims to raise a client company's shareholder value (HR, 2004).

Business processes within a company can be broken down into three categories: core; business critical non-core; and finally non-core, non-critical. Core processes are seldom outsourced, because they are the very essence of the business and the area that requires the most investment. Critical and non-critical non-core processes may be suited for outsourcing to a third party supplier who will invest in them on the company's behalf.

Process management has the highest expected growth rate in outsourcing. Business processing outsourcing is typically the outsourcing of a company's non-core or back-office business processes. Usually those processes are IT enabled (or should be IT enabled) and hence can be transformed by the use of a new or improved technology platform. The appeal of business process outsourcing is that it therefore attempts to involve a new support services model involving cost effective, scaleable, efficient services. The growth in demand for process outsourcing has also seen an expansion in the range of services being provided by suppliers. Processes typically outsourced include finance and accounting, procurement, human resources, and real estate (Honess, 2003).

Business process outsourcing is the factor likely to have the greatest influence over commoditization and maturity of IT infrastructure outsourcing. Business process outsourcing may largely eliminate the IT element in decision making for business unit managers and corporate-level executives looking for cost reduction. Enterprises are more likely to have separate IT and business process contracts than a business process contract that subsumes IT, but this is expected to shift over time with business process outsourcing maturity (Gartner, 2004b).

Anticipating this shift in focus to business process level, outsourcing vendors such as EDS, HP and IBM have already developed strategies based on emerging real-time infrastructures and real-time delivery offerings that are positioned as enablers of real-time enterprise. Each vendor has developed its own vision for real time infrastructure, delivery, enterprise, and template, and branded its vision as follows in 2004: Agile Enterprise (EDS), Adaptive Enterprise (HP), and On Demand Business (IBM). These brands reflect a focus on business value instead of technical value. As IT infrastructure services commoditize and mature, value shifts upward to the business process level (Gartner, 2004b).

Real-time delivery offerings, whether end-to-end or point solutions, require major shifts in outsourcing contracting models, including financing, pricing, service levels, asset management, risk management and standards (Gartner, 2004b).

As of 2004, among the fastest-growing aspects of global outsourcing is business process outsourcing (BPO). BPO began as back-office process arrangements to run finance and accounting operations such as payroll, accounts payable and receivable, financial, insurance, and property accounting. These services have expanded into new areas such as call centers, with staff trained to answer and transact basic service-related areas, including order entry and credit card processing (Clott, 2004).

An important critical success factor in business process outsourcing is knowledge management. The outsourcing promise is to leverage the supplier's superior technical know-how (human capital), superior management practices (structural capital), economies of scale, and increasingly, access to strategic and business advice. This should enable the client to refocus on strategic, core capability and knowledge areas. But Willcocks et al.'s (2004) research into IT outsourcing has shown consistently over the past decade that the prospects have been disappointing for meaningful knowledge management and value creation there from:

- Most clients report their frustration from with endless cost-service debates, and sometimes significant loss of control over their IT destiny and knowledge base.

- Most vendors find it difficult to deliver on their promises of innovation and value added, because of their lack of knowledge about the client's long-term business strategy.

Typically, even on the very big, long-term deals considered strategic vendor relationships, the supplier offers technical know-how for routine solutions, with high performers in short supply. There is little influx of new technical/managerial talent, and disappointing access to the supplier's global capacity and knowledge base. Meanwhile, the client does not thoroughly think through the issues of core capability and retained knowledge. As a result, the client spends much time fire fighting and experiences little value-added or technical/business innovation. Over time, the client loses control over its IT destiny or business process destiny, as knowledge asymmetries develop in favor of the vendor.

The loss of information and knowledge can be traumatic for both outsourcing parties unless specific and purposeful steps are undertaken to develop and sustain new information pathways and capabilities. That is why the nine knowledge transfer mechanisms to be presented below, are so important for success.

In an outsourcing relationship, the vendor will need to manage its intellectual capital so that clients experience efficient and effective knowledge transfers. One of the key authors in the area of intellectual capital is Sveiby (2001) who has developed a knowledge-based theory of the firm to guide in strategy formulation. He distinguished between three families of intangible assets with the outsourcing vendor. The *external structure* family consists of relationships with customers and suppliers and the reputation (image) of the firm. Some of these relationships can be converted into legal property such as trademarks and brand names. The value of such assets in primarily influenced by how well the company solves its customers' problems, and there is always an element of uncertainty here.

The *internal structure* family consists of patents, concepts, models, and computer and administrative systems. These are created by the employees and are thus generally owned by the organization. The structure is partly independent of individuals and some of it remains even if a large number of the employees leave. *The individual competence* family consists of the competence of the professional staff, the experts, the research and development people, the factory workers, sales and marketing — in short, all those that have a direct contact with customers and whose work are within the business idea.

Competence is a term introduced here. Competence can be defined as the sum of knowledge, skills, and abilities at the individual level. With this definition, we say that knowledge is part of competence, and competence is part of intellectual capital.

Figure 10.2. Knowledge transfer within and between families of intangible assets

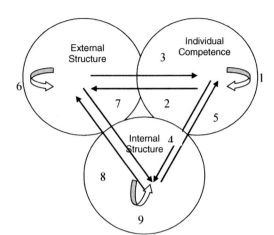

These three families of intangible resources have slightly different definitions when compared to the capital elements. The external structure seems similar to relational capital; the internal structure seems similar to structural capital, while the individual competence seems similar to human capital.

To appreciate why a knowledge-based theory of the firm can be useful for strategy formulation, Sveiby (2001) considers some of the features that differentiate knowledge transfers from tangible goods transfers. In contrast to tangible goods, which tend to depreciate when they are used, knowledge grows when used and depreciates when not used. Competence in a language or a sport requires huge investments in training to build up — managerial competence takes a long time on-the-job to learn. If one stops speaking the language, it gradually dissipates.

Given three families of intangible assets, it is possible to identify nine knowledge transfers. These knowledge transfers can occur within a family and between families as illustrated in Figure 10.2. Each of the nine knowledge transfers in Figure 10.2 can be explained as follows (Sveiby, 2001):

1. *Knowledge transfers between individuals* concern how to best enable the communication between employees within the organization. The strategic question is: how can we improve the transfer of competence between people in the organization? Activities for intellectual capital management focus on trust building, enabling team activities, induction programs, job rotation, and master/apprentice scheme.

2. *Knowledge transfers from individuals to external structure* concern how the organization's employees transfer their knowledge to the outer world. The strategic question is: how can the organization's employees improve the competence of customers, suppliers and other stakeholders? Activities for intellectual capital management focus on enabling the employees to help customers learn about the

products, getting rid of red tape, enabling job rotation with customers, holding product seminars and providing customer education.

3.   *Knowledge transfers from external structure to individuals* occur when employees learn from customers, suppliers and community feedback trough ideas, new experiences and new technical knowledge. The strategic question is: how can the organization's customers, suppliers and other stakeholders improve the competence of the employees? Activities for intellectual capital management focus on creating and maintaining good personal relationships between the organization's own people and the people outside the organization.

4.   *Knowledge transfers from competence to internal structure* concern the transformation of human capital into more permanent structural capital through documented work routines, intranets, and data repositories. The strategic question is: how can we improve the conversion individually held competence to systems, tools, and templates? Activities for intellectual capital management focus on tools, templates, process, and systems so they can be shared more easily and efficiently.

5.   *Knowledge transfers from internal structure to individual competence* are the counterpart of the above. Once competence is captured in a system, it needs to be made available to other individuals in such a way that they improve their capacity to act. The strategic question is: how can we improve individuals' competence by using systems, tools, and templates? Activities for intellectual capital management focus on improving human-computer interface of systems, action-based learning processes, simulations, and interactive e-learning environments.

6.   *Knowledge transfers within the external structure* concern what customers and others tell each other about the services of an organization. The strategic question is: how can we enable the conversations among the customers, suppliers and other stakeholders so they improve their competence? Activities for intellectual capital management focus on partnering and alliances, improving the image of the organization and the brand equity of its products and services, improving the quality of the offering, conducting product seminars and alumni programs.

7.   *Knowledge transfers from external to internal structure* concern what knowledge the organization can gain from the external world and how the learning can be converted into action. The strategic question is: how can competence from the customers, suppliers and other stakeholders improve the organization's systems, tools, processes, and products? Activities for intellectual capital management focus on empowering call centers to interpret customer complaints, creating alliances to generate ideas for new products and research and development alliances.

8.   *Knowledge transfers from internal to external structure* are the counterpart of the above. The strategic question is: how can the organization's systems, tools and processes and products improve the competence of the customers, suppliers and other stakeholders? Activities for intellectual capital management focus on making the organization's systems, tools and processes effective in servicing the customer, extranets, product tracking, help desks and e-business.

9.   *Knowledge transfers within the internal structure* where the internal structure is the backbone of the organization. The strategic question is: how can the organization's systems, tools, processes, and products be effectively integrated? Activities for intellectual capital management focus on streamlining databases, building integrated information technology systems, and improving the office layout.

In addition to these nine knowledge transfer mechanisms, the client has to retain several core capabilities. These ensure the elicitation and delivery of business requirements, the development of technical/business architecture, the managing of external supply, and the coordination and governance of these tasks. In practice, Willcocks et al. (2004) have found all too many client organizations inadequately making these critical, initial knowledge investments.

The traditional IT outsourcing approach restricts creation and leveraging of knowledge concerns only to one specialist area — IT operations. However, much bigger knowledge gains can arise if whole functions or processes that include IT are outsourced. This is the premise of the dramatic growth in business process outsourcing. The knowledge contract of BPO is to outsource IT functions to suppliers that have superior structural and human capital in the areas of business process and specific expertise. Some deals also recognize the need for closer partnering to get closer to the customer: to create and leverage relational capital to both parties' advantage.

In business process outsourcing, the most common types of processes that are being outsourced are in the areas of administration and industry-specific processes. This was the result of a survey conducted by Gartner (2004c) about the use of BPO.

Resource-Based View

The resource-based view argues that firms possess resources, a subset of which enables them to achieve competitive advantage, and a further subset that leads to superior long-term performance. Empirical studies of firm performance using the resource-based view have found differences between firms. Resources that are valuable and rare and whose benefits can be appropriated by the owning (or controlling) firm provide it with a temporary competitive advantage. That advantage can be sustained over longer time periods to the extent that the firm is able to protect against resource imitation, transfer, or substitution (Wade & Hulland, 2004).

Wade and Hulland (2004) define resources as assets and capabilities that are available and useful in detecting and responding to market opportunities or threats. Together, assets and capabilities define the set of resources available to the firm. Assets are defined as anything tangible or intangible the firm can use in its processes for creating, producing, and/or offering its products (goods or services) to a market. Capabilities are repeatable patterns of actions in the use of assets to create, produce, and/or offer products to a market. Assets can serve as inputs to a process, or as the outputs of a process. Assets can be either tangible (e.g., information systems hardware) or intangible (e.g., software licenses). Capabilities transform inputs to outputs of greater worth. Capabilities can include skills, such as technical or managerial ability, or processes, such as systems development or integration.

IT resources can be categorized in different classifications. One categorization distinguishes between IS infrastructure, IS technical skills, IS development, and cost effective IS operations (Wade & Hulland, 2004):

- *IS infrastructure* conveys no particular strategic benefit due to lack of rarity, ease of imitation, and ready mobility. Only proprietary or complex and hard to imitate infrastructures may provide some competitive advantage.

- *IS technical skills* are a result of the appropriate, updated technology skills, relating to both systems hardware and software, that are held by the IS/IT employees of a firm. Such skills do not include only current technical knowledge, but also the ability to deploy, use, and manage that knowledge. Thus, this resource is focused on technical skills that are advanced, complex, and, therefore, difficult to imitate. Although the relative mobility of IS/IT personnel tends to be high, some IS skills cannot be easily transferred, such as corporate-level knowledge assets and technology integration skills, and, thus, these resources can become a source of sustained competitive advantage. This capability is focused primarily on the present.

- *IS development* refers to the capability to develop or experiment with new technologies, as well as a general level of alertness to emerging technologies and trends that allow a firm to quickly take advantage of new advances. Thus, IS development is future oriented. IS development includes capabilities associated with managing a systems development life-cycle that is capable of supporting competitive advantage, and should therefore lead to superior firm performance.

- *Cost effective IS operations* encompasses the ability to provide efficient and cost-effective IS operations on an ongoing basis. Firms with greater efficiency can develop a long-term competitive advantage by using this capability to reduce costs and develop a cost leadership position in their industry. In the context of IS operations, the ability to avoid large, persistent cost overruns, unnecessary downtime, and system failure is likely to be an important precursor to superior performance. Furthermore, the ability to develop and manage IT systems of appropriate quality that function effectively can be expected to have a positive impact on performance.

Chapter XI

Sourcing Practices

IT Outsourcing Performance

The rapidly increasing use of outsourcing for IT services, both in the public and private sectors, has attracted much interest from researchers and practitioners alike. While early studies of IT outsourcing were largely qualitative in nature, more recent studies have attempted to analyze the outcomes achieved in quantitative terms. Domberger et al. (2000) are consistent with the latter, but goes further by modeling the price, performance, and contract characteristics that are relevant to IT outsourcing. A two-equation recursive regression model was used to analyze 48 contracts for IT support and maintenance.

The results did not reveal any quantitatively significant price-performance trade-off, but did suggest that first-term contracts (i.e., the first ever contract awarded by a client for the provision of a particular IT service) were more expensive than repeat contracts. Although competitive tendering did not result in lower prices than directly negotiated contracts, it was associated with comparatively better performance. Well-defined expectations of an organization's IT requirements were also likely to lead to improved performance when the service was outsourced.

Domberger et al. (2000) measured IT outsourcing performance by both desired performance and realized performance. Clients typically have an expectation of service quality prior to awarding a contract. This can be referred to as desired performance. A necessary part of contract management involves an assessment of the realized performance of the contract. The clients responding to the study were asked to rate the desired performance and realized performance of the contracts for each of the following eight service attributes.

1. Service availability and timeliness
2. Out-of-hours availability
3. Response in emergencies
4. Provision at expected cost
5. Delivery to expected quality
6. Accuracy of advise
7. Correctness of error fixes
8. Minimization of system downtime

The original scale for the desired and realized performance ratings was from one to four. A rating of 1 corresponded to not important for the former and unsatisfactory for the latter, while 4 corresponded to very important and excellent, respectively. Ratings that were not reported were filled with zeros to preserve the continuity of the scale on the assumption that they were considered irrelevant or very low in terms of desired or realized performance.

The eight service attributes listed were taken to represent measures of quality. For the purposes of analysis and estimation, a single quality/performance variable was sought. Here there were a number of choices. One possibility was to construct what is called principal components. The first principal component, which explained approximately 50% of the variation in the attributes, is essentially a simple average of the realized ratings. It turned out that the responses were all positively and highly correlated. Thus, the simple average of the ratings attached to the eight attributes represented a simple and readily interpretable choice for a single performance variable.

A second possibility was to consider the realized performance relative to the base, as represented by the desired performance ratings. Constructing a new set of attributes by subtracting the desired from the realized rating for each attribute and contract results in data that has as its first principal component a variable that is essentially the simple average. Once again, this accounted for approximately 50% of the variation in the data. Thus, a second possible proxy for the performance variable is the average of the eight realized minus desired attributes. Rather than choose between these alternative proxies, the results for both realized and differences were reported by Domberger et al. (2000).

Mean of the eight realized performance ratings was 2.97. This result can be interpreted as satisfactory, but not excellent, indicating that the average response by the 48 firms was that they found realized performance to be satisfactory. Mean of the realized minus desired performance ratings was -0.49. The negative mean for this performance variable indicates a slight tendency to under-perform relative to the desired levels of service quality.

IT Outsourcing Relationships

There is no easy answer to the question about what makes a relationship a partnership. Common suggestions that partnership is a close relationship are vague and do not offer much help. In order to give meaning to closeness, one has to consider the degree of integration between the buying and the selling company. The extent of integration between customer and supplier, for example expressed in terms of the specific investments made by either partner, may have an impact on the performance of the relationship (Gadde & Snehota, 2000).

In terms of specific investments made by outsourcing partners, a distinction can be made between tangible assets (buildings, tools, equipment, and processes), and intangibles (time and effort spent on learning the business partner's practices and routines). According to Gadde and Snehota (2000), there is significant evidence that the size of investments dedicated to a specific counterpart significantly correlates with practices commonly associated with strategic partnerships, such as long-term relationship, mutual trust, cooperation, and wide-scope relationships.

Focusing on integration is an important step toward a better understanding of the critical dimensions of relationships. It requires consideration of the actual behavior in relationships, rather than relying on a notion of partnerships as a matter of vaguely defined positive attitudes. We need to elaborate further on the extent of integration in relationships, and so Gadde and Snehota (2000) propose involvement as a relevant concept. Three dimensions of involvement can be distinguished that affect outcomes in relationships: coordination of activities; adaptations of resources; and interaction among individuals. The degree of involvement in the three dimensions can be referred to as activity link, resource ties, and actor bonds.

First, the activities carried out at the vendor and client companies can be more or less tightly coordinated. Examples of tight activity coordination are integrated delivery systems where the vendor and the remaining internal IT function coordinate their activity to provide superior user service. Second, the resources of the companies can be more or less specifically adapted to the requirements of the counterpart. Examples are complementary competencies. Third, the individuals in the companies may interact more or less intensely. Close interaction among individuals in the two organizations make their choices more independent and affect both commitment and trust in the relationship, which in turn affects coordination and adaptations. Some relationships score high on all three of the relationship dimensions, while others only on one or two (Gadde & Snehota, 2000).

The existence of strong links, ties, and bonds describes the degree of involvement of the companies in a relationship. Gadde and Snehota (2000) prefer the concept of involvement rather than integration, because it makes possible a distinction between vendor involvement and client involvement. In this context, high-involvement relationships are characterized by extensive activity links, resource ties, and actor bonds.

High-involvement relationships are costly because coordination, adaptation, and interaction entail costs. Increasing involvement usually means a substantial increase in relationship costs, but may, under certain circumstances, lead to lower direct transaction costs. However, the main rationale for high involvement is either to achieve cost benefits in terms of reduced costs in production, improved flexibility and service levels, or revenue benefits, for instance, through taking advantage of vendor skills and capability to improve the quality of the customer's end product. Increased involvement only makes sense when the consequently increased relationship costs are more than offset by relationship benefits. Reaping these benefits most often requires non-standardized solutions and customer specific adaptations. High-involvement relationships are associated with investment logic (Gadde & Snehota, 2000).

Low-involvement relationships have their rationales as well. They can be handled with limited coordination, adaptation, and interaction costs. Generally, this is the case when the context is stable and the content of the relationship can be standardized. In these situations, the requirements of the customer can be satisfied by use of existing solutions. This means that no specific product or service adaptations are needed, implying that resource ties are minimized. When activity coordination can be limited to standardized services, such as outsourced communication and network operations, the activity links are weak. Finally, when interaction among individuals in the two companies involved can be contained to sales and purchasing administration, the actor bonds will also be limited (Gadde & Snehota, 2000).

Due Diligence

The world of mergers and acquisitions (M&A) has learned the importance of conducting in-depth legal and financial due diligence, yet many acquisitions still fail to live up to expectations. The most common reasons actually relate to flaws in the business strategy of the acquired company rather than tangible shortcomings that the accountants and lawyers can identify. Broadening the scope of due diligence has turned out to be the answer for many private equity investors (Lislie, 2003).

A structured process of evaluating the business strategy of the target company relative to the marketplace improves the chances of any acquisition's success. An in-depth investigation of the market, competitors, customer behavior, consumer attitudes, brand, and company positioning usually sheds light on issues that provide the acquirer with increased confidence to move forward, uncover problems, which lead to a reduced price, or induce walking away. Is the target company positioned properly to capitalize on the key market drivers? How do customers really make their purchase decisions? What are their unmet needs? What are their switching costs? What is the strategy of the competition? How have they chosen to differentiate themselves? The future performance of a target company can be predicted with a higher level of accuracy by having fact-based answers to these questions and many others, not just anecdotal information (Lislie, 2003).

Lislie (2003) argues that the most successful acquirers systematically assess the qualitative aspects of their deals as the first step in the due diligence process. The core competency of the deal team of a private equity group typically revolves around making the single Go/No Go decision regarding investment, based upon the individual (and often contradictory) analyses of the various aspects of due diligence. Suppose that Legal due diligence reveals few concerns; Accounting has many concerns; Environmental has no concerns; Technical says Invest Now! The act of making the decision to invest or not, based on conflicting pieces of evidence is the real core competency.

Global Outsourcing

Kaiser and Hawk (2004) argue that there is currently an evolution of offshore software development from outsourcing and cosourcing. "Financial Insurance Services Company" (FISC) (a pseudonym) is a major U.S. financial services company with thousands of representatives across the country. "Offsource" (a pseudonym) is a leading India-based company providing consulting and IT services to clients globally. Kaiser and Hawk (2004) tell how their eight-year alliance has evolved. The relationship began as a simple pilot of offshore application development outsourcing, aimed at reducing development costs and supplementing in-house IT staff knowledge. It has evolved into a vastly more complex "cosourcing" model, where work is shared. To achieve cosourcing, the two firms had to resolve two major issues. The first was how to keep IT skills and knowledge from draining from FISC. This issue has been resolved by formally linking career development to project assignments and to outsourcer-to-client mentoring. The second issue is how to share work. It has been resolved by creating a dual project management hierarchy, where leadership at each level of a project can be either by FISC or Offsource, depending on the need.- Their experiences provide five recommendations for others on structuring offshore outsourcing relationships: (1) understand where cosourcing is applicable, (2) define and develop the appropriate in-house IT competencies, (3) build trust but avoid building a binding relationship, (4) foster mutual understanding of ethnic and corporate cultures, and (5) map out a progression to cosourcing.

Public administration is changing, and new publication management strategies include the globalization of public services production. Inside government agencies bureaushaping motivations sustain the new public management model approach and create a strong disposition towards embracing radical outsourcing, and residualizing government's implementation roles, a direction reinforced by the marketization of public services. Transnational pressures on nation states to standardize policies will powerfully erode the existing single-country distinctiveness of public service markets. Globalization of public services production is likely for two main reasons (Dunleavy, 1994):

- *Market pressures for globalization.* There are five principal market pressures for globalization of private services production, all of which are likely to have important corollaries or implications for public services production: the contemporary growth of services, changes in technology, new forms of commercial and industrial organization by firms, the development of radical outsourcing, and changes in commodification processes. Radical outsourcing strategies have had far-reaching effects on service growth and the reorganization of corporations by splitting up previously unitary organizational configurations.

- *State pressures for globalization.* Within the public sector, there are analogous pressures for globalization, and some key differentiating features. There are four principal state pressures: the bureau-shaping incentives acting on bureaucrats and public officials, the potential for radical outsourcing in the public sector, the impacts of government procurement rules, and consequent changes affecting the commodification of public services. Radical outsourcing in the public sector entails generalizing best in the world criteria from firms' and corporations' activity to apply also to public service operations.

However, Dunleavy (1994) argues that governments will find it extraordinarily hard to meet the best in the world criterion applied to many or most of their service activities. As large corporations progressively develop and refine their capabilities in current or new implementation areas, they will often be able to acquire extra focus in depth, to make large capital investments, and to reap economies of scale by producing standardized service packages across many different localities, regions, or countries. Unlike most governmental units, corporations are able to change rapidly their scope of operations by merging, setting up partnership deals, or franchising, so that scale-escalation in the corporate economy can rather quickly affect public services production. Major corporations are already emerging in key public service areas, and they will be able to take seriously best in world criteria. In this perspective the prospect of trans-European or trans-global firms becoming major players in defining and developing public services production is likely.

The bureau-shaping model also sheds light on the scope for radical outsourcing inside government. Bureau-shaping incentives have emerged as dominant bureaucratic responses to the end of the postwar growth era in public services employment. Rationally self-interested bureaucrats have little stake in maximizing budgets and expanding empires, as older public choice models suggested. The biggest potential for radical outsourcing lies in a large-scale shift to contracting of delivery agencies, where public officials directly organize implementation of public services (Dunleavy, 1994).

Key Issues for Global IT Sourcing: Country and Individual Factors

Global IT sourcing can be defined as the contracting of part or all of a company's IT functions to either third-party vendors or in-house development centers that are based abroad (Rao, 2004).

Key issues are country factors such as telecommunications infrastructure, legal and security issues, time zone differences and the friction of distance. Individual factors are cultural issues and language issues (Rao, 2004).

Business Process Outsourcing (BPO)

Business process outsourcing often fills human resources (HR) practitioners with fear, but handled properly it can help the HR function become more efficient and strategic, according to HR (2004). Of all the business-related acronyms that are filtering through to the corporate consciousness, BPO — business process outsourcing — is certainly one that appears to be raising interest.

Business process outsourcing, although often seen as the next evolutionary step in IT outsourcing, is also very different from it. BPO is about delegating the ownership, administration, and operation of a process to a specialist third party in order to solve a business problem. And because BPO is about delivering outcomes — higher performing business processes — it aims to raise a client company's shareholder value (HR, 2004).

Business processes within a company can be broken down into three categories: core; business critical non-core; and finally non-core, non-critical. Core processes are seldom outsourced, because they are the very essence of the business and the area that requires the most investment. Critical and non-critical non-core processes may be suited for outsourcing to a third party supplier who will invest in them on the company's behalf.

Strategic Outsourcing Termination

Termination of an IT outsourcing arrangement involves strategic decision-making. General studies of strategic decision making show how rapidly strategic decisions are made in small firms operating within high-velocity environments, and how decision speed is linked to performance. Fast decision makers use more, not less information than do slow decision makers. The former also develop more, not fewer, alternatives, and use a two-tiered advice process. Conflict resolution and integration between strategic managers are also critical to the pace of decision-making. Finally, fast decisions based on this pattern of behaviors lead to superior performance (Elter, 2004).

Managers are engaged in myriads of day-to-day activities in attempting to resolve various strategic and organization issues associated with internal and external uncertainty. Problems and opportunities appear unstructured and incoherent. This makes it difficult for them to define appropriate and coherent means to address the many pressing business issues. Individuals cannot absorb all the information needed to formulate a complete set of alternatives from which to choose. Information may not be available and evaluation may be subject to personal biases. This means that actors' rationality is bounded by the environment in which they operate and their own human limitations. Under such complex and uncertain conditions, typically the case in an IT outsourcing termination situation, strategic plans become of limited value (Elter, 2004).

Researchers increasingly call for a need to explore the detailed processes and practices, which constitute strategic decision-making. Understanding strategizing is a key. Strategizing refers to the continuous formation and transformation of strategic patterns through ongoing and intertwined processes of strategic thinking and strategic acting, with several actors involved, on different layers of the organization (Elter, 2004).

IT outsourcing termination is a strategic issue. The term strategic issue refers to developments or trends that emerge from an organization's internal or external environments recognized by strategic managers as trends or events with significant influence on an organization's prospect of reaching a desired future. Strategic issues can be seen as the problems that actors in an organization engage in getting resolved (Elter, 2004).

Belief Perseverance

Prior beliefs persevere in the face of challenges to data that created those beliefs and even in the face of new data that contradict those beliefs. Many cognitive and motivational processes play roles in belief perseverance. For instance, different people have different reward structures that force different public stances. Politicians know that they get more votes by promising no new taxes than by embarking on expensive programs that have not only long-term payoffs. Such public image management is of little interest here, although it surely accounts for much real-world perseverance. More interesting questions concern factors that influence private beliefs after challenges to those beliefs. Several lines of research provide insight into such belief perseverance phenomena (Anderson & Kellam, 1992).

Research has dealt with three different types of beliefs: self-perceptions, social perceptions, and social theories. This research reveals the importance of *causal reasoning* in perseverance. It shows that when causal reasoning is reduced, so is perseverance. When causal reasoning is enhanced, perseverance is increased. Forcing alternative causal reasoning reduces perseverance. The underlying mechanism appears to be the availability of causal arguments (Anderson & Kellam, 1992).

Numerous studies demonstrate that prior beliefs can bias people's judgments of new data, particularly when the new data are ambiguous. Biased assimilation occurs under many circumstances (Anderson & Kellam, 1992).

Beliefs can be general or specific judgments. Some researchers have distinguished between impression judgments based on memory for specific behaviors vs. recall of impressions formed online as the behaviors were observed. Other researchers distinguished between the automatic and the controlled aspects of stereotypes and prejudice. Finally, some distinguished between the hypothesis-testing aspects of a prior belief and the confirmed beliefs resulting from biased testing of the hypotheses. Several research teams have focused on people's ability to discount subsets of initial information, finding a variety of influential conditions. For instance, to-be-discounted information that has been integrated with to-be-used information is particularly difficult to discount. These various findings are quite different in their specifics, but they all illustrate the importance of seemingly trivial differences in judgmental context (Anderson & Kellam, 1992).

Anderson and Kellam (1992) suggest an additional distinction between two types of judgments that people frequently make. Specific judgments about a particular group or person are typically based on fairly automatic heuristics; the availability of causal theories will play a major role in such judgments. General judgments about a social theory are typically based on a more controlled judgment process that includes a search for relevant data (if there is ample time). Thus, accurate predictions about when perseverance will or will not occur might depend not only on the type of causal reasoning induced prior to the judgment task but on the particular type of judgment as well. Specific judgments will be responsive to new data or challenges to old data only if such challenges increase the availability of alternative causal theories or scenarios. The reason is that in making specific judgments we are typically unaware that we are using implicit social theories. More general judgments are fairly explicit statements of our social theories. As such, they need to match relevant information and thus will tend to be more responsive to contradictory data.

Anderson and Kellam (1992) conducted an experiment where they found that people's general beliefs were influenced by new data but not by explanations. Furthermore, they found that specific predictions about a group of risk preferring and a group of conservative people were influenced by explanation but not by new data.

The importance of social theories in the perseverance of initial beliefs has been demonstrated in a variety of studies. One line of work shows that one route to perseverance is through the biased assimilation of new evidence. Anderson and Kellam (1992) tested the limits of this assimilation process, assessed the simultaneous effects of prior beliefs and new conclusive data, and did so on several types of final beliefs. Their explanation manipulations replicated earlier research findings: Explaining a hypothetical relation between two variables can systematically alter one's beliefs about that relation.

Anderson and Kellam (1992) found limits of biased assimilation. The most obvious were (a) that explanation-induced theories are too weak, too uninvolving, or too unemotional to produce systematic biases in evaluation of new data (b) that the covariaton detection paradigm is not sensitive to biased assimilation processes, and (c) that clear data are not susceptible to biased assimilation processes. Tests of the relative strengths of causal explanations vs. new data produced the most interesting results. Subjects successfully avoided use of explanation-induced theories when asked to give their general opinions. They relied heavily on the data. However, when subjects made more specific judgments, they apparently fell back on more automatic heuristic processes involving the availability of causal explanations. In essence, their stated general opinions did not automatically translate into more specific working judgments.

Naive theories are an interesting area for belief persistence. Naive theories allow people to explain events that have already occurred. More importantly, they predict possible futures. A fascinating feature of naive theories is their ability to survive empirical disconfirmation. Incorrect naive theories, such as racial stereotype explanations of achievement-test score differences, would be relatively harmless if those theories were easily changed. Similarly, incorrect theories about how HIV and AIDS is (and is not) spread would be a minor social issue if direct public persuasion campaigns were effective. The long history of racial prejudice and the short history of HIV and AIDS ignorance both attest to the persevering nature of naive theories (Anderson & Lindsay, 1998).

Anderson and Lindsay (1998) believe there are several processes contributing to theory perseverance. Some are behavioral, some are purely cognitive, and some have their origins in motivation. In all cases, however, they believe that ultimately there is a cognitive mechanism involving causal thinking at work. Perseverance producing processes can be classified into three broad categories. One set involves perceptual and memory processes that lead social perceivers to see stronger support for their naive theories than is actually present in the relevant social data. These are the illusory correlation processes. The second set involves processes that in some way change the data that are brought to bear on evaluation of a person's naive theory. These are referred to as data distortion processes. The third and final set involves heuristic judgment processes that tend to bolster a priori naive theories. These are the available elements processes. These three categories are not mutually exclusive.

Illusory correlations are cases in which people perceive a relation between two variables when in fact there is none, or when the perceived relation is stronger than actually exists. Data distortions are instances in which some action by the perceiver — behavioral or mental — fundamentally changes the data being used to assess the validity of a naive theory (Anderson & Lindsay, 1998).

The third set of perseverance producing processes involves use of some type of availability heuristic in making judgments under uncertainty. In many judgment contexts, the final judgment is based on how easily, quickly, or frequently particular elements can be brought to mind. In different judgment contexts, the type of element involved in the availability judgment varies. More importantly, in many contexts the availability of the key elements is influenced by naive theories, sometimes directly and sometimes indirectly (Anderson & Lindsay, 1998).

Anderson and Lindsay (1998) suggest some solutions to knowledge structure-induced biases. One approach is to make an opposing naive theory available. This can be done through a counter-explanation process in which the person imagines and explains how a different relation is (or might be) true. Several researchers have found that this strategy works. Another approach for reducing bias in everyday judgments involves increasing the motivation of perceivers to come up with the right answers. Fear of invalidity is a possible explanation for reliance on naive theories for judgments. Those individuals who are unconcerned with the validity of their judgments may resort to a quick and dirty method of assessment (i.e., depend on their naive theories or attitudes) rather than conduct a more effortful evaluation of the data. In one study where participants were told that their judgments were going to be evaluated by others made more stimulus-based judgments. A similar effect was found in another study, where increasing pressure to be accurate does not always improve accuracy (Anderson & Lindsay, 1998).

Strategic Risk Behavior

IT outsourcing represents a strategic decision-making involving risk. Risk behavior of client managers will influence outsourcing decisions, governance decisions, and termination decisions.

Risk can be defined as a condition in which decision makers know the possible consequences of the decisions as well as their associated probabilities. In strategic management, it is seldom that all consequences and their probabilities are known. Thus, risk is often used as if it is the same as uncertainty, or unpredictable consequences and/or probabilities. In this sense, strategic management scholars refer to risk as variance in performance beyond the control of decision makers. In recent years, recognition has been growing in the strategy literature that managers conceive of risk only as downside possibilities. That is, managers are more concerned with negative variations in performance, not performance variances as a whole. For our purposes here, we define risk broadly as the unpredictability in decision outcomes. Thus, risk taking would be to undertake consciously tasks, which are associated with uncertain consequences (Das & Teng, 2001a).

Strategic risk behavior constitutes an essential perspective in analyzing strategic behavior. Broadly defined, strategic risk taking refers to corporate strategic moves that cause returns to vary, that involve venturing into the unknown, and that may result in corporate ruin. Considering that risk is a problematic aspect in the management of business organizations, it is important to understand the reasons that lead strategists to engage in risky decision-making behavior (Das & Teng, 2001a).

Extensive research on risk taking carried out by psychologists over the years has resulted in two competing paradigms concerning the attributes of risk taking behavior — one suggested by the personality psychologists who focus on individual differences in risk taking behavior, and the other by the experimental psychologists who deal with risk taking in such terms as subjective expected utility (Das & Teng, 2001a).

The view of the personality psychologists focuses on individual differences in risk taking, so that it ascribes risk behavior mostly to the general traits and dispositional tendencies of decision makers. Scholars have observed that individuals are fairly consistent in their attitudes towards risk — some people seem more comfortable with risk taking than others. Based on such stable individual attribute, researchers differentiate decision makers in terms of their risk propensity — namely, as being either risk averters or risk seekers. Some researchers also believe that a dispositional risk propensity can help explain, largely, the risk behavior of individuals (Das & Teng, 2001a).

In contrast, the experimental psychologists challenge the consistency of such dispositional traits and argue that situational factors have a greater influence on risk taking

Figure 11.1. Strategic risk behaviors based on risk propensity, decision context, and risk horizon (Das & Teng, 2001a)

Risk propensity / *Decision context*	Positive	Negative
Risk avert	Short-range low-risk behavior Long-range low-risk behavior Cell A	Short-range high-risk behavior Long-range low-risk behavior Cell B
Risk seeker	Short-range low-risk behavior Long-range high-risk behavior Cell C	Short-range high-risk behavior Long-range high-risk behavior Cell D

Figure 11.2. Integrated framework of trust, control, and risk in strategic alliances (Das & Teng, 2001b)

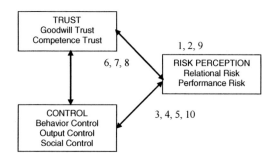

behavior. Unlike other psychological attributes, the risk propensity of decision makers seems to lack constancy across decision situations. Since this view attempts to understand Everyman's risk taking behavior, it regards the external stimulus as more important. Many empirical studies suggest that situational factors such as outcome history and decision framing are salient in determining the riskiness of strategic decisions. Hence, the view of the experimental psychologists — which treats risk taking as situation-contingent — seems to command substantial support (Das & Teng, 2001a).

Since both views have their virtues and considerable empirical support, efforts have been made to integrate them. These studies suggest that the dispositional risk propensity interacts with situational factors in determining risk-taking behavior. In their article, Das and Teng (2001a) present an alternative framework for reconciling the two views on the determinants of strategic risk behavior. Their framework is illustrated in Figure 11.1.

Figure 11.1 illustrates the interplay of two factors — risk propensity and decision context. This framework suggests that decision makers will exhibit high-risk behavior in short-range risk horizons, if the decision context is perceived as a loss position (negative context). The framework further suggests that decision makers will exhibit low-risk behavior in short-range risk horizons, if the decision context is perceived as a gain position (positive context). Furthermore, decision makers who are risk averters will exhibit low-risk behavior in long-range risk horizons. Finally, decision makers who are risk seekers will exhibit high-risk behavior in long-range risk horizons.

In another study, Das and Teng (2001b) developed an integrated framework for trust, control, and risk in strategic alliances, as illustrated in Figure 11.2. Trust and control are inextricably interlinked with risk in strategic alliances such as outsourcing relationships. To understand how partner firms can effectively reduce and manage this risk, we need to examine the interrelationships between trust, control, and risk.

Based on this framework, Das and Teng (2001b) developed the following propositions:

1.   A firm's goodwill trust in its partner firm will reduce its perceived relational risk in an alliance, but not its perceived performance risk.

2.   A firm's competence trust in its partner firm will reduce its perceived performance risk in an alliance, but not its perceived relational risk.

3.   Perceived relational risk in an alliance will be reduced more effectively by behavior control than by output control.

4.   Perceived performance risk in an alliance will be reduced more effectively by output control than by behavior control.

5.   Social control in an alliance will reduce both perceived relational risk and perceived performance risk.

6.   Both output control and behavior control will undermine goodwill trust and competence trust in an alliance.

7.   Social control will enhance both goodwill trust and competence trust in an alliance.

8.   Goodwill trust and competence trust will enhance the effectiveness of all control modes (behavior, output, and social) in an alliance.

9.   Control levels remaining the same, the lower the acceptable relational risk level, the higher the needed goodwill trust level in an alliance. Control levels remaining the same, the lower the acceptable performance risk level, the higher the needed competence trust level in an alliance.

10.   Goodwill trust remaining the same, the lower the acceptable relational risk level, the more will be the use of behavior control and social control in an alliance. Competence trust remaining the same, the lower the acceptable performance risk level, the more will be the use of output control and social control in an alliance.

Das and Teng's (2001b) proposed an integrated framework of trust, control, and risk leading to these ten propositions. Overall, the framework suggests that trust and control are two separate routes to risk reduction in alliances. While trust can be seen as a more intrinsic source for lowering the perception of risk, control may be viewed as a more overt and active way of reducing risk.

Chapter XII

Offshore IT Outsourcing

The shifting geography of business processes can de defined as the third wave of geography-related change in the design and operation of corporations. During the first wave, the improving transportation infrastructure of the 20th century enabled corporations to seek effective production capabilities in increasingly far-flung locations that provided access to new markets and tangible resources — land, local factories, mines, and production workers. During the second wave, as capital markets became global and interconnected in the latter half of the 20th century, corporations began to capitalize on vibrant global financial markets for both debt and equity. Now we are in the midst of a third wave — in which digitized business processes like order processing, billing, customer service, accounts and payroll processing, and design and development can be carried out without regard to physical location (Venkatraman, 2004).

According to Kaiser and Hawk (2004), all executives need to explore offshore outsourcing. Competitors' use, or perceived use, makes evaluation inevitable. Even IT organizations that choose not to use offshore companies must be able to convince their senior management that they have carefully considered the option. Those who do choose to outsource need to decide how they want to work with an offshore organization.

Offshore vs. Onshore IT Outsourcing

Underpinning the move toward outsourcing has been a confluence of structural and theoretical changes in the nature of business and organizations dating back approximately two decades. Theorists have suggested that the changing nature of competition has resulted from two factors: (a) globalization of commerce engendering worldwide competition, and (b) technology developments that have changed basic business processes related to time and distance. Globalization and technology have placed enormous pressure on firms to cut costs and improve efficiency in the interests of self-preservation (Clott, 2004).

Wage rate differentials generate cost savings, but the compelling gains come from pairing savings with top-flight skills. While only a few Asian countries offer enough English-speaking call-center representatives and help-desk functions to deal with foreign customers, many other skills are more abundant in Asia than in Europe and the U.S. China, for example, produces 350,000 graduate engineers every year, compared to 90,000 for U.S. engineering schools. And most leading Indian IT-outsourcing firms operate at level five — the highest degree of expertise — of the IT service capability maturity model, whereas most internal IT departments in the United States operate at levels two or three (Hagel, 2004).

Many skills of Asian companies are distinctive. Product engineers in China and Taiwan, for instance, are more focused on designing for production than are their U.S. counterparts, who tend to emphasize features and product performance (Hagel, 2004).

The combination of low wages and a plentiful supply of skilled applicants make it possible for Asian companies to use managerial practices very different from those generally found in developed economies. To begin with, the best offshore companies invest heavily to recruit the right staff because they can afford to be more selective. Furthermore, there are more managers to staff, so that they can spend more time building the skills of employees (Hagel, 2004).

Offshoring Solutions

As of 2004, among the fastest-growing aspects of global outsourcing is business process outsourcing (BPO). BPO began as back-office process arrangements to run finance and accounting operations such as payroll, accounts payable and receivable, financial, insurance, and property accounting. These services have expanded into new areas such as call centers, with staff trained to answer and transact basic service-related areas, including order entry and credit card processing (Clott, 2004).

Kaiser and Hawk (2004) argue that there is currently an evolution of offshore software development from outsourcing and cosourcing. "Financial Insurance Services Company" (FISC) (a pseudonym) is a major U.S. financial services company with thousands of representatives across the country. "Offsource" (a pseudonym) is a leading India-based company providing consulting and IT services to clients globally. Kaiser and Hawk (2004) tell how their eight-year alliance has evolved. The relationship began as a simple pilot of offshore application development outsourcing, aimed at reducing development costs and supplementing in-house IT staff knowledge. It has evolved into a vastly more complex "cosourcing" model, where work is shared. To achieve cosourcing, the two firms had to resolve two major issues. The first was how to keep IT skills and knowledge from draining from FISC. This issue has been resolved by formally linking career development to project assignments and to outsourcer-to-client mentoring. The second issue is how to share work. It has been resolved by creating a dual project management hierarchy, where leadership at each level of a project can be by either FISC or Offsource, depending on the need. Their experiences provide five recommendations for others on structuring offshore outsourcing relationships: (1) understand where cosourcing is applicable, (2) define and develop the appropriate in-house IT competencies, (3) build trust but avoid building a binding relationship, (4) foster mutual understanding of ethnic and corporate cultures, and (5) map out a progression to cosourcing.

Public administration is changing, and new publication management strategies include the globalization of public services production. Inside government agencies, bureau-shaping motivations sustain the new public management model approach and create a strong disposition towards embracing radical outsourcing, and residualizing government's implementation roles, a direction reinforced by the marketization of public services. Transnational pressures on nation states to standardize policies will powerfully erode the existing single-country distinctiveness of public service markets. Globalization of public services production is likely for two main reasons (Dunleavy, 1994):

- *Market pressures for globalization.* There are five principal market pressures for globalization of private services production, all of which are likely to have important corollaries or implications for public services production: the contemporary growth of services, changes in technology, new forms of commercial and industrial organization by firms, the development of radical outsourcing, and changes in commodification processes. Radical outsourcing strategies have had far-reaching effects on service growth and the reorganization of corporations by splitting up previously unitary organizational configurations.

- *State pressures for globalization.* Within the public sector, there are analogous pressures for globalization, and some key differentiating features. There are four principal state pressures: the bureau-shaping incentives acting on bureaucrats and public officials, the potential for radical outsourcing in the public sector, the impacts of government procurement rules, and consequent changes affecting the commodification of public services. Radical outsourcing in the public sector entails generalizing best in the world criteria from firms' and corporations' activity to apply also to public service operations.

However, Dunleavy (1994) argues that governments will find it extraordinarily hard to meet the best in the world criterion applied to many or most of their service activities. As large corporations progressively develop and refine their capabilities in current or new implementation areas, they will often be able to acquire extra focus in depth, to make large capital investments, and to reap economies of scale by producing standardized service packages across many different localities, regions, or countries. Unlike most governmental units, corporations are able to change rapidly their scope of operations by merging, setting up partnership deals, or franchising, so that scale-escalation in the corporate economy can rather quickly affect public services production. Major corporations are already emerging in key public service areas, and they will be able to take seriously best in world criteria. In this perspective the prospect of trans-European or trans-global firms becoming major players in defining and developing public services production is likely.

The bureau-shaping model also sheds light on the scope for radical outsourcing inside government. Bureau-shaping incentives have emerged as dominant bureaucratic responses to the end of the postwar growth era in public services employment. Rationally self-interested bureaucrats have little stake in maximizing budgets and expanding empires, as older public choice models suggested. The biggest potential for radical outsourcing lies in a large-scale shift to contracting of delivery agencies, where public officials directly organize implementation of public services (Dunleavy, 1994).

Offshore Software Development

In the last several years, offshore outsourcing of software development has grown considerably. As just one example, Accenture has tripled its staff in India in the two years. The current 20% annual growth rate in offshore It work is expected to continue, if not increase, propelled by managerial needs to cut costs and stories in the popular press (Kaiser & Hawk, 2004).

Kaiser and Hawk (2004) describe the steps of offshoring through an example of two fictive companies, FISC and Offsource:

- *Step 1 — Engagement.* To solve the skills shortage and the cost increases, FISC management decided to outsource with an offshore IT firm. FISC began cautiously, initially engaging Offsource in assisting only with a small pilot project. However, management was pleased enough with the results that it involved Outsource in more projects. Offsource delivered well and trust grew between the two organizations. In this step, Offsource staff worked offshore, the work was considered a pilot project, and the contract was for time-and-expense billing. To move beyond pilot offshore outsourcing, FISC would need to rely on Offsource in a meaningful way. This change became reflected in contract negotiations, where time-and-expense billings on new projects became fixed bids.

- *Step 2 — Commitment.* The mode of operating in the early projects was traditional outsourcing, with primarily all the work offshore. As trust built, both firms viewed contract negotiations differently, with some of the later projects becoming fixed bids. Then, FISC committed to the concept of offshoring by giving Offsource its first opportunity to maintain a mission-critical legacy system — the sales representative compensation system for agents built in several years ago. Management would not allow vendors to touch the production data so Offsource had to work on-site at FISC. Furthermore, this on-site support was to be purely technical; the staff would not interact with FISC users. The two IT organizations worked separately, but side-by-side. The FISC assistant support director, who managed the application, had direct contact with her on-site peer, the on-site team leader, which Offsource referred to as an "anchor." But this assistant support manager did not have direct contact with Offsource's on-site or offshore staff—only the anchor did. Unfortunately, this work initially did not go well. In fact, it started out badly because the anchor was "too much of a teachie guy." Once Offsource learned of the communication and personality problem, its management responded quickly, and the relationship improved and grew. Having made the commitment to outsourcing, to gain more value FISC would need to increase interaction with Offsource both on-site and offshore. FISC's management determined that understanding Offsource's corporate and ethnic culture would improve team performance.•

- *Step 3 — Interchange*. The FISC-Offsource relationship moved up a step when some members of FISC's IT staff worked at an Offsource location such as Offsource had been doing at FISC. This interchange began with Offsource's work on a big program that encompassed multiple projects underway at the same time. Offsource's work on the program began as supplementing FISC's IT staff on-site, in combination with offshore staff for much of the implementation work. Billing was for time and expenses. The Offsource staff concentrated on technical design and implementation because they had little understanding of the FISC business. To fill this knowledge gap, Offsource taught these employees the business at classes outside normal working hours. As a result, Offsource began assuming responsibility for a wider range of development tasks, including interfacing with users and defining requirements. This interchange step brought out four personnel issues that FISC and Offsource needed to resolve to gain more value from their relationship. First, the presence of the Indian workers on-site was somewhat disquieting to FISC's IT staff. The Indians tended to work much longer days than their FISC counterparts did. FISC's employees often noted, "Work is their life." Second, as Offsource's staff took on more high-level project work, FISC's IT employees became concerned that Offsource's staff would end up with the important and interesting roles, such as deriving requirements and learning new tools. Third, due to Offsource's expanded role in this interchange step, FISC's employees were not developing certain skills. Fourth, FISC was potentially becoming dependent on Offsource because Offsource's staff increasingly understood the applications better than FISC's employees. If the relationship was terminated, FISC had less knowledge to maintain the systems. The switching costs of moving the work in-house, or to another outsourcer, would be significant, even though outsourcing is supposed to increase flexibility, not decrease it.

- *Step 4 — Cosourcing*. IT cosourcing can be defined as an outsourcer and client melding their IT competencies to accomplish the client's work. That is the approach the two took in this step to address the people concerns raised in the interchange step. Two of the major changes were to: (i) formalize knowledge transfer from Offsource to FISC, and (ii) create a dual project management hierarchy. FISC's employees were increasingly assigned to work with particular Offsource staff, to learn from them. The process of joint teaming, however, led to an unexpected side effect. Sometimes, Offsource team members were the only ones in a position to evaluate some FISC employees. Thus, FISC began to need Offsource's involvement in FISC employee evaluations as well as development — an unusual role for an outsourcer. Once FISC's senior IT executives realized how outsourcing could degrade the staff's IT competencies, they adopted changes to preserve and develop the competencies.

- *Step 5 — Alignment.* Alignment in outsourcing means alignment between two firms in commitment and values. The approach FISC has taken in this step is to ask for Offsource's input on FISC IT strategy on future projects and on how to manage and integrate IT core competencies to contribute to the firm's success. Offsource's participation in senior decision-making is a significant criterion to warrant a more sophisticated step in the cosourcing model. This level of involvement has come only after many years of increasing trust and commitment. One manifestation of this step is becoming evident: Offsource is aligning its balanced business scorecard with FISC's balanced scorecard.

Based on their research, Kaiser and Hawk (2004) have several recommendations for other firms considering cosourcing with an offshore outsourcer. First, the firm must understand where cosourcing is applicable. Second, it must define and develop the appropriate in-house IT competencies. Third, it must build trust but avoid building a binding relationship. Fourth, it must foster mutual understanding of ethnic and corporate cultures. Finally, it must map out a progression of cosourcing.

Benefits and Pitfalls

According to Wright and Boschee (2004), the success of these offshore providers of outsourced IT derives in large part from two economic trends. First, in the wake of the recession, U.S. businesses have focused increasingly on their core skills and outsourced a broad variety of services not integral to their mission, with technology services leading the way. Second, with revenues flat or shrinking, businesses have focused on cutting costs, again with an eye on the high price of technology. The formula of Indian IT companies to capitalize on those trends is simple: excellent technology service at much lower cost.

Much of their reduced cost structure is based on their use of highly skilled Indian technology professionals, who are often paid substantially less in India than technology workers in the U.S. With the U.S. employment marked in a slump — and the once high-flying technology sector leaving a large trail of laid-off American technical workers — politicians and U.S. workers alike have begun complaining bitterly about the flow of outsourced work to offshore providers (Wright & Boschee, 2004).

One major challenge then, is to organize the work is such a way that knowledge can be exchanged between traditional separation lines and across borders. The line of separation is not only between managers and employees, but also between government and private companies, single companies and industry networks, and between research & development units and operational units. Global outsourcing might have major implications on future knowledge based product and service production.

Companies can boost their capital productivity in low-wage environments in three ways (Agrawal et al., 2003):

- *Round-the-clock shifts*. The most obvious way to use the capital infrastructure that account for most of the cost of offshore operations, is to run round-the-clock shifts, even if they mean higher wages for odd hours. This option does not exist in the domestic high-wage environment, where wage premiums offset any capital savings.

- *Cheaper capital equipment*. Some service providers in India are using cheap local labor to develop their own software instead of purchasing more expensive branded products from the global software giants. American Express, for instance, hired programmers to write software to reconcile accounts.

- *Reduced automation*. Some companies have gone a step further and used workers for tasks that would normally be automated at home. A payments processor, for example, might employ people to input checks manually into a computer system instead of using expensive imaging software.

By reaping offshoring's full potential for benefits, companies will find that their new, lower-cost structures open up a variety of opportunities to boost revenue growth. These opportunities will often far exceed the annual cost savings. Some companies, for instance, can now chase delinquent accounts receivable they formerly had to ignore. The new cost position can also be used to develop cheaper products for customers in emerging markets. As companies go further down the road to globalization, the potential to create new markets and redefine industries is enormous (Agrawal et al., 2003).

To avoid the pitfalls of offshoring, Webster (2004) lists the following tips for arranging offshore operations through a vendor:

- Design an exit strategy, such as month-to-month contract terms, for the early stages. Allow yourself to back away if goals are not met.

- Level with employees about domestic job reductions and cost savings, emphasizing competitiveness and any opportunities for new jobs.

- Avoid making your company's core competencies dependent on offshore operations.

- For processes being relocated offshore — whether simple or sophisticated — make sure results, quality, and worker performance can be precisely measured. Then measure them.

- Monitor the work being done for security lapses and performance, preferably by putting some of your own managers on-site.

- Consult international-law specialists about the tax and labor laws that apply where you will be operating, particularly if you are setting up an offshore subsidiary. (For example, in India employees have certain "moral rights" to the property of their companies, unless a contract expressly deletes them.)

- Review domestic accounting regulations pertaining to offshore operations.

- For anyone contemplating outsourcing work to a location thousands of miles away, the start-up is easily the most frightening step. Putting a manager on permanent assignment in the offshore location, as mentioned on the list, allows a company to work through many of the problems that can plague an effort during that phase, and prevent them from recurring (Webster, 2004).

Critical Success Factors of IT Offshoring

Merely replicating processes developed at home is not the way to realize offshoring's full potential. Wages represent 70 percent of call-center costs in the United States, for instance, so these operations are designed to minimize labor by using all available technology. But in low-wage India, that makes little sense, since wages represent only 30 percent of costs, and capital equipment (to provide telecom bandwidth, for example) is often more expensive than it is at home (Agrawal et al., 2003).

The way to reduce the cost of offshore operations even further is to reorganize and reengineer operations to take full advantage of these differences. In a low-wage country, the capital infrastructure — including office space, telecommunications lines, and computer hardware and software — should be used as intensively as possible. For a call center, this approach can reduce onshore operations. The potential value for other offshored functions, like data entry, payroll processing, and financial accounting, is similar (Agrawal et al., 2003).

Social Concerns and Impact on Local Jobs

Global outsourcing is a fast-growing aspect of the world economy. It has been estimated that 3.3 million jobs will move offshore. The strategic benefits for firms can be portrayed as a means to reduce costs, improve asset efficiency, and increase profits. Criticisms of outsourcing have often been in the areas of changing employment patterns, globalization of labor force, and its effects on individuals and organizations. Outsourcing has been called one of the greatest organizational and industry structure shifts of the century, with the potential to transform the way businesses operate (Clott, 2004).

Some proponents believe it will turn firms from vertically integrated structures into virtual organizations and transform existing fixed structures into variable-cost structures where expenses can move up or down as the business climate dictates. For employees, the trend toward outsourcing has been thought to result in a loss of fixed-employment opportunities because of firms seeking to use cheaper labor overseas (Clott, 2004).

Complaints about the flow of outsourced work to offshore providers can have consequences for international outsourcing when labor markets are unionized. Skaksen (2004) found that international outsourcing might give rise to an increase in the wage rate, which implies that home-country workers may become better off, even though jobs are moved out of the country. Potential, or the threat of, global outsourcing also has important implications for the wage rate and the level of employment. Potential but non-realized international outsourcing can be used as a threat by the firm in the wage negotiations with the trade union. Under these circumstances, a marginal decrease in the cost of international outsourcing implies that there is a decrease in the wage rate and an increase in employment and aggregate social welfare.

With respect to the implications of realized global outsourcing, Skaksen (2004) found that a marginal decrease in the cost of such outsourcing, which implies that the firm actually begins to outsource activities, gives rise to an increase in the wage rate and a reduction in employment and aggregate social welfare.

Political Consequences

According to Venkatraman (2004), the new hot topic being debated in boardrooms, at meetings and in Internet discussion groups is offshoring, the practice among U.S. and European companies of migrating business processes overseas to India, the Philippines, Ireland, China and elsewhere to lower costs without significantly sacrificing quality. At first blush, this would seem like nothing new, but the development of a powerful communication infrastructure is making offshoring an increasingly viable and commonly taken option: Nearly two out of three software companies are already involved, and in a number of industries, IT-enabled back-office business processes are prime candidates for such a shift.

According to Venkatraman (2004), the debate about the ethics of offshoring misses the point that it represents the inevitable next generation of business practice. At the heart of the debate is the issue of jobs and wages. As networking technologies have enabled companies to tap into the global marketplace for talent more easily, offshoring has put downward pressure on domestic salaries.

Business Week asked in 2004, "Will outsourcing hurt America's supremacy?" For decades, the U.S. has been the world's technology leader — thanks in large part to its dominance of software. The question now is whether the U.S. can continue to lead the industry as programming spreads around the globe from India to Bulgaria. Optimists see the offshore wave as the latest productivity miracle of the Internet. Companies that manage it well — no easy task — can build virtual workforces spread around the world, not only soaking up low-cost talent, but also tapping the biggest brains on earth to collaborate on complex projects.

According to a survey in the U.S., information technology is the job function that most companies already offshore or plan to offshore (Webster, 2004). Fifty-nine percent of the respondents in the survey said that they already outsource or plan to outsource information technology. On second place was manufacturing with 36%, followed by call centers 31% and accounting 21%.

Major Offshoring Locations

The industry most closely associated with outsourcing has been information technology. IT functions have been outsourced to such an extent that the "New Silicon Valley" centered in and around the city of Bangalore in India, which became a major outsourcing provider for IT functions because of its lower costs and advanced processing skills. This led to the growth of large Indian outsourcing firms such as Infosys, Tata Consultancy, and Wipro. As of 2003, over 500.000 people were employed in the Indian IT industry. Other countries seeking to replicate India's growth as an IT center for U.S. firms were Ireland, Israel, and the Philippines (Clott, 2004).

According to Wright and Boschee (2004), workers and managers in the technology field almost certainly have heard of companies like Infosys, Wipro, Cordiant, Tata, MachroTech, and others. These companies are among many technology shops based in India that have taken over a growing share of technical work outsourced by U.S. and other firms, which use Indian IT providers for software engineering, applications development, customer service call centers, and many other high-tech needs.

In Mumbai, we find the biggest IT-services firm in India. It is Tata Consultancy Services (TCS). Six hundred miles to the southeast, we find one of TCS's rivals, Infosys, in Bangalore. Nearby Infosys, we find Wipro, which wildly exceeded analyst expectations in April 2004 by announcing a 43 percent increase in fourth-quarter net profits, and a 23 percent increase for the full fiscal year. In 1994, Infosys was a $ 10 million company. In 2004, the company had revenues of more than $ 1 billion, growing 100 times larger in 10 years (Webster, 2004).

The records of most of India's other large IT services firms, such as Satyam Computer Services and HCL Technologies, are equally impressive. Figures from India's National Association of Software and Services Companies show that the country's IT industry grew from $ 5 billion in 1997 to $ 16 billion in 2002. That rosy picture plays nicely into Western fears of domination by India's IT firms. But there are problems, such as currency fluctuations, wage inflation, and public grumbling over jobs moving offshore. The biggest threat to Indian IT firms according to Webster (2004), is the threat of competition from such long established IT and outsourcing consultancies as Accenture, IBM Global Services, and EDS.

SECTION III

GOVERNANCE

Chapter XIII

IT Governance as Resource Mobilization

In many organizations, information technology has become crucial in the support, the sustainability, and the growth of the business. This pervasive use of technology has created a critical dependency on IT that calls for a specific focus on IT governance. IT governance consists of the leadership and organizational structures and processes that ensure that the organization's IT sustains and extends the organization's strategy and objectives (Grembergen et al., 2004).

IT governance matters because it influences the benefits received from IT investments. Through a combination of practices (such as redesigning business processes and well-designed governance mechanisms) and appropriately matched IT investments, top-performing enterprises generate superior returns on their IT investments (Weill, 2004).

What is IT Governance?

IT governance can be defined as specifying decision rights and accountability frame-work to encourage desirable behavior in the use of IT (Weill & Ross, 2004). We will use this definition here.

Other definitions are for example: (i) IT governance is the structures and processes that ensure that IT supports the organization's mission. The purpose is to align IT with the enterprise, maximize the benefits of IT, use IT resources responsibly and manage IT risks,

(ii) A structure of relationships and processes to direct and control the enterprise in order to achieve the enterprise's goals by adding value while balancing risk vs. return over IT and its processes, (iii) IT governance is the responsibility of the board of directors and executive management. It is an integral part of enterprise governance and consists of the leadership and organizational structures and processes that ensure that the organization's IT sustains and extends the organization's strategies and objectives, and (iv) IT governance is the system by which an organization's IT portfolio is directed and controlled. IT Governance describes (a) the distribution of decision-making rights and responsibilities among different stakeholders in the organization, and (b) the rules and procedures for making and monitoring decisions on strategic IT concerns (Peterson, 2004).

An extensive definition was presented by the IT Governance Institute (2004) as follows. It is a board or senior management responsibility in relation to IT to ensure that:

- IT is aligned with the business strategy, or in other words, IT delivers the functionality and services in line with the organization's needs, so the organization can do what it wants to do.

- IT and new technologies enable the organization to do new things that were never possible before.

- IT-related services and functionality are delivered at the maximum economical value or in the most efficient manner. In other words, resources are used responsibly.

- All risks related to IT are known and managed and IT resources are secured.

A distinction has to be made between IT management as discussed previously in this book and IT government that we introduce here. IT management is focused on the internal effective supply of IT services and products and the management of present IT operations (Van Grembergen et al., 2004). IT Governance in turn is much broader, and concentrates on performing and transforming IT to meet present and future demands of the business (internal focus) and the business' customers (external focus).

Figure 13.1. Distinction between IT management and IT governance

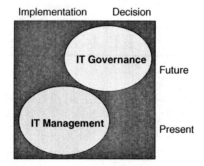

The difference between IT management and IT governance is illustrated in Figure 13.1. While IT management is concerned with implementing IT services at the present, IT governance is concerned with making decisions for the future.

Whereas the domain of IT management focuses on the efficient and effective supply of IT services and products, and the management of IT operations, IT Governance faces the dual demand of (1) contributing to present business operations and performance, and (2) transforming and positioning IT for meeting future business challenges. This does not undermine the importance or complexity of IT management, but goes to indicate that IT Governance is both internally and externally oriented, spanning both present and future time frames. One of the key challenges in IT Governance is therefore how to simultaneously perform and transform IT in order to meet the present and future demands of the business and the business' customers in a satisfying manner (Peterson, 2004).

IT governance encourages desirable behavior in the use of IT. A desirable behavior is one that is consistent with the organization's mission, strategy, values, norms, and culture, such as behavior promoting entrepreneurship, sharing and reuse or relentless cost reduction. IT governance is not about what specific decisions are made. That is management. Rather, governance is about systematically determining who makes each type of decision (a decision right), who has input to a decision (an input right), and how these people (or groups) are held accountable for their role (Weill, 2004).

Good IT governance draws on corporate governance principles to manage and use IT to achieve corporate performance goals. Effective IT governance encourages and leverages the ingenuity of all enterprise personnel in using IT, while ensuring compliance with the enterprise's overall vision and principles. As a result, good IT governance can achieve a management paradox: simultaneously empowering and controlling (Weill, 2004).

All enterprises have IT governance. The difference is that enterprises with effective governance have actively designed a set of IT governance mechanisms (e.g., committees, budgeting processes, approvals, IT organizational structure, chargeback, etc.) that encourage behaviors consistent with the organization's mission, strategy, values, norms, and culture. In these enterprises, when the "desirable behaviors" change, IT governance also changes (Weill, 2004).

IT governance cannot be considered in isolation because it links to the governance of other key enterprise assets (such as financial, human, intellectual property, etc.). Governance of the key assets, in turn, links to corporate governance and desirable behaviors (Weill, 2004).

In the models of *corporate governance,* one can organize the variety of variables and concepts used to describe the complexity of corporate governance mechanisms into two main categories: capital-related and labor-related. The capital-related aspects contain, among others, variables like ownership structure, corporate voting, the identity of owners, and the role of institutional owners. The labor-related aspects refer mainly to the stakeholding position of labor in corporate governance. Here one could mention employee involvement schemes, participatory management, co-determination, etc. (Cernat, 2004).

Corporate Governance

Before we dive into IT outsourcing governance, we must look at the broader issue of corporate governance in enterprises. Corporate governance is concerned with governing key assets, such as (Weill & Ross, 2004):

- *Human assets*: People, skills, career paths, training, reporting, mentoring, competencies, and so on.

- *Financial assets*: Cash, investments, liabilities, cash flow, receivables and so on.

- *Physical assets*: Buildings, plant, equipment, maintenance, security, utilization, and so on.

- *IP assets*: Intellectual property (IP), including product, services, and process know-how formally patented, copyrighted, or embedded in the enterprises' people and systems.

- *Information and IT assets*: Digitized data, information, and knowledge about customers, processes performance, finances, information systems, and so on.

- *Relationship assets*: Relationships within the enterprise as well as relationships, brand, and reputation with customers, suppliers, business units, regulators, competitors, channel partners, and so on.

As we can see from this list, IT outsourcing governance includes not only information and IT assets. IT outsourcing governance is concerned with several of these assets, sometimes even all of these assets. In this perspective, IT outsourcing governance may be as comprehensive in scope as corporate governance.

In governing IT outsourcing, we can learn from good financial and corporate governance. For example, the CFO (chief financial officer) does not sign every check or authorize every payment. Instead, he or she sets up financial governance specifying who can make the decisions and how. The CFO then oversees the enterprise's portfolio of investments and manages the required cash flow and risk exposure. The CFO tracks a series of financial metrics to manage the enterprise's financial assets, intervening only if there are problems or unforeseen opportunities. Similar principles apply to who can commit the enterprise to a contract or a partnership. Exactly the same approach should be applied to IT governance (Weill & Ross, 2004).

The dichotomy market or hierarchy has exercised a dominant influence on the study of forms of governance and their operation for some time. However, in the past two decades there have been large numbers of investigations of intermediate forms of governance. Subsequently it has been recognized that the behavior that occurs within exchanges is not necessarily determined by the forms of governance used, and this points to a need to understand behavior within a variety of exchanges (Blois, 2002).

Contracts in Governance

Blois (2002) defines governance as the institutional framework in which contracts are initiated, monitored, adapted, and terminated. An exchange occurs between two organizations when resources are transferred from one party to the other in return for resources controlled by the other party.

The organization of inter-firm exchanges has become of critical importance in today's business environment. Many scholars have criticized the inadequacies of legal contracts as mechanisms for governing exchange, especially in the face of uncertainty and dependence. Other scholars argue that it is not the contracts per se but the social contexts in which they are embedded that determine their effectiveness. Cannon et al. (2000) investigated the performance implications of governance structures involving contractual agreements and relational social norms, individually and in combination (plural form) under varying conditions and forms of transactional uncertainty and relationship-specific adaptation. Hypotheses were developed and tested on a sample of buyer-seller relationships. The results provide support for the plural form thesis — increasing the relational content of a governance structure containing contractual agreements enhanced performance when transactional uncertainty was high, but not when it was low.

Canon et al. (2000) applied the term legal bonds to refer to the extent to which detailed and binding contractual agreements were used to specify the roles and obligations of the parties. To the extent contracts were characterized in this way, they were less flexible and therefore more constrained in their adaptive properties. Highly detailed contracts were also less likely to possess the kinds of general safeguards that are more effective in thwarting self-interest-seeking behavior under circumstances of ambiguity.

Various perspectives on the nature of contracts as a mechanism of governance may be found in the literature. According to the original transaction cost framework (Williamson, 1979), formal contingent claims contracts (i.e., classical contracts) are inefficient mechanisms of governance in the face of uncertainty because organizations are bounded in their rationality and find it impossible to contemplate all possible future contingencies. For exchanges involving high levels of idiosyncratic investments and characterized by uncertainty, internal organization or hierarchy is predicted to be a more efficient form of governance than the market (Cannon et al., 2000).

However, neoclassical contract law argues that contracts can provide useful governance in exchange relationships even in the face of uncertainty and risk. This tradition of contract law is marked by doctrine and rules that attempt to overcome the difficulties posed by the classical tradition's emphasis on discreteness and presentation of exchange. The new doctrines enable parties to respond to unforeseen contingencies by making adjustments to ongoing exchange and ensuring continuity in their relationships. For example, concepts such as "good faith" and "reasonable commercial standards of fair dealing in the trade" are recognized under the Uniform Commercial Code (UCC) of 1978 in the U.S. as general provisions for contracting behavior that also help to ensure continuity in exchange relationships. Similarly, "gap filler" provisions of the UCC rely on "prior dealings" between parties and "customary practices" across an industry or trading area for completing contract terms intentionally left open or omitted, thus allowing for adjustments to contingencies (Cannon et al., 2000).

However, neoclassical contracts are not indefinitely elastic (Williamson, 1991). Many scholars remain skeptical of how effective even the most carefully crafted contracts can be. It is argued that the scope for drafting rules in contracts to address changing or ambiguous conditions, or the ability to rely on general legal safeguards for controlling commercial conduct, is limited by both practicality and the law itself.

Drawing on these views, Cannon et al. (2000) argue that when a transaction involves relationship-specific adaptations and is (1) subject to dynamic forces and future contingencies that cannot be foreseen or (2) involves ambiguous circumstances where tasks are ill defined and prone to exploitation, the difficulty of writing, monitoring, and enforcing contracts is increased, and their overall governance effectiveness weakened. In each case, efforts to govern the relationship based on detailed and formal contracts — without the benefit of some additional apparatus — are not likely to enhance performance.

Social or relational norms are defined generally as shared expectations regarding behavior. The norms reflect expectations about attitudes and behaviors parties have in working cooperatively together to achieve mutual and individual goals. The spirit of such sentiments is captured by many overlapping types of relational contracting norms. These can be reduced to a core set of five (Cannon et al., 2000):

- *Flexibility.* The attitude among parties that an agreement is but a starting point to be modified as the market, the exchange relationship, and the fortunes of the parties evolve.

- *Solidarity.* The extent to which parties believe that success comes from working cooperatively together vs. competing against one another. It dictates that parties stand by one another in the face of adversity and the ups and downs of marketplace competition.

- *Mutuality.* The attitude that each party's success is a function of everyone's success and that one cannot prosper at the expense of one's partner. It expresses the sentiment of joint responsibility.

- *Harmonization of conflict.* The extent to which a spirit of mutual accommodation toward cooperative ends exists.

- *Restraint in the use of power.* Forbearance from taking advantage of one's bargaining position in an exchange. It reflects the view that the use of power not only exacerbates conflict over time but also undermines mutuality and solidarity, opening the door to opportunism.

Together, these cooperative norms define relational properties that are important in affecting adaptations to dynamic market conditions and safeguarding the continuity of exchanges subject to task ambiguity (Cannon et al., 2000).

Norms represent important social and organizational vehicles of control in exchange where goals are ill defined or involve open-ended performance. They provide a general frame of reference, order, and standards against which to guide and assess appropriate behavior in uncertain and ambiguous situations. In such situations, contracts are often incomplete, and legal remedies can undermine relationship continuity. In contrast, norms motivate performance through focusing attention on the shared values of the partners to safeguard and rely on peer pressure and social sanctions to mitigate the risk of shirking and opportunistic expropriation. Because they involve expectations rather than rigid requirements of behavior, they create a cooperative as opposed to a confrontational environment for negotiating adaptations, thus promoting continuity in exchange (Cannon et al., 2000).

The plural form thesis contends that exchange is best understood as embedded in a complex matrix of economic, social, and political structures and that the governance of exchange relations more often relies on combinations of market, social or authority-based mechanisms than on any one category exclusively. While the plural form thesis is that the various mechanisms in fact work together to reinforce or complement one another in some way, little attention has focused on exactly how these mechanisms actually complement one another (Cannon et al., 2000).

Academic literature and business practice are directing increased attention to the importance of creating value in buyer-supplier relationships. One method for creating value is to reduce costs in commercial exchange. Cannon and Homburg (2001) developed at model that explains how supplier behaviors and the management of suppliers affect a customer firm's direct product, acquisition, and operations costs. The model proposes that these costs mediate the relationship between buyer-supplier relationship behaviors and the customer firm's intentions to expand future purchases from the supplier, as illustrated in Figure 13.2.

Cannon and Homburg (2001) empirically tested all relationships in their model in Figure 13.2. Their findings provide support for the expectation that more complex operational issues at times may require the richer interaction provided in face-to-face communications but at other times may benefit from simpler written exchanges. As expected, the more

Figure 13.2. Model explaining how supplier effect customer costs (Cannon & Homburg, 2001)

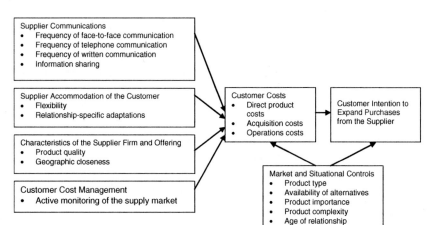

standardized issues typical of product acquisition benefit from more efficient written/ electronic communication.

In contrast, open information sharing by suppliers was not found to be related to a customer firm's costs. The lack of support for these hypotheses may be caused by buying firms' failure to use the information received from suppliers effectively. For example, customer firms may suffer from information overload and be unable to process and act on such information effectively.

Further hypotheses in Figure 13.2 predict the effects supplier accommodation would have on customer costs. The empirical results support the prediction that greater supplier flexibility results in lower acquisition and operations costs. Contrary to the researchers' predictions, higher levels of relationships-specific adaptation did not lead to lower acquisition or operations costs. This may be because many of these adaptations are targeted at enhancing value through increasing the benefits a customer receives, not through cost reduction.

Whereas Canon and Homburg (2001) developed a hypothesis that higher direct product costs would be associated with greater supplier adaptation, the result was statistically significant in the opposite direction. Several factors may explain this unanticipated finding. First, relationship-specific adaptations may evolve into regular business practices with all customers, which may subsequently lower the cost of accommodation. Second, buying organizations may effectively bargain away the premium prices a supplier must initially charge for customized products. Finally, at a more general level, buyers may compensate suppliers through long-term commitments and/or promises of higher sales volume. Typically, such agreements also involve lower prices over time.

As predicted in the model in Figure 13.2, geographic proximity of the supplier's facilities helped lower acquisition costs. The expected effects of quality in lowering the customer's acquisition costs and operations costs were found, but Canon and Homburg (2001) were surprised to find that higher-quality products had lower direct product costs. Possible explanations for the unexpected finding for the product quality-direct product costs relationship can be drawn from the quality literature. It may be that quality operates as an order qualifier and high quality is necessary just to be considered as a supplier but does not allow a supplier to charge higher prices.

Another hypothesis in Figure 13.2 predicts the effects of actively monitoring the supply market on each cost. More active monitoring of the supply market was found to be associated with higher operations costs but not with higher acquisition costs.

A final hypothesis in Figure 13.2 was supported in the empirical data. It predicts that lowering the customer firm's direct product, acquisition, and operations costs leads the customer to expand its business with the supplier. These findings suggest that a supplier's efforts to lower a customer firm's costs can have long-term benefits to suppliers as well.

As IT outsourcing becomes more commonplace, new organizational forms are emerging to facilitate these relationships. Chase Bank has created "shared services" units that compete with outside vendors to furnish services to the bank's own operating units. Delta Airlines has established a "business partners" unit to oversee its relations with vendors. Microsoft outsources almost everything — from the manufacturing of its computer software to the distribution of its software products, thereby focusing the organization on its primary area of competitive advantage: the writing of software code. Still other firms are creating "strategic services" divisions in which activities formerly decentralized into autonomous business units are now being recentralized for outside contracting. As these various approaches suggest, the best ways to structure outsourcing remain the subject of ongoing management debate and media coverage (Useem & Harder, 2000).

As companies devise new forms of organization to assure that outsourcing works as intended, those responsible require a new blend of talents. Rather than issuing orders, managers must concentrate on negotiating results, replacing a skill for sending work downward with a talent for arranging work outward. Thus, the outsourcing of services necessitates lateral leadership, according to Useem and Harder (2000).

Useem and Harder (2000) reached this conclusion about leadership capabilities required for outsourcing through interviews conducted with several companies. What emerged from the interviews and a broader survey was a picture of more demanding leadership environment, even as day-to-day management tasks are streamlined by outsourcing. They found that four individual capabilities encompass much of what is required of managers as outsourcing becomes commonplace:

- *Strategic thinking.* Within the outsourcing framework, managers must understand whether and how to outsource in ways that improve competitive advantage.

- *Deal making.* Outsource process managers must broker deals in two directions simultaneously — securing the right services from external providers and ensuring their use by internal managers.

- *Partnership governing.* After identifying areas suitable for outsourcing through strategic assessment and upon clinching a deal, effectively overseeing the relationship is essential.

- *Managing change.* Forcefully spearhead change is critical because companies are certain to encounter employee resistance.

These four capabilities emerged repeatedly when Useem and Harder (2000) were discussing the essential skills of those responsible for outsourcing decisions, contracting, and oversight. None of these qualities taken singly was found to be unique to outsourcing, but their combination is critical to leading laterally.

Governance and Management Roles

Managers undertake activities to achieve the objectives of the organization. A number of different and sometimes conflicting views of manager's role can be noted. Often, one particular aspect of the manager's job is emphasized to the exclusion of others. In sum, they perhaps cover all the aspects. A role typology is frequently used in studies of managerial work and is genderless.

In the context of IT management, the relevance of six management roles can be identified — leader, resource allocator, spokesman, entrepreneur, liaison and monitor. The following role descriptions can be used:

- *Leader*. As the leader, the manager is responsible for supervising, hiring, training, organizing, coordinating, and motivating a cadre of personnel towards objectives and goals. Literature has emphasized the impact of this role on personnel. This role is mainly internal to the IT function.

- *Resource allocator*. The manager must decide how to allocate human, financial, and information resources to the activities of the IT function. This role emphasizes planning, organizing, coordinating, and controlling tasks and is mainly internal to the IT function.

- *Spokesman*. As a spokesman, the manager extends his/her contacts outside the department to other areas of the organization. This role emphasizes acceptance of the IT function within the organization. Frequently, she or he must cross traditional departmental boundaries and become involved in matters of production, distribution, marketing, and finance.

- *Entrepreneur*. The manager identifies the users' needs and management expectations and develops solutions that change business situations. A major responsibility of the manager is to ensure that rapidly evolving technical opportunities are understood, planned, implemented, and strategically exploited in the organization.

- *Liaison*. In this role, the manager communicates with the external environment. This communication includes exchanging information with external outsourcing stakeholders and vendors. This is an active, external role.

- *Monitor*. This role emphasizes scanning of the external environment to keep up with relevant technical changes and competition. The manager identifies new ideas from resources outside the organization. For example, other companies' outsourcing experiences and plans are scanned. To accomplish this, the manager uses many resources including vendor contacts, professional relationships, and a network of personal contacts.

The six roles are illustrated in Figure 13.3. Leader and resource allocator are roles internal to the IT function. Spokesman and entrepreneur are roles internal to the organization. Monitor and liaison are roles external to the organization.

In terms of decision-making for IT governance, two management roles are visible. First, the resource allocator role is mainly concerned with decisions. The manager must decide how to allocate human, financial, and information resources to the activities of the IT function. Second, the entrepreneur role is mainly concerned with decisions. The manager identifies the users' needs and management expectations and makes decisions concerning solutions that change business situations.

Figure 13.3. Management roles in IT outsourcing projects

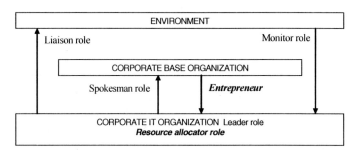

Why is IT Governance Important?

IT Governance matters because it influences the benefits received from IT investments. Through a combination of practices (such as redesigned business processes and well-designed governance mechanisms) and appropriately matched IT investments, top-performing enterprises generate superior returns on their IT investments (Weill, 2004).

Weill and Ross (2004, p. 22) list the following reasons why IT governance is important:

- *Good IT governance pays off.* Among the for-profit firms we studied, the ones pursuing a specific strategy (for example, customer intimacy, or operational excellence) with above-average IT governance performance had superior profits as measured by a three-year industry adjusted return on assets.

- *IT is expensive.* The average enterprise's IT investment is now greater than 4.2 percent of annual revenues and still rising. This investment results in IT exceeding 50 percent of the annual total capital investment of many enterprises. As IT has become more important and pervasive, senior management teams are increasingly challenged to manage and control IT to ensure that value is created. To address this issue, many enterprises are creating or refining IT governance structures to focus better IT spending on strategic priorities.

- *IT is pervasive.* In many enterprises, centrally managed IT is no longer possible or desirable. There was a time when requests for IT spending came only from the IT group. Now IT spending originates all over the enterprise. Some estimates suggest that only 20 percent of IT spending is visible in the IT budget. The rest of the spending occurs in business process budgets, product development budgets, and every other type of budget. Well-designed IT governance arrangements distribute IT decision making to those responsible for outcomes.

- *New information technologies bombard enterprises with new business opportunities.* Foresight is more likely if an enterprise has formalized governance processes for harmonizing desirable behaviors and IT principles.

- *IT governance is critical to organizational learning about IT value.* Effective governance creates mechanisms through which enterprises can debate potential value and formalize their learning. Governance also facilitates learning by formalizing exception processes. Enterprises often learn through exceptions — where a different approach from standard practice is used for good reasons. Effective governance makes learning via exceptions explicit and shares any new practices across the enterprise if appropriate.

- *IT value depends on more than good technology.* In recent years, there have been spectacular failures of large IT investments — major enterprise resource planning (ERP) systems initiatives that were never completed, e-business initiatives that were ill conceived or poorly executed, and data-mining experiments that generated plenty of data but few valuable leads. Successful firms not only make better IT decisions, they also have better IT decision-making processes. Specifically, successful firms involve the right people in the process. Having the right people involved in IT decision making yields both more strategic applications and greater buy-in.

- *Senior management has limited bandwidth.* Senior management does not have the bandwidth to consider all the requests for IT investments that occur in a large enterprise let alone get involved in many other IT-related decisions. If senior managers attempt to make too many decisions, they become a bottleneck. But decisions throughout the enterprise should be consistent with the direction in which senior management is taking the organization. Carefully designed IT governance provides a clear, transparent IT decision-making process that leads to consistent behavior linked back to the senior management vision while empowering everyone's creativity.

- *Leading enterprises govern IT differently.* Top performing firms balancing multiple performance goals had governance models that blended centralized and decentralized decision-making. All top performers' governance had one aspect in common. Their governance made transparent the tensions around IT decisions such as standardization vs. innovation.

Governance of Resources

According to the resource-based theory of the firm, performance differences across firms can be attributed to the variance in the firms' resources and capabilities. The essence of the resource-based theory of the firm lies in its emphasis on the internal resources available to the firm, rather than on the external opportunities and threats dictated by industry conditions. A firm's resources are said to be a source of competitive advantage to the degree that they are scarce, specialized, appropriable, valuable, rare, and difficult to imitate or substitute.

Capabilities and Resources

A fundamental idea in resource-based theory is that a firm must continually enhance its resources and capabilities to take advantage of changing conditions. Optimal growth involves a balance between the exploitation of existing resource positions and the development of new resource positions. Thus, a firm would be expected to develop new resources after its existing resource base has been fully utilized. Building new resource positions is important if the firm is to achieve sustained growth. When unused productive resources are coupled with changing managerial knowledge, unique opportunities for growth are created (Pettus, 2001).

The term resource is derived from Latin, *resurgere*, which means, "to rise" and implies an aid or expedient for reaching an end. A resource implies a potential means to achieve an end, or as something that can be used to create value. The first strategy textbooks outlining a holistic perspective focused on how resources needed to be allocated or deployed to earn rents. The interest in the term was for a long time linked to the efficiency of resource allocation, but this focus has later been expanded to issues such as resource accumulation, resource stocks, and resource flows (Haanaes, 1997).

Firms develop firm-specific resources and then renew these to respond to shifts in the business environment. Firms develop dynamic capabilities to adapt to changing environments. According to Pettus (2001), the term dynamic refers to the capacity to renew resource positions to achieve congruence with changing environmental conditions. A capability refers to the key role of strategic management in appropriately adapting, integrating, and reconfiguring internal and external organizational skills, resources, and functional capabilities to match the requirements of a changing environment.

If firms are to develop dynamic capabilities, learning is crucial. Change is costly; therefore, the ability of firms to make necessary adjustments depends upon their ability to scan the environment to evaluate markets and competitors and to accomplish quickly reconfiguration and transformation ahead of competition. However, history matters. Thus, opportunities for growth will involve dynamic capabilities closely related to existing capabilities. As such, opportunities will be most effective when they are close to previous resource use (Pettus, 2001).

According to Johnson and Scholes (2002), successful strategies are dependent on the organization having the strategic capability to perform at the level that is required for success. So the first reason why an understanding of strategic capability is important is concerned with whether an organization's strategies continue to fit the environment in which the organization is operating and the opportunities and threats that exist. Many of the issues of strategy development are concerned with changing strategic capability better to fit a changing environment. Understanding strategic capability is also important from another perspective. The organization's capability may be the leading edge of strategic developments, in the sense that new opportunities may be created by stretching and exploiting the organization's capability either in ways which competitors find difficult to match or in genuinely new directions, or both. This requires organizations to be innovative in the way they develop and exploit their capability.

In this perspective, strategic capability is about providing products or services to customers that are valued — or might be valued in the future. An understanding of what customers value is the starting point. The discussion then moves to whether an organization has the resources to provide products and services that meet these customer requirements.

By a resource is meant anything that could be thought of as a strength or weakness of a given firm. More formally, a firm's resources at a given time can be defined as those (tangible and intangible) assets that are tied to the firm over a substantial period. Examples of resources are brand names, in-house knowledge of technology, employment of skilled personnel, trade contracts, machinery, efficient procedures, capital etc. According to the economic school, resources include human capital, structural capital, relational capital, and financial capital.

Priem and Butler (2001) find it problematic that virtually anything associated with a firm can be a resource, because this notion suggests that prescriptions for dealing in certain ways with certain categories of resources might be operationally valid, whereas other categories of resources might be inherently difficult for practitioners to measure and manipulate. One example of a resource that might be difficult to measure and manipulate is tacit knowledge. Some have argued for tacit knowledge — that understanding gained from experience but that sometimes cannot be expressed to another person and is unknown to oneself — as a source of competitive advantage.

Another example is the CEO resource. Prescriptions have been made to top managers of poorly performing firms that they are the cause of the problem and should think about voluntarily exiting the firm. This is a case where viewing a CEO as a resource would have more prescriptive implications for boards of directors than for the CEO (Priem & Butler, 2001).

Barney (2002) discusses how value, rarity, imitability, and organization can be brought together into a single framework to understand the return potential associated with exploiting any of a firm's resources and capabilities. The framework consists of the following five steps (Barney, 2002):

1. If a resource or capability controlled by a firm is *not valuable*, that resource will not enable a firm to choose or implement strategies that exploit environmental opportunities or neutralize environmental threats. Organizing to exploit this resource will increase a firm's costs or decrease its revenues. These types of resources are weaknesses. Firms will have either to fix these weaknesses or avoid using them when choosing and implementing strategies. If firms do exploit these kinds of resources and capabilities, they can expect to put themselves at a competitive disadvantage compared to firms that either do not possess these non-valuable resources or do not use them in conceiving and implementing strategies. Firms at a competitive disadvantage are likely to earn below-normal economic profits.

2. If a resource or capability is *valuable but not rare*, exploiting this resource in conceiving and implementing strategies will generate competitive parity and normal economic performance. Exploiting these valuable-but-not-rare resources will generally not create above-normal economic performance for a firm, but failure

to exploit them can put a firm at a competitive disadvantage. In this sense, valuable-but-not-rare resources can be thought of as organizational strengths.

3.   If a resource or capability is *valuable and rare but not costly to imitate*, exploiting this resource will generate a temporary competitive advantage for a firm and above-normal economic profits. A firm that exploits this kind of resource is, in an important sense, gaining a first-mover advantage, because it is the first firm that is able to exploit a particular resource. However, once competing firms observe this competitive advantage, they will be able to acquire or develop the resources needed to implement this strategy through direct duplication or substitution at no cost disadvantage compared to the first-moving firm. Over time, any competitive advantage that the first mover obtained would be competed away as other firms imitate the resources needed to compete. However, between the time a firm gains a competitive advantage by exploiting a valuable and rare but imitable resource or capability, and the time that competitive advantage is competed away through imitation, the first-moving firm can earn above-normal economic performance. Consequently, this type of resource or capability can be thought of as an organizational strength and distinctive competence.

4.   If a resource is *valuable, rare, and costly to imitate*, exploiting this resource will generate a sustained competitive advantage and above-normal economic profits. In this case, competing firms face a significant cost disadvantage in imitating a successful firm's resources and capabilities, and thus cannot imitate this firm's strategies. This advantage may reflect the unique history of the successful firm, causal ambiguity about which resources to imitate, or the socially complex nature of these resources and capabilities. In any case, attempts to compete away the advantages of firms that exploit these resources will not generate above normal or even normal performance for imitating firms. Even if these firms are able to acquire or develop the resources and capabilities in question, the very high costs of doing so would put them at a competitive disadvantage compared to the firm that already possessed the valuable, rare, and costly to imitate resources. These kinds of resources and capabilities are organizational strengths and sustainable distinctive competencies.

5.   The question of organization operates as an adjustment factor in the framework. If a firm with a resource that is *valuable, rare, and costly to imitate, is disorganized*, some of its potential above-normal return could be lost. If the firm completely fails to organize itself to take advantage of this resource, it could actually lead the firm that has the potential for above-normal performance to earn normal or even below-normal performance.

Barney (2001) discusses how value and rarity of resources can be determined. *Value* is a question of conditions under which resources will and will not be valuable. Models of the competitive environment within which a firm competes can determine value. Such models fall into two large categories: (1) efforts to use structure-conduct-performance-based models to specify conditions under which different firm resources will be valuable and (2) efforts to determine the value of firm resources that apply other models derived from industrial organization models of perfect and imperfect competition.

As an example of resource value determination, Barney (2001) discusses the ability of cost leadership strategy to generate sustained competitive advantage. Several firm attributes may be associated with cost leadership, such as volume-derived economies of scale, cumulative volume-derived learning curve economies, and policy choices. These firm attributes can be shown to generate economic value in at least some market settings. The logic used to demonstrate the value of these attributes is a market structure logic that is consistent with traditional microeconomics. After identifying the conditions under which cost leadership can generate economic value, it is possible to turn to the conditions under which cost leadership can be a source of competitive advantage (i.e. rare) and sustained competitive advantage (i.e. rare and costly to imitate).

The resource-based theory postulates that some resources will have a higher value for one firm than for other firms. The reasons why the value of resources may be firm-specific are multiple and include (Haanaes, 1997): the experience of working together as a team, the firm possessing superior knowledge about its resources, the bundling of the resources, and the existence of co-specialized or complementary assets.

The value of a given resource may change over time as the market conditions change, e.g., in terms of technology, customer preferences or industry structure. Thus, it is often argued that firms need to maintain a dynamic, as opposed to static, evaluation of the value of different resources.

Rarity is a question of how many competing firms possess a particular valuable resource. If only one competing firm possesses a particular valuable resource, then that firm can gain a competitive advantage, i.e. it can improve its efficiency and effectiveness in ways that competing firms cannot. One example of this form of testable assertion is mentioned by Barney (2001). The example is concerned with organizational culture as a source of competitive advantage. If only one competing firm possesses a valuable organizational culture (where the value of that culture is determined in ways that are exogenous to the firm), then that firm can gain a competitive advantage, i.e. it can improve its efficiency and effectiveness in ways that competing firms cannot. Both these assertions are testable. If a firm uniquely possesses a valuable resource and cannot improve its efficiency and effectiveness in ways that generate competitive advantages, then these assertions are contradicted. One could test these assertions by measuring the extent to which a firm uniquely possesses valuable resources, e.g. valuable organizational culture, measuring the activities that different firms engage in to improve their efficiency and effectiveness, and then seeing if there are some activities a firm with the unique culture engages in to improve its effectiveness and efficiency — activities not engaged in by other competing firms.

In general, the rarity of a resource is present as long as the number of firms that possess a particular valuable resource is less than the number of firms needed to generate perfect competition dynamics. Of course, there is difficult measurement problems associated with testing assertions of this form. Barney (2001) points out that additional research work is needed to complete the parameterization of the concept of rarity.

Efficient firms can sustain their competitive advantage only if their resources can neither be extended freely nor imitated by other firms. Hence, in order for resources to have the potential to generate rents, they must be rare. Valuable, but common, resources cannot by themselves represent sources of competitive advantage because competitors can access them. Nobody needs to pay extra for obtaining a resource that is not held in limited supply.

In addition to value and rarity, inimitability has to be determined. *Inimitability* can be determined through barriers to imitation and replication. The extent of barriers and impediments against direct and indirect imitation determine the extent of inimitability. One effective barrier to imitation is that competitors fail to understand the firm's sources of advantage. The lack of understanding can be caused by tacitness, complexity, and specificity that form bases for competitive advantage (Haanaes, 1997).

Several authors have categorized resources. A common categorization is tangibles vs. intangibles. Tangibles are relatively clearly defined and easy to identify. Tangible resources include plants, technology, land, geographical location, access to raw materials, capital, equipment, and legal resources. Tangible resources tend to be property-based and may include databases, licenses, patents, registered designs and trademarks, as well as other property rights that are easily bought and sold.

Intangibles are more difficult to define and to study empirically. Intangible resources encompass skills, knowledge, organizational capital, relationships, capabilities and human capital, as well as brands, company and product reputation, networks, competencies, perceptions of quality and the ability to manage change. Intangible resources are generally less easy to transfer than tangible resources, as the value of an intangible resource is difficult to measure (Haanaes, 1997).

Classification of IT Resources for Governance

The resource-based view started to appear in IT research one decade ago. Now IT resources can be compared to one another and, perhaps more importantly, can be compared with non-IT resources. Thus, the resource-based view promotes cross-functional studies through comparisons with other firm resources.

In the beginning of resource-based studies of IT resources, IT was divided into three assets, which together with processes contribute to business value. These three IT assets were labeled human assets (e.g., technical skills, business understanding, problem-solving orientation), technology assets (e.g., physical IT assets, technical platforms, databases, architectures, standards), and relationship assets (e.g., partnerships with other divisions, client relationships, top management sponsorship, shared risk and responsibility). IT processes were defined as planning ability, cost-effective operations and support, and fast delivery. This categorization was later modified to include IT infrastructure, human IT resources, and IT-enabled intangibles.

Wade and Hulland (2004) presented a typology of IT resources, where the IT resources held by a firm can be sorted into three types of processes: inside out, outside in, and spanning. Inside-out resources are deployed from inside the firm in response to market requirements and opportunities, and tend to be internally focused. In contrast, outside-in resources are externally oriented, placing an emphasis on anticipated market requirements, creating durable customer relationships, and understanding competitors. Finally, spanning resources, which involve both internal and external analysis, are needed to integrate the firm's inside out and outside-in resources.

Inside-out resources include IS infrastructure, IS technical skills, IS development, and cost-effective IS operations:

- *IT infrastructure.* Many components of the IT infrastructure (such as off-the-shelf computer hardware and software) convey no particular strategic benefit due to lack of rarity, ease of imitation, and ready mobility. Thus, the types of IT infrastructure of importance are either proprietary or complex and hard to imitate. Despite research attempts to focus on the non-imitable aspects of IT infrastructure, the IT infrastructure resource has generally not been found to be a source of sustained competitive advantage for firms.

- *IT technical skills.* IT technical skills are a result of the appropriate, updated technology skills, relating to both systems hardware and software that are held by the IS/IT employees of a firm. Such skills do not include only current technical knowledge, but also the ability to deploy, use, and manage that knowledge. Thus, this resource is focused on technical skills that are advanced, complex, and, therefore, difficult to imitate. Although the relative mobility of IS/IT personnel tends to be high, some IS skills cannot be easily transferred, such as corporate-level knowledge assets and technology integration skills, and, thus, these resources can become a source of sustained competitive advantage.

- *IT development.* IT development refers to the capability to develop or experiment with new technologies, as well as a general level of alertness to emerging technologies and trends that allow a firm to quickly take advantage of new advances. Thus, IT development includes capabilities associated with managing a systems development life cycle that is capable of supporting competitive advantage, and should therefore lead to superior firm performance.

- *Cost-effective IT operations.* This resource encompasses the ability to provide efficient and cost-effective IS operations on an ongoing basis. Firms with greater efficiency can develop a long-term competitive advantage by using this capability to reduce costs and develop a cost leadership position in their industry. In the context of IS operations, the ability to avoid large, persistent cost overruns, unnecessary downtime, and system failure is likely to be an important precursor to superior performance. Furthermore, the ability to develop and manage IT systems of appropriate quality that function effectively can be expected to have a positive impact on performance.

Outside-in resources include external relationship management and market responsiveness:

- *External relationship management.* This resource represents the firm's ability to manage linkages between the IT function and stakeholders outside the firm. It can manifest itself as an ability to work with suppliers to develop appropriate systems and infrastructure requirements for the firm, to manage relationships with outsourcing partners, or to manage customer relationships by providing solutions, support, and/or customer service. Many large IT departments rely on external partners for a significant portion of their work. The ability to work with and manage these relationships is an important organizational resource leading to competitive advantage and superior firm performance.

- *Market responsiveness*. Market responsiveness involves both the collection of information from sources external to the firm as well as the dissemination of a firm's market intelligence across departments, and the organization's response to that learning. It includes the abilities to develop and manage projects rapidly and to react quickly to changes in market conditions. A key aspect of market responsiveness is strategic flexibility, which allows the organization to undertake strategic change when necessary.

Spanning resources include IS-business partnerships and IS planning and change management:

- *IS-business partnerships*. This capability represents the processes of integration and alignment between the IS function and other functional areas or departments of the firm. The importance of IS alignment, particularly with business strategy, has been well documented. This resource has variously been referred to as synergy, assimilation, and partnerships. All of these studies recognize the importance of building relationships internally within the firm between the IS function and other areas or departments. Such relationships help to span the traditional gaps that exist between functions and departments, resulting in superior competitive position and firm performance. An element of this resource is the support for collaboration within the firm.

- *IS planning and change management*. The capability to plan, manage, and use appropriate technology architectures and standards also helps to span these gaps. Key aspects of this resource include the ability to anticipate future changes and growth, to choose platforms (including hardware, network, and software standards) that can accommodate this change, and to manage effectively the resulting technology change and growth. This resource has been defined variously in previous research as "understanding the business case," "problem solving orientation," and "capacity to manage IT change". It includes the ability of IS managers to understand how technologies can and should be used, as well as how to motivate and manage IS personnel through the change process.

In order to explore the usefulness of the resource-based theory for IT resources, it is necessary to recognize explicitly the characteristics and attributes of resources that lead them to become strategically important. Although firms possess many resources, only a few of these have the potential to lead the firm to a position of sustained competitive advantage. What is it, then, that separates regular resources form those that confer a sustainable strategic benefit?

According to Wade and Hulland (2004), resource-based theorists have approached this question by identifying sets of resource attributes that might conceptually influence a firm's competitive position. Under this view, only resources exhibiting all of these attributes can lead to a sustained competitive advantage for the firm. We have already mentioned Barney's (2001) attributes of value, rareness, inimitability, non-substitutability, combination, and exploration.

In addition, an important seventh attribute is immobile. Once a firm establishes a competitive advantage through the strategic use of resources, competitors will likely attempt to amass comparable resources in order to share in the advantage. A primary source of resources is factor markets. If firms are able to acquire the resources necessary to imitate a rival's advantage, the rival's advantage will be short-lived. Thus, a requirement for sustained competitive advantage is that resources be imperfectly mobile or non-tradable.

To govern IT resources in an efficiently and effectively, it is necessary to understand the strategic attributes of each resource. In Figure 13.4, the table shows an example of how strategic IT resources can be identified. The scale from 1 (little extent) to 5 (great extent) is applied.

In this example, we see that IT infrastructure is the IT resource with the greatest potential to lead to sustained competitive advantage, which would contradict that the IT infrastructure resource has generally not been found to be a source of sustained competitive advantage for firms. On the other hand, cost-effective IT operations have the least potential.

Wade and Hulland (2004) suggest that some of the resources create competitive advantage, while others sustain that advantage. A distinction is made between resources that help the firm attain a competitive advantage and those that help the firm to sustain the advantage. These two types of resource attributes can be thought of as, respectively, ex ante and ex post limits to competition.

Ex ante limits to competition suggest that prior to any firm's establishing a superior resource position, there must be limited competition for that position. If any firm wishing to do so can acquire and deploy resources to achieve the position, it cannot by definition be superior. Attributes in this category include value, rarity, and appropriability.

Ex post limits to competition mean that subsequent to a firm's gaining a superior position and earning rents, there must be forces that limit competition for those rents. Attributes in this category include imitability, substitutability, and mobility.

Figure 13.4. IT resources in terms of strategic importance based on attributes

Attributes / Resources	Valuable	Rare	Exploitable	Inimitable	Non-substitutable	Combinable	Immobile	TOTAL
IT infrastructure	4	2	5	5	2	5	4	27
IT technical skills	4	2	3	3	4	4	3	23
IT development	4	3	3	3	4	3	2	22
Cost-effective IT operations	4	2	3	2	4	3	1	19

Governance as Part of Institutional Economics

A new branch of institutional economics has emerged that is mainly concerned with governance (Williamson, 2000). The new institutional economics argues that institutions are both important and susceptible to analysis. It is based on the assumption that human actors have limited cognitive competence — often referred to as bounded rationality. Given such cognitive limits, complex contracts such as IT outsourcing contracts are unavoidable incomplete. Contractual incompleteness poses problems when paired with the condition of opportunism — which manifests itself as adverse selection, moral hazard, shirking, subgoal pursuit, and other forms of strategic behavior. Because human actors will not reliably disclose true conditions upon request or self-fulfill all promises, contract as mere promise, unsupported by credible commitments, will not be self-enforcing (Willamson, 2000).

Williamson (2000) argues that governance is at level three in the new institutional economics as illustrated in Figure 13.5. He defines governance as play of the game — especially contract by aligning governance structures with transactions. At level 1, we find the social environment, consisting of norms, customs, mores, traditions, and religion. Level 2 is the institutional environment consisting of laws, bureaucracy, and politics. Level 4 is resource allocation and employment, where we also find prices and quantities for resources and incentive alignment for employees.

It is useful for the purposes of perspectives on IT governance to study the hierarchy of Figure 13.5. The solid arrows that connect a higher with a lower level signify that the higher level imposes constraints on the level immediately below. The reverse arrows that connect lower with higher levels are dashed and signal feedback.

Figure 13.5. Economics of institutions

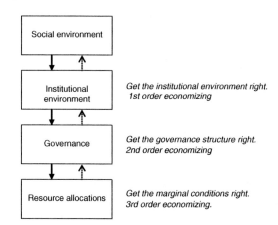

Chapter XIV

IT Governance as Allocation of Decision Rights

Most scholars seem to agree that a critical part of IT governance is allocation of decision rights. Allocation is concerned with identifying decision makers and decision categories.

Decision Makers and Decision Rights

Weill and Ross (2004, p. 58) use political archetypes (monarchy, feudal, federal, duopoly, anarchy) to describe the combinations of people who have either decision rights or input to IT decisions:

1. *Business monarchy.* In a business monarchy, senior business executives make IT decisions affecting the entire enterprise. It is a group of business executives or individual executives (CxOs), including committees of senior business executives (may include CIO). It excludes IT executives acting independently.

2. *IT monarchy.* In an IT monarchy, IT professionals make IT decisions. It is a group of IT executives or individual CIOs.

3. *Feudal.* The feudal model is based on traditions where the princes and princesses or their designated knights make their own decisions, optimizing their local needs. It is business unit leaders, key process owners or their delegates.

4. *Federal.* The federal decision-making model has a long tradition in government. Federal arrangements attempt to balance the responsibilities and accountability of multiple governing bodies, such as country or states. It is c-level executives and business groups (e.g., business units or processes). It may also include IT executives as additional participants. It is equivalent of the central and state governments working together.

5. *IT duopoly.* The IT duopoly is a two-party arrangement where decisions represent a bilateral agreement between IT executives and one other group (e.g., CxO or business unit or process leaders). The IT executives may be a central IT group or team of central and business unit IT organizations.

6. *Anarchy.* Within an anarchy, individuals or small groups make their own decisions based only on their local needs. Anarchies are the bane of the existence of many IT groups and are expensive to support and secure. It can be each individual user.

Peterson (2004) discusses decision makers and decision rights in terms of centralization vs. decentralization. Over the past decade, organizations have set out to achieve the best of both worlds by adopting a *federal* IT governance structure. In a federal IT governance model, IT infrastructure decisions are centralized, and IT application decisions are decentralized. The federal IT governance model thus represents a hybrid model of both centralization and decentralization.

The discussion of whether to centralize or decentralize IT governance is based on a rational perspective of the organization, in which choices are reduced to one of internal efficiency and effectiveness. This view assumes a system of goal consonance and agreement on the means for achieving goals, i.e., rational and logical trade-off between (a) efficiency and standardization under centralization, vs. (b) effectiveness and flexibility under decentralization.

In general, it is assumed that centralization leads to greater specialization, consistency, and standardized controls, while decentralization provides local control, ownership and greater responsiveness and flexibility to business needs. However, flexibility under decentralization may lead to variable standards, which ultimately result in lower flexibility, and specialization under centralization incurs risks due to bounded rationality and information overload (Peterson, 2004).

A federal approach towards IT governance challenges managers in local business units to surrender control over certain business-specific IT domains for the well-being of the enterprise, and to develop business-to-corporate and business-to-IT partnerships. The potential risk in contemporary business environments is that either centralization or decentralization fit the organization into a fixed structure. The challenge is therefore to balance the benefits of decentralized decision-making and business innovation and the benefits of central control and IT standardization (Peterson, 2004).

Figure 14.1. Decision matrix for application proposals

	Profitability Weight = 5		Risk Weight = 3		Suitability Weight = 2		Score	Priority
Proposal A	3	15	6	18	2	4	37	7
Proposal B	4	20	5	15	2	4	39	5
Proposal C	5	25	4	12	7	14	51	3
Proposal D	6	30	3	9	7	14	53	2
Proposal E	7	35	2	6	3	6	47	4
Proposal F	6	30	1	3	3	6	39	5
Proposal G	5	25	4	12	9	18	55	1

Decision Examples

Typically, the number of proposals for new IT applications exceeds the number that can be implemented. Financial constraints, lack of human resources, and other factors may limit the number. Also, financial, human, and other factors will influence the priority of suggested applications. Making decisions about:

* criteria to apply in prioritization,

* use of the criteria to proposals, and

* weight assigned to criteria,

is an important management task. It is illustrated in the table in Figure 14.1. This is an example with seven application proposals A to G. Three criteria are applied: profitability, risk, and suitability in relation to existing IT-systems in the organization. Profitability is assigned highest weight. In this example, proposal A scores three on profitability. When multiplied with the weight of five, the score becomes 15. The total score for proposal A is, resulting in the last priority, making in unlikely for implementation.

Decision-making is related to criteria. For example, in Figure 14.1, more criteria can be used and criteria can be replaced. Decision-making is related to scores assigned to each proposal. Finally, decision-making is necessary when weights are to be applied to criteria.

When needs for change have been identified and proposals for filling gaps have been developed, alternative actions for improving the current situation can be developed. New IS/IT can be developed, acquired, and implemented in alternative ways. Several decisions have to be made when a new IS/IT is chosen. Such decisions are called systems development strategy, and we apply a systems development strategy map to identify appropriate strategies. A systems development strategy map illustrates decisions that have to be made concerning actions for IS/IT as illustrated in Figure 14.2:

* *Use of resources.* One extreme is complete in-house development; the other extreme is a standard package without any changes. There is a fundamental difference for a company between developing the IS/IT itself or buying a standard package in the

marketplace from a software vendor. Between the two extremes, there are some other options. The standard package might be modified, that is, the company or the vendor could make changes to the software package when applied to the company. The decision here will depend on the availability of suitable application packages for the firm's situation.

- *Kind of methodology.* Analytic methodology implies defining the needs of users through intellectual reasoning techniques. Such techniques define stages of systems study, systems design, programming, installation, testing, implementation, and maintenance. Experimental methodology is showing the users alternative computer screens with information and asking for their opinions. This is sometimes called prototyping. Through iterations, we might improve and create even better systems. The decision here will depend on systems complexity and the available time for development.

- *Form of deliverance.* A revolutionary approach implies that everything is delivered at the end of the project, like a big bang. A completely new system is implemented and used. An evolutionary approach implies that changes are gradually taking place over time; changes are implemented in an incremental way. The decision here will depend on available time for development as well as organizational culture for revolution vs. evolution.

- *Participation of users.* A systems project can either be completely expert-driven or completely user-led, or something in between. It is an important part of Scandinavian culture to have user participation. Totally user-led may be difficult, as technical problems will require the assistance of IS/IT experts. The decision here will depend on technical skills needed as well as availability of competent and motivated users.

- *Kind of results.* Product means only the new IS/IT. Process means paying attention to the learning and increased insight gained from participating in the IS/IT development activity. The decision here will depend on systems complexity as well as company culture for learning.

- *Coordination of development.* This scale runs from one-sided systems development to a balanced development of personnel, system, and organization. A completely one-sided systems development may create an efficient technological solution, but it may not work in the organization as personnel and organizational issues were not considered. The decision here will depend on company culture for linking human resources management to information technology management.

The first decision in the systems development strategy map is concerned with use of resources. Over the last two decades, the availability of standard application packages has risen. In most application areas, there are standard packages available today. Most organizations have changed from an in-house development strategy to a standard package strategy. Acquisition of standard application software is a very widespread strategy, especially among small and medium-sized companies that cannot afford large in-house staff for systems development. Large companies may still have the resources

Figure 14.2. Systems development strategy map to identify actions for IS/IT

to cover their own special systems needs. There is a big market for standard application packages. Most companies of small and medium size have bought standard applications for their administrative support functions, many also for their production and marketing systems. As an example, the Norwegian School of Management BI needed a new student administration system. The school bought the standard package BANNER. Because of some special needs for exams and grading, the system had to be modified somewhat.

Generally, the advantages of application package acquisition include:

- Quicker installation providing earlier business benefits

- Reduced costs for development and maintenance

- More reliable cost/benefit analysis

- Know-how built into the package

- Flexibility for changes in business activities

- Well tested, hence fewer errors.

Of course, there are disadvantages and pitfalls as well in acquisitions of application packages. The most common one is that the organization does not carefully enough consider its own needs. It may also be a disadvantage not to have an own IS/IT function to support the system. Costs of adaptation may rise as needs for modifications may cause expensive changes in the package. Generally, disadvantages of package acquisition include:

- Hasty decisions, making an undesirable investment decision

- Underestimation of costs of adaptation of package to the company

- Inappropriate computer operations environment for the package

- Expensive computer operations for the package

- Vendor dependency in areas such as support, modifications and further development

- People have to adapt to the package rather than system adjusted to the people

Even when the company has decided to follow the strategy of acquiring a standard package, it must find out — define — its own needs, that is, the requirements of the desired IS/IT. Without user needs and requirements, it is impossible to choose a standard package. There might be several packages available. First, a comparison between the needs and each package has to be done in order to find out the extent of fit between the two. Then, in the selection, one has to identify the possibilities and the costs of making necessary adjustments. The result of a selection is a temporary choice of one package. Then we have — in more detail — to check if it is possible to make the desired modifications to the package. We also have to check if the initial cost estimate still holds true.

The comparison between the needs and each package can be carried out using the relational model. The *relational model* tells us — step by step — what we have to do to fulfill the requirements of the company if we purchase the temporary selected application package. If we, during the analysis, run into major unanticipated problems, then we have to switch to another package and do the analysis with the new package. The relational model is time-consuming to apply, both for the company and for the software vendor. Therefore we must try to do it only once for each package.

The fit or match between requirements of the company and the package of the software vendor can be measured using the relational model. The goal is to select a package with a good initial fit, and then we can discuss what we can do to improve the fit. Here again we get help from the relational model as parts with poor fit are identified and analyzed. The relational model consists of ten parts as illustrated in Figure 14.3.

The ten parts in the relational model have the following meaning:

1. *Part of the package directly acceptable for the business.* This represents the initial fit between requirements and package.

2. *Part of the package that will make business even more efficient.* These are things we did not consider when making the requirements. When we see the package, we realize that this part can be advantageous to the company.

Figure 14.3. The relational model for evaluation of an application package

8	7	6	4	3	1	2	5		
		6	4	3	1	2	5	9	10

3.   *Part of the package that will have this as a permanent feature, expanded and developed by vendor.* This part of the requirements is not covered by the package. The vendor thinks it is a good idea to incorporate it in the package. The vendor does the changes on his own account. This will be a future feature of the package, available to all vendor customers.

4.   *Part of the package that will be changed to meet requirements, developed by vendor.* This part of the requirements is not covered by the package. The vendor is willing to incorporate this in the software application, but at the expense of the buyer. It is to be decided if this work is to be done at a fixed price or paid by the hour. Payment by the hour introduces an uncertainty in the buying situation. Furthermore, there might be a future problem of maintenance, since it is not certain that the vendor will do it.

5.   *Part of the business that will adapt to package.* This part of the requirements is not covered by the package. The company will give up some of the requirements and do work the way it has to be done with the application package. This is an important decision for both management and users. Some corporate cultures are more willing to adapt to a package than other cultures.

6.   *Part of the package that will be changed to meet requirements, developed by customer.* This is not part of the package. The company buying it will extend the software. This is a very risky task, as it might be difficult to make changes in an unknown package and to maintain those changes over time. It is also risky because the vendor will in the future make changes to the standard package that might affect the homemade part and create further need for software changes.

7.   *Part of requirements that will be developed in-house.* This is not part of the package. These requirements will be met by the customer by making an IS/IT separate and in addition to the package.

8.   *Part of the requirements that will be left unfulfilled.* Neither the vendor nor the customer will develop and program a subsystem to meet these requirements. The vendor will not do it because he may see technical difficulties as well as no market potential for the subsystem. The customer will not do it because he expects to be able to survive without it.

9.   *Part of the package that will not be used.* There can be many reasons for not using this part of the software package in the company. For example, our company may have another application that already has all functions in this part covered in an efficient and effective way.

10. *Irrelevant part of the package.* There can be many reasons for the irrelevance of this part of the software package to the company. For example, our company is in a service industry, while this part of the package is only applicable to manufacturing industry.

Form of deliverance is the third issue in the systems development strategy map. A revolutionary approach implies that everything is delivered at the end of the project, like a big bang. A completely new system is implemented and used. An evolutionary approach implies that changes are gradually taking place over time; changes are implemented in an incremental way. The decision here will depend on available time for development as well as organizational culture for revolution vs. evolution. We can distinguish between the following four forms of deliverance, as illustrated in Figure 14.4:

- *Direct deliverance (cold start)*. At a specific point in time, the old system is terminated and the new system is implemented. The old system can no longer be used, because data for that system are no longer updated. If the new system fails, it will be a painful period without any information system.

- *Double deliverance (parallel)*. For a specific period, both the old system and the new system are run in parallel. This form reduces risks, but it causes higher operating costs for the period.

- *Stepwise deliverance (phased)*. The new system is divided into subsystems, and subsystems are implemented one at a time. When one module in the new system is used, then the equivalent module in the old system is stopped.

- *Pilot deliverance (group wise)*. At a specific point in time, the system is implemented in one part of the organization. For example, the department of mergers and acquisitions in a law firm may be the first part of an organization to use a new system. If the use is successful, then the system spreads to other parts of the organization.

After having completed all decisions the systems development strategy map, we have to make final decisions concerning content of actions and development actions. While content of actions is our final priority of needed changes, development actions is our final systems development strategy.

We are now going to look a little closer at the task of choosing which IS/IT to develop/acquire. An IS/IT should in general be financially justified, and we should use the traditional tools of financial analysis to see if the investment is economically sound. But the following list of reasons for IS/IT projects shows that there might be some IS/IT that can be justified by other reasons than financial ones:

- *Strictly necessary applications*. There might be some that are required by law, for example a new tax law that require changes in the existing financial management system.

- *Strategic applications*. To stay in business we have to do it.

- *Maintenance of existing applications*. Several bugs need fixing now.

- *User requests*. Users have expanded the use of an existing system to new tasks that require systems modification.

- *New areas*. We have to experiment with new technology, such as e-business.

- *Applications that increase efficiency, effectiveness, and competitiveness*. These are the applications that can be freely prioritized for selection.

The economist will look at the development of a new IS/IT or changes made to an existing one as an investment. An investment is characterized by some initial costs (net profit is

Figure 14.4. Four basic approaches to system changeover

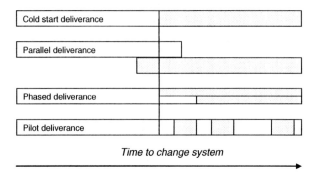

negative) and later some income (net profit is positive). We will have a cash flow with some negative payments first and some positive payments later. Then we can calculate NPV (Net Present Value) or IRR (Internal Rate of Return), and then decide if the investment is worth implementing. If we have several profitable investments, we can decide which one is best.

There are other ways of deciding if an investment is favorable. The ambition might be to have a balanced application portfolio. For example, some IS/IT support cash cows, while other IS/IT support stars and wild cats.

Ward and Griffiths (1996, p. 408) suggest that three factors need to be included in the assessment of priorities for future applications:

•   What is most important to do: benefits to the firm

•   What is capable of being done: resources in the firm

•   What is likely to succeed: risks to the firm

Some companies use a point (or scoring method) when evaluating an IS/IT investment. This can be done by making a list of requirements and then looking at the proposed IS/IT and give points (e.g., 0-5) according to how well the different systems fulfill the requirements. Economic profitability in terms of NPV or IRR might be only one of the requirements. Implemented within a certain time limit might be high on the priority list of users. There might be knockout factors. If the score is zero for such a factor, then the planned system is dropped.

We should try harder to measure the benefits in financial terms. It is not always easy, on the contrary, costs are often much easier to estimate than benefits. There is sometimes the danger of detailed cost analysis and lacking benefits analysis. One approach to benefit analysis is to identify what kind of benefits may be caused by the system. We have earlier discussed efficiency, effectiveness, and competitiveness. Efficiency (E) means doing things right. It is to use a minimum of resources to obtain a predetermined result. Effectiveness (E) means doing the right things. It is to use resources to obtain a desired result. Competitiveness (C) means doing the right things better than the competitors do. In addition to the EEC model, we can look for rationalization (automation) benefits, control (decision) benefits, organizational (redesign) benefits, and market (competitive) benefits as discussed earlier.

The costs are often easier to calculate than the benefits. Costs include development costs, hardware and software costs, operating costs, and maintenance costs. In an investment analysis, we have to distinguish between:

- Actual investment (occurring only once, e.g. development costs and the costs of acquiring hardware and software)

- Yearly operating costs

- Periodic costs (e.g. maintenance costs, which might not appear each year)

A survey of 80 American, British, Australian, and New Zealand companies' practices in approving IS/IT projects showed a variety of criteria used. Support of business objectives was a criteria used by 88 percent of the companies. Budgetary constraints was a criteria used by 68 percent of the companies (Olson, 2001).

Risks have to be considered before taking the final decision on an IS/IT investment. An IS/IT might be associated with more risks than another IS/IT. The typical failures to be considered include:

- *Technical failure.* The IS/IT does not work. The technical quality is low. It may be difficult to integrate different kinds of equipment. Maybe there is too little capacity. Technical problems are often the easiest and cheapest problems to overcome. This is the responsibility of IS/IT experts.

- *Data failure.* The data provide wrong information because of low data quality. The data may be wrong, or the information associated with the data may be misunderstood. The problem can be reduced if data are collected at the source, and the users are motivated. This is the shared responsibility of users and IS/IT help functions.

- *User failure.* Users misunderstand the IS/IT, e.g. because they are not properly trained. This is the responsibility of the IS/IT department.

- *Organizational failure.* IS/IT does not correspond to the needs and tasks of the organization. This is the responsibility of users and management.

- *Failure in business environment.* Inappropriate IS/IT may emerge due to changes in the business environment.

Risk management requires identification of risk categories. Common categories are people issues, project size, control of the project, complexity, novelty, and stability of requirements. Some proposed IS/IT might be associated with more risks than others might. To analyze risk further, it can be helpful to distinguish between two dimensions of risk. The first dimension is concerned with probability, i.e. the chance of something going wrong. The second dimension is concerned with consequence, i.e. the seriousness of problems arising when something goes wrong. The two dimensions are illustrated in Figure 14.5.

Figure 14.5. Risk analysis of proposed IS/IT

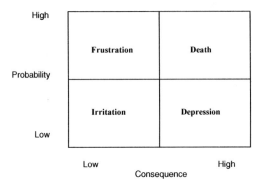

We would like to choose IS/IT with both low risk probability and low risk consequence. In companies with a significant degree of risk aversion, consequence is often considered more important than probability. This can also be observed in society, where nuclear accidents or plane crashes may be associated with very low probability and very high (unacceptable) consequence. Risk analysis of proposed IS/IT should therefore take into account the potential risk aversion of corporate management.

Often, there will be a positive relationship between NPV or IRR and risk. A very risky new IS/IT will typically have a high NPV or IRR. This is illustrated in Figure 14.6. IS/IT with high economic return and low risk will typically be chosen before other IS/IT in the figure. We would like many IS/IT that are runners, we will accept some swimmers and walkers, and we will avoid all troublemakers.

Figure 14.6. Trade-off between economic return and risk of proposed IS/IT

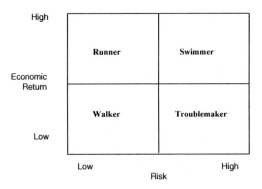

Categories of Decisions

Weill og Ross (2004, p. 27) defined the following decision categories:

1. *IT principles* are a related set of high-level statements about how IT is used in the business. Once articulated, IT principles become part of the enterprise's management lexicon and can be discussed, debated, supported, overturned, and evolved. The hallmark of an effective set of IT principles is a clear trail of evidence from the business to the IT management principles. For Mead Westvaco, architectural integrity (IT principle 2) provides both standardized processes and technologies (business principle 2) and cost control and operational efficiency (business principle 4); rapid deployment of new applications (IT principle 4) promotes alignment and responsiveness to negotiated business requirements (business principle 5); a consistent, flexible infrastructure (IT principle 3) should enable all five business principles. IT principles can also be used as a tool for educating executives about technology strategy and investment decisions.

2. *IT architecture* is the organizing logic for data, applications, and infrastructure, captured in a set of policies, relationships, and technical choices to achieve desired business and technical standardization and integration. By providing a road map for infrastructure and applications (and consequently investment decisions), architecture decisions are pivotal to effective IT management and use. By clarifying how IT supports business principles, IT principles state — implicitly or explicitly — the requirements for process standardization and integration. The key to process standardization is discipline — adherence to a single, consistent way of doing things. Process integration allows multiple business units to provide a single face to a customer or to move seamlessly from one function to another.

3. *IT infrastructure* is the foundation of planned IT capability (both technical and human) available throughout the business as shared and reliable services and used by multiple applications. Foresight in establishing the right infrastructure at the right time enables rapid implementation of future electronically enabled business initiatives as well as consolidation and cost reduction of current business processes. Over investing in infrastructure — or worse, implementing the wrong infrastructure — results in wasted resources, delays, and system incompabilities with business partners. Infrastructure base are the technology components, such as computers, printers, database software packages, operating systems, and scanners. The technology components are converted into useful shared services by a human IT infrastructure composed of knowledge, skills, standards, and experience.

4. *Business applications needs* often has two conflicting objectives — creativity and discipline. Creativity is about identifying new and more effective ways to deliver customer value using IT. Creativity involves identifying business applications that support strategic business objectives and facilitate business experiments. Discipline is about architectural integrity — ensuring that applications leverage and build out the enterprise architecture rather than undermine architectural principles. Discipline is also about focus — committing the necessary resources

to achieve project and business goals. Business application needs decisions require reconciling complex change and opposing organizational forces. Managers responsible for defining requirements must distinguish core process requirements from nonessentials and know when to live within architectural constraints. They must design experiments knowing that actual benefits could be different from anticipated benefits — or if there are no benefits, they must pull the plug. Most importantly, they must know how to design organizational change and then make it happen. Business application needs decisions require creative thinkers and disciplined project managers and are probably the least mature of the five IT decisions.

5.   *IT investment and prioritization* is often the most visible and controversial of the five key IT decisions. Some projects are approved, others are bounced, and the rest enter the organizational equivalent of suspended animation with the dreaded request from the decision makers to "redo the business case" or "provide more information." Enterprises that get superior value from IT focus their investments on their strategic priorities, cognizant of the distinction between "must have" and "nice to have" IT capabilities. IT investment decisions address three dilemmas: (a) how much to spend, (b) where to spend it, and (c) how to reconcile the needs of different constituencies. Probably the most important attribute of a successful IT investment process is ensuring that the enterprise's IT spending reflects strategic priorities. Investment processes must reconcile the demands of individual business units as well as demands to meet enterprise-wide needs. Many enterprises value the interdependence of their business units and support their efforts to invest in IT according to business unit strategy. Most enterprises also emphasize the importance of enterprise-wide efficiencies and even integration. Enterprises that attempt to persuade independent business units to fund shared infrastructure are likely to experience resistance. Instead, business leaders must articulate the enterprise-wide objectives of shared infrastructure and provide appropriate incentives for business unit leaders to sacrifice business unit needs in favor of enterprise-wide needs.

Stakeholders

An important task in establishing and designing IT governance is to identify stakeholders. Stakeholders may be assigned input rights and decision rights.

The stakeholder approach to strategic management was introduced by Freeman (1984). According to Freeman, a stakeholder is any group or individual who can affect, or is affected by, the achievement of a corporation's purpose. Stakeholders include employees, customers, suppliers, stockholders, banks, environmentalists, government, and other groups who can help or hurt the corporation. For each category of stakeholders, groups can be broken down into several useful smaller categories. Freeman's focus was to show how executives could use the stakeholder approach to manage their organization more effectively. In instrumental stakeholder theory, the role of management is seen as achieving a balance between the interests of all stakeholders. For each major strategic issue we must think through the effects on a number of stakeholders, and therefore, we need processes that help take into account the concerns of many groups. It is argued that maintaining an appropriate balance between the interests of all stakeholder groups is the only way to ensure survival of the firm and the attainment of other performance goals. The normative condition is that managers must provide economic and otherwise returns to stakeholders in order to continue engaging in wealth creating activities by virtue of the critical resources stakeholders provide to the firm.

Stakeholder theory is justified on the basis that firms have responsibilities to stakeholders for moral reasons, and that there is no priority of one set of interests over another. Upholding four principles: 1) honoring agreements, 2) avoiding lying, 3) respecting the autonomy of others, and 4) avoiding harm to other, are necessary precondition for efficient working. Thus, stakeholder theories of the firm establish economic relationships within a general context of moral management. Contrary to the traditional understanding of the principal-agent relationship, used in several IT outsourcing studies, a stakeholder orientation will include at least two new dimensions: 1) a number of stakeholder groups, and 2) the interpretation of the four moral principles that underlie stakeholder theory. Neglecting these dimensions, firms will have less satisfied stakeholders, and will show financial performance that is consistently below industry average (Shankman, 1999).

The term stakeholder is a powerful one. This is due, to a significant degree, to its conceptual breath. The term means many different things to many different people and hence evokes praise and scorn from a wide variety of scholars and practitioners of myriad academic disciplines and backgrounds. Such breadth of interpretation, though one of stakeholder theory's greatest strengths, is also one of its most prominent theoretical liabilities as a topic of reasoned discourse. Much of the power of stakeholder theory is a direct result of the fact that, when used unreflectively, its managerial prescriptions and implications are merely limitless. When discussed in instrumental variation (i.e., that managers should attend to stakeholders as a means to achieving other organizational goals such as profit or shareholder wealth maximization) stakeholder theory stands virtually unopposed. Stakeholder theory is a theory of organizational management and ethics. Indeed all theories of strategic management have some moral content, though it is often implicit. Moral content in this case means that the subject matter of the theories is inherently moral topics (i.e., they are not amoral). Stakeholder theory is distinct because it addresses morals and values explicitly as a central feature of managing organizations. The ends of cooperative activity and the means of achieving these ends are critically examined in stakeholder theory in a way that they are not in many theories of strategic management (Phillips et al., 2003).

Managing stakeholders involves attention to more than simply maximizing shareholder wealth. Attention to the interests and well being of those who can assist or hinder the achievement of the organization's objectives is the central admonition of the theory. In this way, stakeholder theory is similar in large degree with alternative models of strategic management, such as resource-based theory. However, for stakeholder theory, attention to the interests and well being of some non-shareholders is obligatory for more than the prudential and instrumental purposes of wealth maximization of equity shareholders. While there are still some stakeholder groups whose relationship with the organization remains instrumental (due largely to the power they wield) there are other normatively legitimate stakeholders than simply equity shareholders alone. According to Phillips et al. (2003), stakeholder theory may be undermined from at least two directions — critical distortion and friendly misinterpretations — at its current stage of theoretical development. Critical distortions include arguments that stakeholder theory is an excuse for managerial opportunism and that stakeholder theory cannot provide sufficiently specific objective function for the corporation. Friendly misinterpretations include arguments that stakeholder theory requires changes to current law and that stakeholder theory is socialism and refers to the entire economy.

According to Phillips et al. (2003), it is commonly asserted that stakeholder theory implies that all stakeholders must be treated equally irrespective of the fact that some obviously contribute more than others to the organization. Prescriptions of equality have been inferred from discussions of balancing stakeholder interests and are in direct conflict with the advice of some experts on organizational design and reward systems. However, corporations should attempt to distribute the benefits of their activities as equitably as possible among stakeholders in light of their respective contributions, costs, and risks. This interpretation of balance is called meritocracy, where benefits are distributed based on relative contribution to the organization. In addition to meritocracy, it has been suggested that stakeholders may usefully be separated into normative and derivative stakeholders. Normative stakeholders are those to whom the organization has a direct moral obligation to attend to their well-being. They provide the answer to seminal stakeholder query "For whose benefit ought the firm be managed?" Typically, normative stakeholders are those most frequently cited in stakeholder discussions such as financiers, employees, customers, suppliers and local communities. Alternatively, derivative stakeholders are those groups or individuals who can either harm or benefit the organization, but to whom the organization has no direct moral obligation as stakeholders. This latter group might include such groups as competitors, activists, terrorists, and the media. The organization is not managed for the benefit of derivative stakeholders, but to the extent that they may influence the organization or its normative stakeholders, managers are obliged to account for them in their decision-making. Far from strict equality, therefore, there are a number of more convincing ways that stakeholder theory may distinguish between and among constituency groups.

Stakeholder theory is a managerial conception of organizational strategy and ethics. The central idea is that an organization's success is dependent on how well it manages the relationships with key groups such as customers, employees, suppliers, communities, financiers, and others that can affect the realization of its purpose. The manager's job is to keep the support of all of these groups, balancing their interests, while making the organization a place where stakeholder interests can be maximized over time. The identification of stakeholder groups is currently among the central debates in the scholarly and popular (Freeman & Phillips, 2002).

Lacity and Willcocks (2000) define a stakeholder as a group of people with aligned interests. The term is widely used and accepted by IT outsourcing practitioners and researchers. However, as indicated by some of the reviewed literature above, stakeholder is defined and used differently in finance (issue of CEO responsibility to shareholders or stakeholders), law (requires ownership), and gaming (person who holds the bets). According to Lacity and Willcocks (2000) there is four distinct client IT stakeholder groups and three distinct supplier IT stakeholder groups. The groups identified are customer senior business managers, customer senior IT managers, customer IT staff, customer IT users, and supplier senior managers, supplier account managers, supplier IT staff. An additional group is the subcontractors. All stakeholder groups are presumed to have significant differences in expectations and goals regarding IT outsourcing. Thus, it is reasonable to propose that upholding the interest of these different stakeholder groups with the principles of moral management will affect the success of IT outsourcing.

Decision Rights Distribution

Weill and Ross (2004) studied both who made each of the five decisions and who provided input to those decisions. They then categorized the enterprise's approach by archetypes of decision makers. Figure 14.7 shows a combination of decision makers and categories of decisions. The most frequent decision maker for each category found by Weill and Ross (2004) is indicated with an X in the table.

IT principles, which set the strategic role for IT across the enterprise, were decided in a variety of ways. Thirty-six percent of enterprises used a duopoly approach (usually IT professionals and the CxOs in a T-shaped duopoly), but business and IT monarchies and federal approaches were also regularly used. Duopolies in general and senior management IT duopolies in particular seem to have gained favor in IT principles decisions because senior managers sense that they must take the lead to ensure that IT aligns with business strategies. Working in partnerships with IT leaders in decision processes establishes realistic expectations for IT and forces clarification of business strategy. The most frequent input to IT principles came from federal management.

Over 70 percent of enterprises relied on IT monarchies to choose *IT architecture*, suggesting that senior managers view architecture more as a technical than strategic issue. Most enterprises attempt to incorporate business strategy considerations into architecture decisions via inputs from federal and duopoly arrangements.

Like architecture, *IT infrastructure* decisions are often made within the IT unit. Almost 60 percent of enterprises used IT monarchies to make infrastructure decisions. This

Figure 14.7. How enterprises govern

	IT Principles	IT Architecture	IT Infrastructure	Business Applications	IT Investments
Business Monarchy					X
IT Monarchy		X	X		
Feudal					
Federal				X	
IT Duopoly	X				
Anarchy					

Figure 14.8. Sample effective IT governance arrangements matrix

	IT Principles	IT Architecture	IT Infrastructure	Business Applications	IT Investment
Business Monarchy					Executive committee subgroup, includes CIO
IT Monarchy		CIO IT leadership (CIO, CIO's office and business unit CIOs)	CIO IT leadership (CIO, CIO's office and business unit CIOs)		
Feudal					
Federal					
IT Duopoly	Executive committee at C levels (CxOs) IT leadership (CIO, CIO's office and business unit CIOs)			Business unit heads (presidents) Business process owners	
Anarchy					

arrangement gives IT independence in designing and pricing service offerings. Input to IT infrastructure decisions typically come from federal arrangements.

People who make *business applications needs* decisions specify the business needs for systems to be acquired or built in the next year or so. Enterprises studied by Weill and Ross (2004) displayed a wide variety of approaches to these decisions. Federal approaches were slightly more popular than duopolies, and there were also substantial numbers of enterprises using feudal and business monarchies. Input to business applications needs decisions were mostly provided through federal arrangements as well.

Three approaches dominated *IT investment and prioritization* decision-making: business monarchies, federal, and duopolies. The there approaches were almost equally popular, but they offer different views of how enterprises ensure maximum value from IT investments. That only nine percent of enterprises place IT investment decisions in the hands of IT professionals reflects the growing awareness that IT investment decisions involve business tradeoffs — decision makers determine which business processes will and will not receive IT support. Input to IT investment and prioritization decisions was mostly provided by federal arrangements.

Nielsen (2004) suggested decision rights distribution as indicated in Figure 14.8. This is a sample effective IT governance arrangement matrix.

Weill and Ross (2004) found significant variation in IT governance arrangements among the 256 firms studied. Each of the five key IT decisions has a choice of six governance

Figure 14.9. Top three overall governance performers (Weill, 2004)

	IT Principles	IT Architecture	IT Infrastructure	Business Applications Needs	IT Investment and Prioritization
Business Monarchy	C	C	C		B C
IT Monarchy		A B	A B		
Feudal					
Federal				A C	
IT Duopoly	A B			B	A
Anarchy					

archetypes, yielding very many possible combinations. The ten most popular combinations accounted for twenty-five percent of the enterprises. Within these ten, Weill (2004) identified the three most effective arrangements, as measured by IT governance performance. These three top governance performers are illustrated in Figure 14.9.

Arrangement A uses duopolies for principles and investment, IT monarchies for infrastructure and architecture, and federal for business application needs. This arrangement requires IT groups that are finely tuned to business needs, with a strong level of trust between the business and IT. The federal model for application needs can capitalize on potential synergies (such as common customers) across business units.

Arrangement B is similar, using a duopoly for application needs and a business monarchy for investment. For enterprises with few synergies, using a duopoly for application needs can work well because there is less need to coordinate across business units. Arrangements A and B are both good starting points for enterprises balancing growth and profitability because the tensions of business units seeking to meet their local customer needs are nicely balanced with senior managers governing IT investments.

Arrangement C is much more centralized, with business monarchies making all decisions except business application needs (which are federal). More centralized approaches are typically used in firms with single business units or where profitability or cost control is a predominant issue. Arrangement C requires business leaders who are interested and well informed about IT issues — often the result of CIOs educating and working closely with the senior management team. Arrangement C is also sensible when major changes are occurring (e.g., mergers, major cost cutting, crises etc.) and decision rights must be tightly held.

According to Weill (2004), Figure 14.9 illustrates how, in the three top performing patterns, the five decision-making approaches fit together to create a total governance design that is reinforcing and balances the tensions inherent in large enterprises. For example, an IT monarchy for IT architecture can be very effective if the architecture is guided by IT principles set by a business monarchy or a duopoly. The IT decision makers focus on creating an integrated and flexible IT architecture guided by the business-driven IT principles set by the senior leaders in the business monarchy.

Weill (2004) identified to *financial* performers and studied how they govern IT. For an enterprise to lead on one specific performance metric (asset utilization, profit, or growth) requires its focus and culture to pursue single-mindedly that goal. Firms that lead their industries in one of these metrics govern IT differently from the leaders on other metrics. They also govern differently from most common governance patters shown in Figure 14.8. And they govern differently from the top *governance*-performing enterprises just described in Figure 14.10, which aim for more balanced performance goals.

Leaders in asset utilization were found typically to use IT duopoly governance for all five IT decisions. In the duopoly model, the IT group plays an important coordinating role because it is one of the few groups that interacts with all business units and can thus see firm-wide opportunities for sharing and reuse across business units, business processes and regions.

According to Weill (2004), firms wanting to lead on asset utilization can learn from these top performers and consider:

- Setting IT principles with a strong flavor of asset utilization and using an IT duopoly consisting of CxOs and the corporate IT group.

- Empowering business/IT relationship managers who focus on achieving business value from IT in their business unit and leveraging the enterprise-wide infrastructure.

- Establishing a technical core of infrastructure and architecture providers who plan and implement the enterprise's technology platform and interact with the business/IT relationship managers.

- Involving IT architects on business unit projects to facilitate IT education of the business leaders and effective use of the shared infrastructure and architecture standards.

- Developing a simple chargeback system and a regular review process to help business unit leaders see the value of shared services.

To analyze IT governance, Weill (2004) suggests that managers map their enterprise's current IT governance onto a matrix similar to the figures used here. Then it can be subjectively assessed whether or not IT governance is encouraging desirable behaviors for the enterprise's performance goals. If not, the appropriate top performers' governance (best practice) can be used as starting-point templates to create a new governance model that is then tailored to the enterprise's culture, structure, strategy and goals.

Chapter XV

IT Governance as Strategic Alignment

Strategy can simply be defined as principles, a broad based formula, to be applied in order to achieve a purpose. These principles are general guidelines guiding the daily work to reach business goals. Strategy is the pattern of resource allocation decisions made throughout the organization. These encapsulate both desired goals and beliefs about what are acceptable and, most critically, unacceptable means for achieving them.

Business Strategy and IS/IT Strategy

While the business strategy is the broadest pattern of resource allocation decisions, more specific decisions are related to information systems and information technology. IS must be seen both in a business and an IT context. IS is in the middle because IS supports the business while using IT.

Business strategy is concerned with achieving the mission, vision and objectives of a company, while IS strategy is concerned with use of IS/IT applications, and IT strategy is concerned with the technical infrastructure as illustrated in Figure 8.1. A company has typically several IS/IT applications. The connection between them is also of great

Figure 15.1. Relationships between strategies at three levels

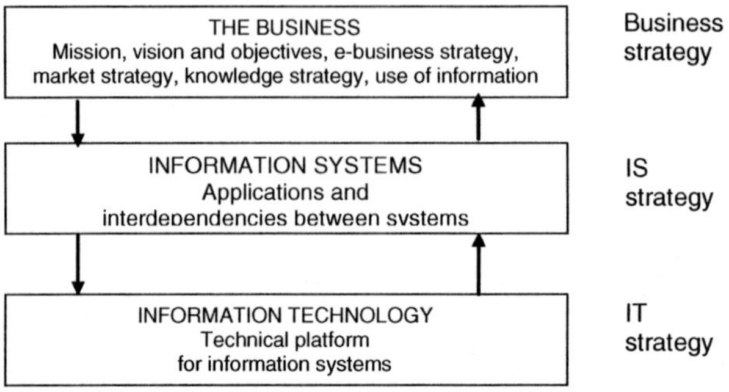

```
┌─────────────────────────────────────────────────┐
│                 THE BUSINESS                      │   Business
│  Mission, vision and objectives, e-business       │   strategy
│  strategy, market strategy, knowledge strategy,   │
│  use of information                               │
└─────────────────────────────────────────────────┘
                    ↓        ↑
┌─────────────────────────────────────────────────┐
│              INFORMATION SYSTEMS                  │   IS
│              Applications and                     │   strategy
│        interdependencies between systems          │
└─────────────────────────────────────────────────┘
                    ↓        ↑
┌─────────────────────────────────────────────────┐
│            INFORMATION TECHNOLOGY                 │   IT
│              Technical platform                   │   strategy
│             for information systems               │
└─────────────────────────────────────────────────┘
```

interest, as interdependencies should prevent applications from being separate islands. Furthermore, the arrows in the illustration in Figure 15.1 are of importance. Arrows from business strategy to IS strategy, and from IS to IT strategy represent the alignment perspective, they illustrate the *what* before *how*. Arrows from IT to IS strategy, and from IS to business strategy represent the extension from *what* to *how* to *what*. This is the impact perspective, representing the potential impacts of modern information technology on future business options.

Necessary elements of a *business strategy* include mission, vision, objectives, market strategy, knowledge strategy, and our general approach to the use of information, information systems, and information technology.

Mission describes the reason for firm existence. For example, the reason for law firm existence is client's needs for legal advice. The mission addresses the organization's basic question of 'What business are we in?' This single, essential, sentence should include no quantification, but must unambiguously state the purpose of the organization and should, just as carefully define what the organization does not do. According to Ward and Griffiths (1996), the mission is an unambiguous statement of what the organization does and its long-term, overall purpose. Its primary role is to set a direction for everyone to follow. It may be short, succinct, and inspirational, or contain broad philosophical statements that tie an organization to certain activities and to economic, social, ethical, or political ends. Values are also frequently stated alongside the mission. Three differing examples of missions are: To help people move from one place to another; to provide medical treatment to sick people; and to enable electronic communication between people.

Vision describes what the firm wants to achieve. For example, the law firm wants to become the leading law firm in Norway. The vision represents the view that senior managers have for the future of the organization; so it is what they want it to become. This view gives a way to judge the appropriateness of all potential activities that the organization might engage in. According to Ward and Griffiths (1996), the vision gives a picture, frequently covering many aspects, which everyone can identify with, of what the business will be in the future, and how it will operate. It exists to bring objectives to life, and to give the whole organization a destination that it can visualize, so that every stakeholder has a shared picture of the future aim.

Objectives describe where the business is heading. For example, the law firm can choose to merge with another law firm to become the leading law firm in Norway. Objectives are the set of major achievements that will accomplish the vision. These are usually small in number, but embody the most important aspects of the vision, such as financial returns, customer service, manufacturing excellence, staff morale, and social and environmental obligations.

Market strategy describes market segments and products. For example, the law firm can focus on corporate clients in the area of tax law.

Necessary elements of an *IS strategy* include future IS/IT applications, future competence of human resources (IS/IT professionals), and future IS/IT organizational structure, and control of the IS/IT function. An important application area is KMS. The future applications are planned according to priorities, how they are to be developed or acquired (make or buy), how they meet user requirements, and how security is achieved. The future competence is planned by types of resources needed, motivation and skills needed (managers, users, IS/IT professionals), salaries, and other benefits. The future IS/IT organization defines tasks, roles, management, and possibly outsourcing.

Necessary elements of an *IT strategy* include selection of IT hardware, basic software, and networks, as well as how these components should interact as a technological platform, and how required security level is maintained. The IT platform consists of hardware, systems software, networks and communications, standards and support form selected vendors.

An *IS/IT strategy* is a combined strategy including business context, the IS in a narrow sense and the technological platform. Necessary elements of an IS/IT strategy include business direction and strategy (mission, vision, objectives, knowledge strategy), applications (knowledge management systems), people (future competence of human resources), organization (future organization and control of IT function), and IT platform (future technical infrastructure). Hence, IS/IT is quite a broad term. The term is broad to take care of all connections and interdependencies in a strategy, as changes in one element will have effect on all other elements, as illustrated in Figure 15.2.

Figure 15.2. IS/IT strategy elements and interdependencies

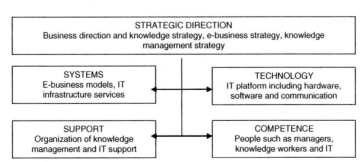

Figure 15.3. Leavitt's Diamond of elements and interrelationships

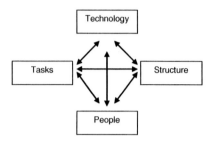

The same thinking is represented in a famous model called Leavitt's Diamond. Everything is connected, and changes in one element affect all the others as illustrated in Figure 15.3. Tasks are performed using systems, structure is important for support functions, and people represent the competence. The Diamond can only create change in desired strategic business direction if all interdependencies between elements are taken care of over time.

Strategic Alignment Model

Henderson and Venkatraman (1993) developed the strategic alignment model as illustrated in Figure 15.4. The concept of strategic alignment is based on two building blocks: strategic fit and functional integration. There are four important perspectives in the strategic alignment model.

Perspective one: Strategy execution. This perspective reflects a notion that business strategy is the driver of both organizational design and IS/IT infrastructure choices. In this perspective, strategic goals are evaluated in terms of how critical business process affect organizational infrastructure and IS/IT infrastructure. This perspective includes emphasis on how possible radical changes in business processes could better support the business strategy.

Needs for change in IS/IT infrastructure is caused by organizational infrastructure, which is influenced by business strategy, as illustrated in the figure for perspective one.

Perspective two: Technology potential. This alignment perspective involves developing an IS/IT strategy in response to a business strategy and using the corresponding choices to define the required IS/IT infrastructure. In contrast to the strategy execution logic of perspective one, this perspective does not use the business strategy to explore or define the organizational structure. Rather, it seeks to identify the best possible IS/IT competencies through appropriate positioning in the IS/IT marketplace. Further, the choices for positioning the firm with respect to key technologies and alliances must be adequately reflected in the design of the internal IS/IT infrastructure.

Figure 15.4. Strategic alignment model

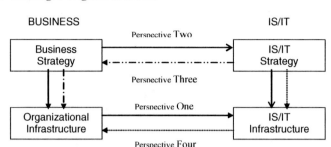

Alignment for this perspective requires that executives understand the impact of business strategy on IS/IT strategy and the corresponding implications for IS/IT infrastructure. The executive management team provides the technological vision to articulate the IT logic and choices that would best support the chosen business strategy. The IT manager should be a technology architect, who efficiently and effectively designs and implements the required IS/IT infrastructure that is consistent with the external component of IS/IT strategy (scope, competencies, and governance). Performance criteria in this perspective are based on technological leadership, with qualitative but insightful benchmarking along a set of critical measures pertaining to positioning in the IS/IT marketplace.

Needs for change in IS/IT infrastructure is caused by IS/IT strategy, which is influenced by business strategy, as illustrated in the figure for perspective two.

Perspective three: Competitive potential. This alignment perspective is concerned with the exploitation of emerging IS/IT capabilities to impact new products and services, influence the key attributes of strategy, as well as develop new forms of relationships. Unlike the two previous perspectives, which consider business strategy as given, this perspective allows the modification of business strategy via emerging IS/IT capabilities. Beginning with three dimensions of IS/IT strategy (i.e., technology scope, systemic competencies, and IT governance), this perspective seeks to identify the most strategic set of options for business and the corresponding set of decisions pertaining to organizational infrastructure.

The specific role for top management to make this perspective succeed is the business visionary, who articulates how the emerging IS/IT competencies and functionality, as well as the changing governance patterns in the IS/IT marketplace, would impact the business strategy. The role of the IT manager, in contrast, is the catalyst, who helps to identify and interpret the trends in the IS/IT environment to assist the business manager's understanding of the potential opportunities and threats from IS/IT. Performance criteria in this perspective are based on leadership, with qualitative and quantitative measurements pertaining to product market leadership.

Needs for change in organizational infrastructure are caused by business strategy, which is influenced by IS/IT strategy, as illustrated in the figure for perspective three.

Perspective four: Service level. This alignment perspective focuses on the need to build a world-class IS/IT service organization. This perspective is often viewed as necessary but not sufficient to ensure the effective use of IS/IT resources in a growing and fast-changing world.

The specific role for top management to make this perspective succeed is the prioritizer, who articulates how best to allocate the scarce resources both within the organization and in the IS/IT marketplace. The role of the IT manager, in contrast, is leadership, with the specific tasks of making the internal IT organization succeed within the operating guidelines from top management. Needs for change in this perspective are found in areas such as customer satisfaction, with qualitative and quantitative measurements with internal and external benchmarking.

Needs for change in organizational infrastructure are caused by IS/IT infrastructure, which is influenced by IS/IT strategy, as illustrated in Figure 9.38 for perspective four.

The strategic alignment model developed by Henderson and Venkatraman (1993) provides a framework to identify needs for change. Applying each of the four perspectives presented above, can lead to identification of needs for change.

Organizational Architect

Sauer and Willcocks (2002) found a need for organizational architects in companies that have moved to e-business to achieve strategic alignment. They identified four partnership principles for relationships between strategists and technologists:

1. *View technology and organization as equal influences.* For example, one company had adopted a single e-business platform combined with its centralization of business-support functions. This company had established three tenets: use a single-instance infrastructure, put the Web first, and consolidate both organizationally and technologically.

2. *Standardize and centralize.* The ability to operate across organizational boundaries is proving essential to flexibility. At a minimum, it requires some standardization and central control.

3. *Manage change intelligently.* It is not enough simply to recognize the importance of partnering organization and technology or even to standardize and centralize. Companies must also create the right drivers for change so that everyone will accept the organizational change that, in turn, helps a platform to succeed.

4. *Match capability and ambition.* Often, either the organization or technology can be serious impediments that an organizational architect must change or work around. Many ambitions are simply not achievable.

Sauer and Willcocks (2002) argue that the existing technology is the starting point for realizing any vision. In the worst cases, the existing technology is a collection of point solutions. Integration is through point-to-point connections that are expensive to build or change and are unreliable. Thus, the company must accommodate any new initiative independently of existing solutions and rarely achieves the desired business synergies within a reasonable budget or time. In the best cases, the existing technology is a coherent platform that is either flexible (custom-built) or dependent (installed to support an already integrated suite of ERP applications).

The organizational architect must understand the enablers and constraints. In ERP, for example, the software vendor helps ensure that the system stays current by offering periodic upgrades. Applications typically grow toward customer-relationship management and supply-chain management. Although ERP is coherent and integrated, if it is tied to the organization's structure when it is installed, it becomes structurally inflexible. The organizational architect works with both strategists and technologists to identify and grow the organizational and technical capabilities needed to see a vision through to its supporting platform (Sauer & Willcocks, 2002).

Chapter XVI

Implementing IT Governance

Enterprises implement their governance arrangement through a set of governance mechanisms and an effective IT governance architecture. Implementation success may be dependent on a variety of factors, such as leadership, relevance, resistance, communication, and planning.

IT Organization and Governance

There is no universal best IT governance structure. Rather, the best IT governance solution for a given firm is contingent on its organizational context. Many research studies point to the importance of organizational context for predicting a firm's IT governance solution.

However, for the most part this literature assumes that firms adopt a uniform IT governance solution for all business units and that this solution can be predicted by context variables at the overall organizational level. This assumption is incorrect in cases where organizations adopt hybrid IT governance solutions.

Hybrid IT Organization

Hybrid IT governance can be defined as management decentralized to some business units, but not to other business units, within the same enterprise. Different governance solutions for different business units within the same firm suggests a growing management interest in customized solutions for different business units in order to exploit the unique capabilities of a given strategic business unit.

By inference, then, context variables at the business unit level need to be addressed to understand why business units within the same firm exhibit the same or different IT governance arrangements. Brown (1997) phrased the following research question: Why do firms adopt a hybrid IS governance form in which centralized and decentralized governance solutions for the management of systems development coexist?

Brown (1997) studied why large, multidivisional firms implement hybrid IT governance solutions in which systems development is decentralized to some business units, but not to others. Study findings suggest that a configuration of four variables characterizes a business unit context conducive to decentralized systems development governance: organic decision-making, high business unit autonomy, a differentiation competitive strategy, and an unstable industry environment.

These findings imply that highly autonomous business units with organic decision-making, that are competing in an unstable industry environment with a differentiation competitive strategy, are likely to control their own systems development resources. Furthermore, the influence of these four variables will be overridden and a deviant governance solution adopted in the presence of perceived deficiencies in IT capabilities by business units that have a culture that places a high emphasis on change.

Horizontal Mechanisms

In response to increased complexity and uncertainty, today's enterprises are adopting organizational designs that balance not only the hierarchical trade-offs of control vs. autonomy, but also a third design criterion: collaboration. Among the design tools for collaboration are horizontal mechanisms, defined as structural and non-structural devices that encourage contacts between individuals in order to coordinate the work of two units.

Horizontal mechanisms directed at collaboration have been utilized in IT management. For example, cross-functional teams and liaison roles have been implemented to achieve collaboration not only across IT units and business units, but also across multiple systems development units under a federal form of IT governance. Brown (1999) identified the following mechanisms:

* *Formal groups*: Steering committees and IT standing teams.

* *Formal roles*: Cross-unit integrators and corporate IT oversight roles.

- *Informal networking practices*: Physical Collocation, interdepartmental events, IT networks.

- *Cross-unit human resource practices*: Job rotations, input to performance reviews.

Determinants of IT Governance

Research studies have sought an answer to the best way of designing IT governance, recognizing that this best way is contingent upon internal and external factors. These studies examined the influence of various determinants, including organization size, business strategy, and business governance structure. The cumulative of these empirical findings indicate that (Peterson, 2004):

- Central IT governance is associated with small-sized organizations following a cost-focused business (competitive) strategy, and characterized by a centralized business governance structure, environmental stability, low information-intensive business products, and low business experience and competency in managing IT.

- Decentral IT governance is associated with large, complex organizations following an innovation-focused business (competitive) strategy, and characterized by a decentralized business governance structure, environmental volatility, high information-intensive business products and processes, and high business experience and competency in managing IT.

Recent empirical evidence indicates that organizations adopt federal IT governance when pursuing multiple competing objectives. Due to the relentless pace and unpredictable direction of change in contemporary business environments, many organizations need to focus on both standardization and innovation, and in the process have adopted a federal IT governance model (Peterson, 2004).

In retrospect, Peterson (2004) finds it clear how and why the federal IT governance model has emerged as the dominant design in contemporary organizations. The federal model is found to capture the best of both worlds — centralized and decentralized. From a strategic perspective, both business and IT are facing multiple, competing objectives to reduce costs, standardize, innovate, and provide customer value. From an organizational perspective, the enterprise architecture is characterized by a dynamic network of integrated business-IT capabilities. The federal IT governance model, by dividing direction and control over IT between central and local offices, across different business and IT constituencies, creates a structure that is consistent with the enterprise architecture, i.e., both stable and dynamic, and enables IT-based strategic differentiation of the business.

The Practice of IT Governance

The "IT Governance Global Status Report" was presented by the IT Governance Institute in 2004. The motivation for the research was to find out how IT governance is perceived, whether the need for it is recognized, how the concept itself is recognized, and which tools or frameworks are considered leaders in the field.

The major findings and messages from the survey and research project can be summarized in seven points (IT Governance Institute, 2004):

1. More than 93 percent of business leaders recognize that IT is important for delivering the organization's strategy.

2. Organizations are suffering from IT operational problems.

3. CIOs recognize the need for better governance over IT. A substantial portion of the IT community (75 percent) is aware of the fact that IT has issues that must be resolved. Surprisingly, an even more substantial part of that community (more than 80 percent) recognizes that IT governance or some (partial) form thereof is required to resolve these issues. This is where the importance of a definition for IT governance comes into play. When asked if they intend to do or plan IT governance measures, only 40 percent replied in the affirmative. However, when they were asked more precise and detailed questions about specific practices, many more replied positively. In other words, they actually do perform these practices the IT Governance Institute considers IT governance — they just do not characterize them by that name.

4. IT governance frameworks are used to align IT strategy and manage IT operational risks. IT governance solutions/frameworks are used mostly for aligning the IT strategy with the overall organization strategy (57 percent) and to manage IT operational risks (53 percent). To what extent, however, it should be mentioned that solutions in this domain are not yet readily available. When looking at the IT governance frameworks known or used, there is no clear winner, internal solutions or specific vendor solutions are more frequently mentioned, followed by ISO9000 and COBIT.

5. Good IT governance helps organizations provide IT value and manage IT risks. COBIT is the preferred way to implement effective IT governance. Process models such as COBIT can substantially help in the realization of effective value and risk management. One of the questions that challenge CIOs — are IT operations running as smoothly, reliably and cost-effective as possible? — can therefore be addressed in large part by a process model like COBIT. COBIT is perceived to be a valuable framework for IT governance by those who are familiar with it (89 percent report themselves very or quite satisfied). Compared to many other organizations, ISACA and ITGI rank highly in perception of experience and implementation ability.

6. Whilst COBIT users may not yet be highly numerous, they are very satisfied. Approximately 18 percent of the responding organizations are aware of COBIT. From a regional perspective, COBIT is least known in North America. Looking at size and industry sector, very large organizations and organizations in the financial

industry are especially aware of COBIT. Almost 30 percent of the organizations that are aware of COBIT are using it, resulting in an overall rate of 5 percent of all organizations using COBIT. Appreciation of most ITGI/ISACA deliverables is very high (between 73 percent and 91 percent indicate they are very or quite satisfied users). Forty-three percent of COBIT users find it easy to implement, whereas 25 percent find this task somewhat difficult.

7.   There is little separation amongst those perceived as top providers of expertise and implementation ability. Large IT consultancy firms and ISACA (COBIT) received the highest ranking in regard to their expertise in IT governance (3.8 out of 5), but Gartner, the Big 4 accounting firms, local professional organizations and ITGI are only a few tenths of a point behind. In rating implementation ability (as opposed to expertise), the respondents placed large IT and consultancy firms at the top of the heap (3.7 out of 5), but ISACA (COBIT), the Big 4 Accounting firms, and local professional organizations were clustered close behind. In summary, there are no clear winners (yet) in the IT governance area. In fact, an amazing one-quarter of respondents do not know of any IT governance provider to assist them.

COBIT is mentioned in several of these points. According to the IT Governance Institute (2004), COBIT has been developed as a generally applicable and accepted standard for good Information Technology (IT) security and control practices that provides a reference framework for management, users, and IS audit, control, and security practitioners.

COBIT, issued by the IT Governance Institute and now in its third edition, is increasingly accepted internationally as good practice for control over information, IT, and related risks. Its guidance enables an enterprise to implement effective governance over the IT that is pervasive and intrinsic throughout the enterprise. In particular, COBIT's Management Guidelines component contains a framework responding to management's need for control and measurability of IT by providing tools to assess and measure the enterprise's IT capability for the 34 COBIT IT processes. The tools include:

- Performance measurement elements (outcome measures and performance drivers for all IT processes)

- A list of critical success factors that provides succinct, nontechnical best practices for each IT process

- Maturity models to assist in benchmarking and decision-making for capability improvements

Control Objectives for Information and related Technology (COBIT) first published in 1996, now in its third edition, is fast becoming a popular and internationally accepted set of guidance materials for IT governance.

According to Guldentops (2004), COBIT groups the 34 processes into four domains:

- *Planning and organization.* This domain covers strategy and tactics, and concerns the identification of the way IT can best contribute to the achievement of the business objectives. Furthermore, the realization of the strategic vision needs to be planned, communicated, and managed for different perspectives. Finally, a proper organization as well as technological infrastructure must be put in place.

- *Acquisition and implementation.* To realize the IT strategy, IT solutions need to be identified, developed or acquired, as well as implemented and integrated into the business process. In addition, changes in and maintenance of existing systems are covered by this domain to make sure that the life cycle is continued for these systems.

- *Delivery and support.* This domain is concerned with the actual delivery of required services, which range from traditional operations over security and continuity aspects to training. In order to deliver services, the necessary support processes must be set up. This domain includes the actual processing of data by application systems, often classified under application controls.

- *Monitoring.* All IT processes need to be regularly assessed over time for their quality and compliance with control requirements. This domain thus addresses management's oversight over the organization's control process and independent assurance provided by internal and external audit or obtained from alternative sources.

Corresponding to each of the 34 high-level control objectives is an Audit Guideline to enable the review of IT processes against COBIT's 318 recommended detailed control objectives to provide management assurance and/or advice for improvement.

The Myths of IT Governance

According to Peterson (2004), IT governance has been the subject of much debate and speculation over the past decades, yet it remains an ephemeral and messy phenomenon, emerging in ever-new forms with growing complexity. Currently there is no consistent, well-established body of knowledge and skills regarding IT governance.

Based on his own definition of IT governance, Peterson (2004) identified several myths that have existed for a long time. He defines IT governance as a system by which an organization's IT portfolio is directed and controlled. For him, IT governance describes (a) the distribution of IT decision-making rights and responsibilities among different stakeholders in the organization, and (b) the rules and procedures for making and monitoring decisions on strategic IT concerns.

IT governance thus specifies the structure and processes through which the organization's IT objectives are set, and the means of attaining those objectives and monitoring performance. IT governance is a second order phenomenon, i.e., governance is the set of decisions about whom and how decisions on strategic IT concerns are made.

The definition also implies that several IT governance myths can be addressed. These myths need to be debunked if business and academic communities are to move forward in their IT governance thinking and IT governance practice. Peterson (2004) identified four major myths:

- **IT governance is the responsibility of the CIO.** While IT governance is certainly an essential element of a CIO's portfolio, the CIO is not the primary stakeholder. Still, too often, corporate executives and business managers assume that the CIO is taking care of IT governance.

- **IT governance is concerned with organizing the IT function.** Traditionally, the IT function has been regarded as a single homogenous function. However, given the widespread proliferation and infusion of IT in organizations, involving, e.g., technical platforms, shared IT services centers, and local business-embedded applications, the notion of a single homogenous IT function is obsolete.

- **IT governance is a new form of old school IT management.** Due to the enduring nature of IT governance, and the perennial, often intractable problems associated with IT value delivery, some may draw the conclusion that IT governance is simply a new form of "old-school" IT management.

- **IT governance focuses on the (de)centralization of IT.** The discussion on the formal allocation of IT decision-making as vested in organizational positions has led to much rhetoric and speculation on the "best way" to organize IT governance, and in the process has rekindled the classical "centralization vs. decentralization" debate.

Implementation Mechanisms

Enterprises implement their governance arrangements through a set of governance mechanisms — structures, processes, and communications. Well-designed, well-understood, and transparent mechanisms promote desirable IT behaviors. Conversely, if mechanisms are poorly implemented, then governance arrangements will fail to yield the desired results. According to Weill and Ross (2004), effective governance deploys three different types of mechanisms:

- *Decision-making structures*: Organizational units and roles responsible for making IT decisions, such as committees, executive teams, and business/IT relationship managers. Decision-making structures are the most visible IT governance mechanisms. They locate decision-making responsibilities according to intended archetypes. Decision-making structures are the natural approach to generating commitment.

- *Alignment processes*: Formal processes for ensuring that daily behaviors are consistent with IT policies and provide input back to decisions. These include IT investment proposal and evaluation processes, architecture exception processes, service-level agreements, chargeback, and metrics. Alignment processes are IT management techniques for securing widespread involvement in the effective management and use of IT. Alignment processes should bring everybody on board both by providing input into governance decisions and by disseminating the outputs of IT decisions.

- *Communication approaches*: Announcements, advocates, channels, and education efforts that disseminate IT governance principles and policies and outcomes of IT decision-making processes. Communication mechanisms are intended spread news about IT governance decisions and processes and related desirable behaviors throughout the enterprise. Firms communicate their governance mechanisms in a variety of ways. Weill and Ross (2004) found that the more management communicated formally about the existence of IT governance mechanisms, how they worked, and what outcomes were expected, the more effective was their governance.

Decision-making structures are the most visible IT governance mechanism that locate decision-making responsibilities according to the intended archetypes (Weill & Ross, 2004):

- *Business monarchy decision-making structures*. IT can enable enterprise strategy only if senior management establishes strategic direction and elaborates an operating model. Enterprises adopt a number of approaches to elicit this direction. Business monarchies — usually in the form of executive committees — often play a role. Enterprises vary considerably in the design of their executive committees. In some enterprises, the CEO works with a small team of top executives to ensure that IT aligns with corporate objectives. Other enterprises focus the attention of a subset of the senior management team on IT issues. The level of senior executive involvement in IT governance evolves as enterprises become savvier in using IT strategically.

- *IT monarchy decision-making structures*. Complementing business monarchies, IT monarchies make most of the world's IT architecture and infrastructure decisions. The two most common implementations of IT monarchies are IT leadership teams and IT architecture committees. IT leadership teams may comprise IT functional heads (operations, architecture, applications etc.), they may be CIOs of business units, or they may be combinations of the two. Architecture committees are usually made up of technical experts. They are responsible for defining standards and, in some cases, granting exceptions. In most cases, the role of the architecture committee is to advise the IT leadership team on architectural issues, but occasionally the architecture committee is a key governance decision-making body.

- *Federal decision-making structures*. Almost 90 percent of enterprises in the Weill and Ross (2004) study indicated that a senior executive committee played a role in IT governance. Where these senior executive teams drew members from all business units, they implemented a federal rather than business monarchy archetype. Because federal structures overtly work to balance enterprise and business unit priorities, they can provide valuable input to IT governance decisions.

- *IT duopoly decision-making structures*. The typical role of business leaders in IT governance is to clarify business objectives and incorporate IT capabilities into strategy formulation. The typical role of IT leaders is to help envision IT-enabled strategies, clarify architectural standards, and design shared infrastructures. The responsibilities of these two groups are obviously intertwined. Formal governance linkages often result in better performance. Linkages are sometimes accomplished through overlapping memberships on IT and business monarchy mechanisms. Alternatively, some enterprises establish duopoly governance arrangements that comprise joint IT and business members. One approach to ensuring business-IT interactions is through a joint decision council. Business-IT relationship managers play an important role in communicating mandates and their implications and supporting the needs of business unit managers while helping them see benefits.

Alignment processes are the next step after decision-making structures in designing IT governance. Key alignment processes include the IT investment approval process, the architecture exception process, service-level agreements, chargeback, project tracking, and formal tracking of business value for IT (Weill & Ross, 2004):

- *IT investment approval process* has the objective of ensuring that IT investments generate significant returns to the enterprise relative to alternative investment opportunities. Most enterprises formalize their IT investment proposal process to ensure that creative ideas and strategic priorities are considered by investment decision makers. Many enterprises use standardized IT investment approval application templates to estimate metrics such as ROI, NPV, and risk for each project.

- *Architectural exception process* is caused by the fact that few enterprises can afford to support every technical platform that the business might find useful. Technology standards are critical to IT — and business — efficiency. Enterprises use the exception process to meet unique business needs and to gauge when existing standards are becoming obsolete. Architecture committees usually have responsibility for establishing standards. In many cases, the architecture committee also takes responsibility for granting exceptions to standards.

- *Service-level agreements* (SLAs) list available services, alternative quality levels, and related costs. Through negotiations between the IT services unit and business units, an SLA leads to articulation of the services IT offers and the costs of the services. These negotiations clarify the requirements of the business units, thereby informing governance decisions on infrastructure, architecture, and business application needs. SLAs force IT units to think like external providers.

- *Chargeback* is an accounting mechanism for allocating central IT costs to business units. Some enterprises use chargeback successfully for aligning decisions on infrastructure, business application needs, and IT investment with business objectives. The purpose of chargeback is to allocate costs so that business unit IT costs reflect use of shared services while the shared services unit matches its costs with the businesses it supports.

- *Project tracking* is a critical step in implementing IT governance. It is critical to develop the discipline to track the progress of individual IT projects. Over 90 percent of enterprises in the Weill and Ross (2004) study indicated that they are tracking project resources consumed. Enterprises use a variety of tools to support project tracking. At top performing enterprises, tracking is just one element of a standard project management methodology.

- *Formal tracking of business value* is meeting the challenge of assessing the value of IT. IT decision makers make more effective decisions as they better understand the value the enterprise receives from IT. Formally tracking the business value of IT enhances organizational learning about the value of IT-enabled initiatives. Because project outcomes are difficult to isolate — particularly when projects are part of larger program goals — increasing numbers of enterprises are formalizing intermediate objectives.

Communication approaches include senior management announcements, formal committees, office of CIO or IT governance, working with nonconformists, and Web-based portals (Weill & Ross, 2004):

- *Senior management announcements* clarifying priorities and demonstrating commitment usually get a great deal of attention throughout an enterprise. As IT becomes more strategic in enterprises, IT governance grows more important. Developing a communication strategy to announce and explain new IT governance processes contributes to achieving the objectives of the governance design.

- *Formal committees* create communication between committee members. Committees often make lower-level governance decisions and carry out high-level decisions. Careful committee assignments are required to involve executives in decisions important to them. Communication within and across committees align the efforts of the committees with other governance initiatives.

- *Office of CIO or IT governance* is often recognized advocate, owner, and organizational home for IT governance. 86 % of participants in the Weill and Ross (2004) study used an office of IT governance or the office of the CIO to communicate governance arrangements. IT governance needs an owner to ensure that individual mechanisms reinforce rather than contradict one another and to communicate governance processes and purposes.

- *Working with nonconformists* means working with managers who stray from desirable behaviors. Rarely do all affected managers enthusiastically embrace IT governance decisions. When managers engage in behaviors that undermine enterprise architecture, disregard IT investment guidelines, duplicate shared infrastructure, or ignore project-tracking standards, they may be demonstrating lack of awareness of governance decisions or an unwillingness to adopt mandated practices.

- *Web-based portals* can be used for communication around IT governance to educate organizational members on IT governance processes, including specific procedures for mechanisms such as investment proposals, architectural exceptions, and service-level agreements. Web-based portals provide a central communications channel for many enterprises. IT governance owners use the portals to make announcements and updates. Some portals have examples of IT investment cases with templates. Other portals have lists of approved It software and hardware with instructions on ordering hardware and software. Portals can also support IT governance by posting metrics from project-tracking systems.

IT Governance Architecture

Distribution of decision rights is not sufficient to achieve successful IT governance. Peterson (2004) argues that a holistic view emphasizes the need to view IT governance as a complex social system interacting with its environment, and consisting of a set of interdependent subsystems that produce a purposeful whole. Complex systems are characterized by reciprocal interdependence, in which decisions made by subunits are mutually dependent and influential, thereby increasing the need to exchange information. In complex governance systems, each decision-making unit presents direct decision contingencies for every other unit. Interacting subsystems in a social system imply that stakeholders are interdependent and need to work together in a coordinated fashion to achieve objectives. A systems thinking approach towards IT governance acknowledges its complex and dynamic nature, and underscores the impotence of personal mastery and mental models, and team learning and shared vision.

The manner in which responsibilities and accountabilities for the IT portfolio are organized and integrated is defined as an IT Governance architecture. An IT Governance architecture describes the differentiation and integration of strategic decision-making for IT. The IT governance architecture specifies the strategic policies and business rules that provide direction to strategic IT decision-making, and plots a path for achieving business objectives. The IT governance architecture describes coordination mechanisms to be applied to decisions. Decisions can be coordinated either by hierarchy or by plan (Peterson, 2004).

Hierarchical coordination describes the hierarchical referral of infrequent situations for which standardized programs have no solution. The hierarchy achieves coordination by having one person (e.g., CxO) take responsibility for the work of others, issuing instructions, and monitoring actions. If the hierarchy gets overloaded, additional levels or positions can be added to the hierarchy.

Plan-based coordination describes the use of standard programs, formal rules, and procedures, and the specification of outputs, goals, and targets. The adoption and use of reporting forms and service level agreements (SLAs) are typical examples of how contemporary organizations coordinate by plan.

Peterson (2004) argues that hierarchical coordination and plan-based coordination only provide limited coordination capability in complex and uncertain environments. Organizations need to develop horizontal integration mechanisms.

Peterson (2004) classified integration strategies for IT governance according to two dimensions. Vertically, integration mechanisms can focus either on integration structures or integration processes. Horizontally, a division is made between formal positions and processes, and relational networks and capabilities. Collectively, this provides the following four types of integration strategies.

Formal integration structures involve appointing IT executives and accounts, and institutionalizing special and standing IT committees and councils. The use of account and/or relationship managers aid IT managers to develop an improved understanding of business needs, and aid in proactive — vs. reactive — behavior by IT managers. Committees and/or executive teams can take the form of temporary task forces — e.g., project steering committees — or can alternatively be institutionalized as an overlay structure in the organization in the form of executive or IT management councils.

Formal integration processes describe the formalization and institutionalization of strategic decision-making/monitoring procedures and performance. Formal integration processes vary with levels of comprehensiveness, formalization, and integration.

Relational integration structures involve the active participation of and collaborative relationships between corporate executives, IT management, and business management. Central to relational integration is the participative behavior of different stakeholders to clarify differences and solve problems in order to find integrative solutions. An example is strategic partnership that reflects a working relationship of long-term commitment.

Relational integration processes describe strategic dialogue and shared learning between principle business and IT stakeholders. Strategic dialogue involves exploring and debating ideas and issues in depth prior to decision-making or outside the pressure of immediate IT decision-making.

We can here see a considerable overlap with the governance mechanisms suggested by Weill and Ross (2004). The three governance mechanisms do in many ways cover these four types of integration strategies. Formal integration structures are similar to decision structures, and formal integration processes are similar to alignment processes. Communication approaches are here divided into relational integration structures and relational integration processes.

Designing an effective IT governance architecture is dependent on both the differentiation and integration of strategic decision-making for IT. Whereas differentiation focuses on the distribution of IT decision-making rights and responsibilities among different stakeholders in the organization, integration focuses the coordination of IT decision-making processes and structures across stakeholder constituencies. The notion of an IT governance architecture emphasizes the need to define and control the interfaces between the separate components of the IT governance system. Designers of IT governance architectures thus need to consider and implement integration strategies and tactics for governing IT effectively (Peterson, 2004).

Critical Success Factors

Governance performance assesses the effectiveness of IT governance in delivering objectives weighted by their importance to the enterprise. Weill and Ross (2004) apply the following four objectives: cost-effective use of IT, effective use of IT for asset utilization, effective use of IT for growth, and effective use of IT for business flexibility. When assessing governance performance, senior managers first identify the relative importance of these four factors in their enterprises and then rate enterprise performance on each factor.

For IT governance success, Weill (2004) identified the following eight critical success factors:

1. *Transparency.* Make each IT governance mechanism transparent to all managers. The more IT decisions are made covertly and off-governance, the less confidence people will have in the structure and the less willing they will be to play by the rules, which are designed to increase enterprise-wide performance.

2. *Actively designed.* Many enterprises have created uncoordinated IT governance mechanisms. These mechanism "silos" result from governance-by-default — introducing mechanisms one at a time to address a particular need (e.g., architecture problems or overspending or duplication). Instead, design IT governance around the enterprise's objectives and performance goals, creating a coherent design that can be widely communicated.

3. *Infrequently redesigned.* Rethinking the entire IT governance design is a major undertaking, so it should be done infrequently and only when desirable behaviors change.

4. *Education about IT governance.* Education to help managers understand and use IT governance mechanisms is critical. Educated users of governance mechanisms are more likely to be accountable for the decisions they make and less likely to second-guess other decisions.

5. *Simplicity.* Effective governance arrangements are simple and attempt to reach a small number of performance goals. The more goals, the harder IT governance is to design and manage because each new goal often requires new governance mechanisms.

6. *An exception-handling process.* Successful businesses continuously forge new opportunities, some of which will not be supported by existing IT decisions. To support these opportunities, IT governance must include a clearly stated exception-handling process — to bring the issues out into the open, allow debate, and most importantly, foster organizational learning.

7. *Governance designed at multiple organizational levels.* In large multi-business-unit enterprises, IT governance is required at several levels. The suggested starting point is enterprise-wide IT governance, driven by a small number of enterprise-wide strategies and goals. Enterprises with different IT needs in divisions, business units, or geographies require a separate but connected layer of IT governance for each entity.

8. *Aligned incentives.* IT governance will only work when the incentive and reward systems are driving desirable behavior.

Chapter XVII

IT Outsourcing Governance

The overall objective of this chapter is to concentrate on the important issues of strategy, structure, and management of IT outsourcing arrangements. Using well-known theoretical perspectives described earlier in this book and experience earned from several business case studies in this book, we present a governance model for successful management of IT outsourcing relationships.

IT outsourcing governance can be defined as specifying the decision rights and accountability framework to encourage desirable behavior in the IT outsourcing arrangement, where resources are transferred from one party to the other in return for resources controlled by the other party. Governance is not about making specific decisions — management does that — but rather determines who systematically makes and contributes to those decisions. Governance reflects broader principles while focusing on the management of the outsourcing relationship to achieve performance goals for both client and vendor. Governance is the institutional framework in which contracts are monitored, adapted, and renewed. Effective outsourcing governance encourages and leverages the ingenuity of the vendor's and client's people in IT usage and ensures compliance with both enterprises' overall vision and values.

The Governance Model

Our governance model is illustrated in Figure 17.1. It consists of five elements (contracts, principles, resources, activities and managers), two main links (terms-exchanges link between contracts and resources, and norms-relationships link between principles and activities), and four local links (roles between contracts and principles, capabilities between principles and resources, efficiencies between resources and activities, and outcomes between activities and contracts).

Contracts provide a legally bound, institutional framework in which each party's rights, duties, and responsibilities are codified and the goals, policies, and strategies underlying the arrangement are specified. *Principles* define decision rights concerning general IT principles, IT infrastructure, IT architecture, business application needs, and IT investments. *Resources* define decision rights concerning human assets, financial assets, physical assets, IP assets, information and IT assets, and relationship assets. *Activities* define decision rights concerning transactions, projects, problem solving and reporting. *Managers* are classified into stakeholder groups of client business management, client IT management, vendor business management, and vendor account man agent.

Exchanges of resources occur through transactions based on contracts. *Terms* for use of resources are defined in contracts. *Norms* create expectations of behavior and imply a certain action and are shared by the actors. Norms are based on principles and they occur in activities. Norms are concerned with flexibility, solidarity, mutuality, harmonization, and power. *Relationships* frame activities based on principles and norms.

Figure 17.1. Governance model

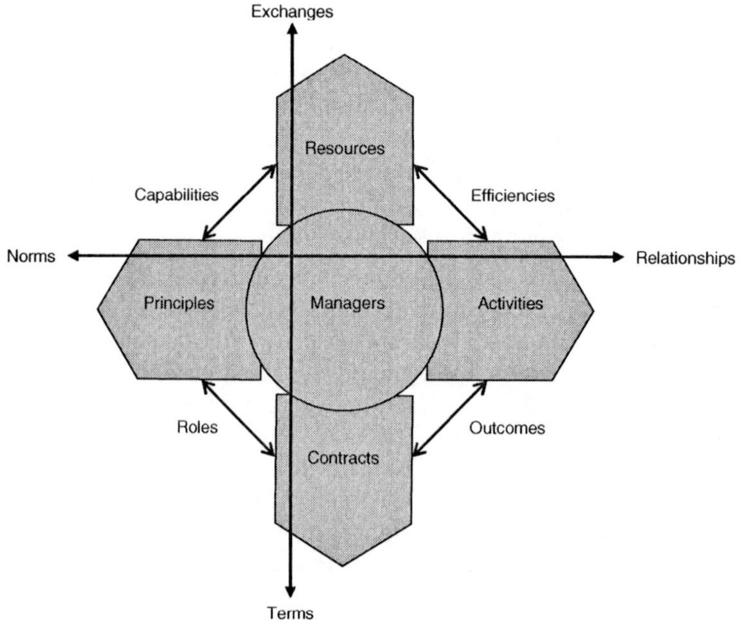

Figure 17.2. The governance model defines decision rights concerning principles

Principles Stakeholders	General principles	IT infrastructure	IT architecture	Business application needs	IT investments
Client business management	Strategic information systems planning decisions	Infrastructure capabilities decisions	Architecture performance decisions	Strategic information systems planning decisions	Financial investments decisions
Client IT management	Technology business alignment decisions	Infrastructure functions decisions	Architecture structure decisions	Information systems decisions	Investment analysis contents decisions
Vendor business management	Service level decisions	Service organization decisions	Service organization decisions	Information systems organization decisions	Financial investments decisions
Vendor account management	Technology decisions	Infrastructure integration decisions	Architecture integration decisions	Technology decisions for information systems	Investment analysis contents decisions

Roles are defined by contracts and carried out when making decisions about principles. Management roles include spokesperson, entrepreneur, personnel leader, resource allocator, monitor, and liaison roles. *Capabilities* enable the use of resources based on principles. *Efficiencies* are determined by the use of resources in activities. *Outcomes* occur in activities that are performance results from contracts.

Figure 17.2 illustrates how managers and principles are related through decision rights. *General principles* are high-level statements about how IT is used in the business. *IT infrastructure* are strategies for the base foundation of budgeted-for IT capability (technical and human), shared throughout the firm as reliable services, and centrally coordinated such as network, help desk and shared data. *IT architecture* is an integrated set of technical choices to guide the organization in satisfying business needs. The architecture is a set of policies and rules that govern the use of IT and plot a migration path to the way business will be done (includes data, technology, and applications). *Business application needs* are concerned with business applications to be acquired and built. *IT investment* and prioritization are decisions about how much and where to invest in IT, including project approvals and justification techniques (Weill & Ross, 2004).

Figure 17.3 illustrates how managers and resources are related through decision rights. *Human assets* are people, skills, career paths, training, reporting, mentoring, competencies, and so on. *Financial assets* are cash, investments, liabilities, cash flow, receivables, and so on. *Physical assets* are buildings, plant, equipment, maintenance, security, utilization, and so on. *IP assets* are intellectual property (IP), including product, services, and process know-how formally patented, copyrighted, or embedded in the enterprises' people and systems. *Information and IT assets* are digitized data, information, and knowledge about customers, processes performance, finances, information systems, and so on. *Relationship assets* are relationships within the enterprises as well as relationships between client and vendor at all levels (Weill & Ross, 2004).

Figure 17.3. The governance model defines decision rights concerning resources

Resource / Stakeholders	Human assets	Financial assets	Physical assets	IP assets	Information and IT assets	Relationship assets
Client business management	Knowledge management decisions	User investment decisions	Tangible assets policy	Intangible assets policy	Strategic information systems planning decisions	Information sharing policy
Client IT management	Internal IT personnel decisions	User technology investment decision	Tangible assets management	Intangible assets management	Technology business alignment decision	Project sharing policy
Vendor business management	Knowledge management decisions	Vendor investment decisions	Tangible assets governance	Intangible assets governance	Service level decisions	Competence sharing policy
Vendor account management	Internal IT personnel decisions	Vendor technology investment decisions	Tangible assets governance	Intangible assets governance	Technology decisions	Knowledge transfer policy

Figure 17.4. Stages of growth in IT outsourcing

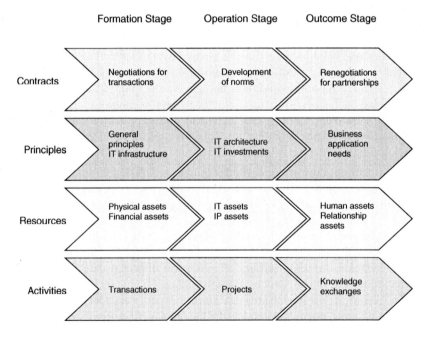

IT outsourcing governance consists of five elements as illustrated in Figure 17.1. Four of these elements are really dimensions of governance, while the remaining element is management, which integrates the four dimensions of governance. In Figure 17.4, the four dimensions of governance are illustrated along the time dimension, defined as the formation stage (vision, evaluation, negotiation), the operation stage (transition, improvement), and the outcome stage (performance, results, goals, objectives).

In the formation stage, contracts are concerned with transactions in the outsourcing arrangement. Later, as relationships and norms develop between vendor and client, contracts will be renegotiated, shifting focus from transactions to relationships and partnerships. While the first contracts will be transactional contracts, later contracts will be relational contracts. Contract work is characterized by progressive contractual work, where focus slowly shifts from transactions to relationships as contract outcomes start to materialize.

It is important to design effective IT outsourcing governance. We defined governance as specifying the decision rights and accountability framework to encourage desirable behavior in an IT outsourcing relationship. Governance performance must then be how well the governance arrangements encourage desirable behaviors and ultimately how well both firms achieve their desired performance goals as vendor and client.

Early on in this book, we presented several IT outsourcing theories. Each theory implies suggestions for managing successful IT outsourcing relationships. As a total set of suggestions and ideas from all theories, these guidelines represent critical success factors after outsourcing. The guidelines can be implemented in the governance model as illustrated in Figure 17.5. We see that resource-based theory and theory of firm boundaries both provide guidelines for resource management. Alliance and partnership theory and relational exchange theory both provide guidelines for principles management. Transaction cost theory, neoclassical economic theory and social exchange theory all provide guidelines for activity management, while contractual theory provide guidelines for contract management. Theory of core competencies, agency theory, and stakeholder theory provide guidelines directly to managers in charge of the outsourcing arrangement.

How to Succeed as a Client

Based on outsourcing theories and practice, we are able to list the following key success factors for a sourcing firm as listed in Figure 17.6.

How to Succeed as a Vendor

Based on outsourcing theories and practice, we are able to list the following key success factors for a source firm as listed in Figure 17.7.

Figure 17.5.   Managing successful IT outsourcing relationships through the governance model based on IT outsourcing theories

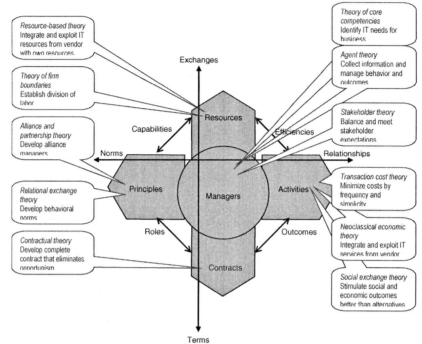

Figure 17.6.   Key success factors for the client in managing successful IT outsourcing relationships based on theories

Theory	How to succeed as a client company in an outsourcing arrangement
Theory of core competencies	We have to define our IT needs and manage IT services from the vendor.
Resource-based theory	We have to integrate and exploit strategic IT resources from the vendor together with our own resources to produce competitive goods and services.
Transaction cost theory	We have to minimize transaction costs by reducing the need for lasting specific IT assets; increase transaction frequency; reduce complexity and uncertainty in IT tasks; improve performance measurements; and reduce dependence on other transactions.
Contractual theory	We must have a complete IT contract based on information symmetry in a predictable environment with occurence adaptation that prevents opportunistic behavior in an efficient collaborative environment with balance of power between client and vendor, where the contract is a management instrument that grants decision rights and action duties.
Neoclassical economic theory	We have to integrate and exploit IT services from the vendor together with our own services to produce competitive goods and services.
Partnership and alliance theory	We have to develop experience with alliances, develop alliance managers, and develop the ability to identify potential vendors.
Relational exchange theory	We have to develop and secure common norms that are relevant to both parties.
Social exchange theory	We have to enable social and economic outcomes in the exchange between the vendor and us such that these outcomes outperform those obtainable in alternative exchanges.
Agency theory	We have to make it easy and inexpensive for ourselves to find out what the vendor is actually doing. In addition, both outcome-based and behavior-based incentives can be used to reduce and prevent opportunistic vendor behavior.
Theory of firm boundaries	We have to implement a strict and rigid division of labor between the vendor and us.
Stakeholder theory	We must create efficient and effective communication with and between stakeholders to secure continued support from all stakeholders, to balance their interests and to make the IT outsourcing arrangement so that all stakeholders achieve their goals.

Figure 17.7. Key success factors for the vendor in managing successful IT outsourcing relationships based on theories

Theory	How to succeed as a vendor company in an outsourcing arrangement
Theory of core competencies	We have to provide complementary core competencies, such as personnel, methodologies, and services, to the client.
Resource-based theory	We have to enable the client to integrate and exploit strategic IT resources from us together with the clients' own resources to produce competitive goods and services.
Transaction cost theory	We have to minimize transaction costs by reducing the need for lasting specific IT assets; increase transaction frequency; reduce complexity and uncertainty in IT tasks; improve performance measurements; and reduce dependence on other transactions.
Contractual theory	We must have a complete IT contract based on information symmetry in a predictable environment with occurrence adaptation that prevents opportunistic behavior in an efficient collaborative environment with balance of power between client and vendor, where the contract is a management instrument that grants decision rights and action duties.
Neoclassical economic theory	We have to enable the client to integrate and exploit IT services from us together with own services to produce competitive goods and services.
Partnership and alliance theory	We have to develop experience with alliances, develop alliance managers, and develop the ability to identify potential clients.
Relational exchange theory	We have to develop and secure common norms that are relevant to both parties.
Social exchange theory	We have to enable social and economic outcomes in the exchange between the client and us such that these outcomes outperform those obtainable in alternative exchanges.
Agency theory	It must be easy and inexpensive for the principal (client) to find out what the agent (vendor) is actually doing. In addition, both outcome-based and behavior-based incentives can be used to reduce and prevent opportunistic behavior.
Theory of firm boundaries	We have to implement a strict and rigid division of labor between the client and us.
Stakeholder theory	We have to create efficient and effective communication with and between stakeholders to secure continued support from all stakeholders, to balance their interests and to make the IT outsourcing arrangement so that all stakeholders achieve their goals.

Chapter XVIII

Knowledge Management in Governance

The knowledge-based view of the firm has established itself as an important perspective in strategic management. This perspective builds on the resource-based theory of the firm. The knowledge-based view of the firm implies that information systems are designed to support knowledge management in organizations.

Knowledge management can be defined as a method to simplify and improve the process of sharing, distributing, creating, capturing, and understanding knowledge in a company. Knowledge management is description, organization, sharing, and development of knowledge in a firm. Knowledge management is managing knowledge-intensive activities in a company. Knowledge management refers to identifying and leveraging the collective knowledge in a company to help the company compete. Knowledge management is a method for achieving corporate goals by collecting, creating and synthesizing and sharing information, insights, reflections, thoughts, and experience. Knowledge management is a discipline focused on systematic and innovative methods, practices, and tools for managing the generation, acquisition, exchange, protection, distribution, and utilization of knowledge, intellectual capital, and intangible assets (Montana, 2000).

The purpose of knowledge management is to help companies create, share and use knowledge more effectively. Effective knowledge management causes fewer errors, less work, more independence in time and space for knowledge workers, fewer questions, better decisions, less reinventing of wheels, improved customer relations, improved service, and improved profitability. Knowledge management is purported to increase both innovation and responsiveness. The recent interest in organizational knowledge has prompted the issue of managing knowledge to the organization's benefit (Alavi & Leidner, 2001).

IS/IT in Knowledge Management

As we trace the evolution of computing technologies in business, we can observe their changing level of organizational impact. The first level of impact was at the point work was done and transactions (e.g., orders, deposits, reservations) took place. The inflexible, centralized mainframe allowed for little more than massive number crunching, commonly known as electronic *data* processing. Organizations became data heavy at the bottom and data management systems were used to keep the data in check. Later, the management *information* systems were used to aggregate data into useful information reports, often prescheduled, for the control level of the organization – people who were making sure that organizational resources like personnel, money, and physical goods were being deployed efficiently. As information technology (IT) and information systems (IS) started to facilitate data and information overflow, and corporate attention became a scarce resource, the concept of *knowledge* emerged as a particularly high-value form of information (Grover & Davenport, 2001).

Information technology can play an important role in successful knowledge management initiatives. However, the concept of coding and transmitting knowledge in organizations is not new: training and employee development programs, organizational policies, routines, procedures, reports, and manuals have served this function for many years. What is new and exciting in the knowledge management area is the potential for using modern information technology (e.g., the Internet, intranets, extranets, browsers, data warehouses, data filters, software agents, expert systems) to support knowledge creation, sharing and exchange in an organization and between organizations. Modern information technology can collect, systematize structure, store, combine, distribute, and present information of value to knowledge workers (Nahapiet & Ghoshal, 1998).

According to Davenport and Prusak (1998), more and more companies have instituted knowledge repositories, supporting such diverse types of knowledge as best practices, lessons learned, product development knowledge, customer knowledge, human resource management knowledge, and methods-based knowledge. Groupware and intranet-based technologies have become standard knowledge infrastructures. A new set of professional job titles — the knowledge manager, the chief knowledge officer (CKO), the knowledge coordinator, and the knowledge-network facilitator — affirms the widespread legitimacy that knowledge management has earned in the corporate world.

The low cost of computers and networks has created a potential infrastructure for knowledge sharing and opened up important knowledge management opportunities. The computational power as such has little relevance to knowledge work, but the communication and storage capabilities of networked computers make it an important enabler of effective knowledge work. Through e-mail, groupware, the Internet, and intranets, computers, and networks can point to people with knowledge and connect people who need to share knowledge independent of time and place.

There is no single information system that is able to cover all knowledge management needs in a firm. This is evident from the widespread potential of IT in knowledge management processes. Rather, knowledge management systems (KMS) refer to a class of information systems applied to managing organizational knowledge. These systems are IT applications to support and enhance the organizational processes of knowledge creation, storage and retrieval, transfer, and application (Alavi & Leidner, 2001).

Requirements from Knowledge Management

The critical role of information technology and information systems lies in the ability to support communication, collaboration, and those searching for knowledge, and the ability to enable collaborative learning. This has implications for information systems design, and the following requirements from knowledge management can be identified:

1. *Interaction between information and knowledge.* Information becomes knowledge when it is combined with experience, interpretation, and reflection. Knowledge becomes information when assigned an explicit representation. Sometimes information exists before knowledge, sometimes knowledge exists before information. One important implication of this two-way direction between knowledge and information is that information systems designed to support knowledge in organizations may not appear radically different from other forms of IT support, but will be geared toward enabling users to assign meaning to information and to capture some of their knowledge in information (Alavi & Leidner, 2001).

2. *Interaction between tacit and explicit knowledge.* Tacit knowledge is knowledge that is hard and sometimes impossible for humans to articulate and communicate. Tacit and explicit knowledge depend on each other, and they influence each other. The linkage of tacit and explicit knowledge suggests that only individuals with a requisite level of shared knowledge are able to exchange knowledge. They suggest the existence of a shared knowledge space that is required in order for individual A to understand individual B's knowledge. The knowledge space is the underlying overlap in knowledge base of A and B. This overlap is typically tacit knowledge. It may be argued that the greater the shared knowledge space, the less the context needed for individuals to share knowledge within the group and, hence, the higher the value of explicit knowledge. IT is both dependent on the shared knowledge space and an important part of the shared knowledge space. IT is dependent on the shared knowledge space because knowledge workers need to have a common understanding of available information in information systems in the organization. If common understanding is missing, then knowledge workers are unable to make use of information. IT is an important part of the shared knowledge space because

information systems make common information available to all knowledge workers in the organization. One important implication of this two-way relationship between knowledge space and information systems is that a minimum knowledge space has to be present, while IT can contribute to growth in the knowledge space (Alavi & Leidner, 2001).

3. *Knowledge management strategy.* Efficiency-driven businesses may apply a stock strategy where databases and information systems are important. Effectiveness-driven businesses may apply a flow strategy where information networks are important. Expert-driven businesses may apply a growth strategy where networks of experts, work processes, and learning environments are important (Hansen et al., 1999).

4. *Combination in SECI processes.* The SECI process consists of four knowledge conversion modes: Socialization, Externalization, Combination, and Internalization. These modes are not equally suited for IS/IT support. Socialization is the process of converting new tacit knowledge to tacit knowledge. This takes place in the human brain. Externalization is the process of converting tacit knowledge to explicit knowledge. The successful conversion of tacit knowledge into explicit knowledge depends on the sequential use of metaphors, analogy, and model. Combination is the process of converting explicit knowledge into more complex and systematic sets of explicit knowledge. Explicit knowledge is collected from inside and outside the organization and then combined, edited and processed to form new knowledge. The new explicit knowledge is then disseminated among the members of the organization. According to Nonaka et al. (2000), creative use of computerized communication networks and large-scale databases can facilitate this mode of knowledge conversion. When the financial controller collects information from all parts of the organization and puts it together to show the financial health of the organization, that report is new knowledge in the sense that it synthesizes explicit knowledge from many different sources in one context. Finally, internalization in the SECI process converts explicit knowledge into tacit knowledge. Through internalization, explicit knowledge created is shared throughout an organization and converted into tacit knowledge by individuals.

5. *Explicit transfer of common knowledge.* If management decides to focus on common knowledge as defined by Dixon (2000), knowledge management should focus on the sharing of common knowledge. Common knowledge is shared in the organization using five mechanisms: serial transfer, explicit transfer, tacit transfer, strategic transfer, and expert transfer. Management has to emphasize all five mechanisms for successful sharing and creation of common knowledge. For serial transfer, management has to stimulate meetings and contacts between group members. For explicit transfer, management has to stimulate documentation of work by the previous group. For tacit transfer, management has to stimulate contacts between the two groups. For strategic transfer, management has to identify strategic knowledge and knowledge gaps. For expert transfer, management has to create networks where experts can transfer their knowledge. These five mechanisms are not equally suited for IT support. Explicit transfer seems very well suited for IT support as the knowledge from the other group is transferred explicitly as

explicit knowledge in words and numbers and shared in the form of data, scientific formulae, specifications, manuals and the like. Expert transfer also seems suited for IT support when generic knowledge is transferred from one individual to another person to enable the person to solve new problems with new methods.

6. *Link knowledge to its uses.* One of the mistakes in knowledge management is disentangling knowledge from its uses. A major manifestation of this error is that knowledge management initiatives become ends in themselves. For example, data warehousing can easily degenerate into technological challenges. The relevance of a data warehouse for decisions and actions gets lost in the turmoil spawned by debates about appropriate data structures.

7. *Treat knowledge as an intellectual asset in the economic school.* If management decides to follow the economic school of knowledge management (Earl, 2001), then intellectual capital accounting should be part of the knowledge management system. The knowledge management system should support knowledge markets where knowledge buyers, knowledge sellers and knowledge brokers can use the system.

8. *Treat knowledge as a mutual resource in the organizational school.* The potential contribution of IT is linked to the combination of intranets and groupware to connect members and pool their knowledge, both explicit and tacit (Earl, 2001).

9. *Treat knowledge as a strategy in the strategy school.* The potential contribution of IT is manifold once knowledge as a strategy is the impetus behind knowledge management initiatives. Once can expect quite an eclectic mix of networks, systems, tools, and knowledge repositories (Earl, 2001).

10. *Value configuration determines knowledge needs in primary activities.* Knowledge needs can be structured according to primary and secondary activities in the value configuration. Depending on the firm being a value chain, a value shop, or a value network, the knowledge management system must support more efficient production in the value chain, adding value to the knowledge work in the value shop, and more value by use of IT infrastructure in the value network.

11. *Incentive alignment.* The first dimension of information systems design is concerned with software engineering (error-free software, documentation, portability, modularity & architecture, development cost, maintenance cost, speed, and robustness). The second dimension is concerned with technology acceptance (user friendliness, user acceptance, perceived ease-of-use, perceived usefulness, cognitive fit, and task-technology fit). The third dimension that is particularly important to knowledge management systems is concerned with incentive alignment. Incentive alignment includes incentives influencing user behavior and the user's interaction with the system, deterrence of use for personal gain, use consistent with organizational goals, and robustness against information misrepresentation (Ba et al., 2001).

According to Earl (2001), the strategic school of knowledge management sees knowledge management as a dimension of competitive strategy. Indeed, it may be seen as the essence of a firm's strategy. Approaches to knowledge management are dependent on management perspective. Distinctions can be made between the information-based perspective, the technology-based perspective, and the culture-based perspective:

- *Information-based perspective* is concerned with access to information. I have a problem, and I am looking for someone in the organization who has knowledge that can solve my problem.

- *Technology-based perspective* is concerned with applications of information technology. We have all this hardware and software in the firm, how can we use this technology to systematize, store and distribute information to knowledge workers.

- *Culture-based perspective* is concerned with knowledge sharing. We are an organization because division of labor makes us more efficient and because we can draw on each other's expertise.

All three perspectives belong in a knowledge management project to be successful. However, the main focus may vary depending on corporate situation. If reinventing the wheel all the time is the big problem, then the information-based perspective should dominate project focus. If the technology in the firm is unable to provide even basic services to knowledge users, then the technology-based perspective should dominate project focus. If knowledge workers are isolated and reluctant to share knowledge, then the culture-based perspective should dominate project focus.

Codification and Personalization Strategy

Some companies automate knowledge management, while others rely on their people to share knowledge through more traditional means. In some companies, the strategy centers on the computer. Knowledge is carefully codified and stored in databases, where it can be accessed and used easily by anyone in the company. These companies have developed elaborate ways to codify, store and reuse knowledge. Knowledge is codified using a people-to-documents approach: it is extracted from the person who developed it, made independent of that person, and reused for various purposes. Knowledge objects are developed by pulling key pieces of knowledge such as interview guides, work schedules, benchmark data, and market segmentation analysis out of documents and storing them in the electronic repository for people to use. This approach allows many people to search for and retrieve codified knowledge without having to contact the person who originally developed it. That opens up the possibility of achieving scale in knowledge reuse and thus of growing the business. Hansen et al. (1999) call this the codification strategy for managing knowledge.

In other companies, knowledge is closely tied to the person who developed it and is shared mainly through direct person-to-person contacts. The chief purpose of computers at such companies is to help people communicate knowledge, not to store it. These companies focus on dialogue between individuals, not knowledge objects in a database. Knowledge that has not been codified is transferred in brainstorming sessions and one-on-one conversations. Knowledge workers collectively arrive at deeper insights by going back and forth on problems they need to solve. These companies invest heavily in building networks of people. Knowledge is shared not only face-to-face, but also over the telephone, by e-mail, and via videoconferences. Networks can be fostered in many ways: by transferring people between offices, by supporting a culture in which knowledge workers are expected to return phone calls from colleagues promptly, by creating directories of experts, and by using knowledge managers within the firm to assist project teams. These firms may also have developed electronic document systems, but the purpose of the systems is not to provide knowledge objects. Instead, knowledge workers scan documents to get up to speed in a particular area and to find out who has done work on a topic. They then approach those people directly. Hansen et al. (1999) call this the personalization strategy for managing knowledge.

Codification and personalization strategy can be contrasted with each other using criteria such as competitive strategy, economic model, knowledge management strategy, information technology, and human resources. The competitive strategy by codification is to provide high quality, reliable, and fast information-systems implementation by reusing codified knowledge. The competitive strategy by personalization is to provide creative, analytically rigorous advice on high-level strategic problems by channeling individual expertise. The economic model for codification strategy can be labeled reuse economics, while the economic model for personalization can be labeled expert economics. Reuse economics implies investing once in a knowledge asset, and then reuse it many times. Expert economics implies charging high fees for highly customized solutions to unique problems.

Knowledge management strategy will either be people-to-documents for codification or person-to-person for personalization. People-to-documents implies developing an electronic document system that codifies stores, disseminates, and allows reuse of knowledge. Person-to-person implies developing networks for linking people so that tacit knowledge can be shared. By codification, the company invests heavily in IT, where the goal is to connect people with reusable codified knowledge. By personalization, the company invests moderately in IT, where the goal is to facilitate conversations and exchange of tacit knowledge. By codification, the human resource approach will be concerned with training people in groups and through computer-based distance learning. By personalization, the human resource approach will be concerned with training people through one-on-one mentoring.

Hansen et al. (1999) found that companies that use knowledge effectively, pursue one strategy predominantly and use the second strategy to support the first. This can be thought of as an 80-20 split: 80% of their knowledge sharing follows one strategy, 20% the other. Executives who try to excel at both strategies of codification and personalization, risk failing at both.

How do companies choose the right strategy for managing knowledge? Competitive strategy must drive knowledge management strategy. Executives must be able to articulate why customers buy a company's products or services rather than those of its competitors. What value do customers expect from the company? How does knowledge that resides in the company add value for customers? Assuming the competitive strategy is clear, managers will want to consider three further questions that can help them choose a primary knowledge management strategy. The three questions developed by Hansen et al. (1999) are concerned with standardized vs. customized products, mature or innovative products, and explicit vs. tacit knowledge.

The first question is: do you offer standardized or customized products? Companies that offer standardized products will fit the codification strategy, while companies that offer customized products will fit the personalization strategy. The second question is: do you have mature or innovative products? Companies that offer mature products will fit the codification strategy, while companies that offer innovative products will fit the personalization strategy.

The final question is: do your people rely on explicit or tacit knowledge to solve problems? Explicit knowledge is knowledge that can be codified, such as simple software code and market data. When a company's employees rely on explicit knowledge to do their work, the people-to-documents approach makes the most sense. Tacit knowledge, by contrast, is difficult to articulate in writing and is acquired through personal experience. It includes scientific expertise, operational know-how, and insights about an industry, business judgment, and technological expertise. When people use tacit knowledge most often to solve problems, the person-to-person approach works best.

Hansen et al. (1999) stress that people need incentives to participate in the knowledge sharing process. The two knowledge management strategies call for different incentive systems. In the codification model, managers need to develop a system that encourages people to write down what they know and to get those documents into the electronic repository. And real incentives – not small enticements – are required to get people to take those steps. The level and quality of employees' contributions to the document database should be part of their annual performance review. Incentives to stimulate knowledge sharing should be very different at companies that are following the personalization approach. Managers need to reward people for sharing knowledge directly with other people.

Stock, Flow and Growth Strategy

Approaches to knowledge management are dependent on knowledge focus in the organization. Distinctions can be made between expert-driven business, experience-driven business and efficiency-driven business:

- *Expert-driven business* solves large, complex, risky, new, and unusual problems for customers. Competitive advantage is achieved through continuous improvisation and innovation. Knowledge workers apply general high-level knowledge to understand, solve, and learn. Learning from problem solving is important to be able to solve the next new and unknown problem for customers. An expert-driven business is characterized by both new problems and new methods for solution.

- *Experience-driven business* solves large and complicated problems for customers. The problems are new, but they can be solved with existing methods in a specific context every time. Competitive advantage is achieved through effective adaptation of existing problem solving methodologies and techniques. Continuous improvement in effectiveness is important to be able to solve the next problem for customers. An experience-based business is characterized by new problems and existing methods for solution.

- *Efficiency-driven business solves* known problems. The quality of the solution is found in fast and inexpensive application to meet customer needs. Competitive advantage is achieved in the ability to make small adjustments in existing goods and services at a low price. An efficiency-driven business is characterized by known problems and known methods for solution.

Few knowledge-intensive firms are only active in one of these businesses. Most firms are active in several of these businesses. For example, medical doctors in a hospital are mainly in the experience-driven business of solving new problems with known methods. Sometimes, they are in the expert-driven business of solving new problems with new methods. Similarly, lawyers in a law firm are often in the expert-driven business, but most of the time in the experience-driven business. In some engineering firms, engineers are often in the efficiency-driven business, but most of the time in the experience-based business.

Knowledge focus will be different in expert-driven, experience-driven, and efficiency-driven businesses. In the expert-driven business, learning is important, while previous knowledge becomes obsolete. In the experience-driven business, know-how concerning problem solutions is important, while knowledge of previous problems becomes obsolete. In the efficiency-based business, all knowledge concerning both problems and solutions is important in an accumulation of knowledge to improve efficiency. These differences lead us to make distinctions between the following three knowledge management strategies of stock strategy, flow strategy and growth strategy:

- *Stock strategy* is focused on collecting and storing all knowledge in information bases in the organization. Information is stored in databases and made available to knowledge workers in the organization and in knowledge networks. Knowledge workers use databases to keep updated on relevant problems, relevant methods, news, and opinions. Information on problems and methods accumulate over time in databases. This strategy can also be called person-to-knowledge strategy.

- *Flow strategy* is focused on collecting and storing knowledge in information bases in the organization as long as the information is used in knowledge work processes. If certain kinds of knowledge work disappear, then information for those work processes become obsolete and can be deleted from databases. This is a yellow-pages strategy where information on knowledge areas covered by individuals in the firm is registered. The link to knowledge sources in the form of individuals is made specific in the databases, so that the person source can be identified. When a knowledge worker starts on a new project, the person will search company databases to find colleagues who already have experience in solving these kinds of problems. This strategy can also be called person-to-person strategy.

Figure 18.1.   Characteristics of knowledge management strategies

Characteristics	Stock strategy	Flow strategy	Growth strategy
Knowledge focus	Efficiency-driven business	Experience-driven business	Expert-driven business
Important persons	Chief knowledge officer Chief information officer Database engineers	Chief knowledge officer Experienced knowledge workers	Management Experts
Knowledge base	Databases and information systems	Information networks	Networks of experts, work processes and learning environments
Important elements	Access to databases and information systems	Access to knowledge space	Access to networks of experts and learning environments
Management task	Collecting information and making it available	Connecting persons to experienced knowledge workers	Providing access to networks
Learning	Efficiency training applying existing knowledge	Experience accumulation applying existing knowledge	Growth training developing new knowledge

- *Growth strategy* is focused on developing new knowledge. New knowledge is developed in innovative work processes taking place when knowledge workers have to solve new problems with new methods for customers. Often, several persons are involved in the innovation, and together they have gone through a learning process. When a knowledge worker starts on a new project, the person will use the intraorganizational and interorganizational network to find information on work processes and learning environments, which colleagues have used success-fully in previous innovation processes.

There is a strong link between these three knowledge management strategies and the three alternatives of expert-driven, experience-driven, and efficiency-driven business. In Figure 18.1, characteristics of the three strategies are presented. Typically, efficiency-driven businesses will apply the stock strategy, while experience-driven businesses will apply the flow strategy, and expert-driven businesses will apply the growth strategy.

Stages of Growth in IS/IT

Stages of knowledge management technology is a relative concept concerned with IT's ability to process information for knowledge work. IT at later stages is more useful to knowledge work than IT at earlier stages. The relative concept implies that IT is more

Figure 18.2.   The knowledge management technology stage model

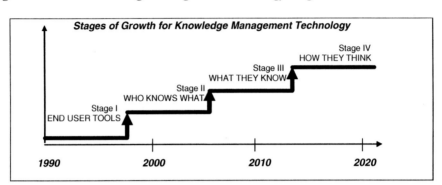

directly involved in knowledge work at higher stages, and that IT is able to support more advanced knowledge work at higher stages.

The knowledge management technology (KMT) stage model consists of four stages. The first stage is general IT support for knowledge workers. This includes word processing, spreadsheets, and e-mail. The second stage is information about knowledge sources. An information system stores information about who knows what within the firm and outside the firm. The system does not store what they actually know. A typical example is the company intranet. The third stage is information representing knowledge. The system stores what knowledge workers know in terms of information. A typical example is a database. The fourth and final stage is information processing. An information system uses information to evaluate situations. A typical example here is an expert system.

The contingent approach to firm performance implies that Stage I may be right for one firm, while Stage IV may be right for another firm. Some firms will evolve over time from Stage I to higher stages as indicated in Figure 18.2. The time axis ranging from 1990 to 2020 in Figure 18.2 suggests that it takes time for an individual firm and a whole industry to move through all stages. As an example applied later in this chapter, the law firm industry is moving slowly in its use of information technology.

Stages of IT support in knowledge management are useful for identifying the current situation as well as planning for future applications in the firm. Each stage is described in the following:

I.   *Tools for end users* are made available to knowledge workers. In the simplest stage, this means a capable networked PC on every desk or in every briefcase, with standardized personal productivity tools (word processing, presentation software) so that documents can be exchanged easily throughout a company. More complex and functional desktop infrastructures can also be the basis for the same types of knowledge support. Stage I is recognized by widespread dissemination and use of end-user tools among knowledge workers in the company. For example, lawyers in a law firm will in this stage use word processing, spreadsheets, legal databases, presentation software, and scheduling programs.

Stage I can be labeled *end-user-tools* or *people-to-technology* as information technology provides knowledge workers with tools that improve personal efficiency.

II. *Information about who knows what* is made available to all people in the firm and to select outside partners. Search engines should enable work with a thesaurus, since the terminology in which expertise is sought may not always match the terms the expert uses to classify that expertise.

According to Alavi and Leidner (2001), the creation of corporate directories, also referred to as the mapping of internal expertise, is a common application of knowledge management technology. Because much knowledge in an organization remains uncodified, mapping the internal expertise is a potentially useful application of technology to enable easy identification of knowledgeable persons.

Here we find the cartographic school of knowledge management (Earl 2001), which is concerned with mapping organizational knowledge. It aims to record and disclose who in the organization knows what by building knowledge directories. Often called Yellow Pages, the principal idea is to make sure knowledgeable people in the organization are accessible to others for advice, consultation, or knowledge exchange. Knowledge-oriented directories are not so much repositories of knowledge-based information as gateways to knowledge, and the knowledge is as likely to be tacit as explicit.

Information about who knows what is sometimes called metadata, representing knowledge about where the knowledge resides. Providing taxonomies or organizational knowledge maps enables individuals to locate rapidly the individual who has the needed knowledge, more rapidly than would be possible without such IT-based support.

Stage II can be labeled *who-knows-what* or *people-to-people* as knowledge workers use information technology to find other knowledge workers.

III. *Information from knowledge workers* is stored and made available to everyone in the firm and to designated external partners. Data mining techniques can be applied here to find relevant information and combine information in data warehouses. On a broader basis, search engines are Web browsers and server software that operate with a thesaurus, since the terminology in which expertise is sought may not always match the terms used by the expert to classify that expertise.

One starting approach in Stage III is to store project reports, notes, recommendations, and letters from each knowledge worker in the firm. Over time, this material will grow fast, making it necessary for a librarian or a chief knowledge officer (CKO) to organize it. In a law firm, all client cases will be classified and stored in databases using software such as Lotus Notes.

An essential contribution that IT can make is the provision of shared databases across tasks, levels, entities, and geographies to all knowledge workers throughout a process (Earl, 2001).

According to Alavi and Leidner (2001), one survey found that 74% of respondents believed that their organization's best knowledge was inaccessible and 68% thought that mistakes were reproduced several times. Such a perception of failure to apply existing knowledge is an incentive for mapping, codifying and storing information derived from internal expertise.

According to Alavi and Leidner (2001), one of the most common applications is internal benchmarking with the aim of transferring internal best practices. To be successful, best practices have to be coded, stored, and shared among knowledge workers.

In addition to (i) best practices knowledge within a quality or business process management function, other common applications include (ii) knowledge for sales purposes involving products, markets and customers, (iii) lessons learned in projects or product development efforts, (iv) knowledge around implementation of information systems, (v) competitive intelligence for strategy and planning functions, and (vi) learning histories or records of experience with a new corporate direction or approach (Grover & Davenport, 2001).

Stage III can be labeled *what-they-know* or *people-to-docs* as information technology provides knowledge workers with access to information that is typically stored in documents. Examples of documents are contracts and agreements, reports, manuals and handbooks, business forms, letters, memos, articles, drawings, blueprints, photographs, e-mail and voice mail messages, video clips, script and visuals from presentations, policy statements, computer printouts, and transcripts from meetings.

IV.   *Information systems solving knowledge problems* are made available to knowledge workers and solution seekers. Artificial intelligence is applied in these systems. For example, neural networks are statistically oriented tools that excel at using data to classify cases into one category or another. Another example is expert systems that can enable the knowledge of one or a few experts to be used by a much broader group of workers requiring the knowledge.

According to Alavi and Leidner (2001), an insurance company was faced with the commoditization of its market and declining profits. The company found that applying the best decision making expertise via a new underwriting process, supported by a knowledge management system based on best practices, enabled it to move into profitable niche markets and, hence, to increase income.

According to Grover and Davenport (2001), artificial intelligence is applied in rule-based systems, and more commonly, case-based systems are used to capture and provide access to resolutions of customer service problems, legal knowledge, new product development knowledge, and many other types of knowledge.

Knowledge is explicated and formalized during the knowledge codification phase that took place in Stage III. Codification of tacit knowledge is facilitated by mechanisms that formalize and embed it in documents, software, and systems.

However, the higher the tacit elements of the knowledge, the more difficult it is to codify. Codification of complex knowledge frequently relies on information technology. Expert systems, decision support systems, document management systems, search engines, and relational database tools represent some of the technological solutions developed to support this phase of knowledge management. Consequently, advanced codification of knowledge emerges in Stage IV, rather than in Stage III, because expert systems and other artificial intelligence systems have to be applied to be successful.

Stage IV can be labeled *how-they-think* or *people-to-systems* where the system is intended to help solve a knowledge problem.

When companies want to use knowledge in real-time, mission-critical applications, they have to structure the information base for rapid, precise access. A Web search yielding hundreds of documents will not suffice when a customer is waiting on the phone for an answer. Representing and structuring knowledge is a requirement that has long been addressed by artificial intelligence researchers in the form of expert systems and other applications. Now their technologies are being applied within the context of knowledge management. Rule-based systems and case-based systems are used to capture and provide access to customer service problem resolution, legal knowledge, new product development knowledge, and many other types of knowledge. Although it can be difficult and labor-intensive to author a structured knowledge base, the effort can pay off in terms of faster responses to customers, lower cost per knowledge transaction, and lessened requirements for experienced, expert personnel (Grover & Davenport, 2001).

Chapter XIX

Case Studies

Rolls-Royce

The primary learning objective of this term paper assignment is to enable you to practice the application of various techniques that are used in the process of developing an IS/IT strategy for an organization. Each of these techniques will be discussed in detail during the face-to-face class sessions with the professors, and they are also described in the textbooks for the course.

Please read carefully the attached case study about IS/IT at Rolls-Royce. Rolls-Royce operates in four global markets — civil aerospace, defense aerospace, marine and energy. It is investing in technology and capability that can be exploited in each of these sectors to create a competitive range of products. Please note that the case study focuses on certain areas of IS/IT at Rolls-Royce, such as electronic commerce (e-commerce), enterprise resource planning (ERP), knowledge management and IT outsourcing. These areas serve as examples of IS/IT at Rolls-Royce.

After reading the case study, please visit the company's web pages at www.rolls-royce.com to get a better understanding of the company's services, operations, positioning and strategic situation. Also visit the web pages of other similar international companies, to see how they are positioned differently in strategic terms and in terms of the services they offer. You may also want to do some library research about how various other companies are responding to the challenge of e-commerce as well.

Given the challenge of e-business technology to global companies, your task is to develop an IS/IT strategy document for Rolls-Royce using the Y model. Feel free to introduce assumptions about the company (based on what you know about other international companies) and use any other publicly available information you find.

You must follow three sequential steps in developing the IS/IT strategy. The first step is concerned with analysis. The second step is concerned with choice (selection and decision), while the final step is concerned with implementation.

Your paper MUST be based on the Y model for strategy work as described in your two textbooks, and you should do the strategy work according to the following stages:

1. Describe the current situation
2. Describe the desired situation
3. Analyze the needs for change (focus specifically on the e-commerce, e-business, knowledge management, and IT outsourcing challenges facing the company)
4. Search for alternative actions
5. Select actions and make an action plan
6. Think about the implementation challenges the company will face.

At the very least, the IS/IT strategy document in your term paper should have the following table of contents:

1. Introduction

    Purpose (what kind of plan and how will it be used)

    Assumptions (about Rolls-Royce that you are making)

    The e-commerce challenge to international companies as well as e-business, knowledge management, and outsourcing challenges

2. Current IS/IT Situation

    (Here you must apply between 2 to 5 specific methods)

3. Desired Business Situation

    (Here you must apply between 2 to 5 specific methods)

4. Needs for Change (Make sure you provide a specific list)

5. IS/IT Strategy and Recommended Actions

6. Expected Implementation Challenges (and how you would deal with them)

7. Your Process

A one-page description about how you went about developing the IS/IT strategy and your opinion about the methods you used and the process you followed.

You are also welcome to add other sections if you think it is helpful, but you are not allowed to go beyond the maximum 25 page limit for the assignment as additional pages will be ignored.

Please note that Rolls-Royce has an outsourcing agreement and relationship with EDS. A discussion of and recommendation for the future of outsourcing at Rolls-Royce should be included in your term paper.

Your IS/IT strategy must follow the stages of the Y model and should incorporate at appropriate stages of the Y model future opportunities and priorities for e-commerce, e-business, knowledge management systems, and IS/IT outsourcing. You should also discuss general sourcing options for Rolls-Royce in the future and appropriate IT governance mechanisms.

Please make your IS/IT strategy for the whole of Rolls-Royce. Your role is to act as an external management consultant to Jonathan Mitchell, who is director of business process improvement in the company. You can assume that you have been asked by Jonathan Mitchell to develop the IS/IT strategy document and that he will be the first reader of your document. You are not allowed to contact Jonathan Mitchell.

E-Commerce, ERP, Knowledge Management, and Outsourcing at Rolls-Royce

This case was prepared by professor Petter Gottschalk in 2004 based on several sources, for the purposes of term paper discussion rather than to illustrate either effective or ineffective handling of business and IS/IT situations.

 **History of Rolls-Royce**

1884 – Rolls-Royce grew from the electrical and mechanical business established by Henry Royce in 1884. Royce built his first motor car in 1904 and in May of that year met Charles Rolls, whose company sold quality cars in London. Agreement was reached that Royce Limited would manufacture a range of cars to be exclusively sold by CS Rolls & Co — they were to bear the name Rolls-Royce.

 1906 – Success with the cars led to the formation of the Rolls-Royce Company in March 1906 and to the launch of the six-cylinder Silver Ghost, which, within a year, was hailed as 'the best car in the world'.

1914– At the start of the First World War, in response to the nation's needs, Royce designed his first aero engine – the Eagle, providing some half of the total horsepower used in the air war by the allies. The Eagle powered the first direct transatlantic flight as well as the first flight from England to Australia – both in the Vickers Vimy aircraft.

1931 – The late 1920s saw Rolls-Royce develop the 'R' engine to power Britain's entry in the International Schneider Trophy seaplane contest. It established a new world air speed record of over 400 mph in 1931. Subsequently it established new world records on both land and water. More importantly, as subsequent events were to prove, it gave

Rolls-Royce the technological base to develop the Merlin, which Royce had begun to work on before his death in 1933.

1940 – The Merlin powered the Hawker Hurricane and Supermarine Spitfire in the Battle of Britain. Demand for the Merlin during the Second World War transformed Rolls-Royce from a relatively small company into a major contender in aero propulsion.

1944 – In parallel, Rolls-Royce began development of the aero gas turbine, pioneered by Sir Frank Whittle. The Welland engine entered service in the Gloster Meteor fighter in 1944, and Rolls-Royce had the confidence immediately after the war to commit itself to the gas turbine, in which it had a technological lead.

1953 – Rolls-Royce entered the civil aviation market with the Dart in the Vickers Viscount. It was to become the cornerstone of the universal acceptance of the gas turbine by the airline industry. The Avon-powered Comet became the first turbojet to enter transatlantic service and in 1960, the Conway engine in the Boeing 707 became the first turbofan to enter airline service.

1959 – The other major manufacturers in Britain between the wars were Armstrong Siddeley, Blackburn, Bristol, de Havilland, and Napier. The leader among these was Bristol, which, in 1959, merged with the motor car and aero-engine maker Armstrong Siddeley. Three other smaller engine companies were absorbed into Bristol Siddeley and Rolls-Royce in 1961. Finally, the capability of the British aero-engine industry was consolidated when Rolls-Royce and Bristol Siddeley merged in 1966.

1960s – With the emergence of the wide body airliners in the late 1960s, Rolls-Royce launched the RB211 for the Lockheed L-1011 Tri-Star.

1971 – Early problems with the RB211 led to the company being taken into state ownership, and the flotation of the motorcar business in 1973 as a separate entity. The three-shaft turbofan concept of the RB211 has now established itself at the heart of the Rolls-Royce world-class family of engines.

1987 – Rolls-Royce returned to the private sector, undergoing a number of mergers and acquisitions to create the only company in Britain capable of delivering power for use in the air, at sea and on land.

1990 – In 1990, Rolls-Royce formed an aero engines joint venture with BMW of Germany. Rolls-Royce took full control of the joint venture from January 2000. The legal name of the company is now Rolls-Royce Deutschland Ltd & Co KG.

1995 – Allison Engine Company in Indianapolis was acquired. Allison brought with it major new civil engines including the AE3007 for Embraer's new regional jet, and existing, successful defense programs.

1998 – Rolls-Royce Motor Cars was sold by Vickers to Volkswagen, although BMW hold the rights to the name and the marquee for use on Rolls-Royce cars, having acquired the rights from Rolls-Royce plc for £40m in 1998. BMW took over responsibility for Rolls-Royce cars from the beginning of 2003.

1999 – Rolls-Royce took full control of its oil and gas joint venture, Cooper Rolls, with the acquisition of the rotating compression equipment interests of Cooper Energy Services. It also acquired National Airmotive in California, a major repair and overhaul facility now part of Rolls-Royce Engine Services. The 1990s ended with the £576m acquisition of Vickers plc, which with primarily the Ulstein (Norway) and Kamewa products and capabilities joining the Rolls-Royce existing gas turbine activities, transformed Rolls-Royce into the global leader in marine power systems.

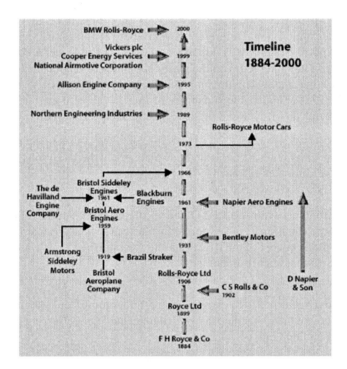

Rolls-Royce in China

Rolls-Royce and Chinese aerospace representatives signed a collaborative agreement involving a new regional jet application for the Rolls-Royce BR710 engine on November 1, 2001 (Rolls-Royce, 2001). A Memorandum of Understanding (MoU), signed by representatives of Rolls-Royce Deutschland and the China Aviation Industry Corporation (AVIC), involves the potential use of the 14,000lb - 17,000lb thrust BR710 on China's new ARJ21 regional jet. The ARJ series, currently in the early stages of development, consists of a 70-90 seat family of aircraft.

The MoU was signed during the state visit to the People's Republic of China by the German Chancellor, Gerhard Schroeder. BR700 series engines are produced by Rolls-Royce at the company's Dahlewitz facilities near Berlin.

John Cheffins, President - Civil Aerospace, Rolls-Royce, said, "This is an exciting opportunity in an expanding market sector in which Rolls-Royce is building a market-leading position. The B710 is the ideal partner for new generation regional and corporate jets. Our relationships with China's aerospace industry are well established and highly valued and this agreement will build on them."

Under a separate agreement, AVIC and the Chinese Aeronautical Establishment will work with Rolls-Royce Deutschland and the German Aerospace Centre on a joint study of aerodynamic issues involving the new aircraft and the fuselage-mounted engine installation.

The BR710 has worldwide success. The engine has been selected for the Bombardier Global 5000 super-large business jet, the newest member of the BR710-powered Bombardier Global Express series.

The BR710 is also flying with the Gulfstream V and V-SP ultra-long-range business jets, and has been selected for the BAE Systems Nimrod MRA4, the UK's new maritime reconnaissance aircraft. Another member of the BR700 series, the more powerful BR715, is the sole power plant for the Boeing 717 100-seat regional jet.

Rolls-Royce 2004

Rolls-Royce operates in four global markets - civil aerospace, defense aerospace, marine and energy. It is investing in technology and capability that can be exploited in each of these sectors to create a competitive range of products. The famous aircraft engine maker also makes marine engines and land based turbines.

The success of these products is demonstrated by the company's rapid and substantial gains in market share over recent years. The company now has a total of 54,000 gas turbines in service worldwide. The investments in product, capability, and infrastructure to gain this market position create high barriers to entry.

Rolls-Royce has a broad customer base comprising more than 500 airlines, 4,000 corporate and utility aircraft and helicopter operators, 160 armed forces and more than 2,000 marine customers, including 50 navies. The company has energy customers in nearly 120 countries. Rolls-Royce employs around 35,000 people, of which 21,000 are in the UK. Forty percent of its employees are based outside the UK - including 5,000 in the rest of Europe and 8,000 in North America.

The large installed base of engines generates demand for the provision of services. A key element of the company's strategy is to maximize services revenues, which have increased by 60 percent over the past five years, by the provision of a comprehensive portfolio of services.

Annual sales total nearly £6 billion, of which 50 percent are services revenues. The order book is over £18 billion, which, together with demand for services, provides visibility as to future activity levels.

The most modern family of engines is the Trent series, which are also powerful three-shaft turbofan engines similar to the RB211, and are used to power the Airbus A330, A340-500/600. The Trent series of engines offer greater thrust, long-range flight capabilities and economical operating and maintenance costs. The Rolls-Royce Power Generation Market includes both electrical and nuclear power, which also includes marine applications, such as providing power plants for nuclear and naval vessels. Rolls-Royce is a truly global business offering a range of first class world leading products. It has facilities over 14 different countries and also offers first rate after sales services, covering mechanical overhauls and spare part distribution.

Rolls-Royce plc is a global company providing power for land, sea, and air. The company has established a balanced business, with leading positions in civil aerospace, defense aerospace, marine and energy markets, where its core technology can be applied over a broad range of products and services.

Its aerospace businesses have customers in over 150 countries, including more than 500 airlines, 2.400 corporate and utility operators and 160 armed forces, using both fixed and rotary wing aircraft.

Rolls-Royce is the global leader in marine power systems, with a broad product range and full systems integration capability. More than 2.000 commercial marine customers and over 30 navies use Rolls-Royce propulsion and products. In energy markets, the company is investing in new products and capabilities for the oil and gas industry and power generation.

Rolls-Royce pioneered gas turbine technology for aerospace, power generation and marine propulsion, and is involved in the major future programs in these fields, including the WR-21 marine engine, leading-edge water jet propulsion systems, and combat engines for Eurofighter Typhoon and the Joint Strike Fighter.

Dr. Jonathan Mitchell
Director of Business Process Improvement
Rolls-Royce plc

Dr. Jonathan Mitchell joined Rolls-Royce in January 2003 as Director of Business Process Improvement, with responsibility for the Rolls-Royce Centers of Competency, the Quality function and for Information Technology.

Prior to that Jonathan had 13 years at Glaxo – now known as GlaxoSmithKline – with a number of roles in the Information Technology Division. In the mid-1990s, he took a leading role in creating combined IT and molecular biology teams, which addressed the emerging opportunities in Genomics. After the merger with SmithKline Beecham in 2000, Jonathan focused on integrating the computing infrastructures of the two companies.

Before Glaxo, Jonathan spent five years in BP Exploration, mainly in the development of computer systems to aid oil explorations. He also helped shape the technical strategy for Exploration computing following the merger of BP and Britoil in 1990.

Jonathan holds a first degree in Geology from the University of Exeter and a Ph.D. from the University of Wales. He was elected as a Fellow of the Geological Society in 1982.

Jonathan is married with two children. In his spare time, he enjoys classical music and sailing. He is 44.

E-Commerce at Rolls-Royce

Exostar

Roll-Royce has integrated more than 180 of its suppliers on an Internet-based system called Supplypass, which connects manufacturers, suppliers, and customers. Rolls-Royce uses the exchange to find suppliers and assign projects. The Internet exchange is from Exostar of Herndon. Rolls-Royce is transmitting electronic planning schedules, goods receipts, reports, and invoices over the connection, said Richard Harris, program manager at Exostar for Rolls-Royce.

It took less than three months to bring more than 180 suppliers online to transact business via the Exostar marketplace. Rolls-Royce global supply chain now has a single scheduling system. Richard Harris said, "The successful integration of these suppliers paves the way for the introduction of other electronic transactions."

Another 150 suppliers will be registered with Exostar, bringing the direct procurement supplier base to 330. "The acquisition program used to integrate these suppliers into Exostar demonstrates the potential of the Internet to train as well as trade, saving precious time and money," said Stephen O'Sullivan, Exostar's executive vice-president of sales.

Exostar is owned by Rolls-Royce, BAE Systems, Lockheed Martin, Boeing, and Raytheon. Rolls-Royce PLC became the fifth founding partner in Exostar in 2001, bringing an engine maker's perspective to the aerospace industry's largest procurement and supply-chain management Internet exchange.

Due diligence on the initiative began in February 2001 and negotiations concluded during the June 8-9 weekend. Rolls-Royce announced its participation June 15 in London and Exostar followed with an announcement June 18 at the Paris air show. Rolls Royce's actual participation in the Exostar exchange occurred in the third quarter.

The announcement came a week after Exostar announced two executive changes: the abrupt departure of its president and CEO, Andy Plyler, and the appointment of Paul Kaminski, former undersecretary of Defense for acquisition and technology, as non-executive chairman. Company officials said the two events were unrelated.

Plyler became CEO in January. His appointment triggered the hiring of other senior executives, including Ken Possenriede as chief financial officer. He will function as CEO while a search is conducted for Plyler's replacement. His resignation was immediate, "to pursue other business opportunities." Company insiders expressed shock at his leaving.

Since its start in March 2000, Exostar's original aerospace founders — BAE Systems, Boeing, Lockheed Martin and Raytheon — have been searching for one or two additional strategic partners.

One obvious way for Exostar to broaden its manufacturing reach was to name a second European-based manufacturer to join BAE Systems. Most attention focused on EADS, the French-German-Spanish company that is BAE Systems' investment partner in Airbus and Europe's largest aerospace concern. The two sides talked, but apparently, the EADS partners could not agree on an exchange strategy and, especially, on joining one so heavily weighted toward American companies.

Meanwhile, BAE Systems senior executives were courting Rolls-Royce. The fit would be doubly advantageous. Exostar was well represented in military/civil airframe, space, and avionics/electronics manufacturing, but lacked an engine maker.

General Electric's corporate policy is not to invest in outside exchanges, and Pratt & Whitney was already an investor in the Cordiem exchange as a business unit of United Technologies Inc.

Rolls-Royce was free of such constraints and looking for an exchange. It conducted a competitive analysis of other exchanges and began due diligence with Exostar in February. The fact that it chose Exostar is regarded as a validation of the exchange's strategy by Exostar officials.

Stephen O'Sullivan, Exostar's executive vice president for new business development and a former executive vice president of BAE Systems Regional Aircraft North American Operations, conducted the due diligence.

Rolls-Royce CEO John Rose said Exostar won because of its "procurement and collaboration capabilities, overall value to Rolls-Royce, and industry-leading position." As a founding partner, Rolls-Royce will invest the same as the four original partners, a sum said to be in the tens of millions of dollars.

The addition of Rolls-Royce means that Exostar's combined membership represents more than 250 procurement systems and 40,000 suppliers. "Our focus is to connect them," said Ludo Van Vooren, Exostar's vice president for communications.

In an April report on the top trading exchanges in 11 industries, AMR Research named Exostar as best among the aerospace and defense sector because of "its notable progress toward [its members'] collective vision of becoming the collaborative hub for aerospace."

With Rolls-Royce onboard, it is unclear whether Exostar needs an additional founding partner, although it continues to talk to "all the major players in the industry" about using the exchange. "Rolls-Royce was very strategic for us," Van Vooren said. "We're not going around the globe trying to sell off a piece of the baby."

Despite its size, Exostar is still largely an exchange for its founding members. Van Vooren said the founders are establishing the procurement and sell-side of the exchange, but the process of signing up their collective supply network will take time. That is largely because to use effectively it raises strategic questions as to whether they can retain their legacy systems or need to replace them with an XML standard connection from a specialist like Ariba or CommerceOne, which built Exostar's trading platform. The first these supplier procurement systems were being set up in 2001. Within two years, all 250 should be in place, he said.

The greatest volume of Exostar's Web transactions have shifted from the "low hanging fruit" of purchasing indirect materials for general business support to the more complex requirements of direct materials actually used in manufacturing.

After months of meeting with the founders' suppliers, about 4,000 of them were using the exchange. As of June, they were conducting some 20,000 transactions a week, Van Vooren said.

Exostar had three products in operation at that time: SupplyPath, its browser-based method for suppliers to receive electronic purchase orders; MachineLink, its XML-based link for suppliers and buyers to the exchange (instead of going through a browser), and Auctioneer, the mechanism for one of the exchange's most successful activities. Exostar conducts about five auctions a week, mostly reverse auctions on direct products, construction work, and services.

Two more products were in the wings. ProcurePass is an onramp for buyers to sell to companies using the exchange for procurement. ForumPass is the exchanges branded name for its Windchill ProjectLink collaboration tool.

The addition of Rolls-Royce — maker of the Trent engine family — as a strategic partner widens Exostar's position among European manufacturers.

Logistics

TNT Logistics has won a five-year contract renewal with Rolls-Royce to manage the inbound flow of aerospace parts from 110 suppliers based in the UK, Europe, and America.

The two companies won Motor Transport's 2003 Supply Chain Technology Award and have worked together for three years.

The award winning partnership has an IT offering including in-cab technology, barcode scanning of items at all stages of the cross-dock operation.

The partnership has saved 2.7 million road miles a year in the UK.

Aviall Inc. is pointing to a $3 billion spare-parts distribution contract it won last month as proof that its new IT infrastructure is starting to pay off after a previous mainframe migration project nearly caused disaster three years ago.

The 10-year contract, under which Dallas-based Aviall will sell and distribute spare parts for a widely used aircraft engine from Rolls-Royce PLC, took effect on Jan. 2. Aviall CIO Joe Lacik last week said the deal — the largest of its kind in the firm's history — would have been impossible without the systems that his staff largely finished putting in place during the fall.

Aviall and London-based Rolls-Royce already had a separate, much smaller distribution deal in place. But one of the keys to the new contract, Lacik said, was Aviall's improved ability to offer technology-driven services such as sales analysis and demand forecasting down to the line-item level to manufacturers.

Lacik said Aviall spent $30 million to $40 million to install new enterprise resource planning (ERP), supply chain, customer relationship management, and e-business applications from five software vendors, including St. Paul, Minn.-based Lawson Software Inc. and San Mateo, Calif.-based Siebel Systems Inc.

The distributor of aviation and marine products also deployed application integration software from Sybase Inc., in Emeryville, Calif., to tie the systems together. Most of the pieces are in place, except for Siebel's order entry software and some of the integration links, Lacik said. Those are scheduled to be rolled out later this year, he added.

The IT makeover, which began two years ago, was a gamble for Aviall following a near-disastrous migration from its mainframe systems to a highly customized set of Lawson ERP applications, completed in early 1999.

Training, software, and implementation issues related to that project were blamed for a big drop in sales. Extensive manual work-arounds were required, and the company's CEO eventually left. Lacik came in to run IT at the start of 2000.

The applications from Lawson were perfectly sound but had not been designed to handle the huge amount of tracking numbers that Aviall needed to maintain on the parts it sells, Lacik said. The company unplugged much of the Lawson system and continued to use pieces of its mainframe applications while developing the new multivendor architecture.

According to Lacik, the distribution and supply chain services made possible by the new applications have helped Aviall minimize lost sales despite the down economy and the Sept. 11 terrorist attacks. He said the systems have also cut costs to the point where the architecture has probably already paid for itself, although Aviall has yet to calculate its return on investment.

"No question that there has been a complete turnaround from the company that was potentially for sale a few years ago and losing market share," said Peter Arment, an analyst at JSA Research Inc., a Newport, R.I.-based aerospace research firm.

Arment said it is difficult to say exactly how much credit IT deserves. But the system changes have made the company more efficient and contributed to an improvement in its profit margins, he added.

ERP at Rolls-Royce

ERP

In the 1990s innovations in information technology led to the development of a range of software applications aimed at integrating the flow of information throughout a company, and these commercial software packages were known as Enterprise Systems. During this period, one particular enterprise system called ERP caught the attention of some of the world's largest companies. It has been estimated that businesses around the world have been spending almost $10 billion per year on ERP systems. ERP aims to integrate business processes through the support of an integrated computer information system.

ERP allows the corporate management of a business, and aims to integrate individual functional systems such as manufacturing, finance, procurement, and distribution. The systems allow companies to replace their existing information systems and also help to standardize the flow of management information.

ERP uses Internet technologies to integrate the flow of information from internal business functions as well as information from customers and suppliers. The system uses a relational database management system, within client/server network architecture, to capture valuable management data. The key principle behind the system involves entering the data from a series of modular applications only once. Once stored, the data automatically triggers the update of all related information within the system. The systems can support virtually all areas of an organization, across business units, departmental functions, and plants. The development of an ERP system within a large manufacturing organization requires the integration of working practices and the information systems.

Companies that use ERP can gain a competitive advantage from the way they implement the system and then exploit the resulting data. Many companies that have installed ERP have claimed to be more nimble within the marketplace than their competitors with hard-to-change custom made systems.

ERP systems offer companies the following three major benefits:

• Business process automation

• Timely access to management information

• Improvement in the supply chain via the use of E-communication and E-commerce

SAP

Five former IBM employees originally founded systems, applications, and products in data processing (SAP) in Mannheim, Germany in 1972. Their aim was to produce standard software application programs that could integrate with each other to form a business solution. SAP has been dedicated to produce products that improve the return on information gathered by an organization. The company began its life with the name

'Systemanalyse Und Programmentwicklung' and eventually became known as SAP.

SAP's first product known as R/2 was built and prototyped for a subsidiary of ICI. The system they produced was simply known as system 'R', which stands for 'Real-time' processing. This system was fully integrated and could be used on the IBM mainframe. The R/2 solution was launched in 1979 and was developed for a computer mainframe environment, at the time it was perceived as the most comprehensive system available to businesses in the world, and it received great interest from industries in the 1980s.

SAP saw the potential for the delivery of information to the end-user via the PC, so SAP reinvented and developed their product further by developing a business solution for the client/server architecture environment; this became known as R/3 and was released in 1992. In the 1990s, SAP and its R/3 solution would go on to become the dominant ERP solution, and become one of the world's biggest software houses.

SAP R/3 applications are a range of software modules. They can be used either alone or combined to form business solutions. SAP state that their R/3 applications offer comprehensive functionality for all standard business needs within an enterprise. SAP R/3 uses a programming language called advanced business application programming (ABAP).

The following are SAP R3's 12 application modules: financial accounting, treasury, controlling, enterprise controlling, investment management, production planning, materials management, quality management, project system, human resource management, sales and distribution, and plant maintenance and service management.

Rolls-Royce

Rolls-Royce used over 1500 systems before the ERP project was started, many of which were developed internally by Rolls-Royce over the last two decades. These legacy systems were expensive to operate and difficult to maintain and develop. They did not provide accurate, consistent, and accessible data that was required for good and timely decision-making and performance assessment (e.g. delivery performance, quality metrics). These ageing systems often did not lend themselves fully to a modern manufacturing environment. Some of the legacy systems were so old that they had year 2000 compliance problems. Work within Rolls-Royce was functionally orientated and various departments worked in isolation (Yusuf et al. 2004).

The last major manufacturing system to be developed and implemented by Rolls-Royce was MERLIN, which stands for mechanized evaluation of resources, logistics and inventory, the system was basically a scheduling system that ran on MRPII system principles. The system was developed in the 1980s and, although it was capable, it was prone to manual manipulation. One particular down fall of the system was the lack of communication between individual sites. MERLIN often had difficulty communicating with another manufacturing system named IBIS, which stands for inventory based instructing system. IBIS was an older manufacturing system that was used at the Bristol and Ansty facilities. Work in progress was often transferred between sites and could not be tracked accurately, often causing inventory and stock take problems.

An additional system named corporate cost accounting (CCA) was used to monitor financially transactions, which covered pipeline inventory and inter-site transport. Rolls-Royce also had a range of individual systems for controlling and monitoring commercial, financial and procurement functions, these systems had problems interfacing with each other, as they had different databases and file formats. The legacy systems did not allow Rolls-Royce to establish direct, online communication with customers, partners, and suppliers. In fact, these systems did not support significant growth of the business and were not sufficiently agile to keep pace with the changing business environment.

The ERP project consisted of a management team of specialists from the external outsourcing company EDS. EDS also had the specialized talents of SAP consultants. Within the project team were specialist internal managers and staff that had vital knowledge of cross-functional business relationships and experience of the old internal systems. In conjunction with this team, each operational business unit (OBU) had its own ERP planning team, which was responsible for implementing working changes and training. The project implementation problems can be grouped into three areas of cultural, business and technical difficulty.

Cultural Problems

The implementation project team expected a high acceptance of the system in areas that provide just as good or better functionality than the old system. However, some functions and processes might not get the full appreciation the legacy systems once had. The project team decided to resolve this by illustrating the improvements made to the company as a whole, thus breaking the traditional segregation of OBUs and departments. The original implementation plan was increased in an attempt to address training and cultural changes. Training took the form of organized seminars, which were split into two distinct groups of specialists and mass users. The specialist training was carried out and conducted by SAP and was technically based. These specialist experts then in turn trained expert users. The remaining training for end-users was conducted internally in collaboration with EDS consultants. The training carried out within the seminars was supported by demonstrations within the workplace, along with information meetings and presentations to relay information to all employees about the changes of working practices. In all, more than 10,000 people would have been trained.

Business Problems

SAP R/3 requires a fairly rigid business structure for it in order to work successfully. The participants of cross-functional workshops soon understood that their working practices must be adjusted in order to fit SAP, ultimately changing the way Rolls-Royce does business. They achieved this by using an internal business process re-engineering (BPR) program. The program consisted of four steps, the first involved drawing and mapping the current processes. The second step involved identifying any problems or issues raised from the mapped process. The third step involved applying some of these issues to a demonstration of SAP, to identify potential problems within the new system. The fourth step involved the re-mapping or modification of the processes in line with SAP. The modifications to the Rolls-Royce business process meant that the SAP R/3 software need not be modified. Modifications to the software would have been extremely expensive both in terms of implementation resources and the fact that newer software versions would be difficult to install in a modified system. SAP named this unmodified software implementation 'Vanilla SAP'.

Technical Problems

The main technical problems that Rolls-Royce has encountered have been with the accuracy of data. The new system requires the retrieval of old data from the legacy systems that has to be normalized, screened and stored in a sensible data format within the new systems data repository. The duplication of data was a major concern that Rolls-Royce had to address. In some special areas the old systems was kept running until such time as they could be phased out by the new systems, and to do this EDS built interfaces between the systems. The CAD system used by Rolls-Royce remained the same, as the process to alter the file formats would be too expensive and require use of valuable resources that are needed for the core implementation.

Rolls-Royce has nine principal business processes, which when taken together describe everything the company does. Figure 19.1 is a schematic representation of the business processes and the interfaces.

Rolls-Royce decided to adopt and utilize the SAP solution offered for the aerospace and defense industry. The SAP aerospace and defense industry solution is the market leader in its industry and is highly configurable for flexible 'vanilla' implementation. Predetermined implementation points from the Rolls-Royce Steering Committee and Implementation Team defined the release strategy for the project. Any future third party software products must first be accredited by SAP to safeguard the upgrade process and would require a justified business case. Business reports that are generated by SAP have to be

Figure 19.1. Rolls-Royce business processes and interfaces

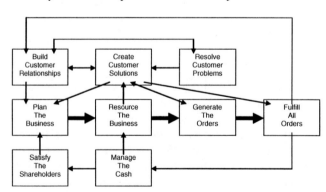

fully justified in a business case, which follows a standard format for internal use. Data entering the project has to be identified, validated, cleaned, loaded, archived, and then maintained within a Data Warehouse.

Rolls-Royce has estimated that over 1000 additional PCs will be required and the total cost for the network infrastructure was about two million pounds. The company required over 6000 SAP licenses for users across all the business. The server was provided by Sun Microsystems and in excess of two Terabytes of disk space. The system required almost 35 weekly MRP runs cascaded by plant. A UNIX server bridges the data from legacy systems and testing and training required an NT server.

Knowledge Management at Rolls-Royce

The company has 300 airline customers. The problem was that repairs of jet engines are time critical. 20 million pages of technical documentation were not easily accessible. A knowledge management project was launched to reduce repair time and improve maintenance planning. Rolls-Royce decided to expand its intranet with maintenance-oriented tables of contents.

SPEDE

SPEDE is a powerful combination of methodologies and software tools that enable businesses to formalize the capture and deployment of their knowledge assets. SPEDE has grown rapidly within Rolls-Royce and forms a major plank in its knowledge management strategy (Watson, 2001).

KTC

The Knowledge Technology Centre (KTC) was set up at the University of Nottingham in the UK to both apply, assess and evolve ideas from knowledge engineering and the SPEDE project to knowledge management within Rolls-Royce.

Towards the end of 1997, Rolls-Royce identified the relevance of early findings from SPEDE to its own Knowledge Management program and embarked upon a bilateral program with the University of Nottingham to exploit Knowledge Acquisition (KA) techniques for the rapid development of components of the Rolls-Royce Capability Intranet.

Rolls Royce's Capability Intranet is intended to become the company's quality system, providing quick and easy access to all the latest information needed by staff in order to complete tasks accurately and reliably including the capture of lessons learned and evolving best practices. The scope of the Capability Intranet spans business processes, manufacturing processes, product definitions, technical skills, and training. It includes quality manuals, working practices, information about technologies and capabilities and specific examples of good (and bad) practice based on real case examples.

A technology transfer program was conceived in early 1998 whereby established KA tools and techniques could be applied and evaluated within the context of developing knowledge-rich web sites for the Rolls-Royce Capability Intranet. The program has involved a series of coached projects, typically comprising two company employees on assignment to a special facility based at the University of Nottingham for a period of twelve weeks. Sixteen groups have so far passed through the facility amounting to thirty-eight Rolls-Royce employees. At the moment, twelve Rolls-Royce employees are on the program, though this is expected to rise significantly over the next year as personnel and facilities are expanded.

PC-PACK Knowledge Acquisition Toolkit

PC-PACK is a portable PC-based knowledge engineering workbench comprising an integrated set of software tools and representations that have been found useful in a range of knowledge engineering projects. PC-PACK comprises 14 tools. The subset of tools found to be most useful in Rolls-Royce is as follows:

- *a protocol editor*: this allows the annotation of interview transcripts, notes and documentation in a variety of formats;
- *a hypertext tool:* this allows more sophisticated annotation, and the creation of a linked set of topics or concepts to provide documentation of knowledge fragments acquired by the other tools;
- *a laddering tool:* this facilitates the creation of hierarchies of knowledge elements such as concepts, attributes, processes and requirements;
- *a control editor:* this facilitates the building of process control diagrams;
- *a card sort tool*: this facilitates the grouping of objects or concepts into classes, using the metaphor of sorting cards into piles;
- *a repertory grid tool:* this uses personal construct theory to identify attributes in the domain, and to group objects or concepts according to how similar they are with respect to these attributes;
- *an entity-relationship tool*: this allows the user to construct compact networks of relations between concepts;
- *HTML generator*: this publishes hypertext pages in HTML form.

The PC-PACK tool set can be used in a variety of ways, depending on the domain and goals in question. Its primary use is by experienced knowledge engineers when producing the Knowledge Document (conceptual model of expertise) for a KBS.

A typical scenario includes a series of KA sessions between the knowledge engineer and domain experts, progressing from natural to more contrived techniques. Many of the tools in PC-PACK support the contrived KA techniques typically used by experienced knowledge engineers.

Each KA session is tape-recorded and transcribed verbatim. The transcripts are analyzed using the Protocol Analysis tool to identify knowledge elements such as concepts, processes, attributes, and values. These elements are then classified into hierarchical graphs using the Laddering tool. The Control Editor tool permits data flow and control flow representations to be constructed. Successive KA sessions become increasingly structured and focus upon appending, modifying, and validating knowledge previously elicited. Annotations, explanations, and notes are recorded in hypertext pages associated with each knowledge element.

PC-PACK is designed to be used during KA sessions and validation plenary sessions to elicit feedback on previously constructed knowledge models. Such tools as the Matrix tool, Card Sort tool, and Repertory Grid tool help elicit new concepts, attributes, and classes if required.

A cycle of analysis, model building, and acquisition and validation sessions is repeated until the experts and knowledge engineer are satisfied that the ontology constructed in PC-PACK represents that required to fulfill the goals of the project.

This is a brief coverage of one use of PC-PACK. It does not assume any previous knowledge has been gathered, or that any generic knowledge can be applied. In reality, the aim would be to reuse as much previously acquired knowledge as possible in the form of ontologies, generic models, and process libraries.

PC-PACK has been used extensively within the SPEDE project to assist in the acquisition of best practice and business process knowledge. Elsewhere, it is being used in a number of organizations to support such activities as brainstorming, knowledge auditing, knowledge sharing, group elicitation, and decision-making.

The main aim for Rolls-Royce is the rapid capture of internal best practice for dissemination throughout the organization at minimum cost and in particular without taking valuable experts away from their normal work to write detailed technical papers. By developing an internal pool of knowledge engineering skills, all additional knowledge gained stays within the company rather than leaving with external consultants.

KM Strategy

The approach to knowledge management within Rolls-Royce has been to promote a knowledge-sharing environment. Person-to-person based approaches, such as communities of practice and after-action reviews, are used and are driven by the realization that it is only feasible and economically viable to capture a portion of an expert's useful knowledge. This is emphasized by the observation that even where reference material is widely used, engineers (people working creatively to solve problems) request information or advice from other people 66 percent of the time. It is also significant that in a high proportion of the requests, the problem is clarified and the engineer's request for information is modified.

Where knowledge can be standardized, the benefit justifies the extra effort required to capture that knowledge and create knowledge documents that guide people in carrying out processes. These knowledge documents appear as good-practice guides, standards, procedures and training material, which are frequently published on the internal web. The knowledge-acquisition and modeling process is a cost-effective approach to creating these knowledge documents. Where knowledge is stable, and speed or repeatability is of great economic value, then additional knowledge capture and development of knowledge-based systems can be justified. Although knowledge capture is unlikely to fully replace the need for direct contact with experts, it does succeed in making the transferal of expertise more routine.

Knowledge Acquisition and Modeling

During the 1980s, industry recognized that the loss of key experts was a problem. Projects were undertaken where knowledge engineers would acquire knowledge from experts and computerize it via an expert system. The task involved a variety of disciplines, such as computer science, artificial intelligence, psychology, and human factors. Significant technical achievements were made at this time. The knowledge base, where rules and facts acquired from the experts were held, was separate from the inference engine that deduced conclusions from the knowledge base. Declarative styles of programming were developed to represent knowledge (Moss, 2004).

Despite these advances, issues still remained. One difficulty was acquiring sufficient knowledge from an expert to make the system useful. Methods for ensuring the quality and maintainability of knowledge were needed. Inference problems also existed; for example, there was no way of deriving results based on alternative assumptions or to maintain truth when an assumption was abandoned. During this period, there was also a commercial proliferation of tools, although in some cases and for some tools this was short-lived or they were of poor quality.

During the 1990s tools became available that significantly improve the inference and representation issues faced. The 1990s also saw the development of methods to formalize knowledge acquisition and the subsequent creation of a computer system. These methods of knowledge acquisition aim to improve:

- *Maintainability* — By structuring knowledge and making it readable by humans, changes could be easily made and systematically incorporated into the system.

- *Visibility* — By making the system seem less like a black box to the user, Rolls-Royce reduced the risks associated with the loss of skills and retained innovation opportunities.

- *Validation* — Experts were able to check knowledge directly rather than having to run the system before gaining access to knowledge.

- *Cost* — As knowledge was more likely to be complete prior to being coded for the computer system the cost of rework was reduced.

These formalized methods produce a platform-independent knowledge model that is an explicit representation of Rolls-Royce knowledge. The knowledge model defines the concepts and their attributes, which are typically organized hierarchically by classification or composition. Additional links give navigation via process steps, for example. Formal methods include CommonKADS (a large general-purpose methodology for expert systems), Moka (aimed at knowledge-based engineering (KBE) systems), and Kamp (where the envisaged product is a document, Web site or manual rather than a computer system). Project management, knowledge acquisition, and knowledge modeling in these methods are similar but modified to suit the planned product.

Expert systems and KBE systems deliver executable software and their creation is resource intensive. Kamp however delivers a human-readable record and is a cost-effective option where the resources or benefits are insufficient to justify an expert or knowledge-based-engineering system.

Kamp

Kamp is a comprehensive method for capturing and publishing knowledge that is suitable for staff members that are not experts in knowledge engineering or knowledge management. The method enables these employees to capture knowledge from experts and publish it as a document. Kamp also provides close support from a coach together with a web definition of what the method is. The web definition is itself presented in Kamp form and therefore provides both guidance and an example.

The method brings together a number of roles and defines what is expected from each one. It also brings to bear techniques from relevant disciplines. Project management (which uses a gated process), psychology (which contributes the knowledge acquisition methods), information engineering, and artificial intelligence (which contribute the knowledge-modeling approaches) have an impact here. The synthesis originated in a collaborative-research project involving computer scientists and psychologists.

Integration into Rolls-Royce processes and organization is also important. For example, it is beneficial for engineers on the graduate-training program to undertake Kamp projects in departments they are joining. Similarly, Rolls-Royce can use the method to acquire knowledge from experts prior to their retirement.

There are a number of benefits that Kamp has delivered to Rolls-Royce, such as accelerated learning, increased availability of expertise, improved response times, reduced risk from sudden loss of expertise and improved quality.

The most active role within Kamp is the knowledge engineer, who is the only full-time member of the project. The remaining roles are part time: the customer identifies the business benefit and owns the topic on behalf of the company, the coach is experienced in knowledge engineering and guides the knowledge engineer throughout the project, the knowledge manager has overall responsibility, experts provide and validate the knowledge, and the intended users are interviewed early on to understand what knowledge should be captured and how it should be delivered.

Outsourcing at Rolls-Royce

The first outsourcing was done in 1996. What had happened up to that point was that the then CIO had done a study of the capability of the IT function, and particularly with the needs he expected the business to have on IT as the company was rapidly growing in the '90s. He had seriously doubted about the in-house teams ability, both on capability prospective and scale prospective. So, he recommended that they look outside for a partner that would be able to deal with those aspects.

Outsourcing Case Study: Rolls-Royce
VNUNet.com
Friday, December 05, 2003

While Rolls-Royce's mega outsourcing deal with EDS has brought continuity and reliable IT operations, it has also revealed some of the risks of a long-term exclusive relationship.

The aircraft engine and car manufacturer struck its first outsourcing agreement for infrastructure operations and programme delivery with EDS in 1996.

A new exclusive $2.1bn (£1.2bn) deal was agreed in 2000, covering 90 per cent of IT services for Rolls-Royce, extending until 2012.

Rolls-Royce has retained a small team of senior IT and contract management staff and specialised in-house developed code expertise.

Meanwhile, EDS has helped the company move from the mainframe as the central solution to an outsourced hosted environment. "We couldn't do it without help," admits Luc Schmitz, IT director at Rolls-Royce.

EDS is also responsible for developing ebusiness systems, infrastructure, network, systems, applications and end-user support.

Schmitz says having one global deal for multi-source arrangements has had "lots of positive effects".

"We have enjoyed a continuity factor with very stable operations. We also have a predictable turnover of IT staff so there is no rockiness," he says.

Three years into the contract, Schmitz says availability remains high and critical IT programmes, such as the rollout of a major single-entity SAP programme, have been delivered.

However, Schmitz admits there is a downside. "There have been challenges in aligning goals. It was bumpy," he says.

He advises companies taking a similar route to make long-term provisions through strict annual and quarterly plans informed by business value.

"There is a risk in having a monopolistic contract with 90 per cent of IT estates outsourced. The original contractual scope is a snapshot. Long-term agreements will struggle to survive based on the original scope definition," he says.

Risks are minimised by "keeping things fresh and changing the EDS management team periodically", he adds.

Rolls-Royce also has an open procurement provision as part of the contract, which reduces prices "if IBM or Accenture offer better value for money," says Schmitz. "Cost savings are made by having a four-year price book and then re-negotiating."

EDS also gives performance guarantees, and benchmarking is facilitated by a third party. But mistakes have been made.

"Outsourcing IT architects was a step too far," says Schmitz. "We ceased to be an intelligent customer, and were no longer able to define our IT requirement. We will transfer them back over the next year."

Willingness to adapt to unexpected events is also important for success.

"The scope of the contract with EDS changed after 11 September. We had to re-plan as demand fell. We focused less on ebusiness and more on e-enablement, providing for online meetings, for example," says Schmitz.

That was the original premise, which then lead to the standard process of tendering with customer specifications and the ultimate selection of the best bidder. They went through a very standard procurement process of defining all the pieces that needed to be outsourced defining what was required, and then inviting bids to the standard request for proposal (RFP). All the big players were involved in bidding.

The whole lot was outsourced at that point from the then aerospace business. And the staff was transferred to EDS (Electronic Data Services) with a relatively thin level of management kept inside RR.

There was a review of the contract in 2000 and another review in 2002. It was a ten-year deal originally with breakpoints. The deal in 2000 was well publicized (see VNUNet.com), which was then a 12-year deal. The intention was to put a long-term arrangement in place and build a pretty close relationship.

The criteria that were laid out for the selection of vendor were pretty clear around maximum service levels, around being able to handle large skilled contracts of that size, and also pretty clear around costs. EDS had generally been competitive on costs, and they demonstrated certainly that they could provide capability for large scaled contracts.

What is generally outsourced is the basic operation of the complete infrastructure — the management of networks, data centers, servers, and so on. RR outsourced the application support for most major applications, the application development function for IT components of projects, and telecommunications and cell phones.

What's not been outsourced is the overall accountability for project management. They believe in RR that they are very good in doing projects. For example, they launched ten major civil aerospace engine projects in the last ten years. Each of them with a value of more than half a billion pounds, and they have all been successful. RR owns the project management overall, and they also own the IT architecture. And RR owns various niche areas of IT, things like the development of internal software at the control level, say control systems for jet engines. In terms of the EDS arrangement, not all aspects of the business are included. The Commercial Marine division is maintained as a stand-alone liability.

UPS Logistics and Maersk Logistics

The objective of this student assignment is the written presentation of a difficult question in a clear manner. Therefore, clarity in the organization of the paper and logical flow is as important as substance. It is not expected that groups cover all issues in the literature. It is extremely important that a group's own thinking is the base.

The group report should be entitled "IS/IT Strategy for UPS Logistics Group" or "IS/IT Strategy for Mercantile Logistics". It should address and discuss how IS/IT can support the business.

The primary learning objective of this term paper assignment is to enable students to practice the application of various techniques that are used in the process of developing an IS/IT strategy for an organization. Each of these techniques will be discussed in detail during the face-to-face class sessions with the professor, and they are also described in the textbook and the handouts for the course.

Please read carefully the attached case studies about UPS Logistics Group and Mercantile Logistics. After reading the case studies, please visit the companies' web pages to get a better understanding of the companies' services, operations, positioning and strategic situation. Also visit the web pages of other similar international companies to see how they are positioned differently in strategic terms and in terms of the services they offer. You may also want to do some library research about how various other companies are responding to the challenges of e-commerce, e-business, knowledge management systems, and IT outsourcing as well. Now you choose which of the two cases you will use for your group assignment.

Feel free to introduce assumptions about the company (based on what you know about other international companies) and use any other publicly available information you find.

You must follow three sequential steps in developing the IS/IT strategy. The first step is concerned with analysis. The second step is concerned with choice (selection and decision), while the final step is concerned with implementation. Your paper must be based on the Y model for strategy work as described in your handouts.

Introduction to Shipping Management

In shipping management, the need for strategic planning has emerged for several reasons:

1. Globalization and developments in the world seaborne trade have produced severe competitive pressures for the maritime industry. The decline in freight rates, the need for investment either to apply new technologies or to improve quality services present the industry with the task of applying competitive strategies.

2. The main measures of market-orientation namely the customer focus, gathering systematic information about the market and the competitors and integrating the inter-functional efforts to create higher customer value have to be adopted by the maritime companies to compete effectively in the global market place.

3. The customers of the maritime industry, namely the shippers, are in requirement of lower prices and higher service quality.

4. Measures concerning safety management and environmental issues have to be included in strategic planning.

Computerization is today driving the maritime industry and its interface with other sectors:

1. Traders are demanding greater added value.

2. Computerization enables adequate control, monitoring and tracking of global operations.

3. Containerization requires stable and advanced information systems.

4. Ports are becoming fully computerized operations.

5. Shipbrokers are becoming fully computerized operations.

6. Ship management is becoming a fully computerized operation.

Computerization is today enabling the maritime industry and its interface with other sectors:

1. Control functions embracing accounts, documentation, communication in the form

of messages and letters, cargo booking, reservation, allocation and consignment, and inventory.

2.   Managerial planning and decision-making, including voyage estimating and feasibility studies. Voyage calculations need port data, cargo data, cargo handling technique data, and vessel data.

In shipping management, maritime logistics is important. Recently, e-logistics has emerged as a driving force of change in shipping management.

Logistics is that part of the supply chain process that plans, implements, and controls the efficient, effective flow and storage of goods, services, and related information from the point of origin to the point of consumption in order to meet customers' requirements. *Logistics management* is the process of managing logistics to achieve the established logistics goals of the company.

Supply chain involves all processes that a company uses to conceive, design, produce, and deliver products or services successfully to customers, including receipt of payment. It is a vastly broader term than logistics.

E-logistics was introduced to increase value to customers, partners, and suppliers through expanded service offerings, to improve communication channel with established market, to open new segments and niches, to improve efficiency and to reduce costs through automation. E-logistics will bring three areas of functionality:

•   Increased pipeline visibility, e.g. global inventory management

•   Improved collaboration between all supply chain participants

•   Improved functionality in managing global supply chains, e.g. applications that can be downloaded, e.g. booking in transport, trade compliance in trade management, finance, and duty paid landed costs, etc.

The significant increase in global electronic logistics over the next years will be driven by several forces, including value added to customers/partners/suppliers, low cost, and improved Internet functionality. Supply chain visibility creates information transparency using the Internet with an open standard infrastructure. Supply chains will loose their fat, because it will be impossible to hide and protect high profit activities over time.

An important implication of e-logistics is that shippers will have to focus on supply chain process improvements as a major source of competitive advantage to compete globally. Increasingly this process improvement will be enabled by web-based information technology. Carriers and other providers of logistics services must assess the impact these emerging logistics offerings have on their business and develop an appropriate strategic response.

Logistics outsourcing is the management of two or more interrelated logistics activities to an external provider, enabling the shipper to focus on core competencies and to receive enhanced cost and/or service value.

International freight forwarder is usually an asset light entity; it acts as the agent of both the shipper and the carrier. Common activities are cargo rate referral and booking, arranging for cargo delivery to port or terminal, preparing and delivering private and government documentation, e.g. letters of credit, insurance, shippers export declaration, and for assuring regulatory compliance. Compensation is customarily a combination of fees paid by the shipper for specific services rendered and commissions paid by the selected carrier. Many forwarders have established a customs brokerage capability.

Third party provider acts on behalf of shippers and may possess some assets, especially distribution or transport equipment. Normally payment is directly from shippers, with few or no commissions paid by carriers. Third party providers stand apart from traditional providers as carriers and freight forwarders because of their ability to manage broad cross-functional processes, e.g. order fulfillment. Generally, compensation is in the form of management fees and performance incentives, e.g. increased order fill rates, reduced order cycle times, increased productivity, and lower total costs.

Fourth party provider is a non-asset (few or no transport, equipment, or distribution facilities) based entity engaged by large global shippers to oversee and manage a wide variety of third party providers. Fourth party providers are expected to possess a comprehensive overview of logistics and its separate functions, understand the supply chain and specific industry sectors, have process reengineering and consulting capabilities, and regularly employ state of the art technology and systems tools. Compensation is likely to be a combination of management fees, performance incentives, and profit sharing with the shipper.

There is a globalization of markets in maritime logistics. There is growth in numbers and size of global companies, standardization of products and services on a global basis, and reduction of the number of players in each phase of the supply chain. There is reduction in the number of competitors and increased market shares remaining, global division of tasks and skills, and transportation and logistics share of the value chain will increase significantly.

The survivors in the future global markets will be characterized by customer loyalty, production costs equal to or lower than competitors, control over supply and distribution, products and services differentiated from the competitors, customer awareness, and supply chain integration in terms of process management and IT integration along the supply chain.

Wilh. Wilhelmsen has more than 140 years of experience in international shipping. The WW Group's area of business is international maritime activities with a central base in Norway. The corporate organization consists of Wallenius Wilhelmsen Lines, Barber International, and Barwil Agencies. Examples of ships owned by the WW Group are the Ro/Ro vessel Texas, Taronga with the stern ramp, and the car carriers Nosac Takara and Takasago.

Shipping management as the management of a ship is closely related to the type and size of shipping organization. The traditional organization was based on the sailing era, in which the ships departed on an adventure around the world. The typical shipping company of today consists of a shore-based organization and a ship based organization. The main processes of the company are (i) voyage charter, (ii) time charter, (iii) bareboat charter, and (iv) pool agreement (Wijnolst and Wergeland, 1997).

Ship management also involves the management of the ship in the sense of keeping the ship in good condition and providing the competent crew at the right time. This requires a competent shore based staff, but also ship based personnel that are able to solve problems on their own (Wijnolst and Wergeland, 1997).

In shipping, there are four shipping markets trading in different commodities (Stopford, 1997):

1. The *new building market* where the shipowner orders the ship. The purchaser entering the new building market may have several different motives. He may need a vessel of a certain size and specification and nothing suitable is available on the secondhand market. Another possibility is that the ships are needed for an industrial project. Steel mills, power stations, and other major industrial projects are generally developed with specific transportation requirements met by new buildings. Some large shipping companies have a policy of regular replacement of vessels. Finally, speculators may be attracted by incentives offered by shipbuild-ers short of work - low prices and favorable credit are examples. The shipyards form a large and diverse group. There are about 250 major shipyards in the world. The negotiation is complex. Occasionally an owner will appoint a broker to handle the new building, but many owners deal direct.

2. The *freight market* where the shipowner charters the ship. The shipowner comes to the market with a ship available, free of cargo. The ship has a particular speed, cargo capacity, dimensions, and cargo handling gear. Existing contractual commit-ments will determine the date and location at which it will become available. The shipper or charterer may be someone with a volume of cargo to transport from one location to another or a company that needs an extra ship for a period of time. Often the principal (i.e. the owner or charterer) will appoint a shipbroker to act for him. The broker's task is to discover what cargoes or ships are available; what the owners/charterers want to be paid; and what is reasonable given the state of the market. With this information, they negotiate the deal for their client, often in tense competition with other brokers. Four types of contractual arrangement are com-monly used. Under a voyage charter, the shipowner contracts to carry a specific cargo in a specific ship for a negotiated price per ton. A variant of the same theme is the contract of affreightment, in which the shipowner contracts to carry regular tonnages of cargo for an agreed price per ton. The time charter is an agreement between owner and charterer to hire the ship, complete with crew, for a fee per day, month, or year. Finally, the bare boat charter hires out the ship without crew or any operational responsibilities.

3. The *sale and purchase market* where the shipowner tries to sell the ship. Typically, the ship will be sold with prompt delivery, for cash, free of any charters, mortgages, or maritime liens. Occasionally it may be sold with the benefit (or liability) of an ongoing time charter. The ship owner's reasons for selling may vary. He may have a policy of replacing vessels at a certain age; the ship may no longer suit his trade; or he may think prices are about to fall. Most sale and purchase transactions are carried out through shipbrokers. The procedure for buying/selling a ship can be subdivided into the following five stages: putting the ship on the market, negotia-tion of price and conditions, memorandum of agreement, inspections, and the

closing where the ship is delivered to its new owners who simultaneously transfer the balance of funds to the seller's bank.

4.   The *demolition market* where the shipowner finally sells the ship. The customer is a scrap yard. Usually the sale is handled by a broker and large broking companies have a demolition desk specializing in this market.

The Case of UPS Logistics Group

The UPS Logistics Group is a wholly owned, but independently managed subsidiary of UPS. The purpose of the logistics offerings is to build close relationships with users, offering a variety of services that can be integrated into their various operational processes. The company recognized that virtually all industries were under enormous pressure to improve performance and adapt to the imperatives of the information age. The changes that firms would undertake to achieve these goals included an increased focus on improving supply chain processes.

UPS Logistics aims to identify, develop, market, and implement the services necessary to accommodate this perceived need in the marketplace. The five principle businesses that comprise the Logistics Group are discussed briefly here:

- *UPS Worldwide Logistics*. This business provides solutions to re-engineer and manage supply chains — from supplier through manufacturer, distributor, dealer or end consumer. Personnel are capable of analyzing, diagnosing, recommending and implementing solutions for customers that reduce supply chain costs and improve customer service. In this capacity Worldwide Logistics forms teams that include industrial engineers, telecommunications consultants, call center specialists, transportation experts, software systems integrators and developers, high-tech repair technicians, logistics consultants and operations managers around the globe.

- *Transportation Services Group*. This business provides comprehensive transportation services custom-tailored to meet the customer's individual requirements. It provides transportation management, intermodal services and dedicated contract carriage, as well as network analysis and re-engineering, lane and mode optimization, carrier selection and routing, performance reporting, claims administration, on-site management and other value-added services. Much of the activity of the Transportation Services Group is centered on transportation management.

- *Service Parts Logistics*. This business provides comprehensive services for companies that seek to outsource their service parts and repair works. Service Parts Logistics offers network planning and management, worldwide service parts depots and repair centers, integrated information systems, call centers and customer service expertise for post-sales support.

- *Business Communications Services*. This business specializes in providing a comprehensive package of customer care solutions. It offers support for call center services, e-commerce, quality measurement, and telecommunications consulting. This business is facilitated by the confidence business customers have in the UPS brand name. It draws upon the firm's global presence, technical expertise, reputation for reliability, and financial stability. Teams of telecommunications experts, engineers, and other customer-oriented personnel are drawn upon to design, redesign, and manage all or part of these support areas that customers may want to farm out to outside providers.

- *Technology Services.* Leveraging the billions of dollars that UPS has been spending on information technology development over the past decade, Technology Services claims to offer state of the art systems to track bits and bytes of data that affect the flow of goods, capital and customer information. It employs a large group of developers, systems integration experts, telecommunications consultants, software engineers and IS network managers. It offers solutions that involve integration across the supply chain, connecting trading partners, transportation carriers, and customers.

UPS Logistics Group will help small shippers, especially those selling products via the Internet. UPS e-Logistics will offer a package of services from warehousing to order fulfillment to customer service for small and medium-sized companies that sell their products on the Web.

UPS Logistics has focused on developing products and solutions to improve the operational efficiency of the clients' logistics department. This concentrated focus has resulted in the development of industry leading software solutions that enable highly efficient order-to-delivery processes. The solutions include street-level, real time wireless dispatch, GPS tracking and on time delivery, which in turn update about the delivery process status and better planning on the delivery schedule.

In view of the nature of the business conduct, UPS Logistics Technologies can be considered as a value shop under the value configuration. The value of the company is created by providing the logistic solution to solve the problems of their clients.

The main assets of the value shop are competence professional and high level of knowledge about certain sectors. The value shops most of the time refers to the professional service firm such as law firm and hospital. UPS Logistics Technologies is another good example of value shop, where it provides solution to the client logistic problem.

UPS as such has the value configuration of a value chain, since UPS services are integrated, multi-modal services that accelerate and simplify freight shipments from international factories through custom to multiple retail stores or end customers' doorsteps anywhere in the world with one point of contact and single bill.

IS/IT can make contributions to business performance in many ways:

- To improve coordination by synchronizing the entire interaction between vendors, customers and suppliers and not just optimizing small piece of the process

- To have a massive technology network to help capture and use real time information

- To develop an extensive portfolio of flexible services and to manage both business to business and consumer to consumer returns

- To extend existing software applications linking many business processes and extending easy UPS access to thousands of additional businesses around the globe

- To meet customers' individual needs in terms of convenience, transit times, compatible technology and price.

- To have a more transparent movement of goods inside corporate supply chains as well as the movement of packages within the UPS global network

DIAD — Deliver Information Acquisition Device — is the company's new driver terminal that features built in cellular, wireless LAN and Bluetooth short-range wireless systems. The DIAD IV driver terminal, a compact suggested device powered by Windows includes a Global Positioning System (GPS) receiver, a bar code scanner, and a color screen. The short-range Bluetooth wire system in the DIAD IV is designed to communicate with peripheral devices that the company may integrate such as printers and credit card readers.

The Bluetooth systems had to operate in the same 2.4 GHz band in order to communicate with the customer's computers. Supporting software to support messaging will also have to be considered to make it easier to communicate with the customers' PCs. UPS started a large scale test operated by AT&T wireless service and will also have many existing systems to support the technology.

UPS Logistics operates on Value Chain Enterprise System (VCES), which looks at an enterprise as an integrated system, addressing the interactions between the demand and supply chain and focusing on end-to-end optimization as the goal. It combines the cost minimizing capabilities of supply chain management and the revenue maximizing objectives of dynamic pricing and demand management.

An analysis of strengths, weaknesses, opportunities, and threats (SWOT) could result in the following figure (Figure 19.2).

Figure 19.2. SWOT analysis for UPS Logistics Group

	Internal	External
Positive	Substantial assets and performance Major freight carrier Innovative logistics provider Low cost, efficient, and global services Reliable service over entire range of modes State of the art IS/IT STRENGTHS	Market growth, revenue growth Promote e-business Promote e-logistics Expand client base by smaller shippers One-stop centre for total service Integrated supply chain management OPPORTUNITIES
Negative	WEAKNESSES Not vessel operating common carrier (VOCC) No authority to enter confidential agreements Certain remote areas of the world inaccessible Lack of infrastructure locally High cost of assets maintenance	THREATS VOCCs offering comprehensive supply chain Competitors using electronic portal systems Trend to 4PL by other major 3PLs Government legislation (homeland security) Terrorist attacks causing disruption of service

The Case of Maersk Logistics

Mercantile Logistics was one of multiple operating units of the A.P. Møller Group. Mercantile had 1890 employees in 110 offices in 60 countries. The business strategy was to develop capabilities in many major markets in order to handle growing needs of large, sophisticated global manufacturers, wholesalers, and retailers. The company could integrate into a shipper's value chain.

Mercantile took over the management of 90.000 square meter Torsvick warehouse of the giant Swedish furniture manufacturer and retailer IKEA. Although IKEA owns the facility and the fixed assets, Mercantile provides staff and materials handling equipment. The deal took 18 months of negotiations and preparatory work. According to management, this unique agreement is based upon an open book principle, gain sharing, and agreed efficiency improvement program. It must meet a number of service parameters, such as lead-time, utilization of vehicles, quality, inventory accuracy, and handling capacity.

Mercantile has many customers. Some of the ones that the firm highlights in its literature and Web sites are Reebok (U.S. footwear), Genesco (U.S. footwear), IKEA (Swedish furniture), Grundfos (Danish pumps), KF (Swedish-coop association), and Otto (German online shopping). As is customary in the freight forwarding and maritime container industries, some accounts may be designated as key corporate accounts. Most, however, are probably accounts of local, country, or regional offices.

Information technology is important to the business. One of the most important information systems is MODS — Mercantile Operations and Documentation System. MODS produces standard operations and documentation data. The system operates based on purchase orders and uses EDI — electronic data interchange.

Other important systems are LOG*IT (Logistics Information Technology) and M*Power. These appear to be fairly standard systems that most progressive freight forwarders would operate today. LOG*IT is designed to be integrated directly into the customer's management systems. It claims to have capability to provide visibility of the complete logistics process, from order placement to final individual delivery.

M*Power appears to be an enhancement of LOG*IT, offering significant graphical improvement. M*Power is an information system package customized according to the customer's business agreement with Mercantile. Mercantile has entered an aggressive stage of systems development. It focuses on significant expansion of M*Power to integrate thousands of suppliers through global supply lines. The World Wide Web is central to this.

The strategic intent of Mercantile is to provide basic infrastructure for handling global business, i.e. global container transport, with logistics capabilities to handle complete supply chain requirements of some of the world's largest companies. This probably will include multiple modes, including air cargo.

Mercantile wants to expand customer base beyond consumer manufacturers and retail. The company is developing increasingly sophisticated supply chain information systems that will provide advanced solutions to customers.

Mercantile Logistics changed name to Maersk Logistics after a merger with Sealand Logistics in 2000. The Web site is www.maersk-logistics.com. Maersk Logistics is a recognized leader in the international logistics market. The company provides customized and integrated solutions for supply chain management, warehousing and distribution — as well as value added services, ocean freight, and airfreight transportation.

Maersk Logistics operates in more than 70 countries with 110 offices and employs over 4,500 people with specialist knowledge of their local markets. The company is part of the A.P. Møller-Maersk Group, which has more than 60,000 employees in over 125 countries around the world.

At Maersk Logistics, management recognizes that there is much more to transportation than moving cargo from port to port. They argue that they have the expertise to understand the nature and dynamics of customer business and the services to support customers' entire supply chain with a seamlessly integrated end-to-end solution — from procurement and pick-up of raw materials to the delivery at the customer's doorstep.

The company offers following products and services to its customers in its endeavors to offer complete solution for their supply chain logistics management: forwarding services, ocean freight, warehousing and distribution, inventory management, and integrated solutions labeled as "supply chain management" encompassing the before mentioned services.

Maersk Logistics' current *mission* is to be a strategic partner in integrated logistics management for their customers. The *business strategy* is to develop capabilities in major markets and specific industries to cater to the growing needs of global manufacturers, wholesalers and retailers by first integrating itself into its customers' value chain and second, to extend its reach to the supply chains of their customers' upstream and downstream associates.

Maersk Logistics *strategic intent* is to position itself at the core of their customers' value web, orchestrating the flow of information, goods and services by having the requisite infrastructure, IS/IT architecture and work processes to handle the complete supply chain requirements of their customers.

Just like any other industry, Maersk Logistics is also faced with developments of the technological era, which brings about following challenges:

- Competitive pressures of low cost at high value to the customers

- Declining freight rates so survival and growth on transportation services alone is not possible

- High productivity and service quality to customer

- Demand for greater transparency of interconnected operations, thereby pressure on reducing margins

- Plus many more related to above challenges for enhancements of IS/IT assets

These challenges can be met by applying IS/IT such as:

- Introduce knowledge-based systems for supporting value enhancement objectives

- Develop and share knowledge for supply chain management with key customers

Figure 19.3. SWOT analysis for Maersk Logistics

Internal	External
Positive Experience in sea freight and logistics Ability to handle commodity cargo Extensive Maersk network Highly skilled and educated staff Creative and resourceful management Financial stability and strength STRENGTHS	Economic boom (more cargo) Security leading to better service quality Cheaper to enter airfreight (budget airlines) New fields (oil, gas, etc.) in line with Maersk Seamless integrated supply chains Globalization creates opportunities OPPORTUNITIES
WEAKNESSES Limited customer base Air freight business (business and market) Lack of own land logistics support No cutting edge technology **Negative** High cost labor	THREATS Strong newcomer competitors with lines Customer expectations to supply chains Price pressures Possible economic recession Security threat (increased operation cost)

- Enhance decision support systems at tactical and strategic management layers

- Enhance scheduling and optimization functionalities within information systems

- Review information systems in the context of new products in the market and upgrade current infrastructure to minimize costs and maximize efficiency of data processing, information extraction, notification, and communication to all users.

An analysis of strengths, weaknesses, opportunities, and threats (SWOT) could result in the Figure 19.3.

Telecom Italia Mobile, Netcomand Colt Telecom Group

Introduction to Telecom Management

The value configuration of a value network as described in Chapter I uses a mediating technology to link customers, e.g. telecommunication companies and banking firms. A telecom company as a value network has three primary activities: network promotion and contract management, service provisioning, and infrastructure operations. The value of a product is determined by network externality when it increases with the number of product users. Thus, network externalities lead to demand-side economies of scale.

The mobile phone industry is a clear example of an industry built around a mediating technology. Fjeldstad et al. (2004) focused on three factors that will affect the nature of strategic action within the mobile phone industry: market concentration, time evolution, and market penetration.

First, market concentration is a critical determinant of competitive behavior that reduces industry rivalry. Network externalities create additional dependencies among rival firms. Second, from a product-life-cycle perspective, the evolution of time shapes firm-level strategy and should affect industry competition when there are strong first-mover advantages, particularly in industries with strong network externalities. Finally, market penetration, as an indicator of network-externality effects, is a key driver of subscription and service usage value in value networks because it better reflects the degree of connectivity within the respective countries. The connectivity relevant to users is higher for a given number of subscribers in a small Nordic country than in a large country (Fjeldstad et al., 2004).

Telecom companies have to compare and choose between two strategic actions: cooperation vs. competition. Industry-accumulated and firm-specific market penetrations are key determinants of competitive behavior in network industries. Early competitive action aimed at influencing standards is important. Equally important is managing expectations to benefit from network externalities and the associated lock-in effects to appropriate the value created. The value of the service increases with network size. As a result, companies can be expected to compete most fiercely to achieve critical mass when market penetration is still low (Fjeldstad et al., 2004).

Cooperation vs. Competition

Expectations play a significant part in the determination of market shares. The network that customers expect to be large will become large, because the customers' willingness to pay for membership is higher. Once the network attains critical mass, the relative positions are more or less fixed and the network industry is on its equilibrium path. Networks therefore become more stable once the market reaches a high degree of penetration. This inertia means that there is less likelihood of purely competitive moves occurring. Correspondingly, strategic actions are more likely to be collaborative in their nature in markets with greater penetration. This was confirmed in an empirical analysis of the European mobile phone industry, where *the probability of a strategic action being cooperative rather than competitive increases with market penetration* (Fjeldstad et al., 2004).

Firms are less likely to engage in competitive moves if they feel that their competitors will retaliate. Furthermore, the probability of firms engaging in competitive moves decreases as the negative consequences of the competitors' responses increase. The likelihood of retaliation is likely to be related to interdependence and market concentration. The effect of concentration on the probability of collaborative actions (vs. competitive moves) should be even stronger in the case of network industries. Network externalities increase the benefits to large firms in an industry because by providing large firms with the opportunity for monopoly rents from incompatible products. When services are not fully compatible, including because of on-net/off-net price differentiation, a smaller firm is at a disadvantage vis-à-vis a larger one and, the payoff from enjoying a significant position in a concentrated industry can be considerable. When industry concentration is high, competitors cannot disregard the terms of access to the customer base of their fewer and stronger full-coverage competitors. This was confirmed in an empirical analysis of the European mobile phone industry, where *the probability of a strategic action being cooperative rather than competitive increases with market concentration* (Fjeldstad et al., 2004).

As the mobile phone industry evolves, a number of alliances fall into place and the number of unexplored collaborative options is reduced. Technological developments should also lead to fiercer competition with time. Industry-level learning effects may allow some firms to gain cost advantages and technological leaders may want to favor communication inside their own network above cross-network communication. The ability to exploit such effects by the individual firm would favor incompatibility and non-collaboration. Hence, as time passes, moves become increasingly hostile. This was confirmed in an empirical analysis of the European mobile phone industry, where *the probability of a strategic action being cooperative rather than competitive decreases as the industry becomes older* (Fjeldstad et al., 2004).

Cooperation allows for the sharing of development costs, while benefits from network externalities in new service layers are made possible by inter-operable technology and service agreements. Cooperation is beneficial in that it increases traffic within established networks. Companies may favor cooperative over purely competitive moves when subscriber bases become more stable (Fjeldstad et al., 2004).

Cooperation vs. competition is an important input to IS/IT strategy work. This clarification of cooperation or competition is important in stage 2 of the Y model. If the desired business situation in stage 2 of the Y model is concerned with cooperation, then the addition of new service layers will be a joint investment with competitors. If the desired business situation in stage 2 is concerned with competition, then the addition of new service layers will have to be completely financed by the firm.

An appropriate method for analyzing the desired business situation at this stage of the Y model is SWOT analysis. Datamonitor (2004a) conducted such a study of Telecom Italia Mobile SpA (TIM).

Telecom Italia Mobile SpA

TIM is one of Europe's top five mobile telecommunications operators. The company has a customer base of around 26 million subscribers in Italy, and through equity stakes in other carriers it serves over six million customers in other parts of the world. TIM is headquartered in Rome, Italy.

Telecom Italia Mobile generated revenues of 12 billion euro in 2003, a growth of 8%. TIM is one of Europe's top five mobile telecommunications operators. Fifty-five percent owned by the former Italian telephone monopoly operator, Telecom Italia, TIM focuses solely on the provision of mobile communications services. The company serves around 40 million customers worldwide. A recent alliance formed between the company, Orange, Telefonica and T Mobile should present the company more opportunities internationally.

Datamonitor's (2004a) SWOT analysis of TIM is shown below. One of the strengths of TIM is the *market leader* position in Italy. TIM is the largest mobile telecommunications company in Italy, ahead of industry rivals such as Vodafone Omnitel and Wind Infostrada. Market leadership enables TIM to maintain a high level of brand awareness, and helps the company to combat more effectively new entrants into the market.

	Positive outcome	Negative outcome
Present outcome	**Strengths** Market leader in Italy M-Services Multi-national UMTS licences	**Weaknesses** TIM PCS in Brazil Market maturity Reliance on Italy
Future outcome	**Opportunities** 3G Innovations Alliances Expansions	**Threats** Strong competition Exchange rates South America Health risks

SWOT analysis of Telecom Italia Mobile

Another strength of TIM is *m-services*. TIM's m-services data product offering has enabled the company to protect its share of the Italian market. TIM was the first company in Italy to launch such a service and achieved an early mover advantage because of this. M-services such as MMS also create another revenue stream for TIM, making the company less reliant on voice revenues.

TIM being *multinational* has operations throughout Europe, the Mediterranean basin and South America. The company's entry into a number of foreign markets will help to raise awareness of the TIM brand on a global scale. TIM's overseas operations will also help to reduce the company's reliance on the Italian mobile market for its revenues.

A final strength in the SWOT analysis is *UMTS licenses*. TIM has acquired UMTS licenses in Italy and Greece. These licenses will enable TIM to offer 3G communication services in the future in these countries. 3G communication services could be an important source of revenue for TIM in the future years.

The first weakness is *TIM PCS in Brazil*. The company's TIM PCS operations in Brazil have incurred higher start up costs than expected. These operations are expected to continue to generate high start up costs and losses over the next few years. These sustained losses in the Brazilian market will affect the company's profits as a whole.

The company's medium term growth has been limited by the *market maturity* of its domestic Italian market, which has a penetration rate of around 90%. This market maturity will leave little room for TIM to increase its subscriber numbers, revenues, and profits in Italy over future years.

A third weakness is *reliance on Italy*. The company is dependent on its domestic market of Italy for over 80% of group revenues and over 90% of gross operating income. This huge reliance on one market can be a weakness of the company, as any negative factor adversely affecting the Italian market would significantly hurt the company as a whole.

Demand for *3G* services is expected to increase over the next few years, as 3G becomes more commercially viable. This represents an opportunity for Telecom Italia Mobile. The demand for 3G will be stimulated by factors such as increasing use of mobile data, and the arrival of cheap, mass-market 3G handsets. TIM should look to develop and rollout its 3G communications services in Italy and Greece to match the growth in demand in order to generate increased revenues and profits in the future.

Technological *innovations* are another opportunity. Technological innovations have played an important part in the evolution of the mobile communications industry. It is very likely that this trend will continue in the future. TIM must look to keep pace with new industry innovations that will occur if it wants to defend its market leadership in Italy.

Another opportunity is the alliance with Telefonica Moviles, Orange, and T-Mobile. The commercial *alliances* should benefit TIM in a number of ways and will create opportunities for the company to generate enhanced revenues in the future. The alliance aims at increasing the four operators' quality of service and competitiveness on international markets leveraging on their complementary footprints. The alliance also aims to exploit the synergies for the creation of new products, services and handsets, which will increase TIM's and the other operator's sales potential while achieving economies of scale and improving efficiency levels.

International *expansions* are the final opportunity for TIM. TIM has sought international expansion in recent years, yet is still very reliant on its domestic market of Italy. The company is in a good position to leverage its strong Italian market position on a global scale. The recent merger of Aria and Aycell has increased the company's opportunities in Turkey and should allow the company to increase its market share there. TIM has also seen good growth in its Latin American markets and further acquisitions and alliances in foreign markets would present many good opportunities for the company for future growth.

The first threat is concerned with *strong competition*. TIM faces strong competition in the Italian mobile market from a number of companies. The company's main competitors at present are Vodafone Omnitel (19 million subscribers) and Wind Infostrada (11 million subscribers). Vodafone Omnitel is emerging as a significant threat to TIM's market leadership in Italy after improving its marketing activities and developing its Vodafone Live! product, which will pose a threat to TIM's M-Services. All of these companies will combine to take away sales and market share from TIM.

Another threat is interest and foreign currency *exchange rates*. As a global company operating in a number of markets worldwide, TIM can be vulnerable to certain external factors. Fluctuating interest and foreign currency exchange rates can have a significant impact on TIM's earnings. Unstable currency markets in Latin America can adversely affect the company and can be difficult to plan for.

The volatile nature of the economies of *South America* will pose a significant threat to TIM. TIM has substantial operations in South America and any downturn in the economies of these countries will affect TIM's revenues in the region. The volatile nature of the economies of South America markets was seen when the Venezuelan economy was badly affected by fluctuations in oil prices. Venezuela is one of the South American countries in which TIM operates. TIM has also recently been involved in a legal case with Brazil Telecom over alleged espionage, which may affect the company's public image.

The final threat is concerned with *health risks*. The growing concern over the links between radiation, cancer and the usage of mobile phones is a threat that could possibly lead to new government legislation making it difficult for mobile service providers to extend network capabilities. The concern over health risks is itself a factor that may reduce demand for TIM's products should advancements in medical technology further concerns over the links between the use of mobile phones and cancer.

Based on this SWOT analysis, IS/IT can be identified that can exploit strengths and opportunities and avoid weaknesses and threats.

Netcom in Norway

-Nobody is good at everything, says IT department manager Bjørn Tore Gullord. When NetCom outsourced large parts of their Intel-based operations, they acknowledged, "Others are better at this!" (Spilling, 2004).

NetCom chose Ementor as outsourcing partner the winter of 2003. –For several years Ementor had delivered outsourcing services to NetCom, and we had good experiences with them. They had built credibility and trust, which assured us they would be capable of handling an expanded range of our services, continues Bjørn Tore Gullord.

Different outsourcing approaches are being used. Within the areas of UNIX and "billing," they use on-site services as a supplement to internal resources. Servicedesk, on-site support of clients and management of the telephony solution, everything is outsourced to Ementor, as well as monitoring and management of large parts of the Intel-servers. —What we have gained is better cost control, greater flexibility when it comes to Netcom's development, and better quality. None is good in everything — IT-operation is better done by others, claims Gullord.

The contract runs for three years, and encompasses operations of large parts of Netcom's ict-platform; e-mail, file, print, applications, hardware, user support, backup, and all clients totaling 800 users. In addition, Ementor operates Netcom's call center solution CIC. The outsourcing agreement supports all of NetCom, including customer support centers in Oslo, Trondheim and regional offices.

-We are proud of this prestigious agreement that has substantial requirements on service-period (uptime) and quality, says Operations director Tore Haugeland in Ementor. NetCom has an SLA agreement with 99.5 % uptime for the terminal server solution, and 99.9 % uptime for the call center solution. — NetCom's choice of working with Ementor proves our competitive outsourcing services, and our capability of handling large and complex outsourcing agreements. This partnership strengthens Ementors ambitions of strong growth and domination in this market, continues Haugeland.

NetCom is the second largest mobile operator in Norway, and the Norwegian part of TeliaSonera. The company offers mobile telecommunication solutions in Norway, and is an innovative company known for its creativity and focus on customer needs. NetCom's head office is placed in Oslo, with branch offices in Trondheim, Bergen, Stavanger, Kristiansand, and Tønsberg. Total number of employees is approximately 740.

COLT Telecom Group plc

COLT specializes in the provision of high bandwidth data, Internet, and voice services to business and government customers in Europe (Datamonitor, 2004b). The company operates an integrated IP based pan European network linking the financial and business centers of Europe, providing a range of telecommunications services to corporate and carrier customers. COLT is one of the leading pan-European providers and has a 20,000 kilometers integrated network that directly connects over 9,000 buildings in 32 major cities in 13 countries. COLT is headquartered in London, UK.

For fiscal year 2003, COLT generated revenues of £ 1.1 billion, an increase of 14% over the previous year's revenues of £ 1 billion. The company reported a net loss of £ 124 million for 2003 compared with a loss of £ 718 million in 2002.

Datamonitor's (2004b) SWOT analysis of COLT is shown below. One of the strengths of COLT is *increased turnover*. COLT posted increased revenues for the 2003 fiscal year. Company turnover exceeded £ 1 billion for the first time in 2002 after rising 14% during the year.

	Positive outcome	Negative outcome
Present outcome	**Strengths** Increased turnover Business success Local level services	**Weaknesses** Execute strategy Performance Pricing pressures
Future outcome	**Opportunities** Industry consolidation Economic recovery Global reach Non-switched services	**Threats** Telecoms spending Competition Regulated industry

SWOT analysis of COLT Telecom Group

Another strength of COLT is *business success*. COLT experienced some success in its business operations during the 2002/3 fiscal year. The company increased its IP VPN, directly connected and eBusiness customer bases, as well as connecting a further 1.000 buildings to its network and increasing its offerings in the high bandwidth services sector. These factors again demonstrate that COLT's business strategy is proving to be successful in certain areas.

A final strength is *local level services*. The company continues to leverage its local presence and market knowledge. Over the past year, COLT has taken the opportunity to centralize a number of its operations and support functions. However, the company has never lost sight of the fact that the majority of its customers are local. The company has kept in place local management, sales and customer service capability. The tight control of the behind the scenes activities combined with service delivery at the local level is the main feature that has enabled to provide the best possible service and at the same time improve operating efficiencies.

The first weakness is ability to *execute strategy*. Due to past performance, the greatest strategic risk in the short to medium term is COLT's ability to execute successfully an up-selling strategy into its corporate customer base, thereby increasing margins and lowering capital intensity. Furthermore, there are longer-term concerns over the cannibalization of voice over IP (VOIP) and corporate virtual private network (VPN) migration on existing revenue streams and the lack of a mobility strategy.

Another weakness is non-switched revenues *performance*. COLT's non-switched revenues have only grown at a low-single-digit rate in the last two quarters, compared to 8% for the previous three quarters. This is due to a combination of factors, including increased cancellations, poor non-switched order book, continued pricing pressure and a 23% churn in sales force.

Furthermore, *pricing pressures* is affecting performance significantly. Pricing pressure continues to hinder European telecoms operators, with COLT's prices declining by 10% per annum for local and national non-switched revenues and 25% per annum for international non-switched revenues. The pricing environment for switched revenues is far less severe, with pricing declines of 2-5% per annum. Constant pricing pressures are forecast and current expectations regarding declines are conservative given that no new entrants are expected across all of COLT's revenue streams.

Industry consolidation is an opportunity for COLT. Industry consolidation provides COLT with an opportunity to build its business. A number of companies operating in the sector are expected to go out of business as the industry begins to consolidate. This will leave fewer companies competing within the industry. This will give COLT the opportunity to increase its share of the market either by acquiring the assets of bankrupt companies or by winning the customers who previously were serviced by those companies that have gone out of business. This trend was seen in the European market following the demise of KPNQwest.

Another opportunity is *economic recovery*. COLT's revenue streams are highly geared to a cyclical recovery and that any improvement in current economic trends should be beneficial. This is due to COLT's corporate customer base, which is more cyclical than that of its incumbent peers (which have defensive residential revenue streams). COLT is therefore expected to benefit relatively more in an economic recovery. COLT is also well positioned to benefit from a pick-up in cyclical demand due to its significant exposure to a recovery in the financial services sector (33% of corporate revenues) and geographic regions such as Germany (35% of total revenues), France (15%), Spain (10%) and Italy (10%).

COLT could choose to extend its *global reach* in order to generate increased revenues and profits in the future. The company could extend its network into other European countries or into other areas of the world. At present, it seems unlikely that COLT will choose to pursue such a strategy due to the unfavorable conditions affecting the telecoms industry. However, if the industry experiences an upturn in fortunes, global expansion remains a possibility for COLT.

It is estimated that there will be a growth in *non-switched services* over the coming years, as demand for local, national and international Internet bandwidth services from retail customers is expected to increase. COLT should position itself to take advantage of any growth within this industry sub segment in order to generate increased sales. COLT is already active in the non-switched services segment and the company should look to leverage its expertise in this area in order to take advantage of segment growth.

The reduction in *telecoms spending* remains a big problem for all organizations competing in the sector. The reduction in spending by COLT's customers is a reflection of the business prospects of COLT's customers, as well as the economic outlook in general. The downturn will continue to affect COLT's earnings and profits until a recovery is seen. This can be exasperated further by fluctuating interest and foreign currency exchange rates that will also have a significant impact on COLT's earnings.

Another threat is *competition*. COLT operates in a highly competitive and rapidly changing market and competes with a variety of organizations that offer services similar to those it offers. The market in which the company operates includes a variety of participants including many big name players such as BT and Cable & Wireless. Many of these competitors have significantly greater financial, technical and marketing resources, generate greater revenue and have greater name recognition than COLT does. Recent shifts away from sector-specific regulation to greater reliance on the Competition Act by regulators are also likely to mean more competitors entering the market, further strengthening competition to the company.

As a *regulated industry*, COLT will always be affected by changes in the regulatory environment, which may include changes in factors such as pricing regulation. These changes may then affect the revenues and profits generated by the company. Ofcom's policies and potential policies as the new single authority in regulation in UK telecommunications will be very important to how the business operates in the future.

Interfirm Relations

We learned from the study by Fjeldstad et al. (2004) that telecom firms make the choice between competition and cooperation. When telecom firms choose cooperation, they enter interfirm relations.

Andersen and Fjeldstad (2003) studied interfirm relations. Interfirm relations and the institutional arrangements that parties deploy to support exchange exist within the context of value systems. A value system consists of all the activities and firms that create and deliver value to the end customer. The value system describes the division of labor among firms and defines the exchanges relevant for integration of end value. Value system properties are potentially important determinants of interfirm relations because the organization of exchanges is likely to depend on the properties of the objects exchanged.

Interconnections between competing firms increase the value of their respective and combined services, but equalize services value. Alliances within the telecommunication extend the reach of their services, but also reduce differentiation among the firms. Closeness to customers has been cited as basis for dividing competition and cooperation in other types of industries. How do the actors deal with competition in the mediation value system, where no layer is closer to the customer than the others do? Can IS/IT help?

The network externality literature addresses the conditions under which firms have motives to cooperate through service compatibility and interconnect. Under some conditions, the firms both need each other strongly in phases of industry and service developments and have strong motives to compete in establishing their own network. The inter-actor relationships are highly complex. What are the time and context-dependent dynamics of mediator relationships? Can IS/IT help?

The strong requirements for access and interconnectivity in network industries affect the relationship between the firms and their nonmediating suppliers. For example, while the retailers of terminals and bundled subscriptions have motives to sell as many subscriptions as possible, the network operators must try to avoid churn, i.e. short-term subscription and re-subscription from frequent provider switching. How can these particular operator-retailer relationships be structured? Can IS/IT help?

Conclusions

Information systems strategy is concerned with the planning, use, control and benefits of IS and IT in business and public organizations. While a business strategy is the broadest pattern of resource allocation decisions, more specific decisions are related to information systems and information technology. IS must be seen both in a business and an IT context.

An e-business strategy is combining the perspectives of strategists and technologists by identifying e-business models that are aligned with business strategy and IS strategy.

Necessary elements of a business strategy include mission, vision, objectives, market strategy, knowledge strategy, and our general approach to the use of information, information systems and information technology.

Necessary elements of an IS strategy include future IS/IT applications, future competence of human resources (IS/IT professionals), and future IS/IT organizational structure, and control of the IS/IT function. Important application areas include electronic business and knowledge management. Future applications are planned according to priorities, how they are to be developed or acquired (make or buy), how they meet user requirements, and how security is achieved.

Changes are currently affecting IS strategy. Major changes are concerned with e-business, knowledge management, sourcing, and governance. Electronic business has integrated information systems in business models. Knowledge management enables e-business, sourcing, and governance. Sourcing represents new approaches to hierarchical and market based supply of IT services. Finally, IT Governance is specifying decision rights that were previously assigned to strategy project management.

This book was based on the premise that it is difficult, if not impossible, to manage a modern business or public organization without at least some knowledge of the planning, use, control, and benefits of information systems and information technology. Managers need to have an understanding of strategy development, including the current technology situation, the current and desired business situation, the need for changes, the application portfolio, and organizational and human resource issues in the area of information technology.

Furthermore, managers need to have an understanding of emergent perspectives that influence their role. Sourcing makes their relationship role more important, while governance makes their decision-making role more important.

This book combined strategy development (process) with theories of the firm, e-commerce and e-business, knowledge management systems and IS/IT outsourcing (content). This book presented emerging perspectives that influence strategy work, such as IT sourcing and IT governance.

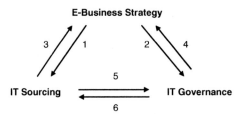

The main perspectives of e-business strategy, IT sourcing and IT governance are linked in different ways. As illustrated in the figure, we can identify the following six links:

1. *E-business strategy influencing IT sourcing.* For example, an e-business model requiring more IT infrastructure services may cause the need for new sourcing options to satisfy emerging infrastructure requirements.

2. *E-business strategy influencing IT governance.* For example, an e-business strategy focusing on standardization may cause decision rights to move from business unit managers to corporate level staff function.

3. *IT sourcing influencing e-business strategy.* For example, the outsourcing vendor has developed a new e-business architecture that is optimal for the organization.

4. *IT governance influencing e-business strategy.* For example, corporate management has implemented a hands-off role for them selves and left IT governance completely to business unit executives. Consequently, e-business models will be designed and implemented, contingent upon business unit requirements, rather than corporate requirements.

5.   *IT sourcing influencing IT governance.* The more complicated sourcing arrangements in terms of the number of sources and the number of services, the more people and functions will have to be included in the governance arrangements.

6.   *IT governance influencing IT sourcing.* For example, the more decision rights are preserved within the organization, the less partnership and the more transaction-based sourcing will be taking place.

The need for an e-business strategy changes as an organization evolves. Earl's (2001) six stages of evolving end at the final stage of transformation, where the company has successfully made the journey of e-business. In this long-term perspective of company development, the "e-" is a temporary phenomenon.

Strategy, sourcing, and governance, on the other hand, are no temporary phenomena. That is why strategy, sourcing and governance should also be understood independent of the "e-," as illustrated in this book.

References

Afuah, A. (2003). Redefining firm boundaries in the face of the Internet: Are firms really shrinking? *Academy of Management Review, 29*(1), 34-53.

Afuah, A., & Tucci, C. L. (2003). *Internet business models and strategies* (2nd ed.). New York: McGraw-Hill.

Agrawal, V., Farrell, D., & Remes, J.K. (2003). Offshoring and beyond. *McKinsey Quarterly*, 4. Retrieved from web11.epnet.com

Alavi, M., & Leidner, D. E. (2001). Knowledge management and knowledge management systems: Conceptual foundations and research issues. *MIS Quarterly, 25*(1), 107-136.

Amit, R., & Zott, C. (2001). Value creation in e-business. *Strategic Management Journal, 22*, 493-520.

Andal, A., Cartwright, P. A., & Yip, G. S. (2003, Summer). The digital transformation of traditional businesses. *MIT Sloan Management Review*, 34-41.

Andersen, E., & Fjeldstad, Ø. D. (2003). Understanding interfirm relations in mediation industries with special reference to the Nordic mobile communication industry. *Industrial Marketing Management, 32*, 397-408.

Anderson, C. A., & Kellam, K. L. (1992). Belief perseverance, biased assimilation, and covariation detection: The effects of hypothetical social theories and new data. *Personality and Social Psychology Bulletin, 18*(5), 555-565.

Anderson, C. A., & Lindsay, J. J. (1998). The development, perseverance, and change of naive theories. *Social Cognition, 16*(1), 8-30.

Anderson, S. W., Glenn, D., & Sedatole, K. L. (2000). Sourcing parts of complex products: evidence on transaction costs, high-powered incentives and ex-post opportunism. *Accounting, Organizations and Society, 25*, 723-749.

Ang, S. (1993). *The etiology of information systems outsourcing.* Doctoral dissertation, University of Minnesota.

Ang, S., & Straub, D. W. (1998). Production and transaction economics and IS outsourcing: A study of the U.S. banking industry. *MIS Quarterly, 22*(4), 535-552.

Armstrong, C. P., & Sambamurthy, V. (1999). Information technology assimilation in firms: The influence of senior leadership and IT infrastructures. *Information Systems Research, 10*(4), 304-327.

Artz, K. W., & Brush, T. H. (2000). Asset specificity, uncertainty and relational norms: an examination of coordination costs in collaborative strategic alliances. *Journal of Economic Behavior & Organization, 41*, 337-362.

Awad, E. M. (2002). *Electronic commerce — From vision to fulfillment.* NJ: Prentice Hall.

Ba, S., Stallaert, J., & Whinston, A. B. (2001). Research commentary: Introducing a third dimension in information systems design — The case of incentive alignment. *Information Systems Research, 12*(3), 225-239.

Barney, J. B. (2001). Is the resource-based "view" a useful perspective for strategic management research? Yes. *Academy of Management Review, 26*(1), 41-56.

Barney, J. B. (2002). *Gaining and sustaining competitive advantage.* NJ: Prentice Hall.

Barthélemy, J. (2003). The seven deadly sins of outsourcing. *Academy of Management Executive, 17*(2), 87-100.

Blois, K. (2002). Business to business exchanges: A rich descriptive apparatus derived from MacNeil's and Menger's analysis. *Journal of Management Studies, 39*(4), 523-551.

Boyd, B. K., & Reuning-Elliott, E. (1998), A measurement model of strategic planning, *Strategic Management Journal, 19*, 181-192.

Brown, C. V. (1997). Examining the emergence of hybrid IS governance solutions: Evidence from a single case site. *Information Systems Research, 8*(1), 69-94.

Brown, C. V. (1999). Horizontal mechanisms under differing IS organization contexts. *MIS Quarterly, 23*(3), 421-454.

Cannon, J. P., Achrol, R. S., & Gundlach, G. T. (2000). Contracts, norms, and plural form governance. *Journal of the Academy of Marketing Science, 28*(2), 180-194.

Cannon, J. P., & Homburg, C. (2001). Buyer-supplier relationships and customer firm costs. *Journal of Marketing, 65*, 29-43.

Cernat, L. (2004). The emerging European corporate governance model: Anglo-Saxon, continental, or still the century of diversity? *Journal of European Public Policy, 11*(1), 147-166.

Chang, K., Jackson, J., & Grover, V. (2003). E-commerce and corporate strategy: An executive perspective. *Information & Management, 40*, 663-675.

Chatzkel, J. (2002). A conversation with Göran Roos. *Journal of Intellectual Capital, 3*(2), 96-117.

Christensen, C. M., & Raynor, M. E. (2003). *The innovator's solution.* Boston: Harvard Business School Press.

Clott, C. B. (2004). Perspectives on global outsourcing and the changing nature of work. *Business and Society Review, 109*(2), 153-170.

Collis, D. J., & Montgomery, C. A. (1997). *Corporate strategy — Resources and the scope of the firm.* Chicago: Irwin, McGraw-Hill.

Computerworld. (2005, January). Premier 100 IT Leaders 2005.

Das, T. K., & Teng, B. S. (2001a). Strategic risk behaviour and its temporalities: Between risk propensity and decision context. *Journal of Management Studies, 38*(4), 515-534.

Das, T. K., & Teng, B. S. (2001b). Trust, control, and risk in strategic alliances: An integrated framework. *Organization Studies, 22*(2), 251-283.

Datamonitor. (2004a). *Telecom Italia Mobile SpA (TIM) — Company profile.* Datamonitor Europe, LondonRetrieved from www.datamonitor.com

Datamonitor. (2004b). *COLT Telecom Group plc — Company profile.* Datamonitor Europe, LondonRetrieved from www.datamonitor.com

Davenport, T. H., & Prusak, L. (1998). *Working knowledge.* Boston: Harvard Business School Press.

Dixon, N. M. (2000). *Common knowledge.* Boston: Harvard Business School Press.

Domberger, S., Fernandez, P., & Fiebig, D. G. (2000). Modelling the price, performance and contract characteristics of IT outsourcing. *Journal of Information Technology, 15*, 107-118.

Dunleavy, P. (1994). The globalization of public services production: Can government be 'best in world'? *Public Policy and Administration, 9*(2), 36-65.

Earl, M. J. (2000). Evolving the e-business. *Business Strategy Review, 11*(2), 33-38.

Earl, M. J. (2001). Knowledge management strategies: Toward a taxonomy. *Journal of Management Information Systems, 18*(1), 215-233.

Eisenhardt, K. M. (1985). Control: Organizational and economic approaches. *Management Science, 31*(2), 134-149.

Else, S. E. (2002). Strategic sourcing and federal government transformation. *Information Knowledge Systems Management, 3*, 31-52.

Elter, F. (2004). *Strategizing in complex contexts.* Series of Dissertations 7/2004, Norwegian School of Management BI.

Evans, P., & Wurster, T. S. (1999, November-December). Getting real about virtual commerce. *Harvard Business Review,* 85-95.

Fahey, L., Srivastava, R., Sharon, J. S. & Smith, D. E. (2001). Linking e-business and operating processes: The role of knowledge management. *IBM Systems Journal, 40*(4), 889-907.

Fjeldstad, Ø. D., Becerra, M., & Narayanan, S. (2004). Strategic action in network industries: an empirical analysis of the European mobile phone industry. *Scandinavian Journal of Management, 20*, 173-196.

Freeman, R. E. (1984). *Strategic Management. A Stakeholder Approach.* Boston: Pitman.

Freeman, R. E., & Phillips, R. A. (2002). Stakeholder theory: A libertarian defence. *Business Ethics Quarterly, 12*(3), 331-349.

Gadde, L. E., & Snehota, I. (2000). Making the most of supplier relationships. *Industrial Marketing Management,* 29, 305-316.

Galanter, M., & Palay, T. (1991). *Tournament of lawyers, the transformation of the big law firms.* Chicago: The University of Chicago Press.

Gartner (2004a). *Worldwide IT services market definitions guide, 3Q03, Gartner Dataquest guide.* Gartner Group, Surrey, TW20 9AW, UK.

Gartner (2004b). Key forces shape outsourcing market. *Gartner Dataquest.* Retrieved from www.gartner.com

Gartner (2004c). Life sciences firms rely on business process outsourcing. *Gartner Report.* Retrieved from www.gartner.com

Gilley, M. K., & Rasheed, A. (2000). Making more by doing less: An analysis of outsourcing and its effects on firm performance. *Journal of Management, 26*(4), 763-790.

Gottschalk, P., & Khandelwal, V. K. (2002). Global comparison of stages of growth based on critical success factors. *Journal of Global Information Management, 10*(2), 42-51.

Grant, R. M. (2002). *Contemporary strategy analysis* (4th ed.). MA: Blackwell Publishing.

Grant, R. M. (2003). Strategic planning in a turbulent environment: Evidence from the oil majors. *Strategic Management Journal, 24*, 491-517.

Grover, V., & Davenport, T. H. (2001). General perspectives on knowledge management: Fostering a research agenda. *Journal of Management Information Systems, 18*(1), 5-21.

Grover, V., & Malhotra, M. K. (2003). Transaction cost framework in operations and supply chain management research: Theory and measurement. *Journal of Operations Management, 21*, 457-473.

Grover, V., & Ramanlal, P. (1999). Six myths of information and markets: Information technology networks, electronic commerce, and the battle for consumer surplus. *MIS Quarterly, 23*(4), 465-495.

Grover, V., & Saeed, K. A. (2004). Strategic orientation and performance of Internet-based businesses. *Information Systems Journal, 14*, 23-42.

Grover, V., Teng, T. C., & Cheon, M. J. (1998). Towards a theoretically-based contingency model of information systems outsourcing. In L. P. Willcocks, & M. C. Lacity (Eds.), *Strategic Sourcing of Information Systems: Perspectives and Practices* (pp. 79-101). London: John Wiley & Sons.

Guldentops, E. (2004). Governing information technology through COBIT. In W. Van Grembergen (Ed.), *Strategies for information technology governance* (pp. 269-309). Hershey, PA: Idea Group Publishing.

Haanaes, K. B. (1997). *Managing resource mobilization: Case studies of Dynal, Fiat Auto Poland and Alcatel Tecom Norway.* PhD series 9.97, Copenhagen Business School, Copenhagen, Denmark.

Hagel, J. (2004). Offshore goes on the offensive. *McKinsey Quarterly, 2*, 82-92.

Hancox, M., & Hackney, R. (2000). IT outsourcing: Frameworks for conceptualizing practice and perception. *Information Systems Journal, 10*, 217-237.

Hann, J., & Weber, R. (1996). Information systems planning: A model and empirical tests. *Management Science, 42*(7), 1043-1064.

Hansen, M. T., Nohria, N., & Tierny, T. (1999, March-April). What's your strategy for managing knowledge? *Harvard Business Review*, 106-116.

Hayes, J., & Finnegan, P. (2005). Assessing the potential of e-business models: Towards a framework for assisting decision-makers. *European Journal of Operational Research, 160*, 365-379.

Henderson, J. C., & Venkatraman, N. (1993). Strategic alignment: Leveraging information technology for transforming organizations. *IBM Systems Journal, 32*(1), 4-15.

Hirshheim, R., & Lacity, M. (2000). The myths and realities of information technology insourcing. *Communications of the ACM, 43*(2), 99-107.

Hitt, M. A., Bierman, L., Shimizu, K., & Kochhar, R. (2001). Direct and moderating effects of human capital on strategy and performance in professional service firms: A resource-based perspective. *Academy of Management Journal, 44*(1), 13-28.

Honess, S. (2003). Business process outsourcing. In J. Angel (Ed.), *Technology outsourcing* (pp. 208-229). London: The Law Society.

Hopkins, W. E., & Hopkins, S. A. (1997). Strategic planning — financial performance relationships in banks: A causal examination. *Strategic Management Journal, 18*(8), 635-652.

HR. (2004). Exercising due diligence in recruitment outsourcing. *Strategic HR Review, 3*(3), 10-11.

IT Governance Institute (2004). IT Governance Global Status Report. *IT Governance Institute,* Rolling Meadows, Illinois. Retrieved from www.itgi.org

Jensen, M. C., & Meckling, W. H. (1976). Theory of the firm: Managerial behavior, agency costs and ownership structures. *Journal of Financial Economics, 3*(4), 305-360.

Johnson, G., & Scholes, K. (2002). *Exploring corporate strategy.* Harlow, Essex, UK: Pearson Education, Prentice Hall.

Julien, P. A., & Ramangalahy, C. (2003, Spring). Competitive strategy and performance of exporting SMEs: An empirical investigation of the impact of their export information search and competencies. *Entrepreneurship Theory and Practice,* 227-245.

Kaiser, K. M., & Hawk, S. (2004). Evolution of offshore software development: From outsourcing to cosourcing. *MIS Quarterly Executive, 3*(2), 69-81.

Kaplan, R. S., & Norton, D. P. (2004). *Strategy maps.* Boston: Harvard Business School Press.

Kern, T., Willcocks, L. P., & Heck, E. V. (2002). The winner's curse in IT outsourcing: Strategies for avoiding relational trauma. *California Management Review, 44*(2), 47-69.

King, W. R., & Malhotra, Y. (2000). Developing a framework for analyzing IS sourcing. *Information & Management, 37*, 323-334.

King, W. R., & Teo, T. S. H. (1997). Integration between business planning and information systems planning: Validating a stage hypothesis. *Decision Sciences, 28*(2), 279-308.

Lacity, M. C., & Willcocks, L. P. (1998). An empirical investigation of information technology sourcing practices: Lessons from experience. *MIS Quarterly, 22*(3), 363-408.

Lacity, M. C., & Willcocks, L. P. (2000). Relationships in IT outsourcing: A stakeholder perspective. In R. W. Zmud (Ed.), *Framing the domains of IT management: Projecting the future through the past* (pp. 355-384). Cincinnati, OH: Pinnaflex Educational Resources.

Lambe, C. J., Wittmann, C. M., & Spekman, R. E. (2001). Social exchange theory and research on business-to-business relational exchange. *Journal of Business-to-Business Marketing, 8*(3), 1-36.

Langfield-Smith, K., & Smith, D. (2003). Management control systems and trust in outsourcing relationships. *Management Accounting Research, 14*, 281-307.

Laudon, K. C., & Laudon, J. P. (2005). *Essentials of management information systems – Managing the digital firm* (6th ed.). Upper Saddle River, NJ: Pearson Education.

Lee, J. N., Miranda, S. M., & Kim, Y. M. (2004). IT outsourcing strategies: Universalistic, contingency, and configurational explanations of success. *Information Systems Research, 15*(2), 110-131.

Levina, N., & Ross, J. W. (2003). From the vendor's perspective: Exploring the value proposition in information technology outsourcing. *MIS Quarterly, 27*(3), 331-364.

Linder, J. C. (2004, Winter). Transformational outsourcing. *MIT Sloan Management Review*, 52-58.

Lislie, C. (2003, Winter). Outsource a core competency? Why private equity groups are outsourcing business strategy due diligence. *The Journal of Private Equity*, 72-75.

Loewendahl, B. R. (2000). *Strategic management of professional service firms* (2nd ed.). Copenhagen Business School Press, Copenhagen, Denmark.

Luo, Y. (2002). Contract, cooperation, and performance in international joint ventures. *Strategic Management Journal, 23*, 903-911.

Maister, D. H. (1993). *Managing the professional service firm*. New York: Free Press.

Miller, C. C., & Cardinal, L. B. (1994). Strategic planning and firm performance: A synthesis of more than two decades of research. *Academy of Management Journal, 37*(6), 1649-1665.

Mintzberg, H. (1994). *The rise and fall of strategic planning*. New York: The Free Press.

Montana, J. C. (2000, July). The legal system and knowledge management. *The Information Management Journal*, 54-57.

Moss, M. (2004, February). Knowledge acquisition and modelling. *Knowledge Management Magazine*, 19-22.

Nahapiet, J., & Ghoshal, S. (1998). Social capital, intellectual capital, and the organizational advantage. *Academy of Management Review, 23*(2), 242-266.

Nayyar, P. R. (1993). On the measurement of competitive strategy: Evidence from a large multiproduct U.S. firm. *Academy of Management Journal, 36*(6), 1652-1669.

Nielsen, K. B. (2004, October). *Reality of IS Lite — and more.* EXP Client presentation, Gartner Group. Retrieved from www.gartner.com

Nolan, R. L. (1979, March-April). Managing the crises in data processing. *Harvard Business Review*, 115-126.

Nonaka, I., Toyama, R., & Konno, N. (2000). SECI, Ba and leadership: A unified model of dynamic knowledge creation. *Long Range Planning, 33*(1), 5-34.

Olson, D. L. (2001). *Introduction to information systems project management.* New York: McGraw-Hill.

Pearlson, K. E. (2001). *Managing and using information systems: A strategic approach.* London: Wiley & Sons.

Peppard, J., Lambert, R., & Edwards, C. (2000). Whose job is it anyway? Organizational information competencies for value creation. *Information Systems Journal, 10*, 291-322.

Peterson, R. R. (2004). Integration strategies and tactics for information technology governance. In W. Van Grembergen (Ed.), *Strategies for information technology governance* (pp. 37-80). Hershey, PA: Idea Group Publishing.

Pettus, M. L. (2001). The resource-based view as a developmental growth process: Evidence from the deregulated trucking industry. *Academy of Management Journal, 44*(4), 878-896.

Phillips, R., Freeman, R. E., & Wicks, A. C. (2003). What stakeholder theory is not. *Business Ethics Quarterly, 13*(4), 479-502.

Porter, M. E. (1985). *Competitive strategy.* New York: The Free Press.

Porter. M. E. (2001, March). Strategy and the Internet. *Harvard Business Review*, 63-78.

Priem, R. L., & Butler, J. E. (2001). Is the resource-based "view" a useful perspective for strategic management research? *Academy of Management Review, 26*(1), 22-40.

Quinn, J. B. (2000, Summer). Outsourcing innovation: The new engine of growth. *Sloan Management Review,* 13-28.

Ramachandran, K., & Voleti, S. (2004). Business process outsourcing (BPO): Emerging scenario and strategic options for IT-enabled services. *Vikalpa, 29*(1), 49-62.

Rao, M. T. (2004, Summer). Key issues for global IT sourcing: Country and individual factors. *Information Systems Management Journal*, 16-21.

Robson, W. (1997). *Strategic management & information systems* (2nd ed.). London: Prentice Hall.

Rolls-Royce. (2001). *Rolls-Royce signs agreement for new Chinese regional jet.* News release. Retrieved from www.rolls-royce.com

Ross, J. W., & Westerman, G. (2004). Preparing for utility computing: The role of IT architecture and relationship management. *IBM Systems Journal, 43*(1), 5-19.

Sambamurthy, V., & Zmud, R. (2000). Research commentary: The organizing logic for an enterpise's IT activities in the digital era — A prognosis of practice and a call for research. *Information Systems Research, 11*(2), 105-114.

Sambamurty, V., & Zmud, R. (2004, March). *Steps toward strategic agility: Guiding corporate transformations.* Presentations, Michigan State University and University of Oklahoma.

Sauer, C., & Willcocks, L. P. (2002, Spring). The evolution of the organizational architect. *MIT Sloan Management Review*, 41-49.

Schilling, M. A., & Steensma, H. K. (2002). Disentangling the theories of firm boundaries: A path model and empirical test. *Organization Science, 13*(4), 387-401.

Shankman, N. A. (1999). Reframing the debate between agency and stakeholder theories of the firm. *Journal of Business Ethics, 19*(4), 319-334.

Sheehan, N. T. (2002, April). *Reputation as a driver in knowledge-intensive service firms.* Series of Dissertations, Norwegian School of Management, Sandvika, Norway.

Skaksen, J. R. (2004). International outsourcing when labour markets are unionized. *Canadian Journal of Economics, 37*(1), 78-94.

Spilling, P. (2004, May 21). *The case of Netcom.* Personal e-mail from business developer Peter Spilling at outsourcing vendor Ementor in Oslo, Norway.

Stabell, C. B., & Fjeldstad, Ø. D. (1998). Configuring value for competitive advantage: On chains, shops, and networks. *Strategic Management Journal*, 19, 413-437.

Steensma, H. K., & Corley, K. G. (2001). Organizational context as a moderator of theories on firm boundaries for technology sourcing. *Academy of Management Journal, 44*(1), 271-291.

Stewart, T. A. (1997). *Intellectual capital: The new wealth of organizations.* London: Nicholas Brealy Publishing.

Stopford, M. (1997). *Maritime economics* (2nd ed.), London: Routledge.

Susarla, A., Barua, A., & Whinston, A. B. (2003). Understanding the service component of application service provision: An empirical analysis of satisfaction with ASP services. *MIS Quarterly, 27*(1), 91-123.

Sveiby, K. E. (2001). A knowledge-based theory of the firm to guide in strategy formulation. *Journal of Intellectual Capital, 2*(4), 344-358.

Tiwana, A. (2000). *The knowledge management toolkit — Practical techniques for building a knowledge management system.* New York: Prentice Hall.

Turban, E., King, D., Lee, J., Warkentin, M., & Chung, H. M. (2002). *Electronic commerce: A managerial perspective.* Sidney, Australia: Pearson Education, Prentice Hall.

Useem, M., & Harder, J. (2000, Winter). Leading laterally in company outsourcing. *Sloan Management Review*, 25-36.

Van Grembergen, W., De Haes, S., & Guldentops, E. (2004). Structures, processes and relational mechanisms for IT governance. In W. Van Grembergen (Ed.), *Strategies for information technology governance* (pp. 1-36). Hershey, PA: Idea Group Publishing.

Venkatraman, N. V. (1994, Winter). IT-enabled business transformation: From automation to business scope redefinition. *Sloan Management Review*, 74-86.

Venkatraman, N. V. (2004, Spring). Offshoring without guilt. *Sloan Management Review*, 14-16.

Wade, M., & Hulland, J. (2004). The resource-based view and information systems research: Review, extension, and suggestions for future research. *MIS Quarterly*, *28*(1), 107-142.

Ward, J., & Griffiths, P. (1996). *Strategic planning for information systems*. Wiley Series in Information Systems, London: Wiley & Sons.

Watson, K. (2001). *KTI and Rolls-Royce to SPEDE up knowledge adoptions*. Retrieved from www.ktiworld.com

Webster, S. (2004, June). Offshore. *CFO*, 45-76.

Weill, P. (2004) *Don't Just lead, govern: How top-performing firms govern IT*. Research article, Center for Information Systems Research, CISR WP No. 341, Sloan School of Management, Massachusetts Institute of Technology (MIT).

Weill, P., & Ross, J. W. (2004). *IT governance*. Boston: Harvard Business School Press.

Weill, P., Subramani, M. & Broadbent, M. (2002, Fall). Building IT infrastructure for strategic agility. *MIT Sloan Management Review*, 57-65.

Weill, P., & Vitale, M. R. (1999). Assessing the health of an information systems applications portfolio: An example from process manufacturing. *MIS Quarterly*, *23*(4), 601-624.

Weill, P., & Vitale, M. R. (2001). *Place to space, migrating to ebusiness models*. Boston: Harvard Business School Press.

Weill, P., & Vitale, M. R. (2002). What IT infrastructure capabilities are needed to implement e-business models? *MIS Quarterly Executive*, *1*(1), 17-34.

Wijnolst, N., & Wergeland, T. (1997). *Shipping*. Delft University Press, The Netherlands.

Willcocks, L., Hindle, J., Feeny, D., & Lacity, M. (2004). IT and business process outsourcing: The knowledge potential. *Information Systems Management*, *21*(3), 7-15.

Williamson, O. E. (1979). Transaction-cost economics: The governance of contractual relations. *The Journal of Law and Economics, 22*, 233-261.

Williamson, O. E. (1981, December). The modern corporation: Origins, evolution, attributes. *Journal of Economic Literature*, 1537-1568.

Williamson, O. E. (1991). Comparative economic organization: The analysis of discrete structural alternatives. *Administrative Science Quarterly, 36*, 269-296.

Williamson, O. E. (2000). The new institutional economics: Taking stock, looking ahead. *Journal of Economic Literature, 38*, 595-613.

Wit, B. D., & Meyer, R. (2004). *Strategy — Process, content, context* (3rd ed.). London: Thomson Learning.

Wright, S., & Boschee, K. (2004). The offshore IT provider is under fire — Will the US company be next? *Employee Relations Law Journal, 30*(1), 60-64.

Yusuf, Y., Gunesakaran, A., & Abthorpe, M. S. (2004). Enterprise information systems project implementation: A case study of ERP at Rolls-Royce. *International Journal of Production Economics, 87,* 251-266.

Zack, M. H. (1999). Developing a knowledge strategy. *California Management Review, 41*(3), 125-145.

About the Author

Dr. Petter Gottschalk is a professor of information and knowledge management in the Department of Leadership and Organizational Management at the Norwegian School of Management in Oslo, Norway. His executive experience includes positions of CIO at ABB Norway and CEO at ABB Datacables and at the Norwegian Computing Center. He earned his MBA in Germany, MSc in the United States, and DBA in the UK. Professor Gottschalk teaches at Fudan University in Shanghai, Nanyang University in Singapore, and the Arab Academy in Egypt. His book entitled *Managing Successful IT Outsourcing Relationships* was published by IRM Press in 2006.

Index

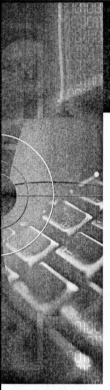

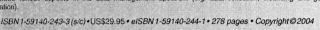